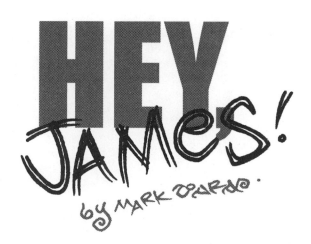

HEY, JAMES!

by MARK TATULLI.

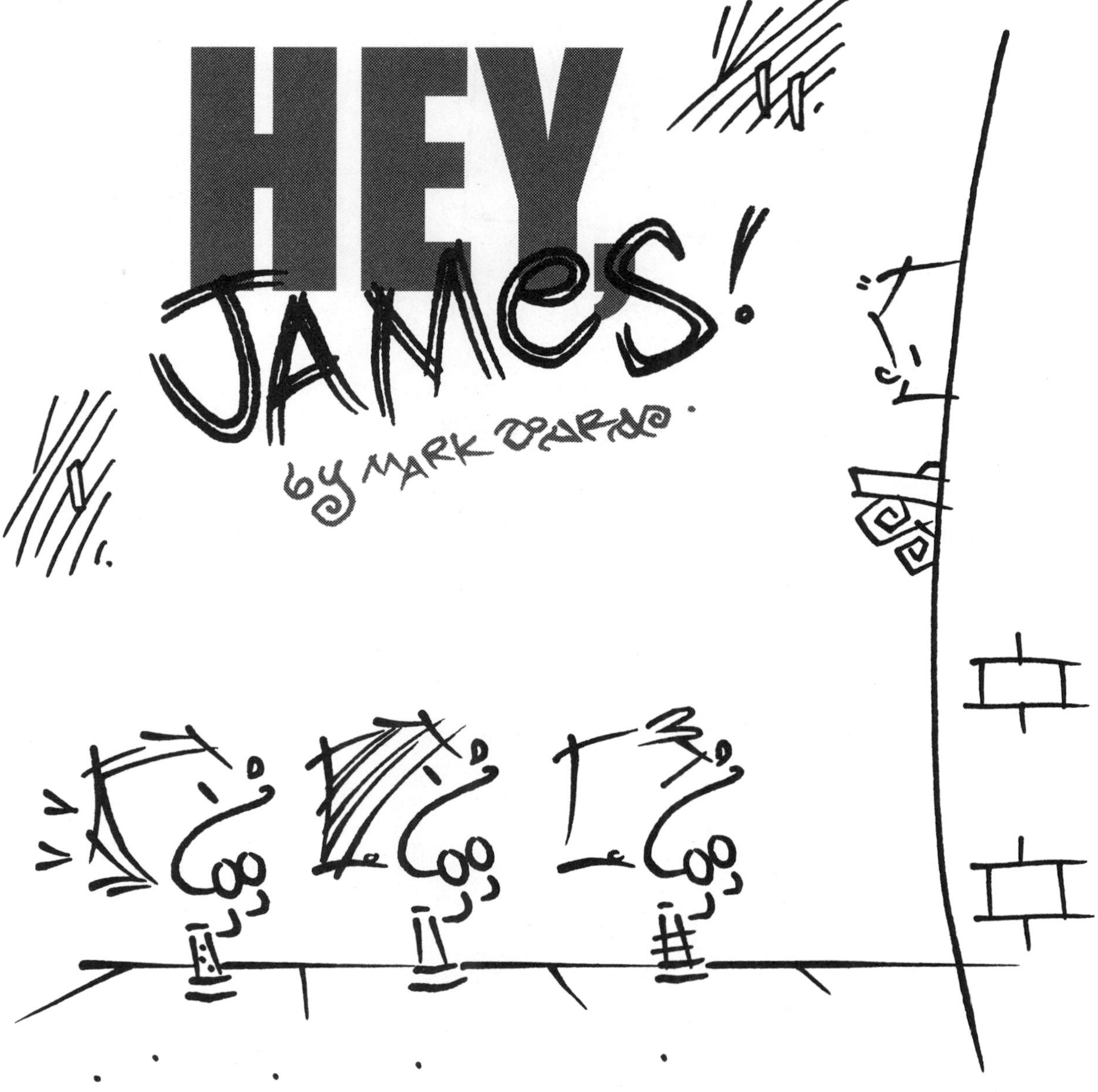
HEY
James!
by MARK TONRA

Andrews McMeel Publishing

Kansas City

FOR SARAH & JAMES!

Thanks to: Sparky, Segar, Herriman, Wilde, Seuss, Thoreau, Blyth, Sendak , and Picasso.
Without whom: Erin, Sue, Lee, Andrews McMeel, uclick, and Universal Press Syndicate.

www.JamesFans.com

www.uComics.com

ISBN: 0-7407-3308-7

Library of Congress Control Number: 2002113728

03 04 05 06 07 BBG 10 9 8 7 6 5 4 3 2 1

───── **ATTENTION: SCHOOLS AND BUSINESSES** ─────

Andrews McMeel books are available at quantity discounts with bulk purchase
for educational, business, or sales promotional use. For information, please write
to: Special Sales Department, Andrews McMeel Publishing, 4520 Main Street,
Kansas City, Missouri 64111.

Foreword

It's true. It happens. Sometimes.

James Tonra
January 2003

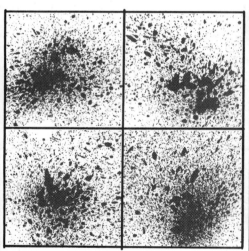

GREAT ART IS OFTEN MISUNDERSTOOD.

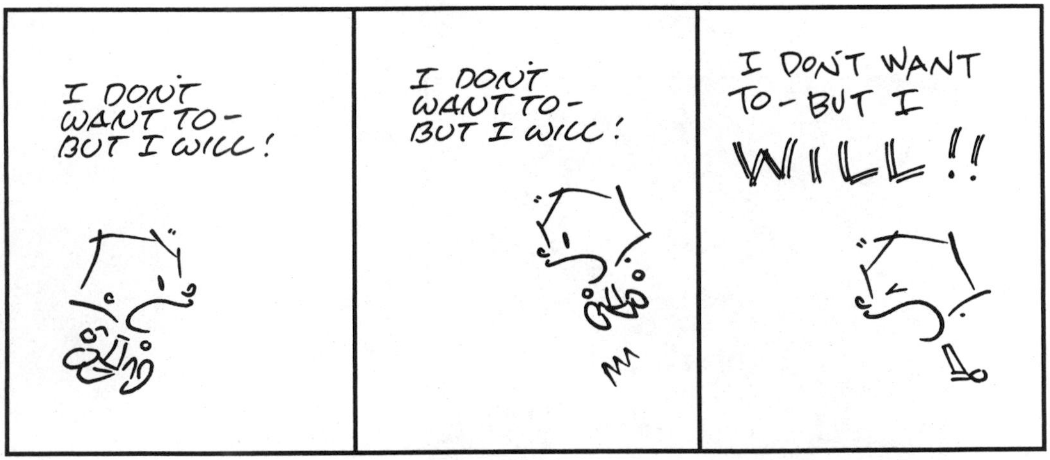
I DON'T WANT TO- BUT I WILL!
I DON'T WANT TO- BUT I WILL!
I DON'T WANT TO- BUT I WILL!!
IT'S A LIFESTYLE I CAN'T DEFEND.

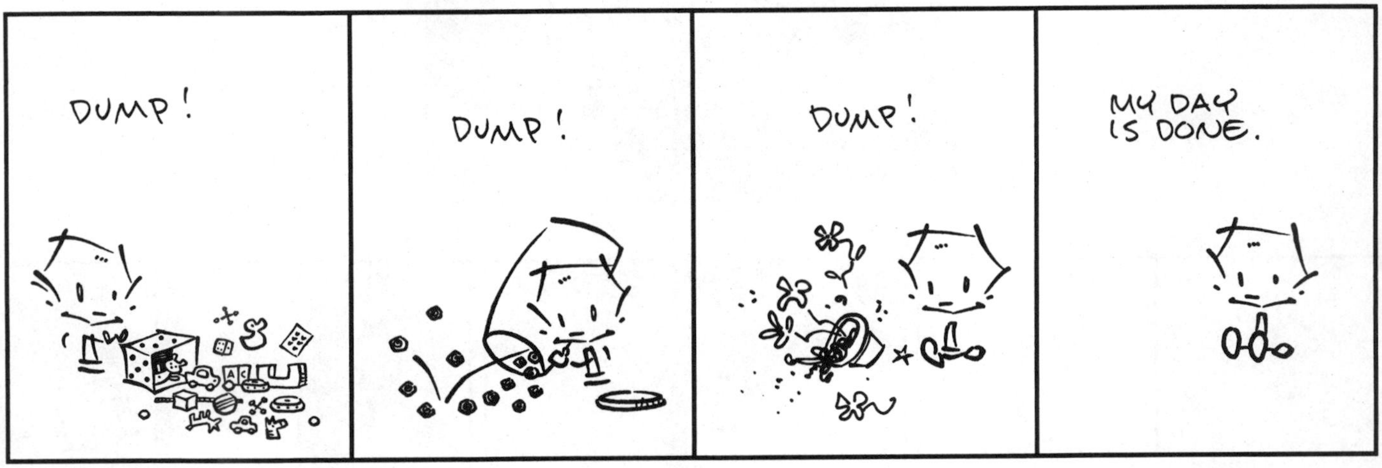
DUMP!
DUMP!
DUMP!
MY DAY IS DONE.

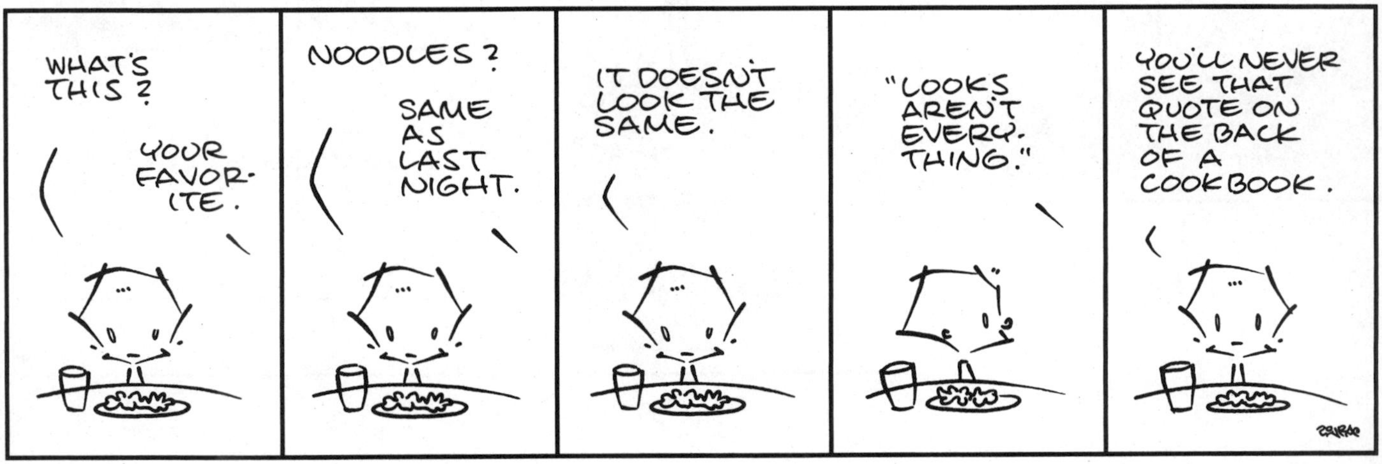
WHAT'S THIS?
YOUR FAVOR-ITE.
NOODLES?
SAME AS LAST NIGHT.
IT DOESN'T LOOK THE SAME.
"LOOKS AREN'T EVERY-THING."
YOU'LL NEVER SEE THAT QUOTE ON THE BACK OF A COOKBOOK.

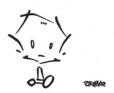

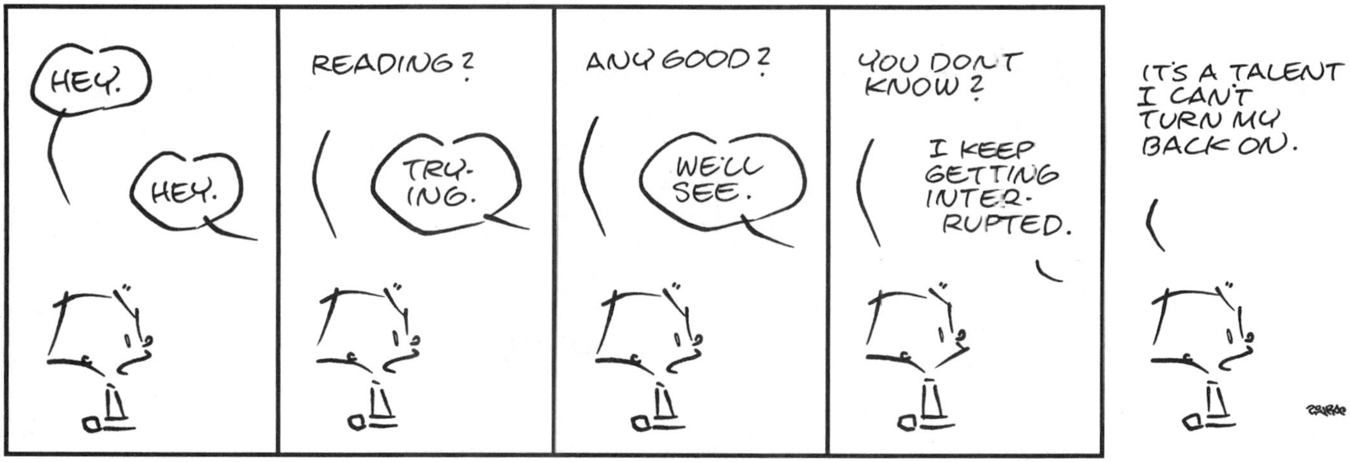
HEY.
HEY.
READING?
TRY-ING.
ANY GOOD?
WE'LL SEE.
YOU DON'T KNOW?
I KEEP GETTING INTER-RUPTED.
IT'S A TALENT I CAN'T TURN MY BACK ON.

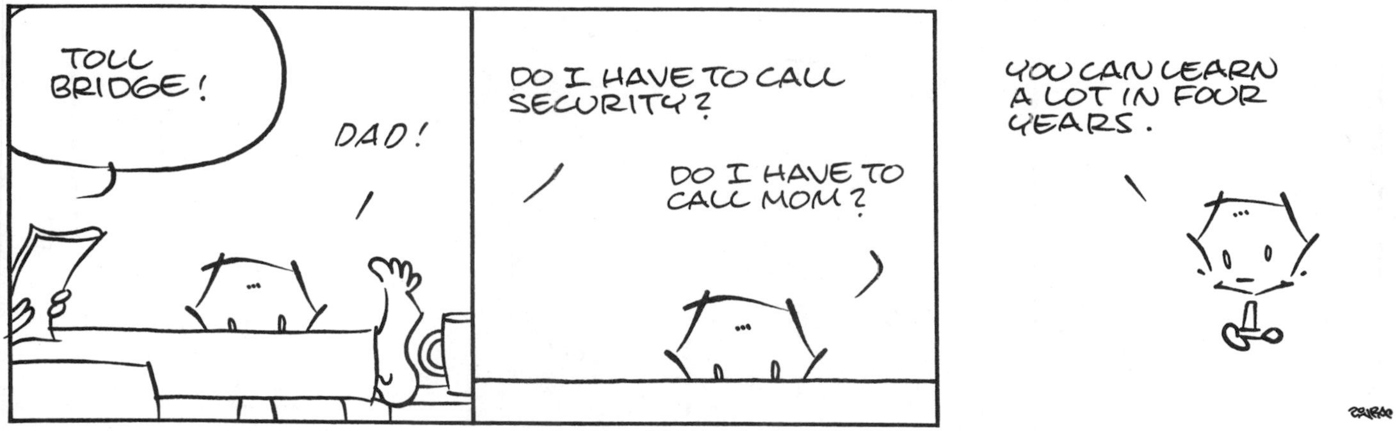
TOLL BRIDGE!
DAD!
DO I HAVE TO CALL SECURITY?
DO I HAVE TO CALL MOM?
YOU CAN LEARN A LOT IN FOUR YEARS.

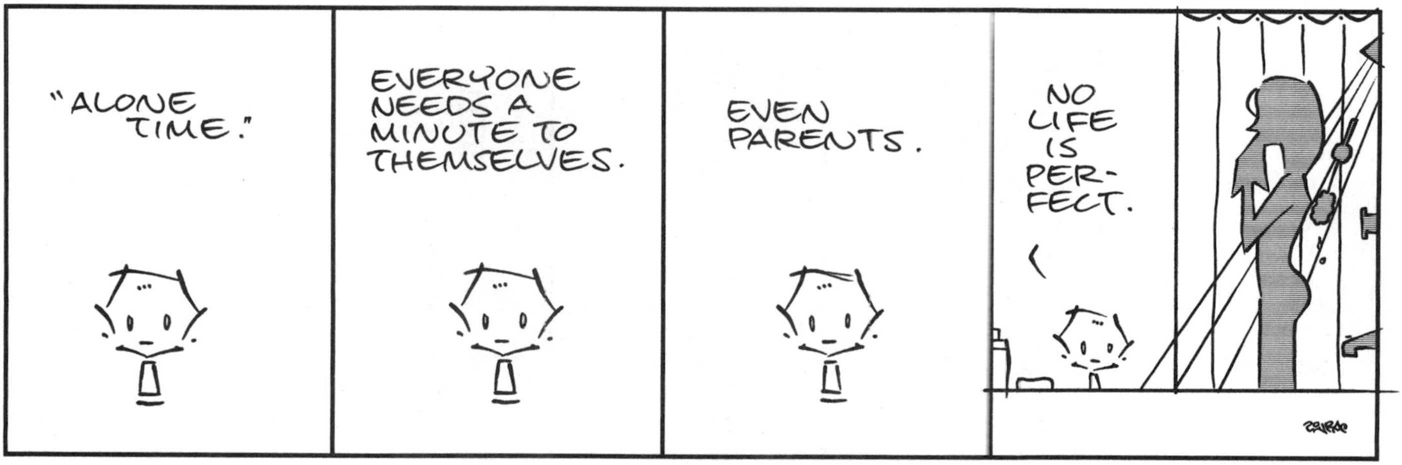
"ALONE TIME."
EVERYONE NEEDS A MINUTE TO THEMSELVES.
EVEN PARENTS.
NO LIFE IS PER-FECT.

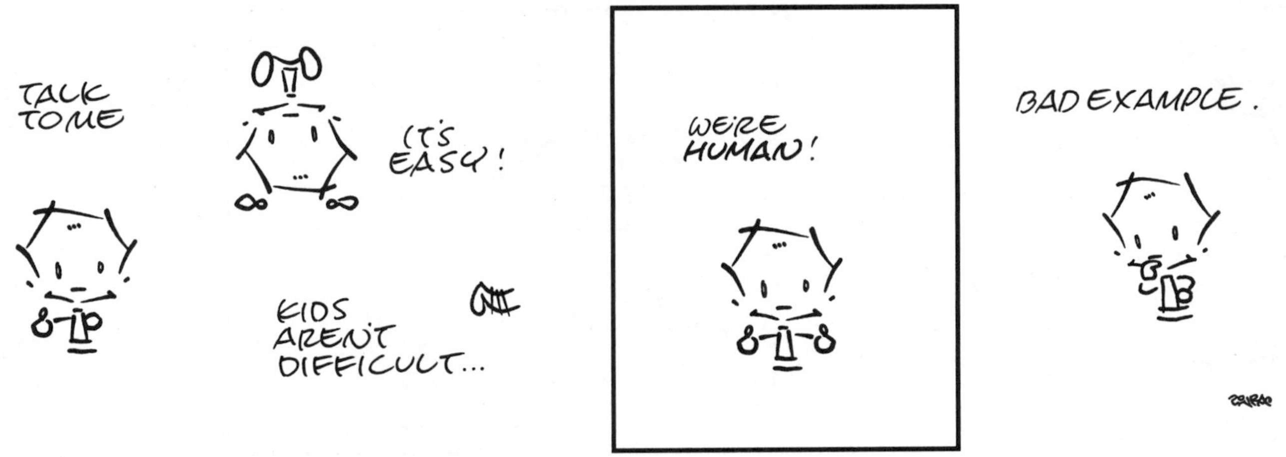
TALK TO ME
IT'S EASY!
KIDS AREN'T DIFFICULT...
WE'RE HUMAN!
BAD EXAMPLE.

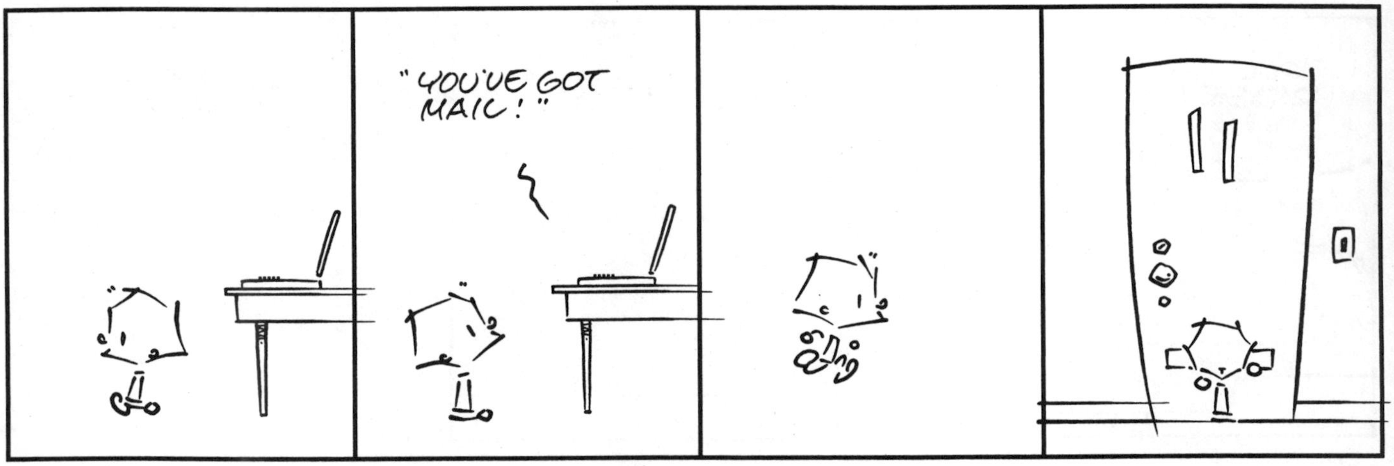
"YOU'VE GOT MAIL!"

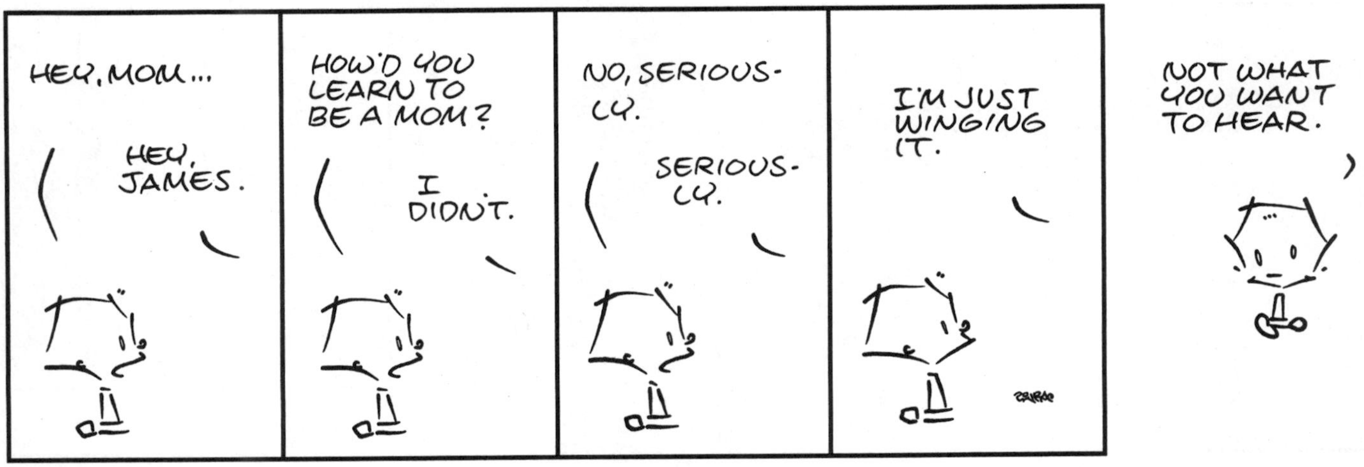
HEY, MOM...
HEY, JAMES.
HOW'D YOU LEARN TO BE A MOM?
I DIDN'T.
NO, SERIOUS-LY.
SERIOUS-LY.
I'M JUST WINGING IT.
NOT WHAT YOU WANT TO HEAR.

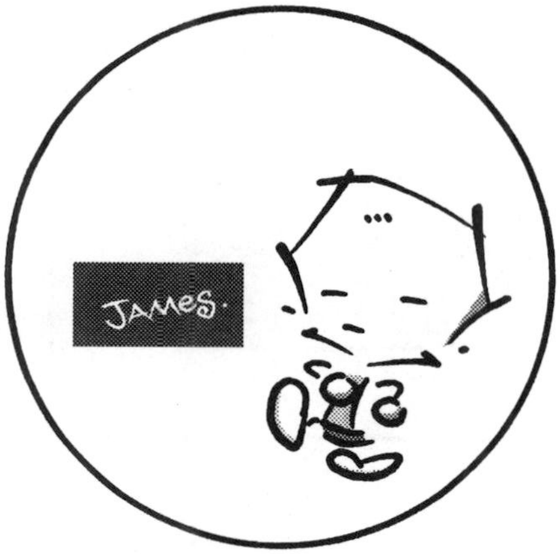
JAMES.

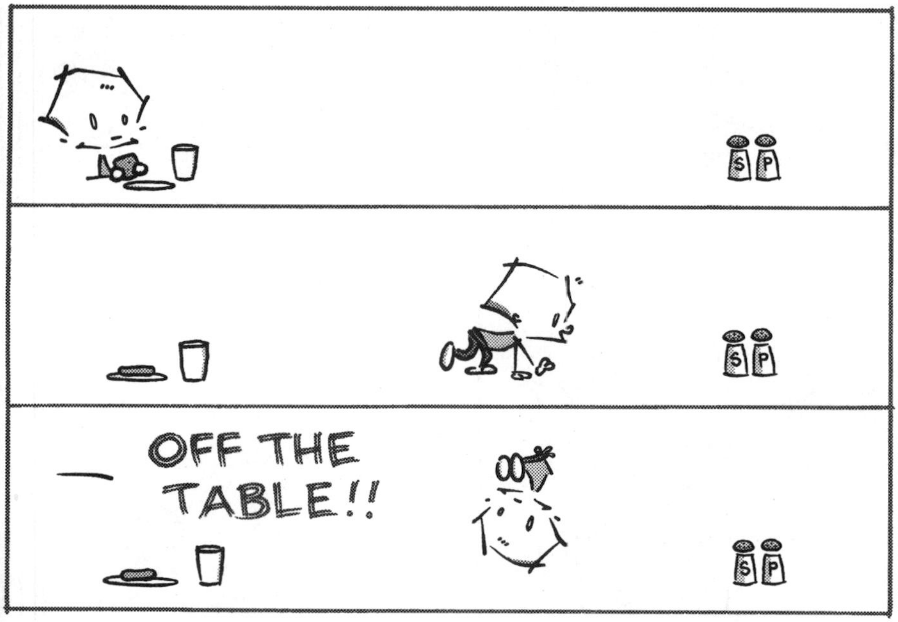
— OFF THE TABLE!!

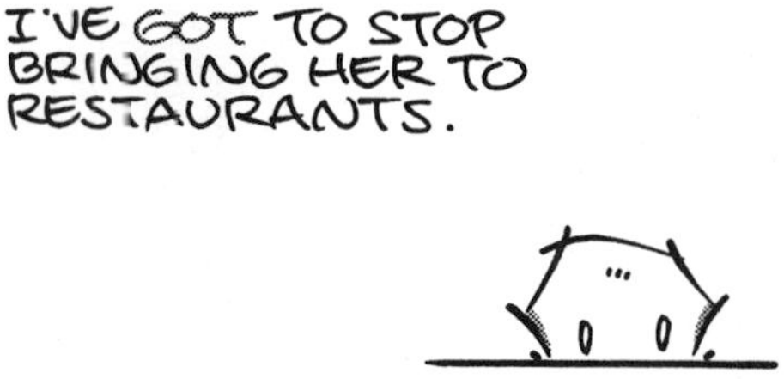
I'VE GOT TO STOP BRINGING HER TO RESTAURANTS.

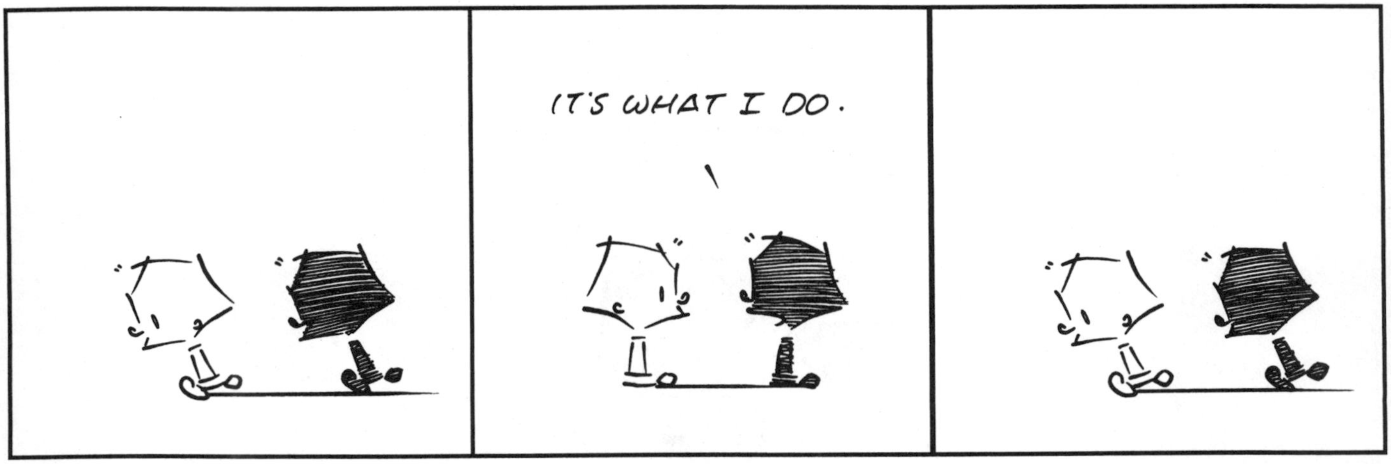
IT'S WHAT I DO.

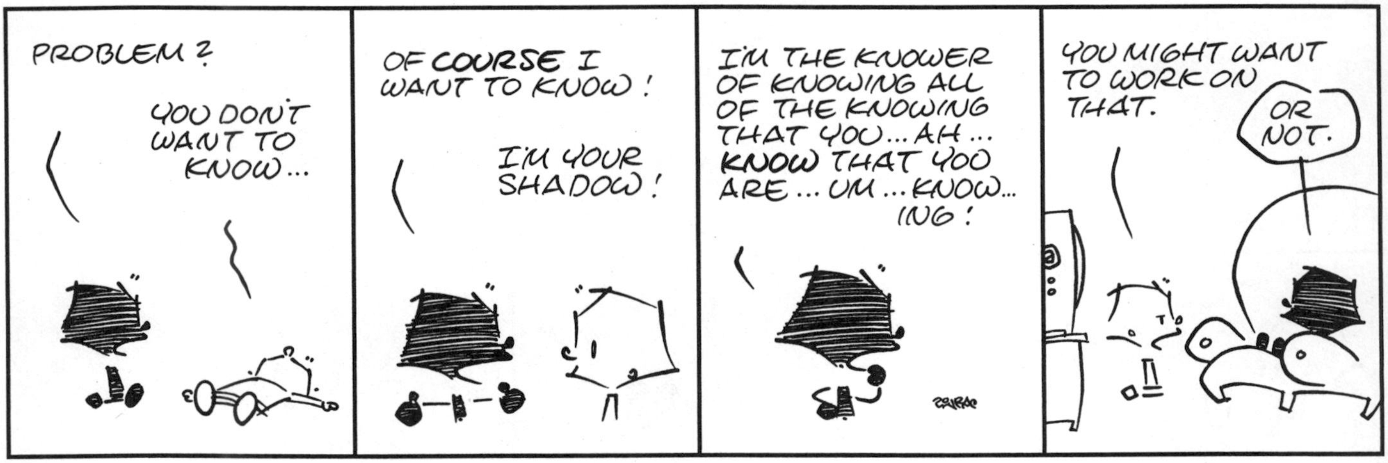
PROBLEM?
YOU DON'T WANT TO KNOW...
OF COURSE I WANT TO KNOW!
I'M YOUR SHADOW!
I'M THE KNOWER OF KNOWING ALL OF THE KNOWING THAT YOU... AH... KNOW THAT YOU ARE... UM... KNOW... ING!
YOU MIGHT WANT TO WORK ON THAT.
OR NOT.

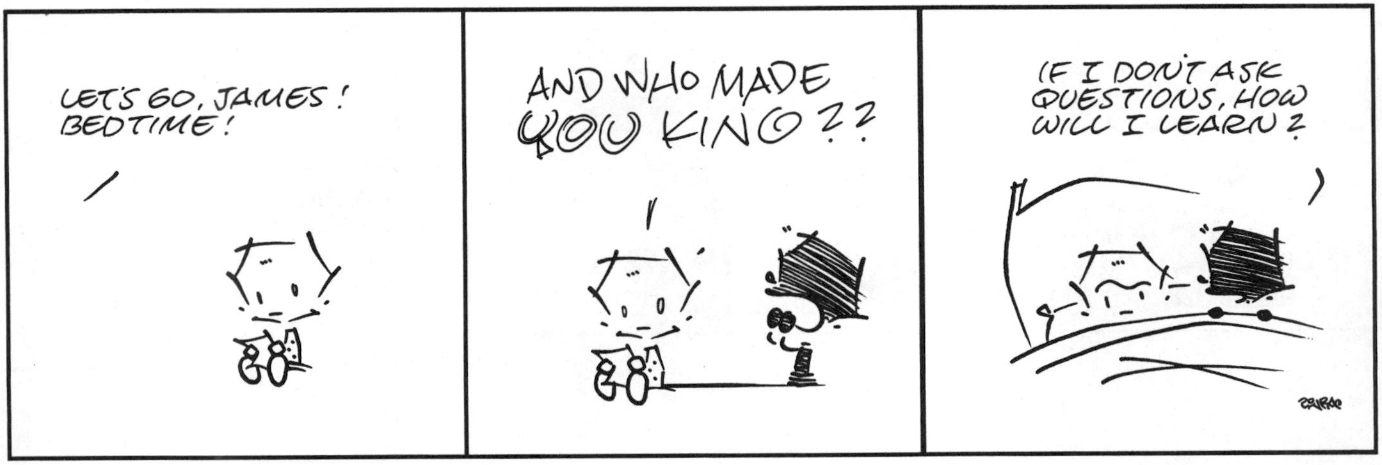
LET'S GO, JAMES! BEDTIME!
AND WHO MADE YOU KING??
IF I DON'T ASK QUESTIONS, HOW WILL I LEARN?

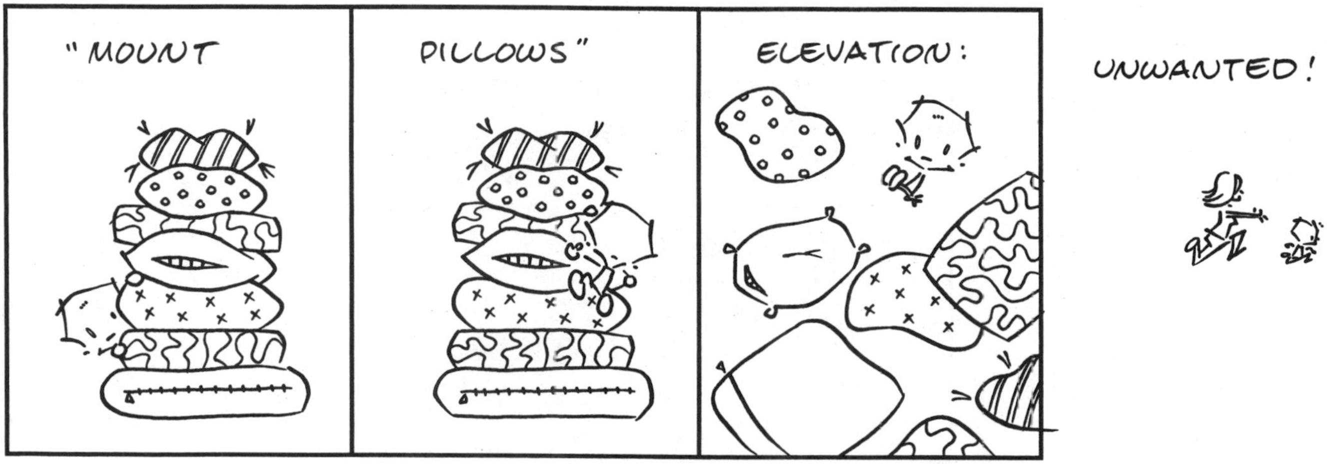
"MOUNT
PILLOWS"
ELEVATION:
UNWANTED!

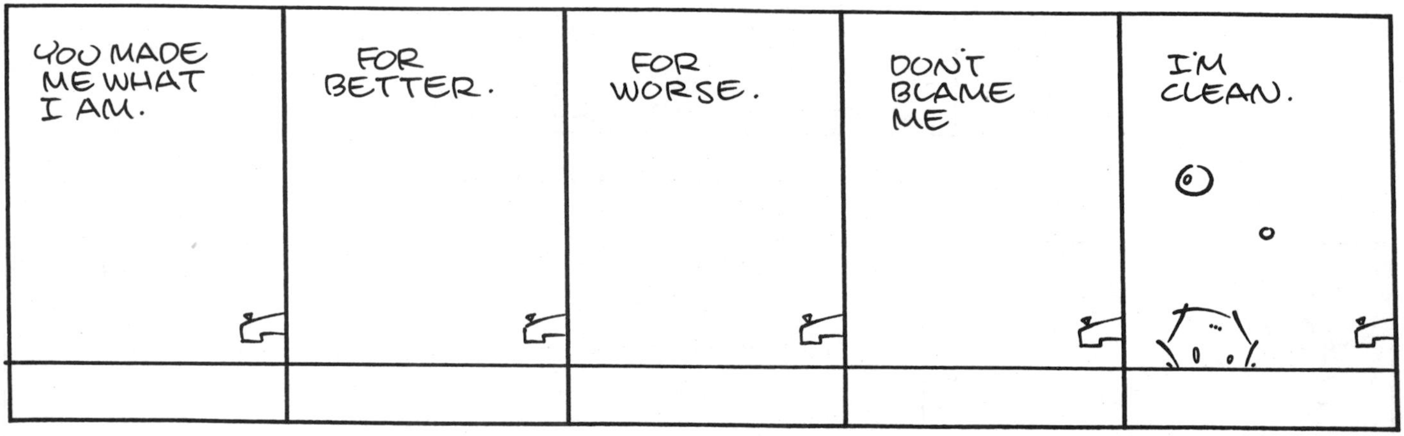
YOU MADE ME WHAT I AM.
FOR BETTER.
FOR WORSE.
DON'T BLAME ME
I'M CLEAN.

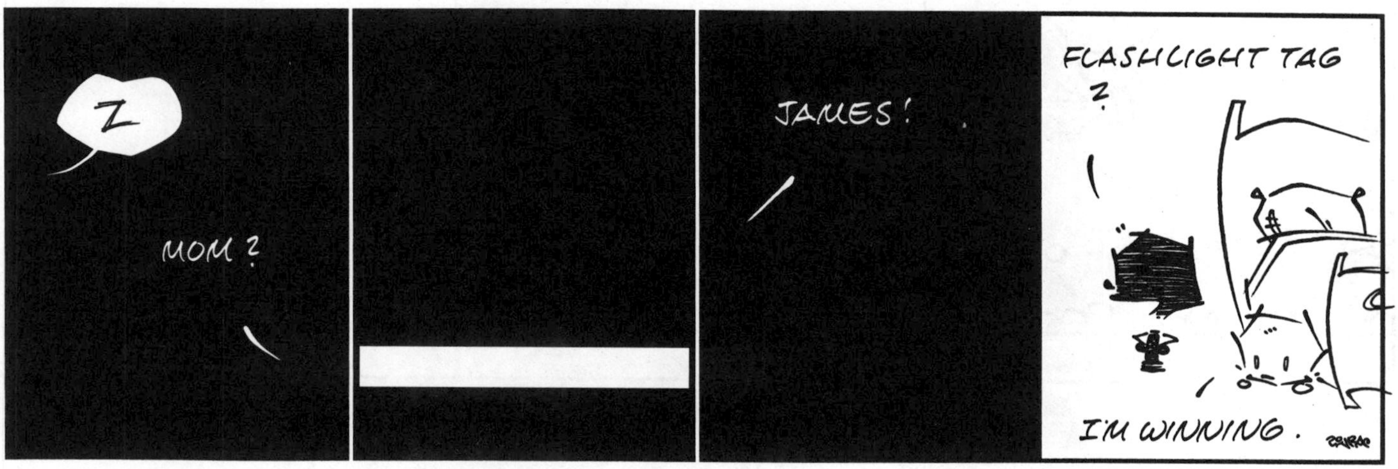
Z
MOM?
JAMES!
FLASHLIGHT TAG
Z
I'M WINNING.

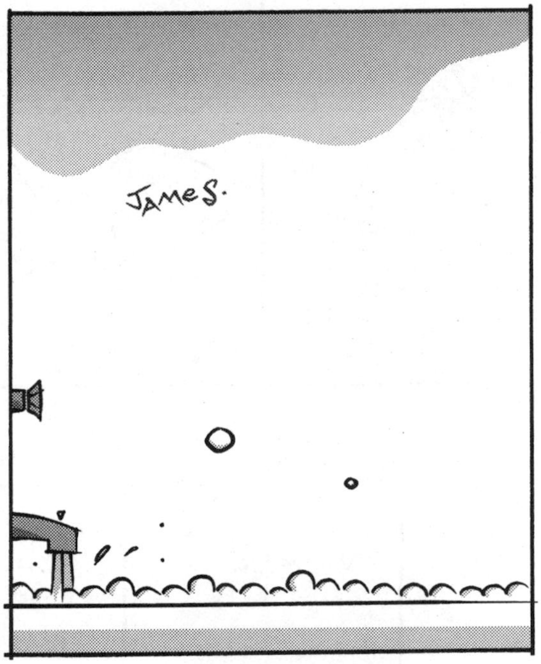
JAMES.

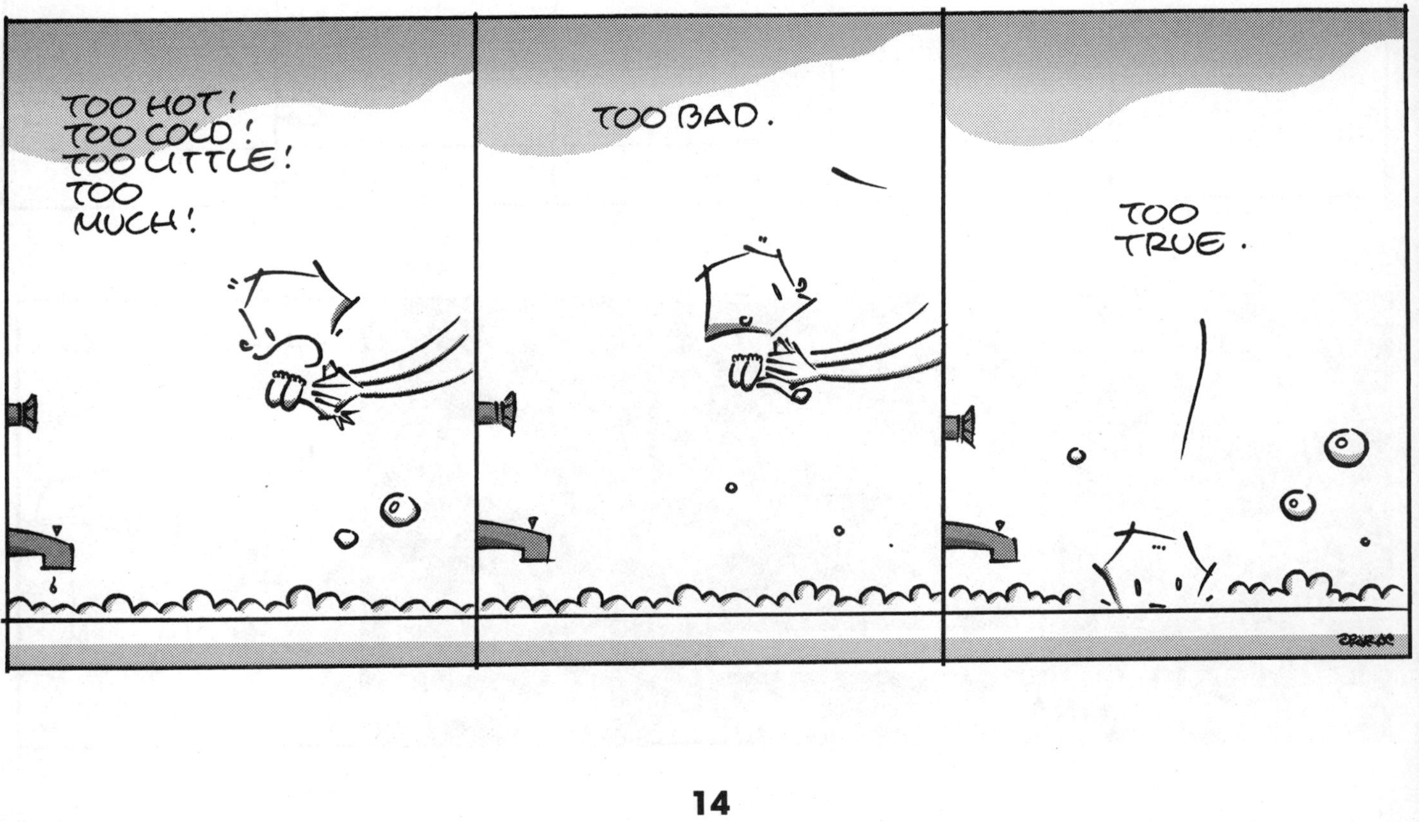
TOO HOT!
TOO COLD!
TOO LITTLE!
TOO MUCH!
TOO BAD.
TOO TRUE.

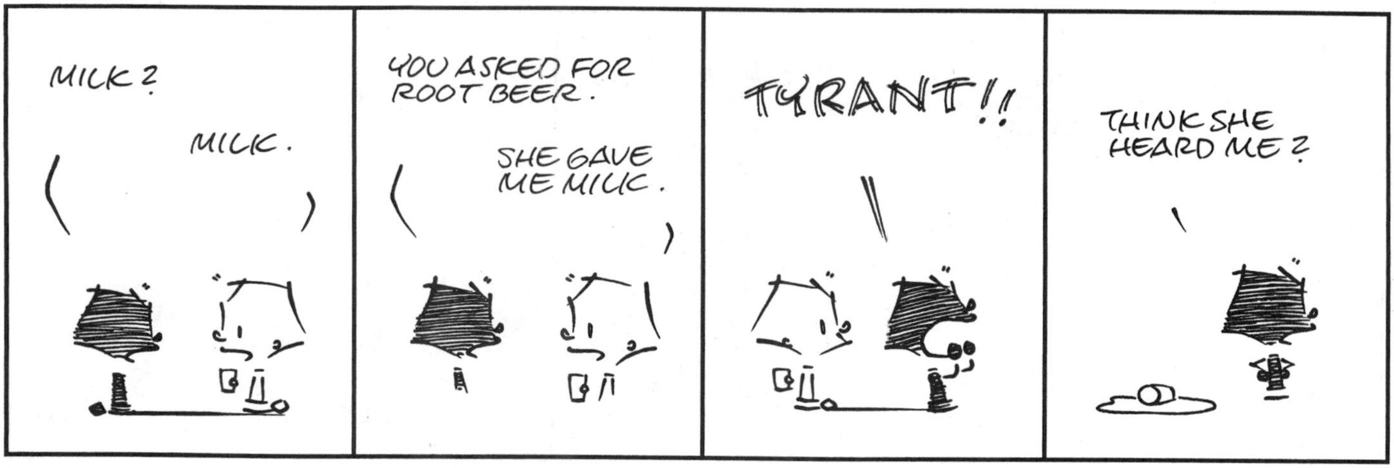
MILK?
MILK.
YOU ASKED FOR ROOT BEER.
SHE GAVE ME MILK.
TYRANT!!
THINK SHE HEARD ME?

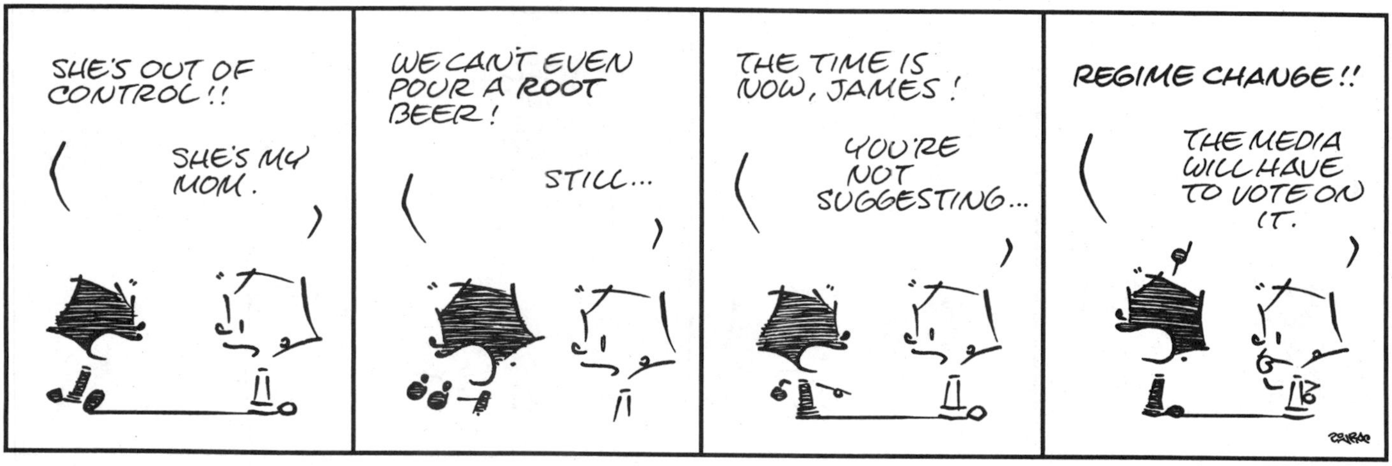
SHE'S OUT OF CONTROL!!
SHE'S MY MOM.
WE CAN'T EVEN POUR A **ROOT** BEER!
STILL...
THE TIME IS NOW, JAMES!
YOU'RE NOT SUGGESTING...
REGIME CHANGE!!
THE MEDIA WILL HAVE TO VOTE ON IT.

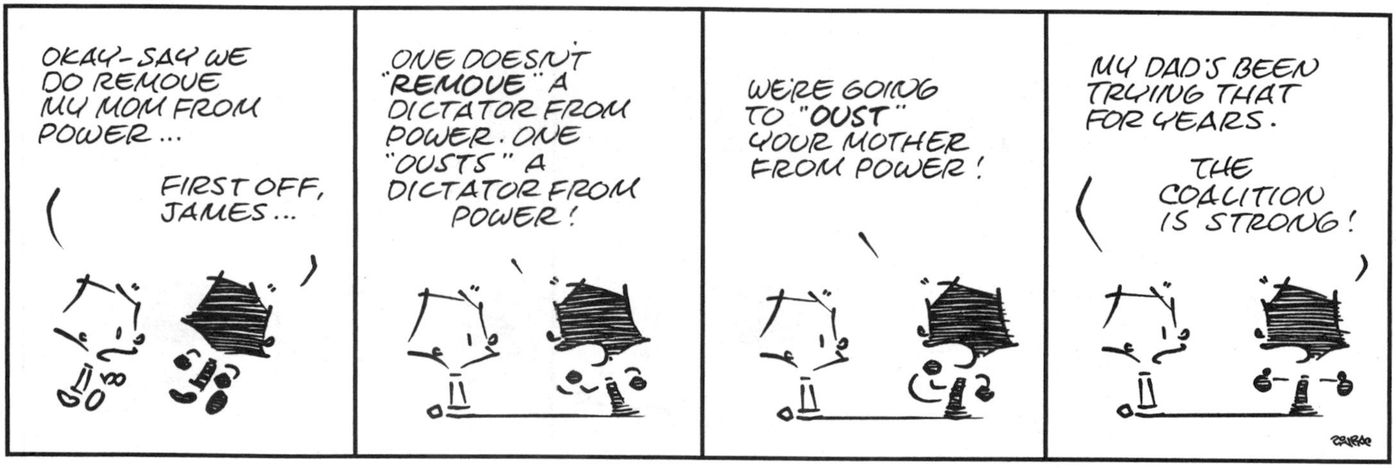
OKAY-SAY WE DO REMOVE MY MOM FROM POWER...
FIRST OFF, JAMES...
ONE DOESN'T "**REMOVE**" A DICTATOR FROM POWER. ONE "OUSTS" A DICTATOR FROM POWER!
WE'RE GOING TO "**OUST**" YOUR MOTHER FROM POWER!
MY DAD'S BEEN TRYING THAT FOR YEARS.
THE COALITION IS STRONG!

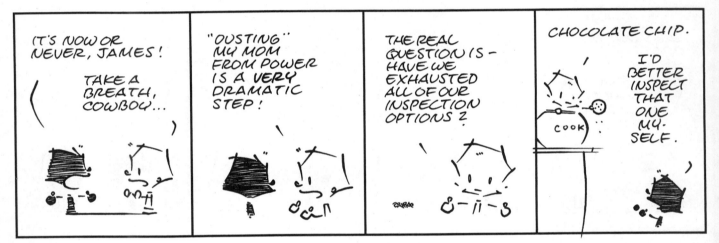
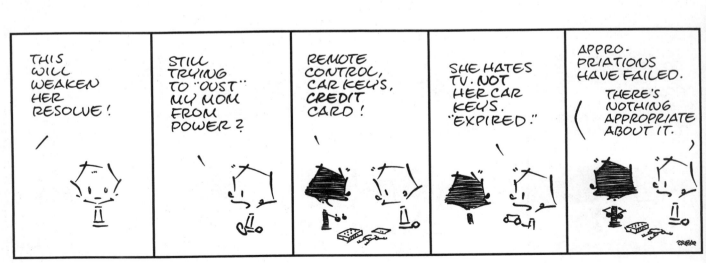

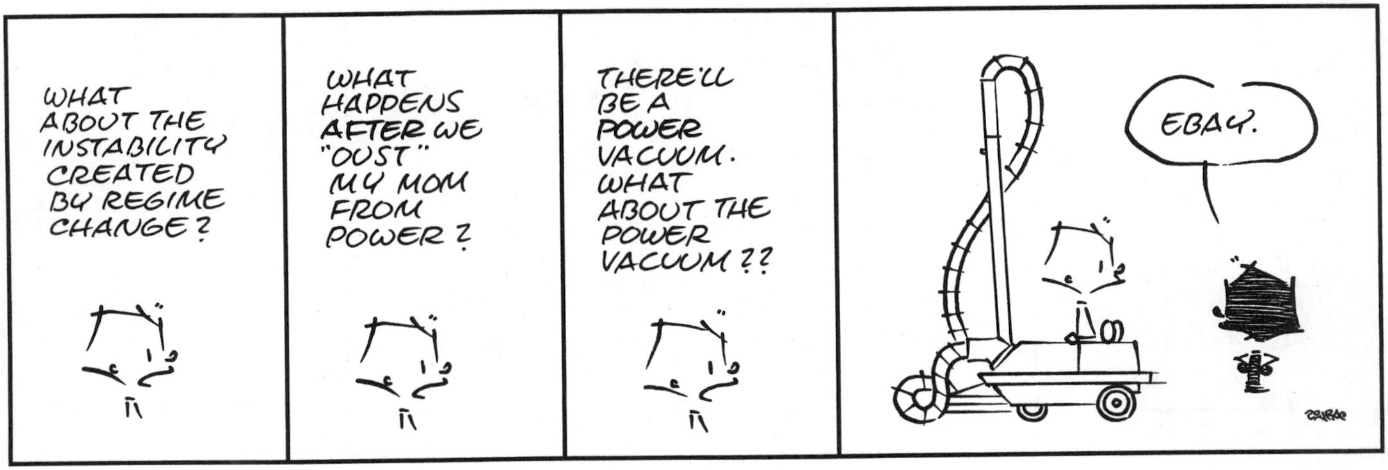

Panel 1: WHAT ABOUT THE INSTABILITY CREATED BY REGIME CHANGE?

Panel 2: WHAT HAPPENS AFTER WE "OUST" MY MOM FROM POWER?

Panel 3: THERE'LL BE A POWER VACUUM. WHAT ABOUT THE POWER VACUUM??

Panel 4: EBAY.

Panel 5: IT'S NOW OR NEVER, JAMES! TAKE A BREATH, COWBOY...

Panel 6: "OUSTING" MY MOM FROM POWER IS A VERY DRAMATIC STEP!

Panel 7: THE REAL QUESTION IS – HAVE WE EXHAUSTED ALL OF OUR INSPECTION OPTIONS?

Panel 8: CHOCOLATE CHIP. I'D BETTER INSPECT THAT ONE MY-SELF. COOK

Panel 9: THIS WILL WEAKEN HER RESOLVE!

Panel 10: STILL TRYING TO "OUST" MY MOM FROM POWER?

Panel 11: REMOTE CONTROL, CAR KEYS, CREDIT CARD!

Panel 12: SHE HATES TV. NOT HER CAR KEYS. "EXPIRED."

Panel 13: APPRO-PRIATIONS HAVE FAILED. THERE'S NOTHING APPROPRIATE ABOUT IT.

16

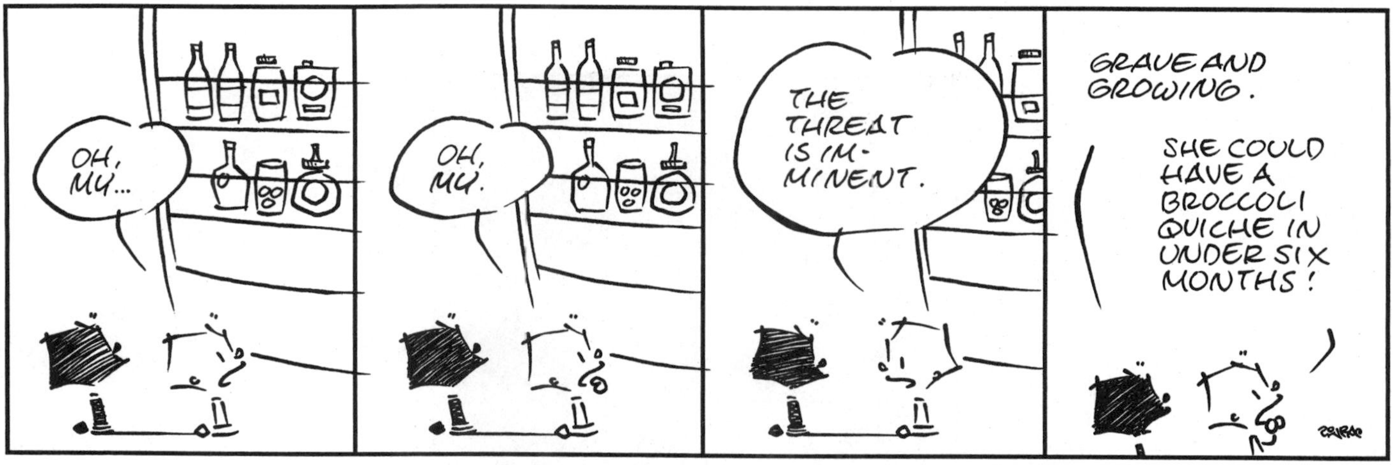
OH, MY...
OH, MY.
THE THREAT IS IMMINENT.
GRAVE AND GROWING.
SHE COULD HAVE A BROCCOLI QUICHE IN UNDER SIX MONTHS!

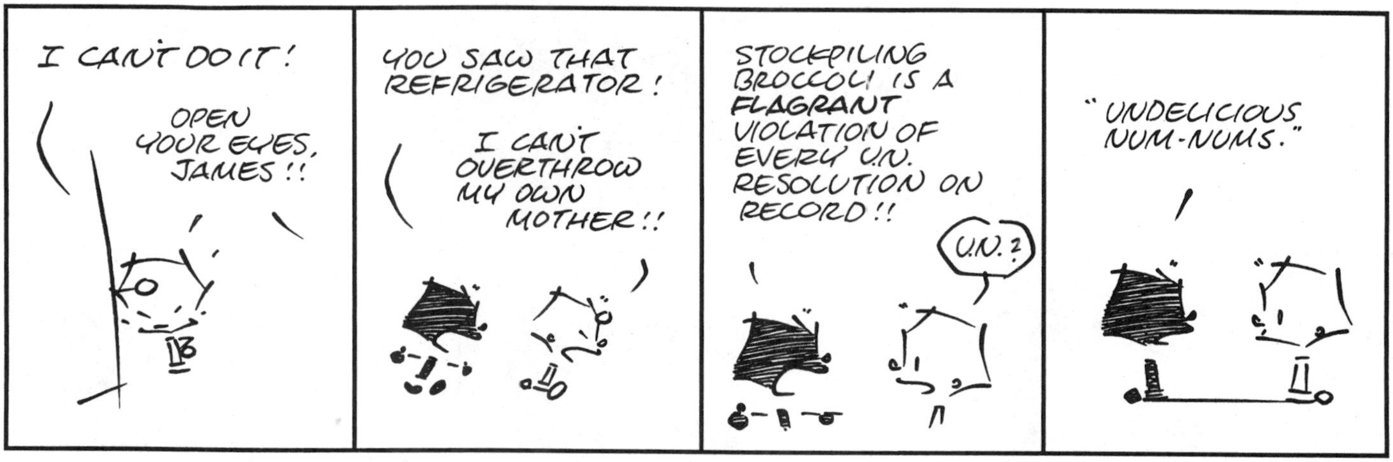
I CAN'T DO IT!
OPEN YOUR EYES, JAMES!!
YOU SAW THAT REFRIGERATOR!
I CAN'T OVERTHROW MY OWN MOTHER!!
STOCKPILING BROCCOLI IS A **FLAGRANT** VIOLATION OF EVERY U.N. RESOLUTION ON RECORD!!
U.N.?
"UNDELICIOUS NUM-NUMS."

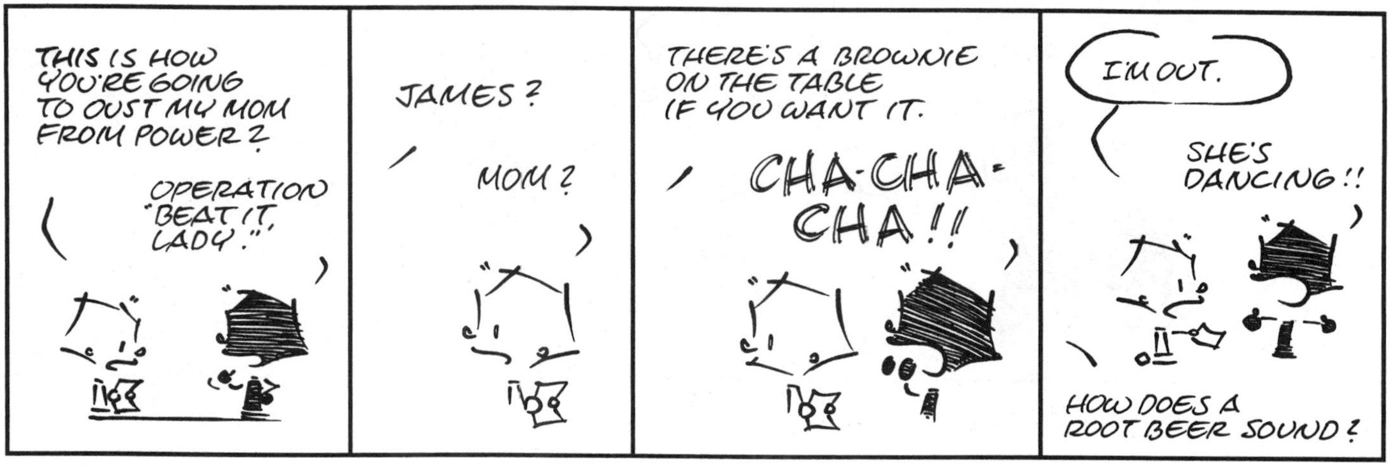
THIS IS HOW YOU'RE GOING TO OUST MY MOM FROM POWER?
OPERATION "BEAT IT, LADY."
JAMES?
MOM?
THERE'S A BROWNIE ON THE TABLE IF YOU WANT IT.
CHA-CHA-CHA!!
I'M OUT.
SHE'S DANCING!!
HOW DOES A ROOT BEER SOUND?

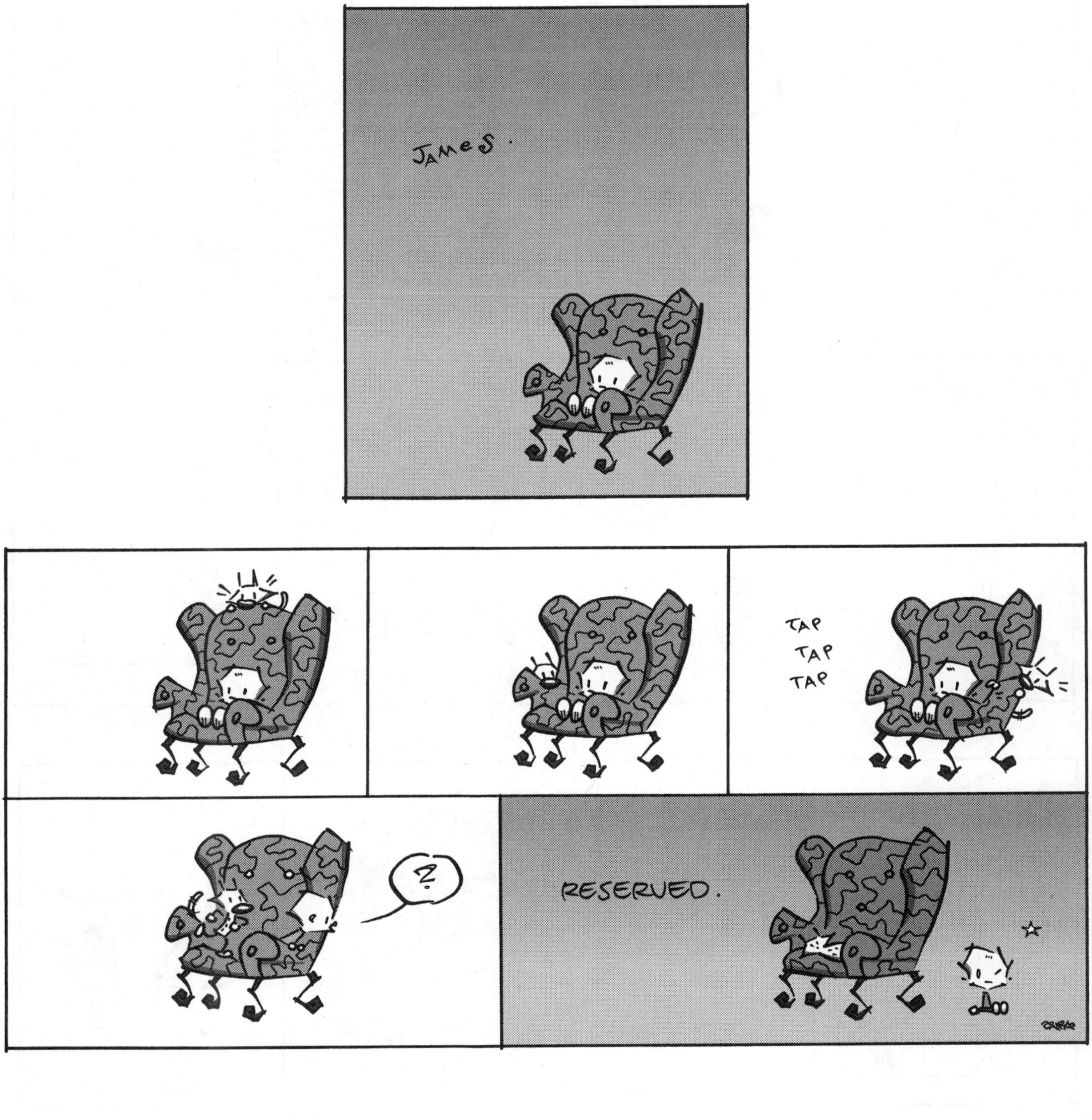
JAMES.
TAP
TAP
TAP
?
RESERVED.

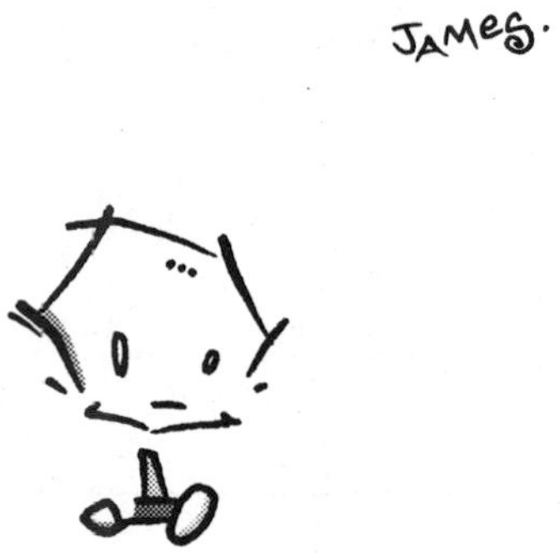
JAMES.

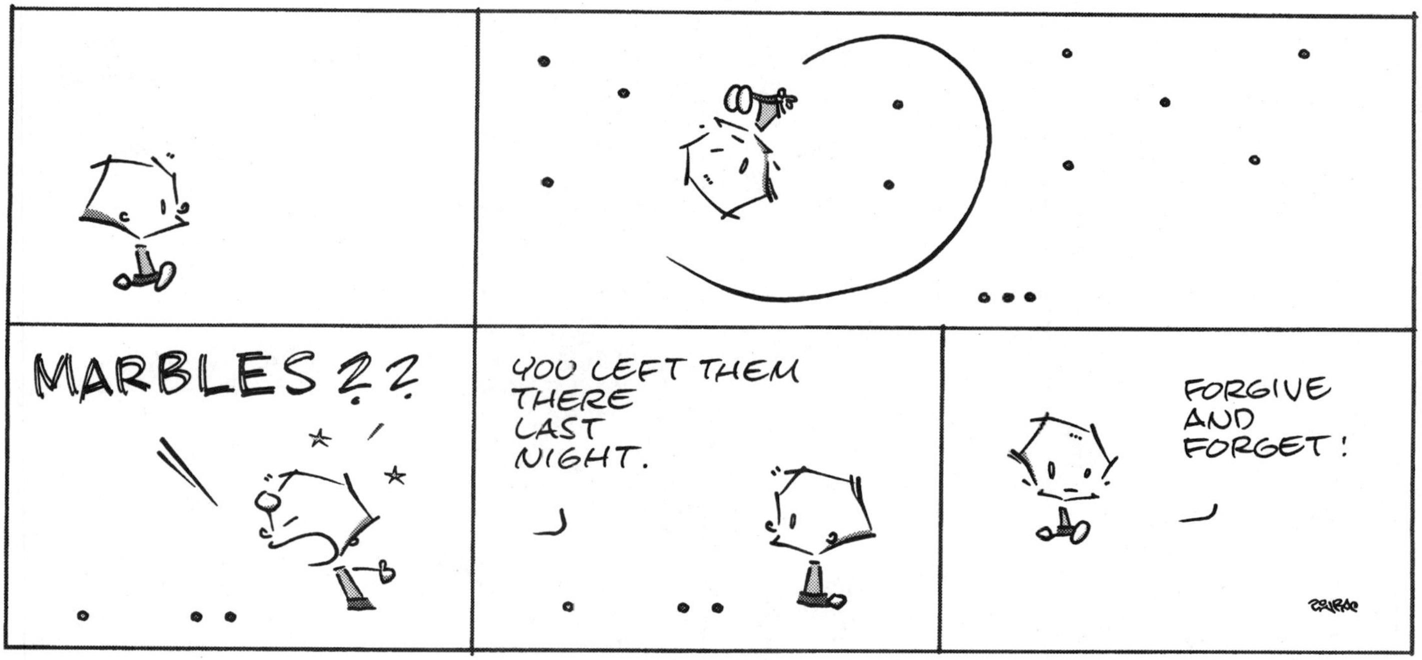
MARBLES ? ?
YOU LEFT THEM THERE LAST NIGHT.
FORGIVE AND FORGET!

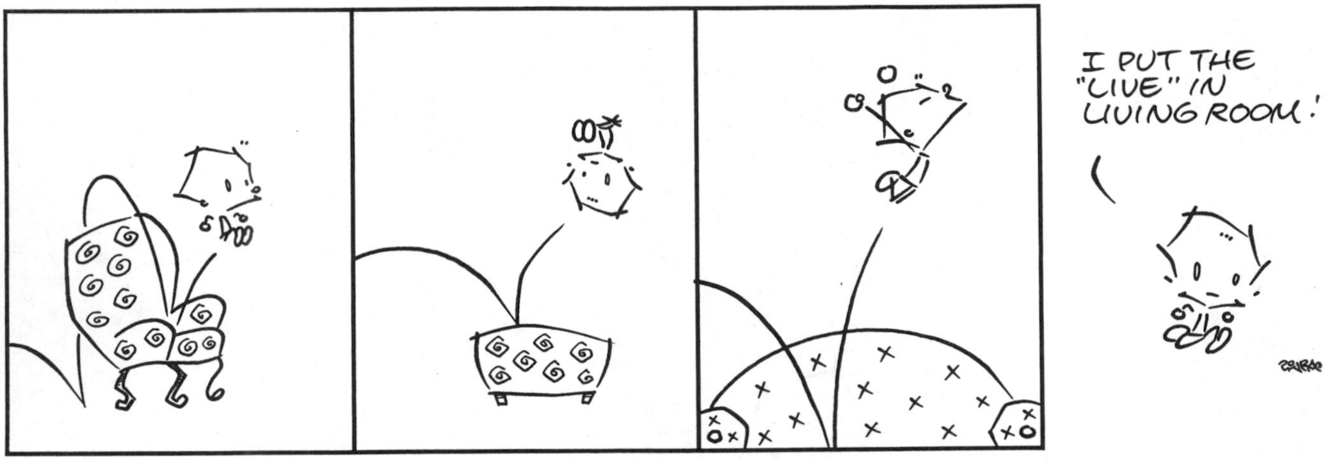
I PUT THE "LIVE" IN LIVING ROOM!

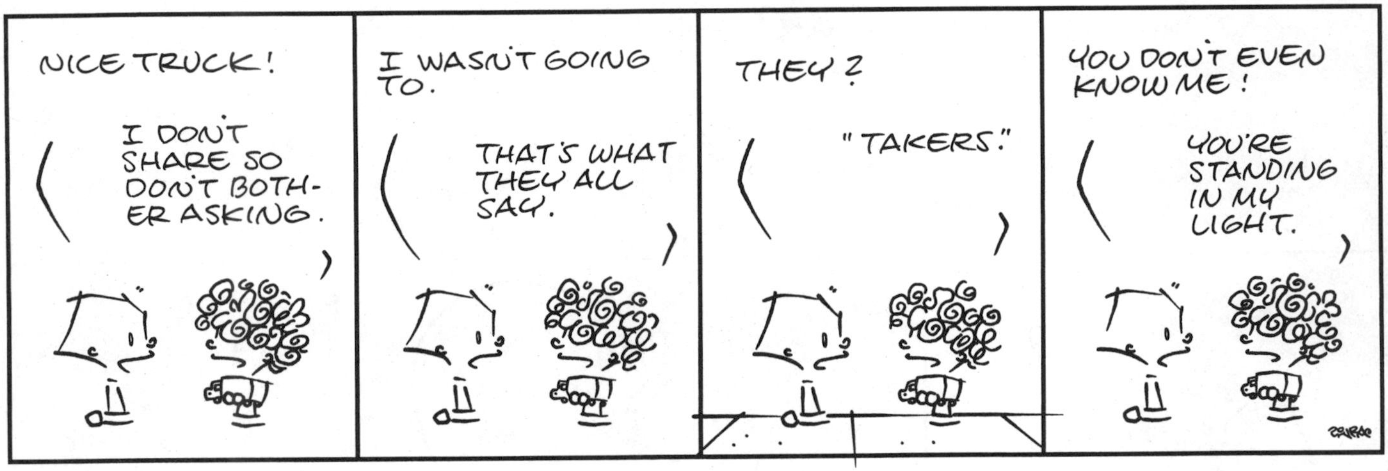
NICE TRUCK!
I DON'T SHARE SO DON'T BOTHER ASKING.
I WASN'T GOING TO.
THAT'S WHAT THEY ALL SAY.
THEY?
"TAKERS."
YOU DON'T EVEN KNOW ME!
YOU'RE STANDING IN MY LIGHT.

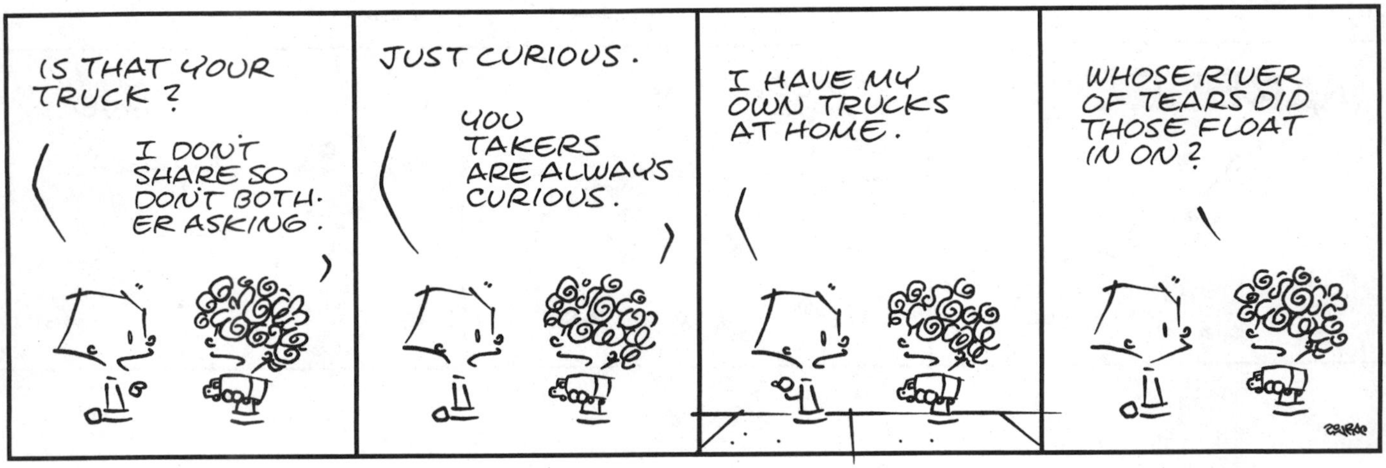
IS THAT YOUR TRUCK?
I DON'T SHARE SO DON'T BOTHER ASKING.
JUST CURIOUS.
YOU TAKERS ARE ALWAYS CURIOUS.
I HAVE MY OWN TRUCKS AT HOME.
WHOSE RIVER OF TEARS DID THOSE FLOAT IN ON?

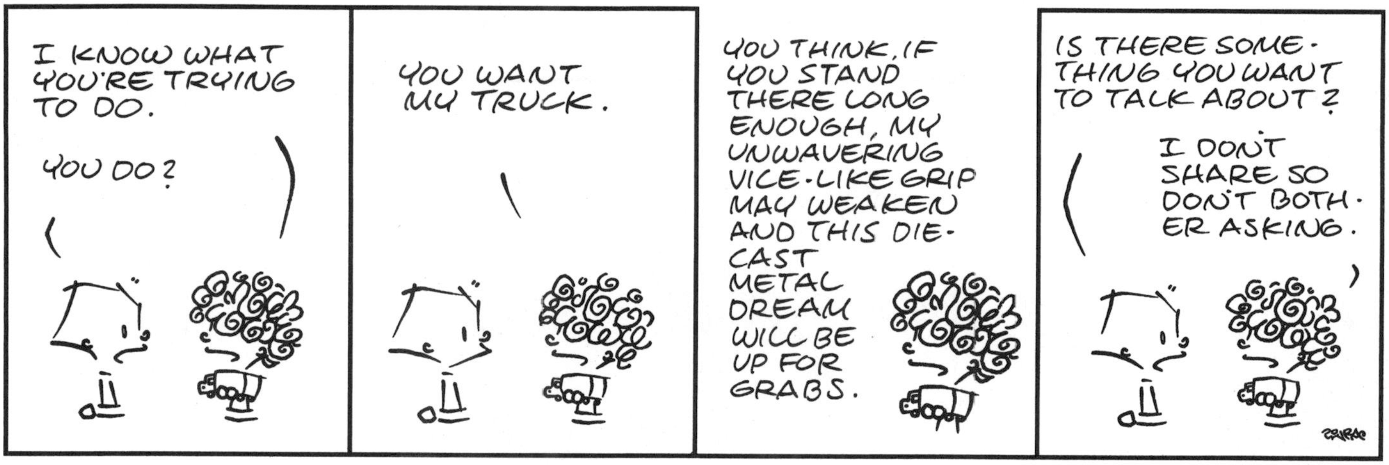
I KNOW WHAT YOU'RE TRYING TO DO.
YOU DO?
YOU WANT MY TRUCK.
YOU THINK, IF YOU STAND THERE LONG ENOUGH, MY UNWAVERING VICE-LIKE GRIP MAY WEAKEN AND THIS DIE-CAST METAL DREAM WILL BE UP FOR GRABS.
IS THERE SOMETHING YOU WANT TO TALK ABOUT?
I DON'T SHARE SO DON'T BOTHER ASKING.

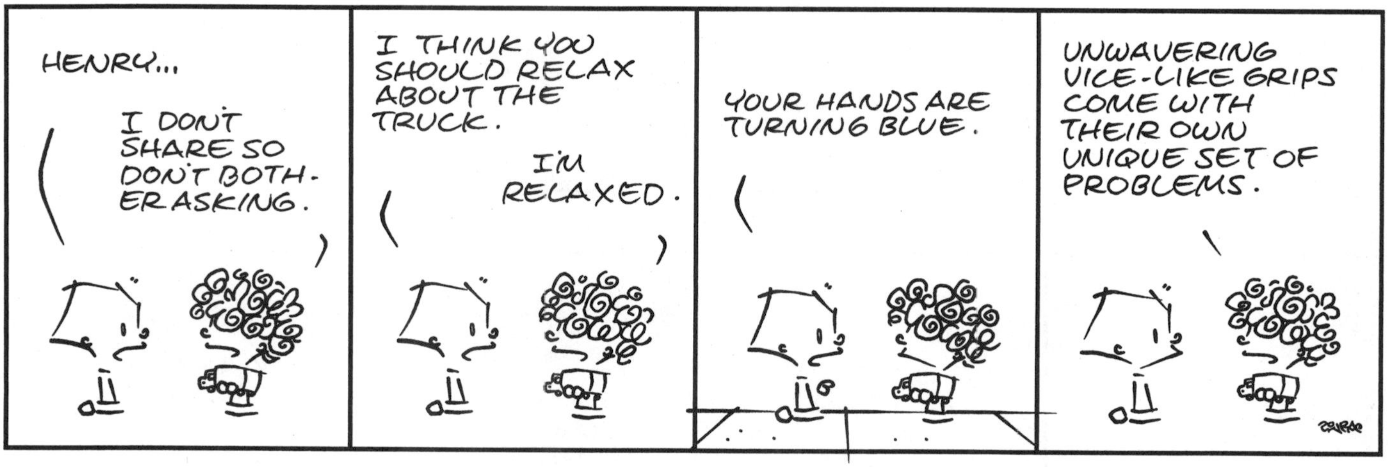
HENRY...
I DON'T SHARE SO DON'T BOTHER ASKING.
I THINK YOU SHOULD RELAX ABOUT THE TRUCK.
I'M RELAXED.
YOUR HANDS ARE TURNING BLUE.
UNWAVERING VICE-LIKE GRIPS COME WITH THEIR OWN UNIQUE SET OF PROBLEMS.

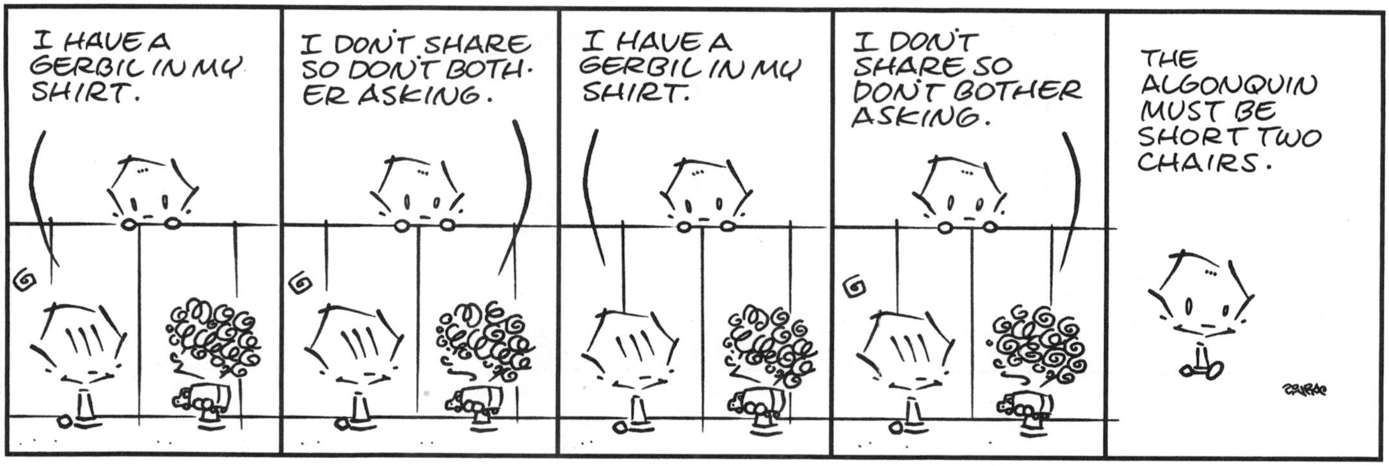
I HAVE A GERBIL IN MY SHIRT.
I DON'T SHARE SO DON'T BOTHER ASKING.
I HAVE A GERBIL IN MY SHIRT.
I DON'T SHARE SO DON'T BOTHER ASKING.
THE ALGONQUIN MUST BE SHORT TWO CHAIRS.

JAMES.

WORK?
I DON'T WANT TO WORK TODAY!
I WORKED FOUR MONTHS AGO...
LAST YEAR.
I'M ALL ABOUT BALANCE...

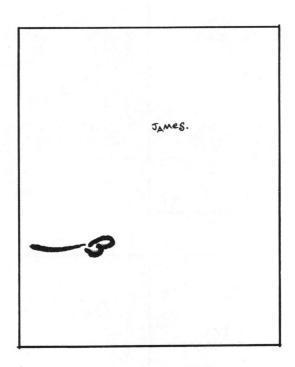

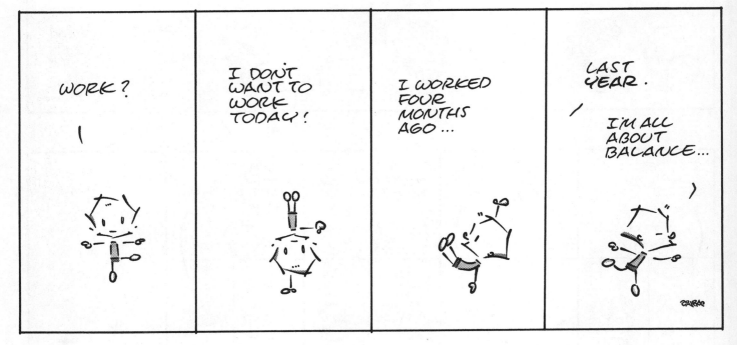

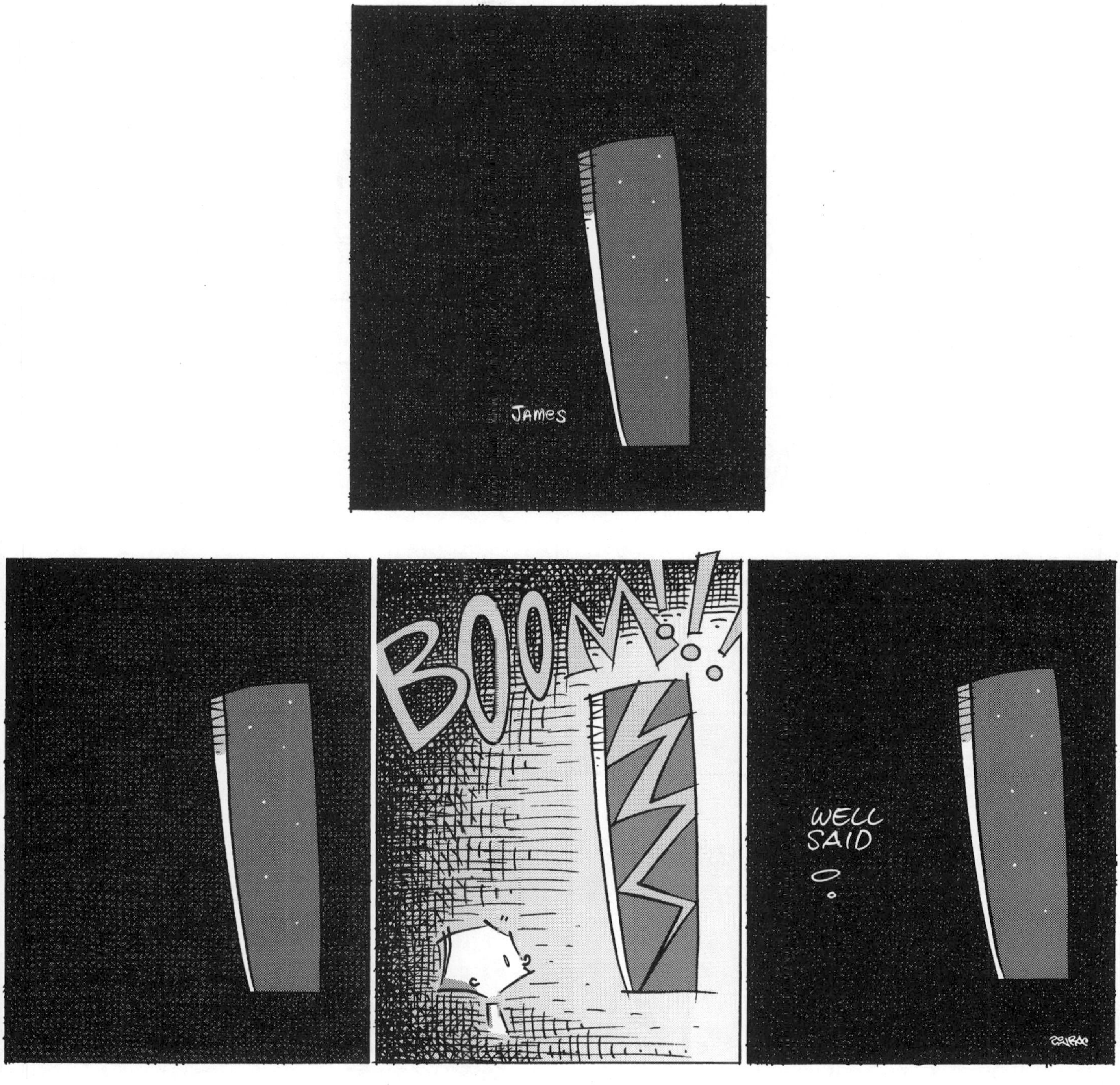
JAMES
BOOM!!
WELL SAID

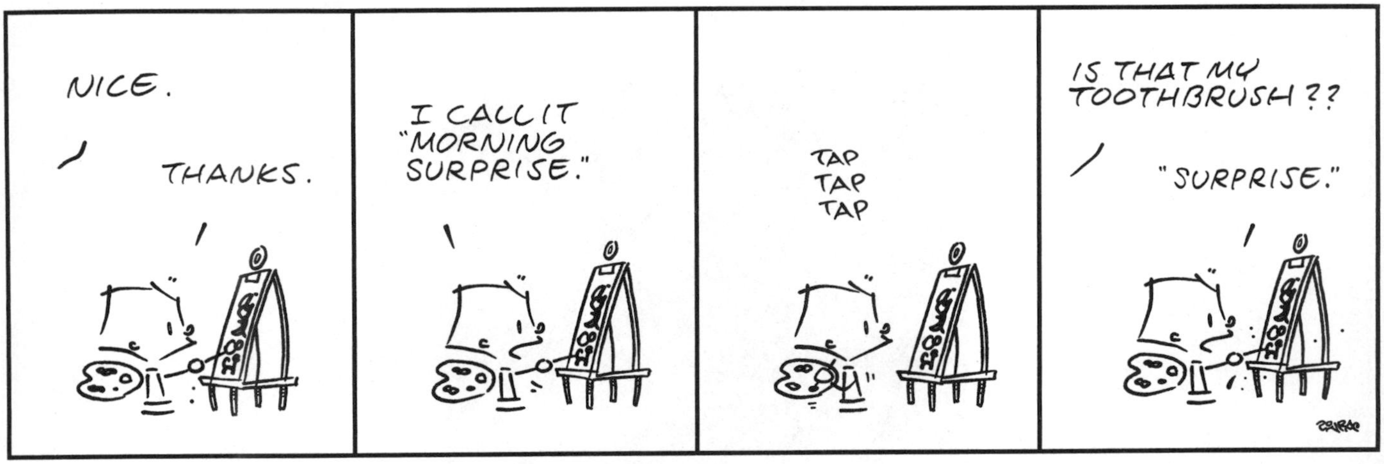
NICE.
THANKS.
I CALL IT "MORNING SURPRISE."
TAP TAP TAP
IS THAT MY TOOTHBRUSH??
"SURPRISE."

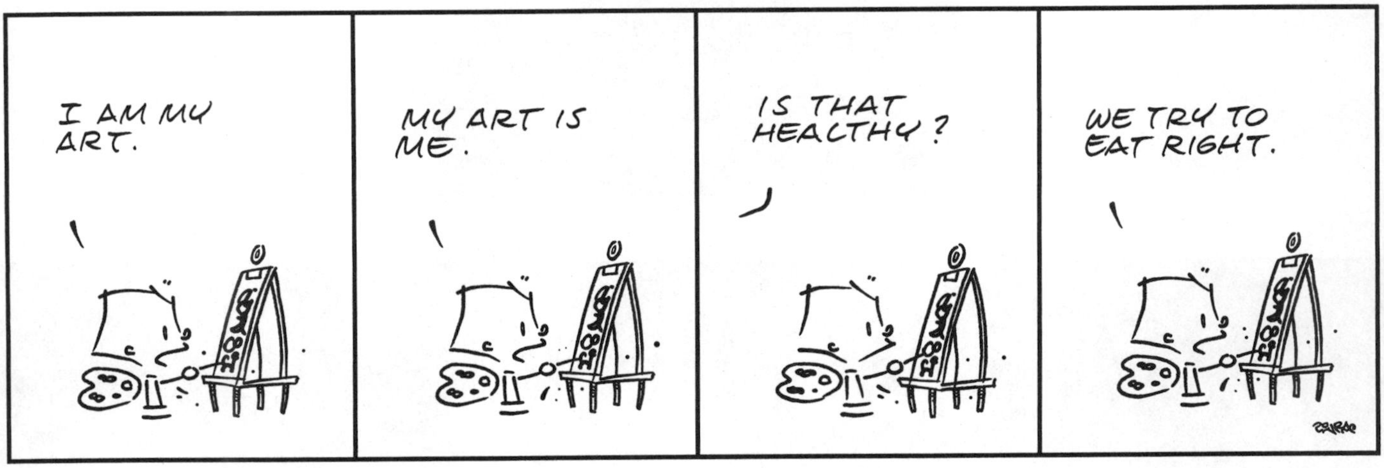
I AM MY ART.
MY ART IS ME.
IS THAT HEALTHY?
WE TRY TO EAT RIGHT.

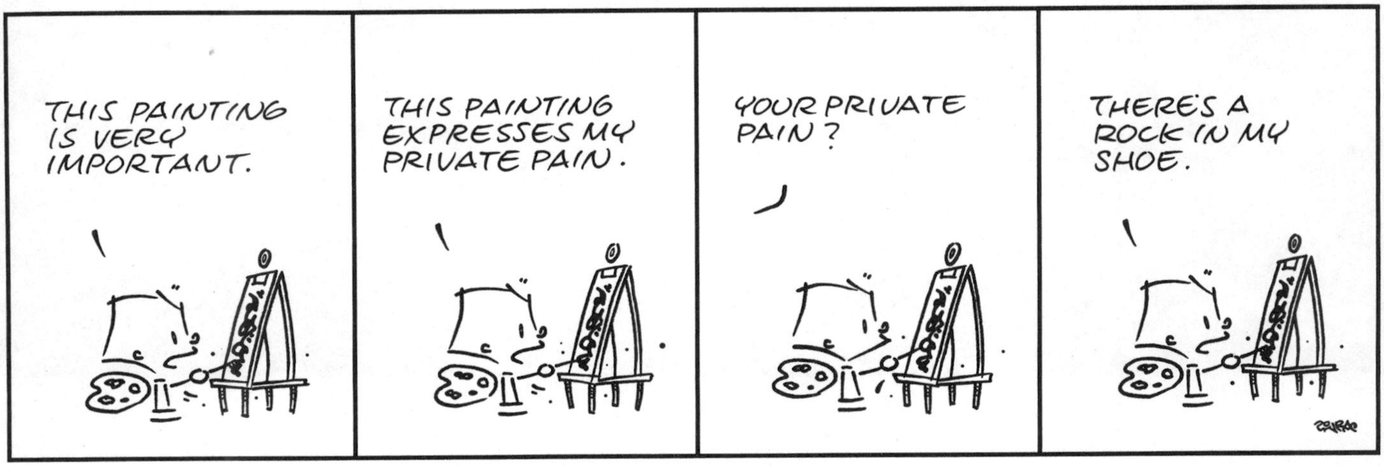
THIS PAINTING IS VERY IMPORTANT.
THIS PAINTING EXPRESSES MY PRIVATE PAIN.
YOUR PRIVATE PAIN?
THERE'S A ROCK IN MY SHOE.

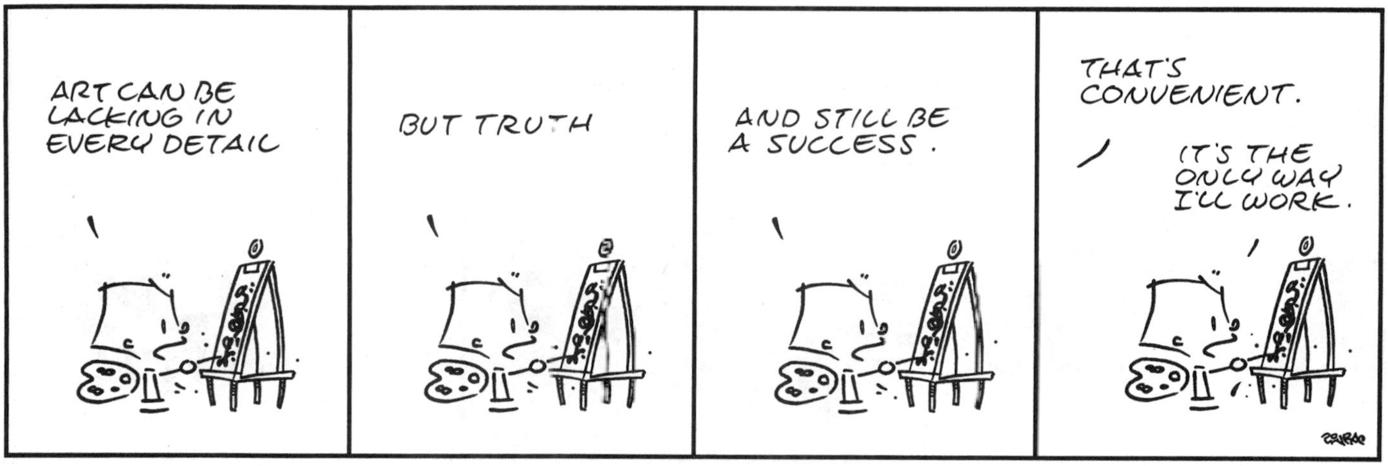
ART CAN BE LACKING IN EVERY DETAIL
BUT TRUTH
AND STILL BE A SUCCESS.
THAT'S CONVENIENT.
IT'S THE ONLY WAY I'LL WORK.

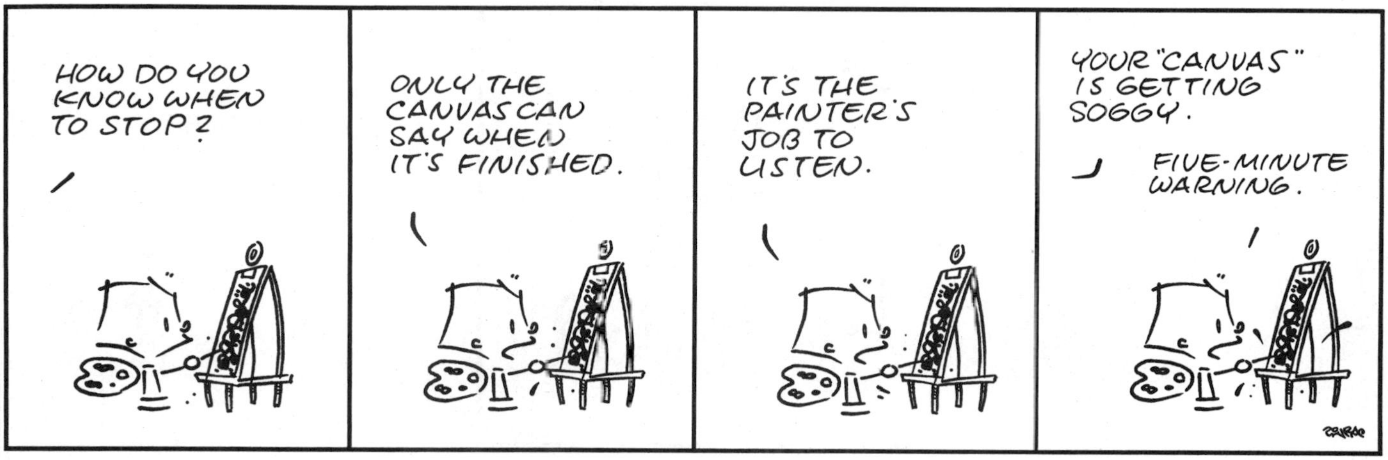
HOW DO YOU KNOW WHEN TO STOP?
ONLY THE CANVAS CAN SAY WHEN IT'S FINISHED.
IT'S THE PAINTER'S JOB TO LISTEN.
YOUR "CANVAS" IS GETTING SOGGY.
FIVE-MINUTE WARNING.

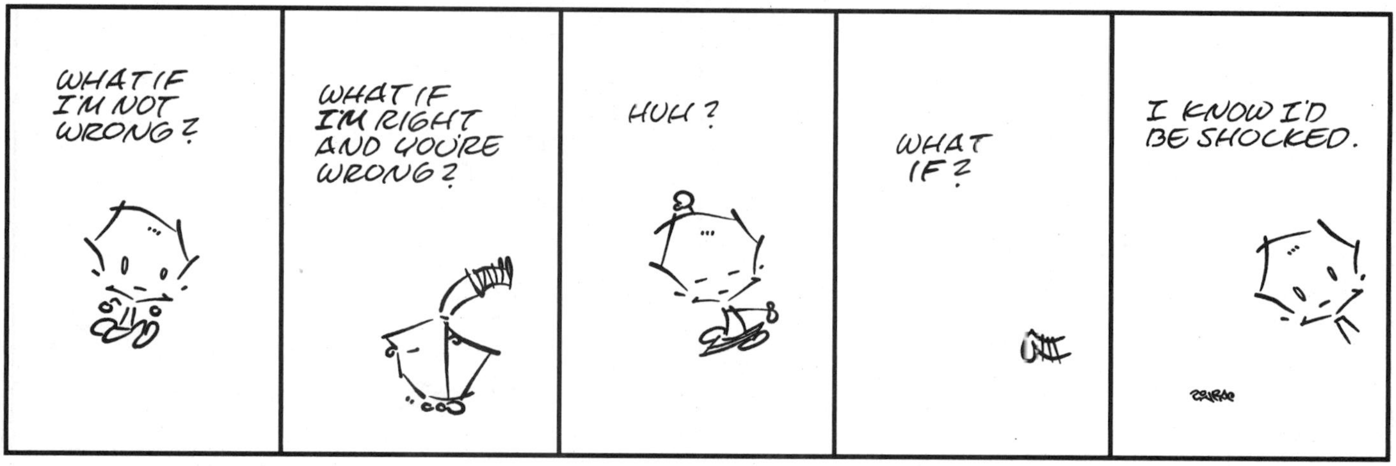
WHAT IF I'M NOT WRONG?
WHAT IF I'M RIGHT AND YOU'RE WRONG?
HUH?
WHAT IF?
I KNOW I'D BE SHOCKED.

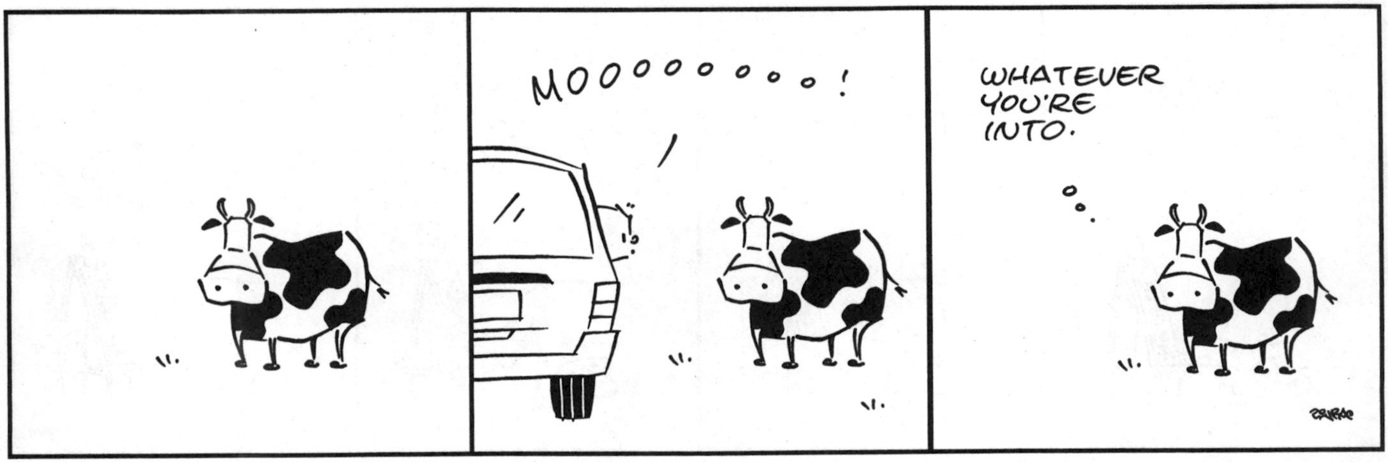
MOOOOOOOOO!
WHATEVER YOU'RE INTO.

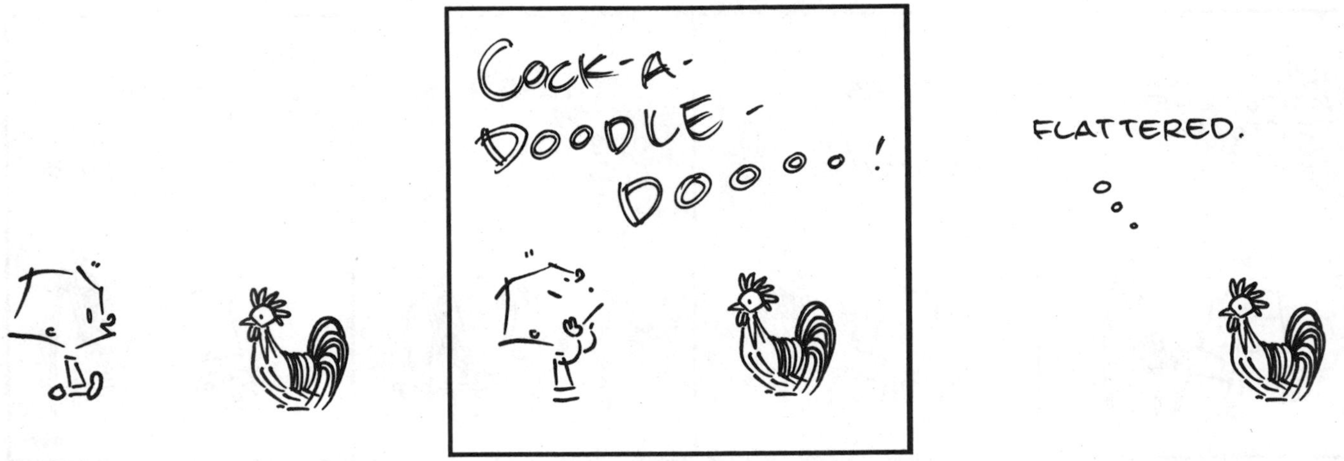
COCK-A-DOODLE-DOOOOO!
FLATTERED.

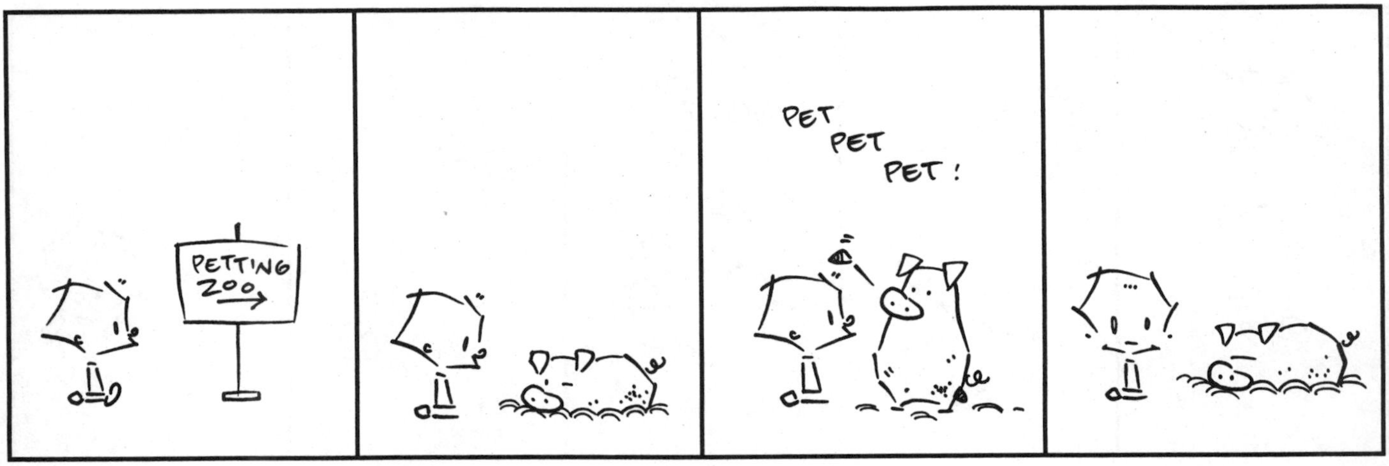
PETTING ZOO
PET PET PET!

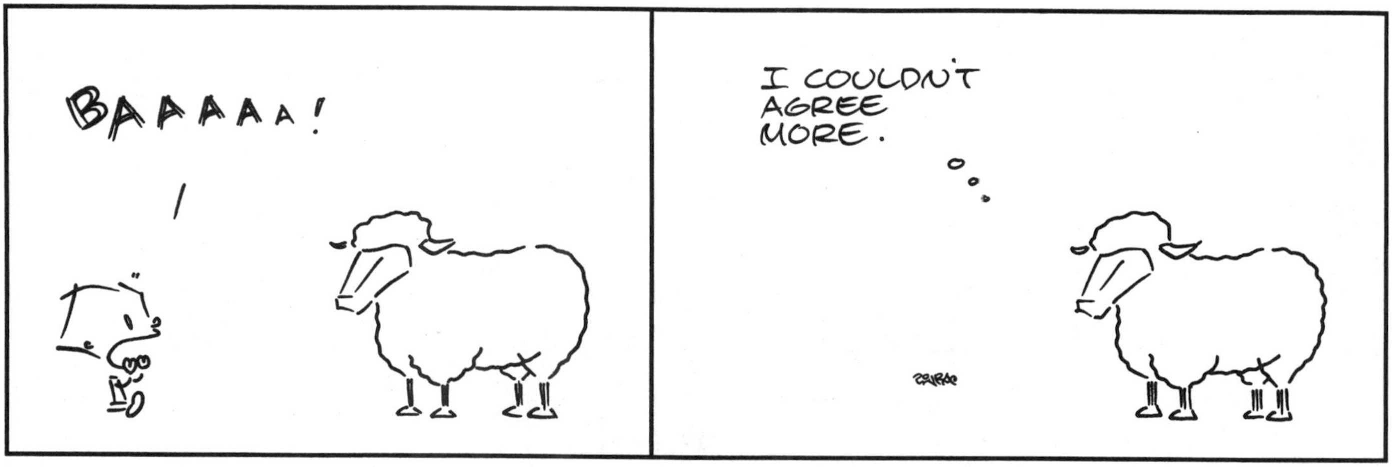
BAAAAA!
I COULDN'T AGREE MORE.

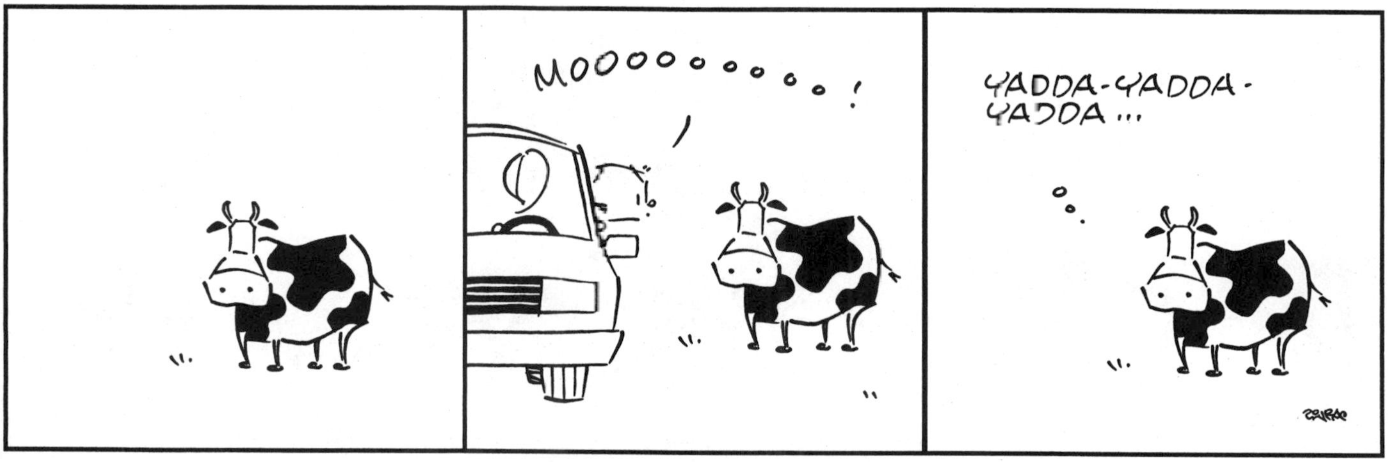
MOOOOOOOOOOO!
YADDA-YADDA-YADDA...

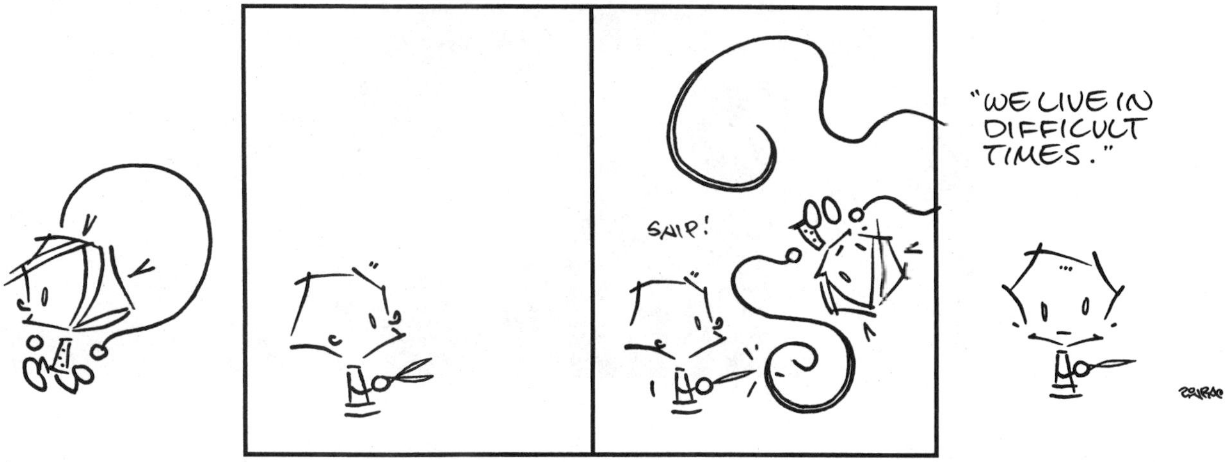
SNIP!
"WE LIVE IN DIFFICULT TIMES."

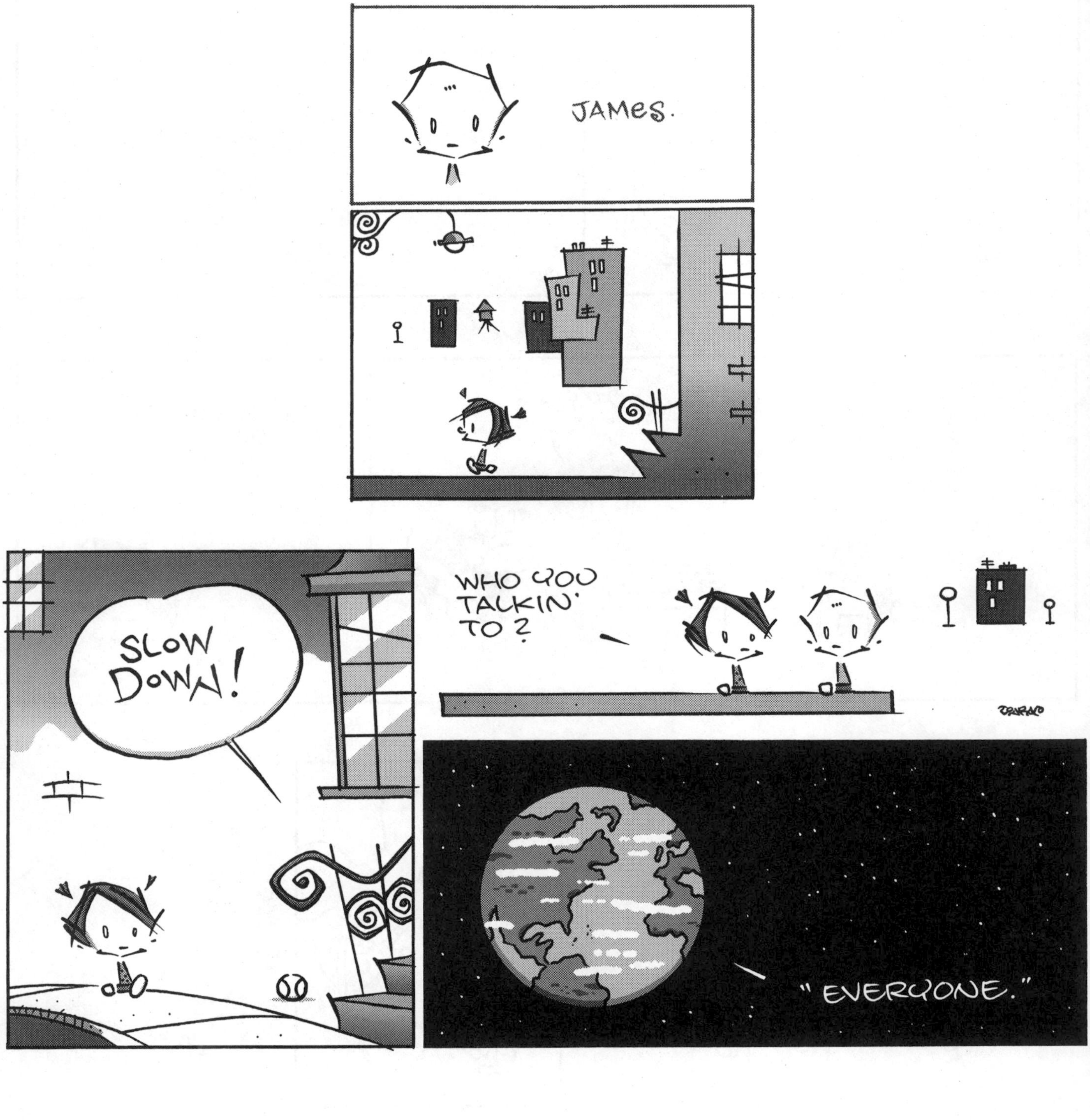
JAMES.
SLOW DOWN!
WHO YOU TALKIN' TO?
"EVERYONE."

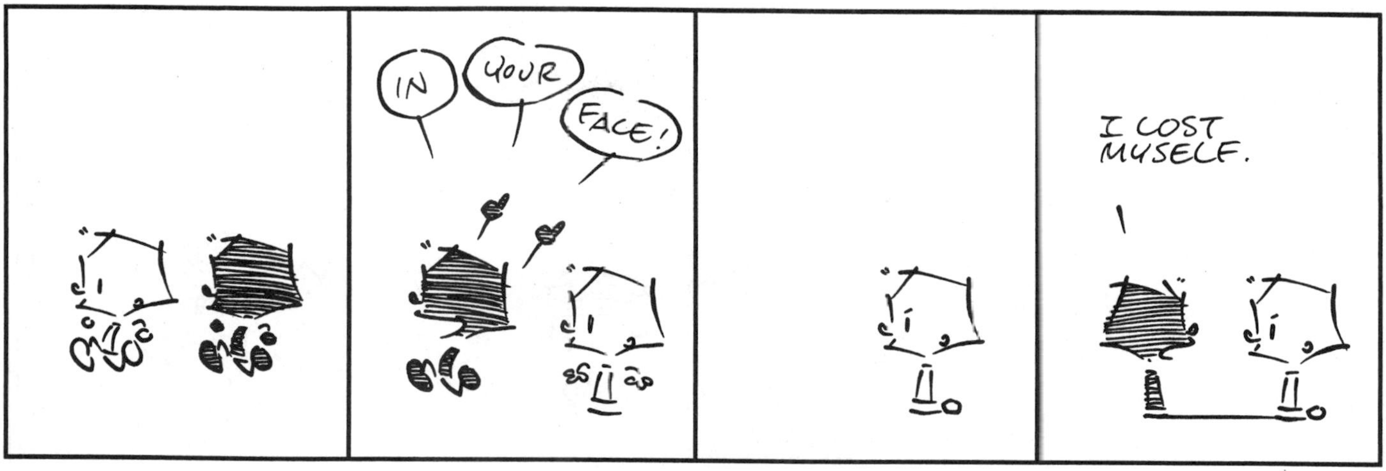
IN
YOUR
FACE!
I LOST MYSELF.

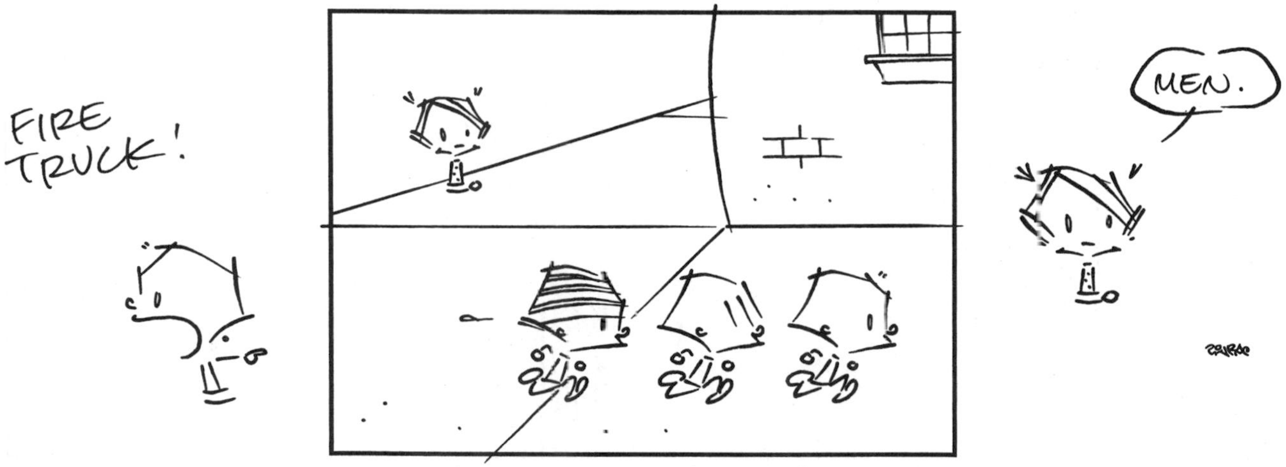
FIRE TRUCK!
MEN.

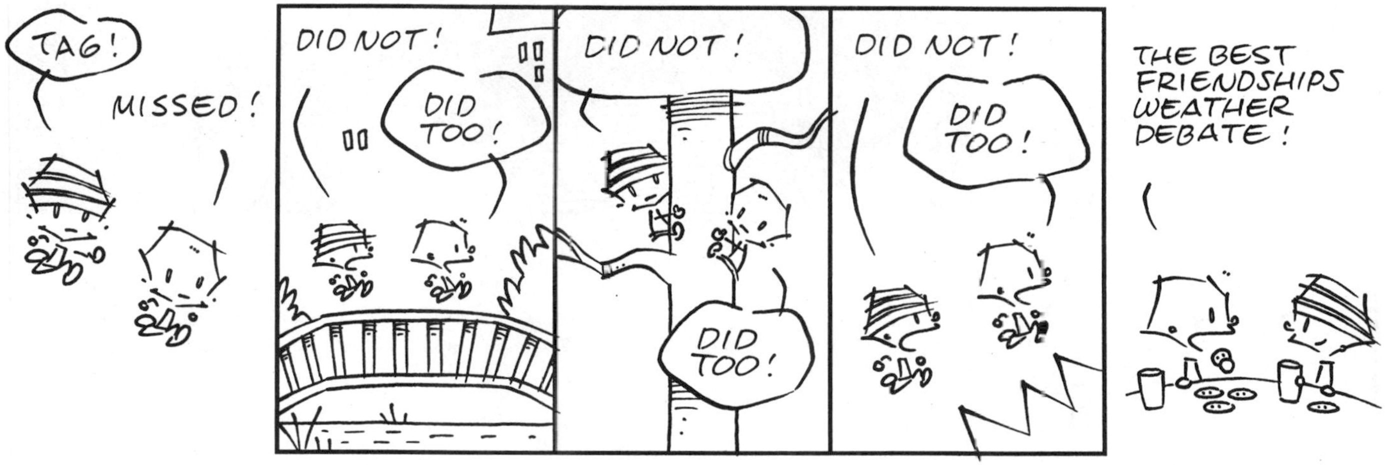
TAG!
MISSED!
DID NOT!
DID TOO!
DID NOT!
DID TOO!
DID NOT!
DID TOO!
THE BEST FRIENDSHIPS WEATHER DEBATE!

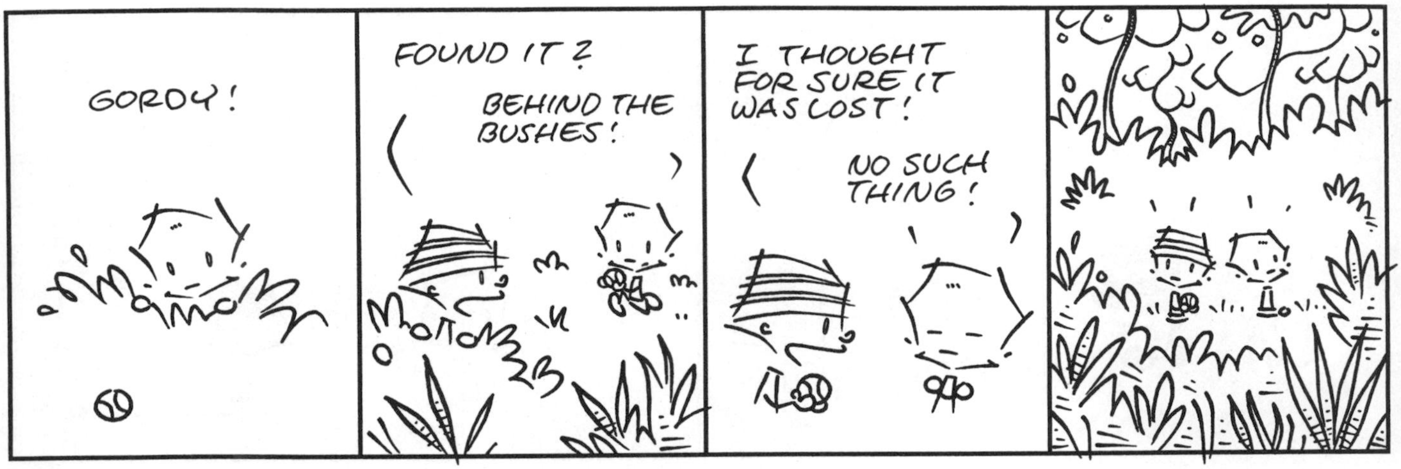
GORDY!
FOUND IT?
BEHIND THE BUSHES!
I THOUGHT FOR SURE IT WAS LOST!
NO SUCH THING!

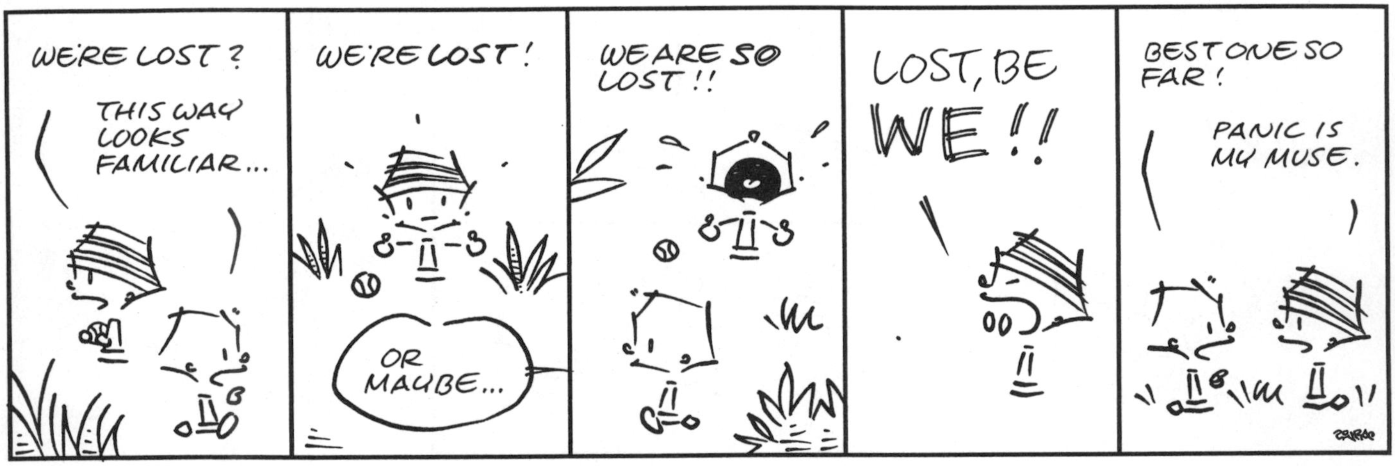
WE'RE LOST?
THIS WAY LOOKS FAMILIAR...
WE'RE LOST!
OR MAYBE...
WE ARE SO LOST!!
LOST, BE WE!!
BEST ONE SO FAR!
PANIC IS MY MUSE.

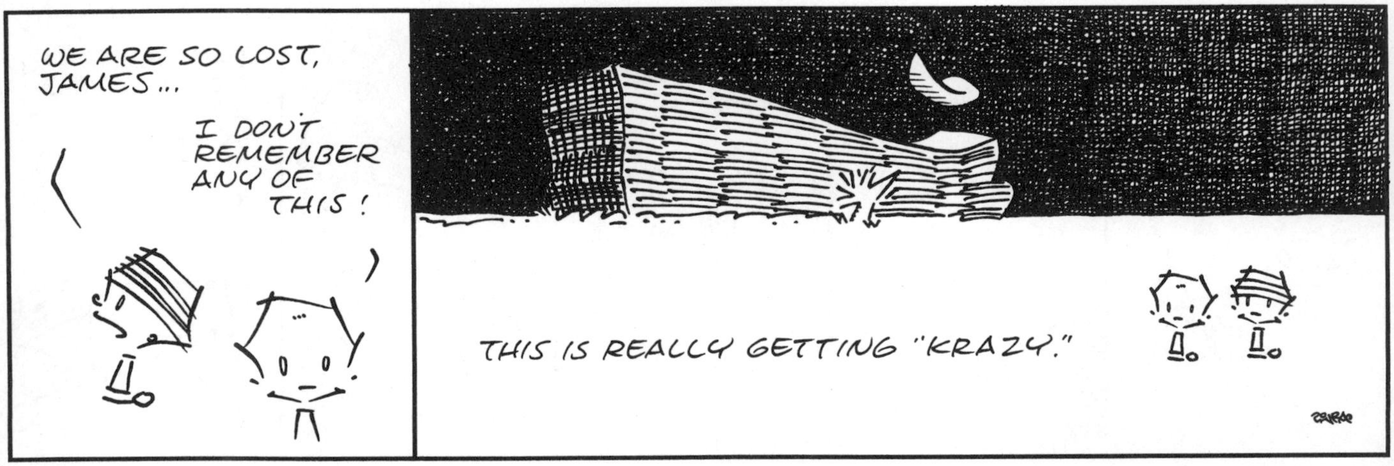
WE ARE SO LOST, JAMES...
I DON'T REMEMBER ANY OF THIS!
THIS IS REALLY GETTING "KRAZY."

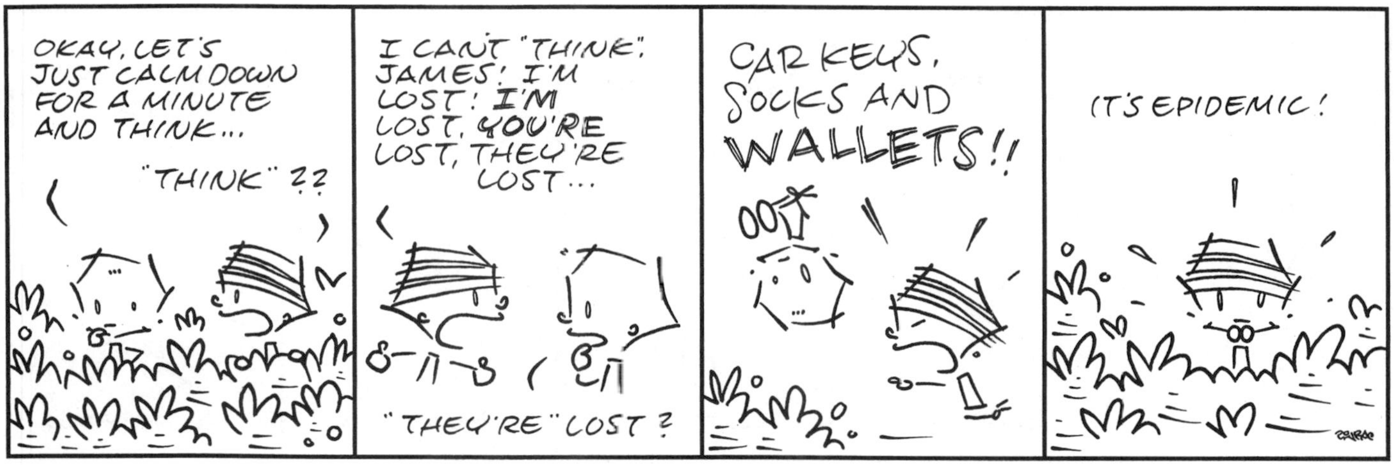
OKAY, LET'S JUST CALM DOWN FOR A MINUTE AND THINK...
"THINK"??
I CAN'T "THINK", JAMES! I'M LOST! I'M LOST, YOU'RE LOST, THEY'RE LOST...
"THEY'RE" LOST?
CAR KEYS, SOCKS AND WALLETS!!
IT'S EPIDEMIC!

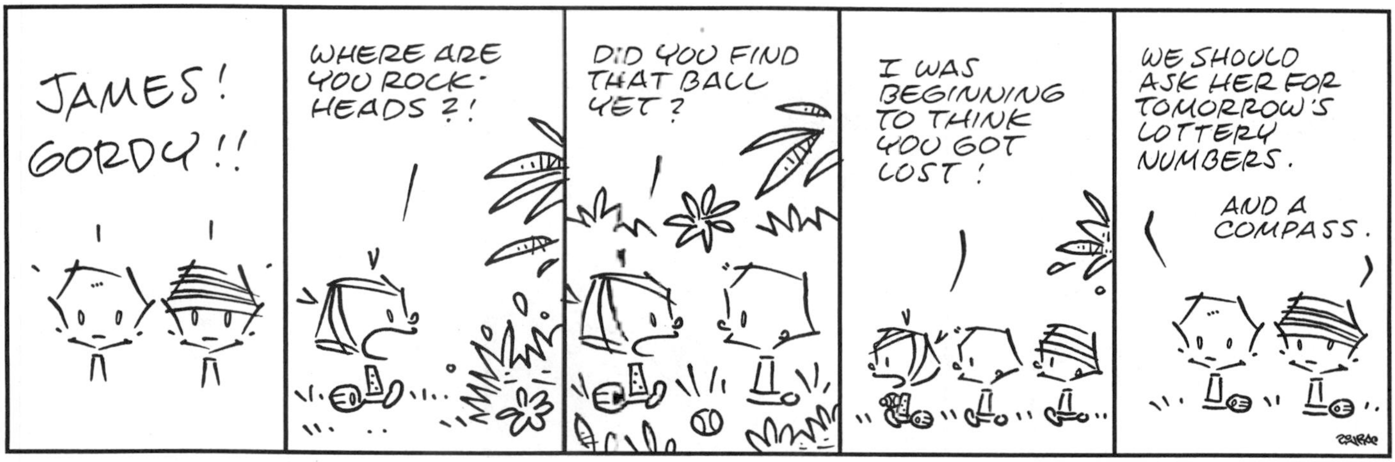
JAMES! GORDY!!
WHERE ARE YOU ROCK-HEADS?!
DID YOU FIND THAT BALL YET?
I WAS BEGINNING TO THINK YOU GOT LOST!
WE SHOULD ASK HER FOR TOMORROW'S LOTTERY NUMBERS.
AND A COMPASS.

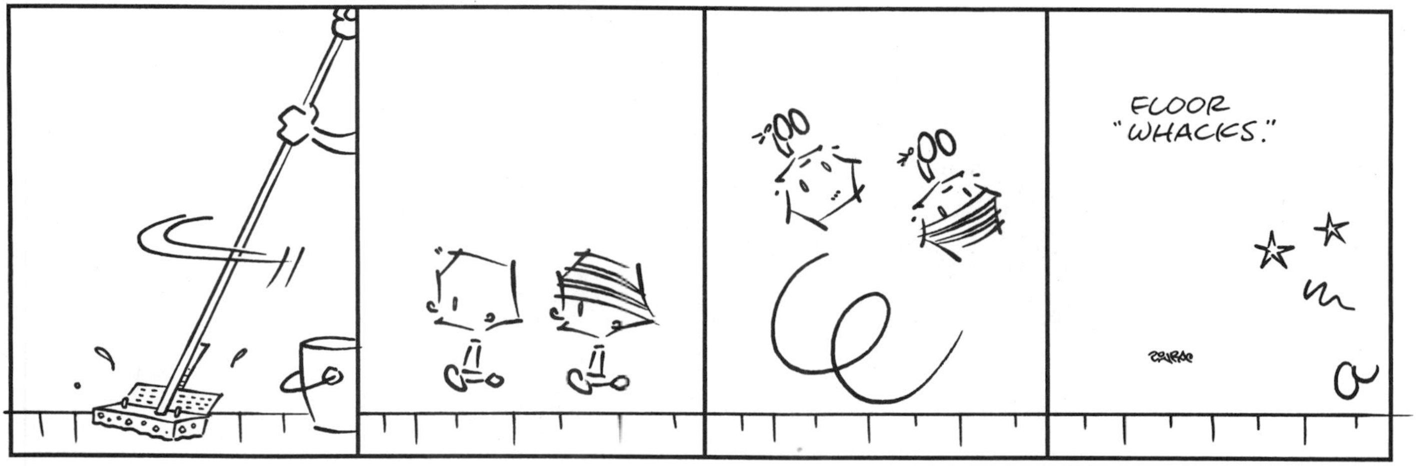
FLOOR "WHACKS."

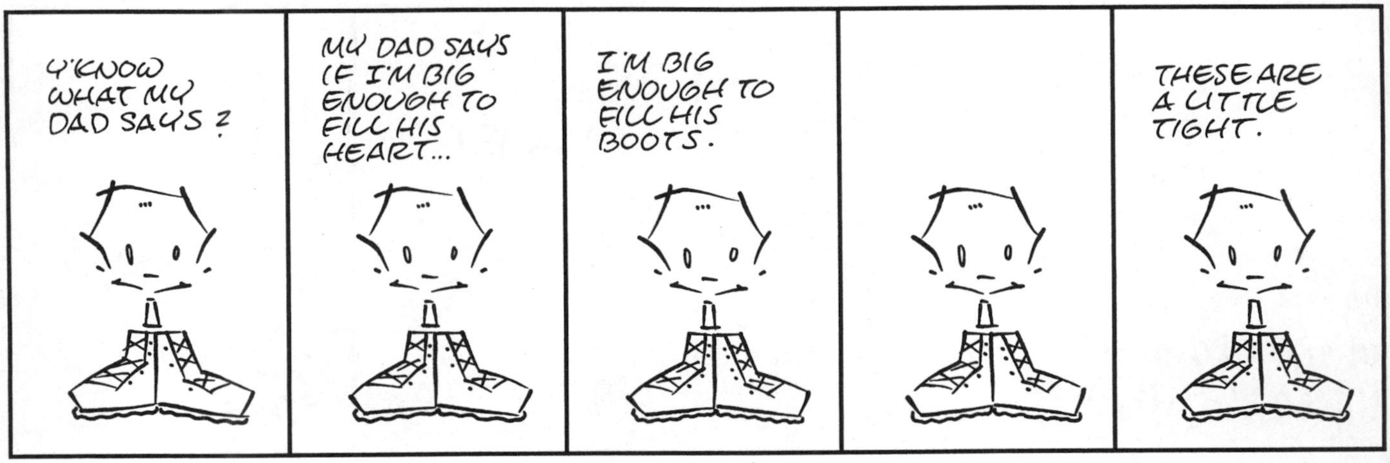
Y'KNOW WHAT MY DAD SAYS?
MY DAD SAYS IF I'M BIG ENOUGH TO FILL HIS HEART...
I'M BIG ENOUGH TO FILL HIS BOOTS.
THESE ARE A LITTLE TIGHT.

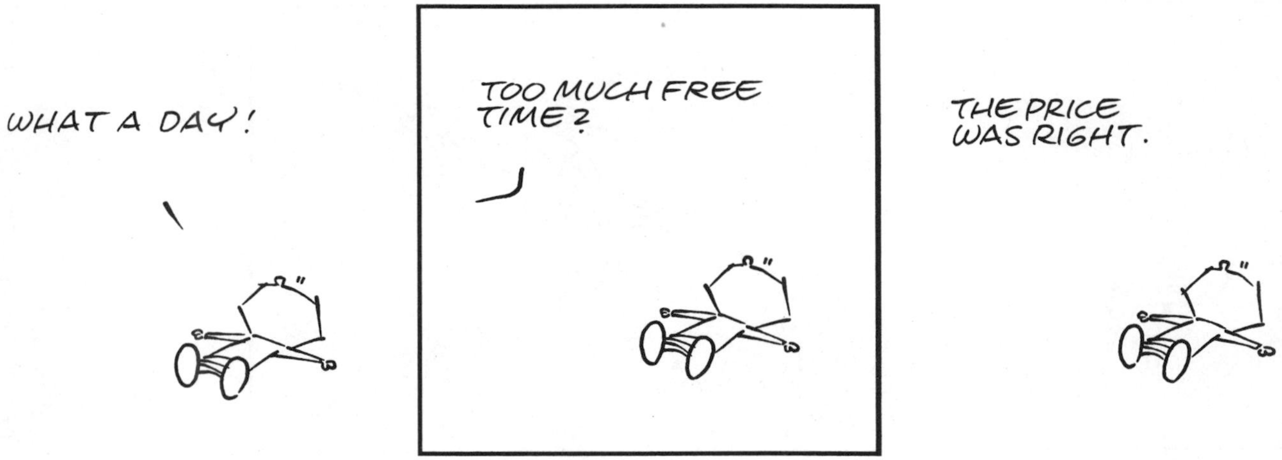
WHAT A DAY!
TOO MUCH FREE TIME?
THE PRICE WAS RIGHT.

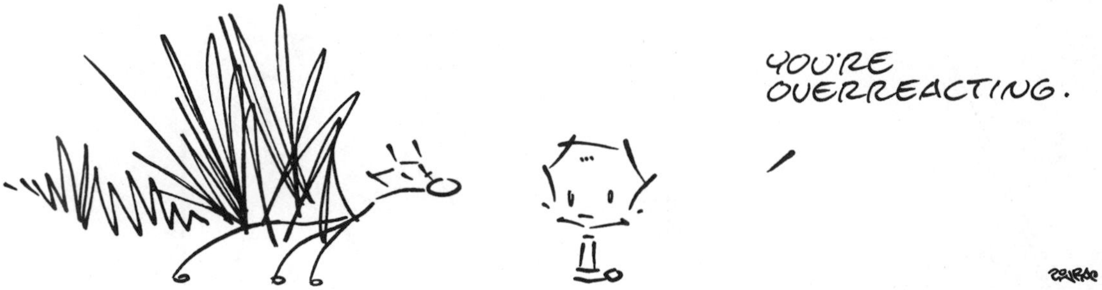
YOU'RE OVERREACTING.

HEY.
HEY.
BAD DREAM?
DELIGHTFUL DROOLING GOOGALIE MONSTERS.
"DELIGHTFUL"?
THEIR WORDS, NOT MINE.

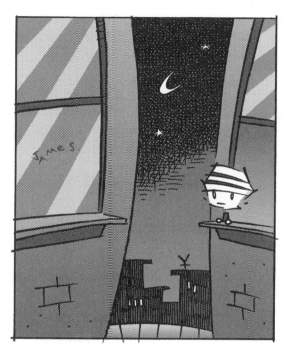

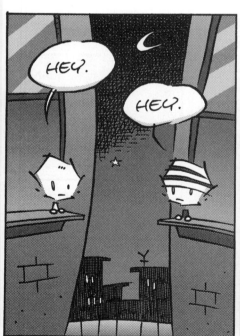

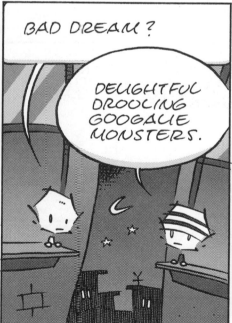

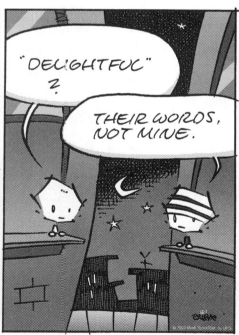

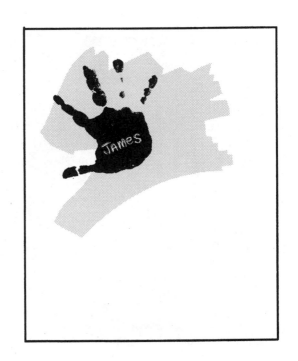

TRUE OR FALSE?

| I'LL HELP! | HE STARTED IT. | NOT TIRED! | I DIDN'T KNOW. |
| IT'S NOT WHAT IT LOOKS LIKE. | YES. | NO. | THE CAT DID IT. |

ANSWER: "THE TRUTH IS RARELY PURE, AND NEVER SIMPLE."

34

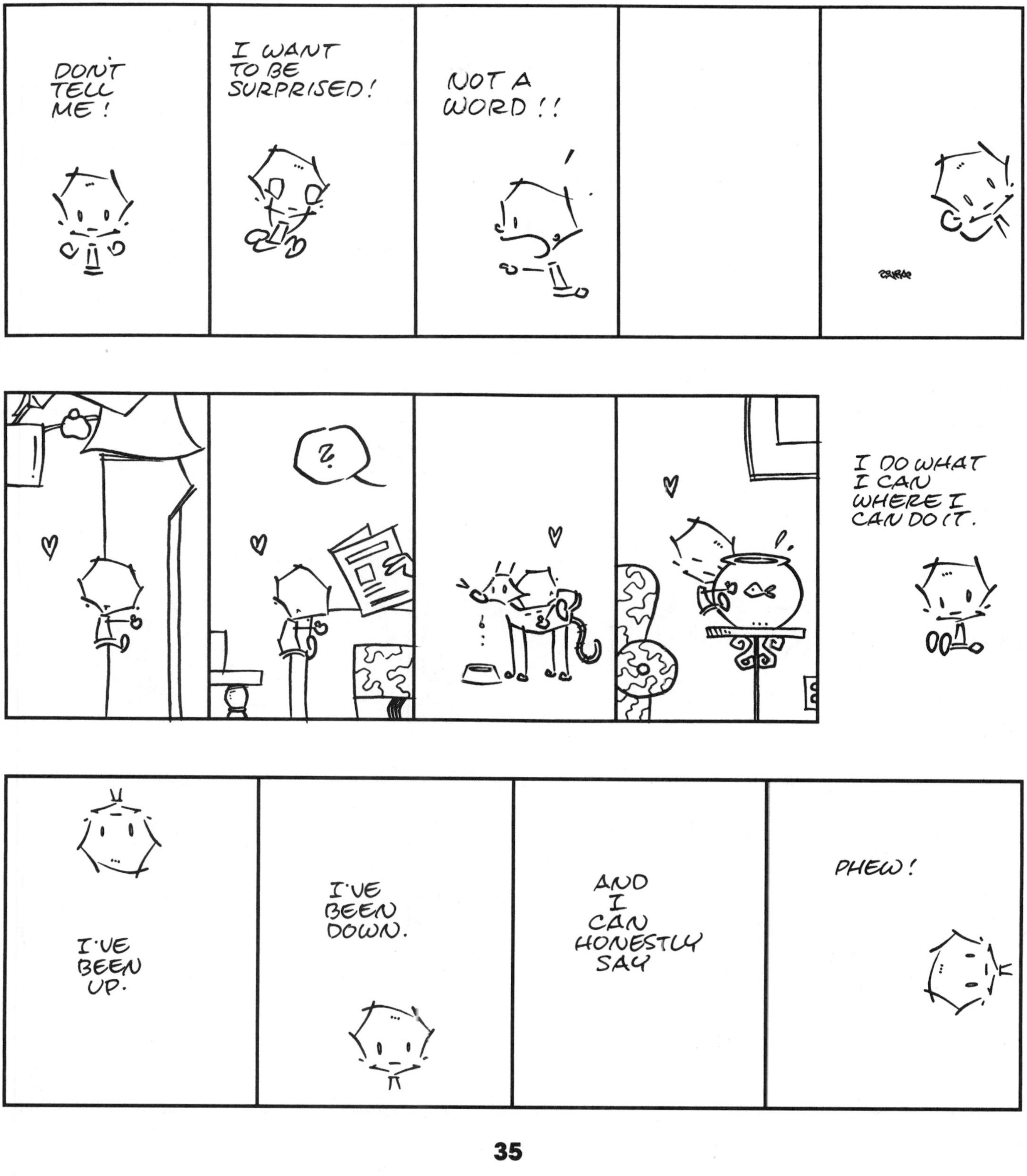
DON'T TELL ME!
I WANT TO BE SURPRISED!
NOT A WORD!!
?
I DO WHAT I CAN WHERE I CAN DO IT.
I'VE BEEN UP.
I'VE BEEN DOWN.
AND I CAN HONESTLY SAY
PHEW!

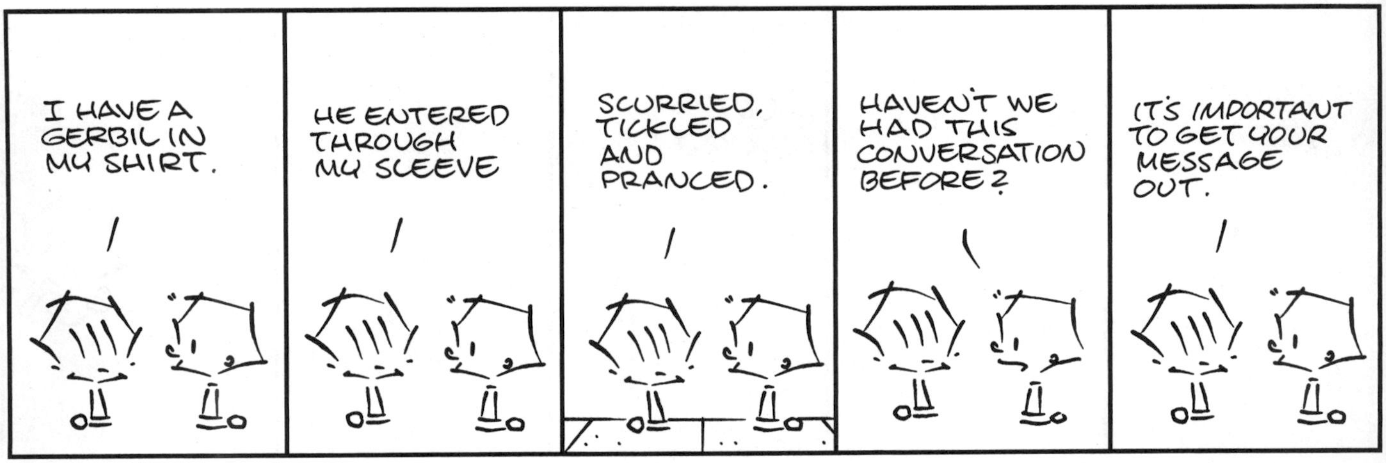
I HAVE A GERBIL IN MY SHIRT.
HE ENTERED THROUGH MY SLEEVE
SCURRIED, TICKLED AND PRANCED.
HAVEN'T WE HAD THIS CONVERSATION BEFORE?
IT'S IMPORTANT TO GET YOUR MESSAGE OUT.

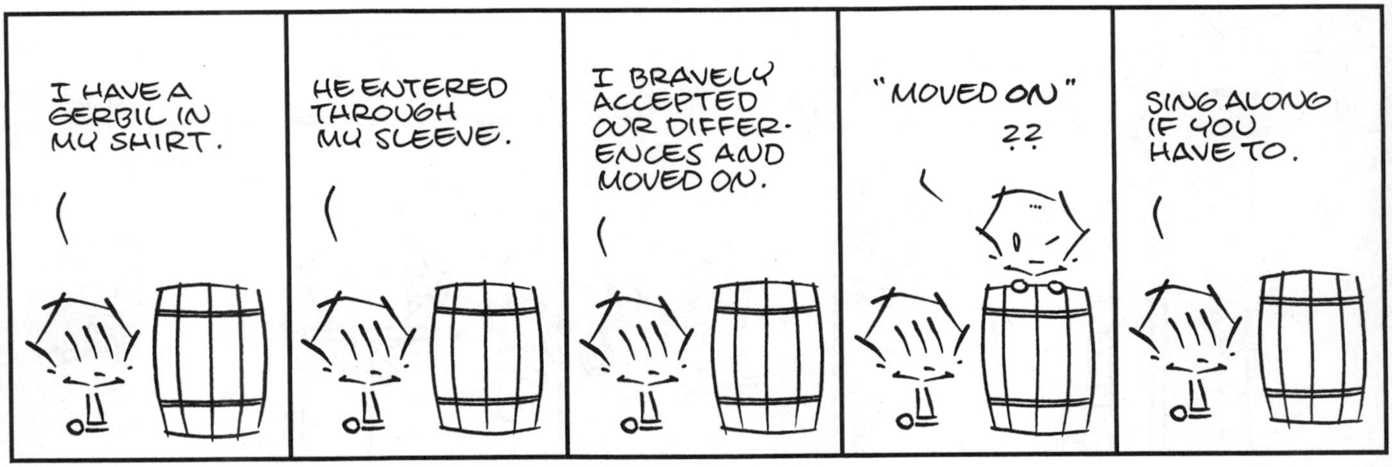
I HAVE A GERBIL IN MY SHIRT.
HE ENTERED THROUGH MY SLEEVE.
I BRAVELY ACCEPTED OUR DIFFERENCES AND MOVED ON.
"MOVED ON"
??
SING ALONG IF YOU HAVE TO.

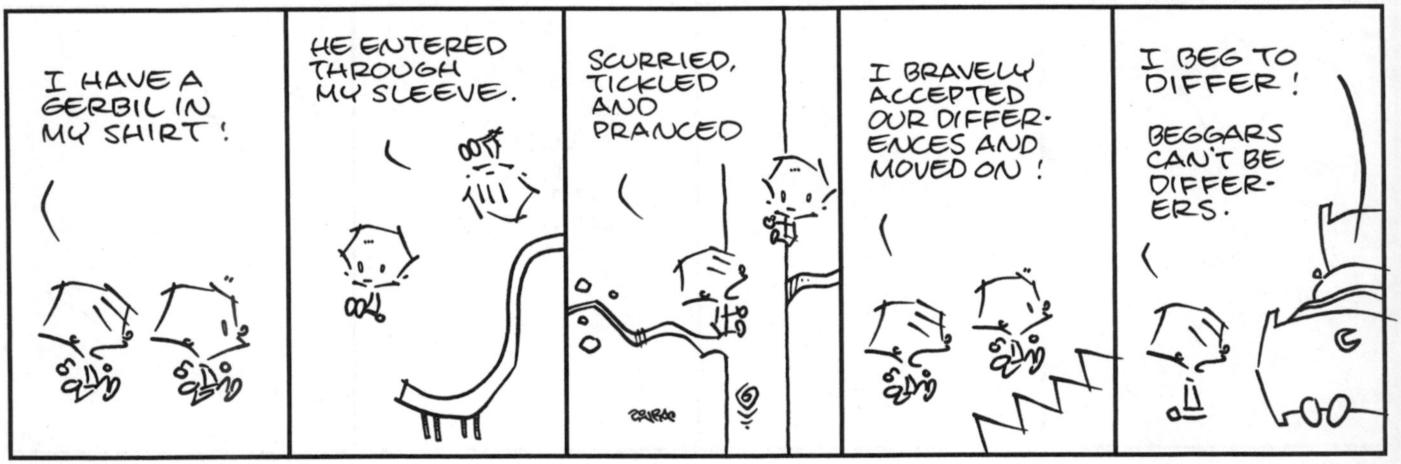
I HAVE A GERBIL IN MY SHIRT!
HE ENTERED THROUGH MY SLEEVE.
SCURRIED, TICKLED AND PRANCED
I BRAVELY ACCEPTED OUR DIFFERENCES AND MOVED ON!
I BEG TO DIFFER!
BEGGARS CAN'T BE DIFFERERS.

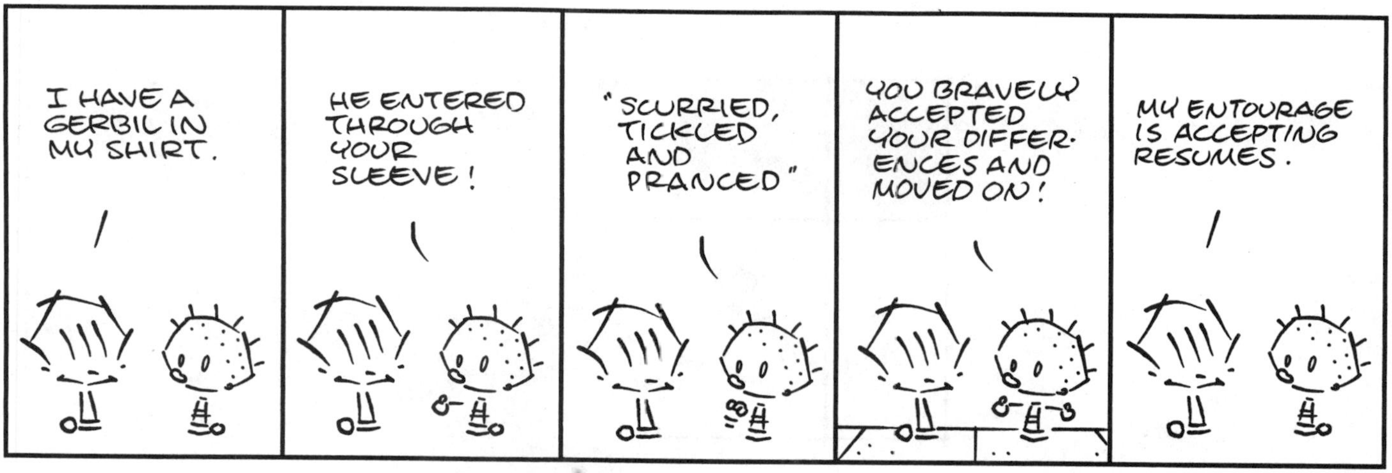
I HAVE A GERBIL IN MY SHIRT.
HE ENTERED THROUGH YOUR SLEEVE!
"SCURRIED, TICKLED AND PRANCED"
YOU BRAVELY ACCEPTED YOUR DIFFERENCES AND MOVED ON!
MY ENTOURAGE IS ACCEPTING RESUMES.

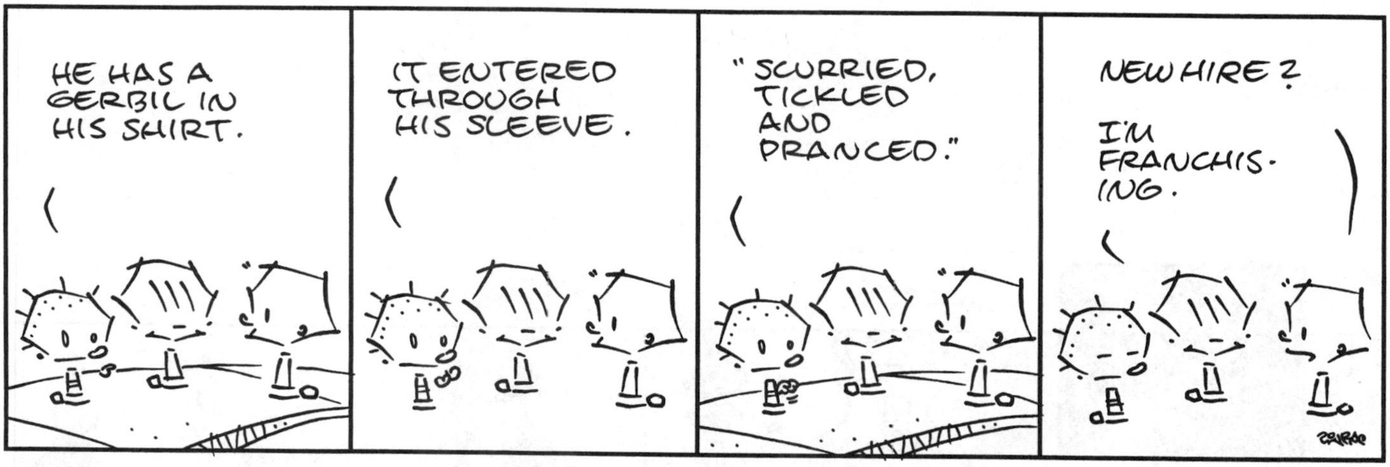
HE HAS A GERBIL IN HIS SHIRT.
IT ENTERED THROUGH HIS SLEEVE.
"SCURRIED, TICKLED AND PRANCED."
NEW HIRE?
I'M FRANCHISING.

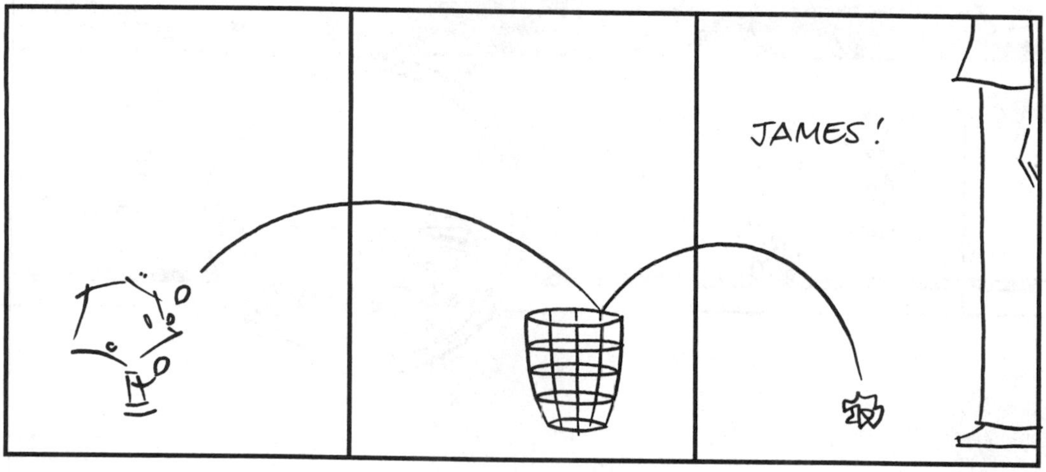
JAMES!

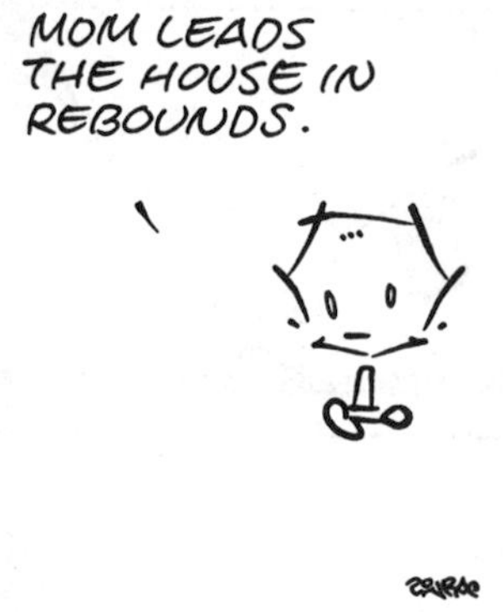
MOM LEADS THE HOUSE IN REBOUNDS.

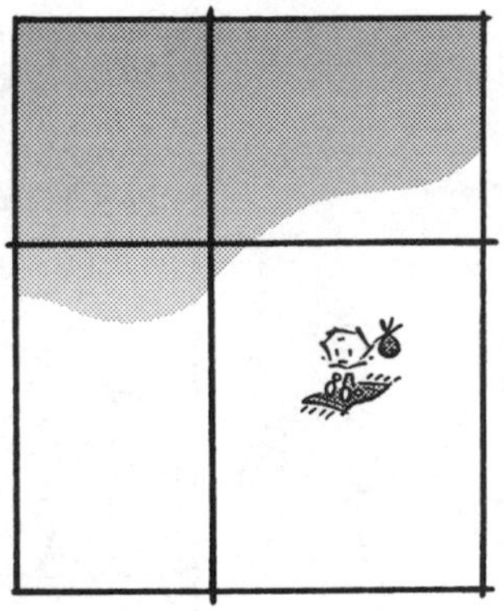

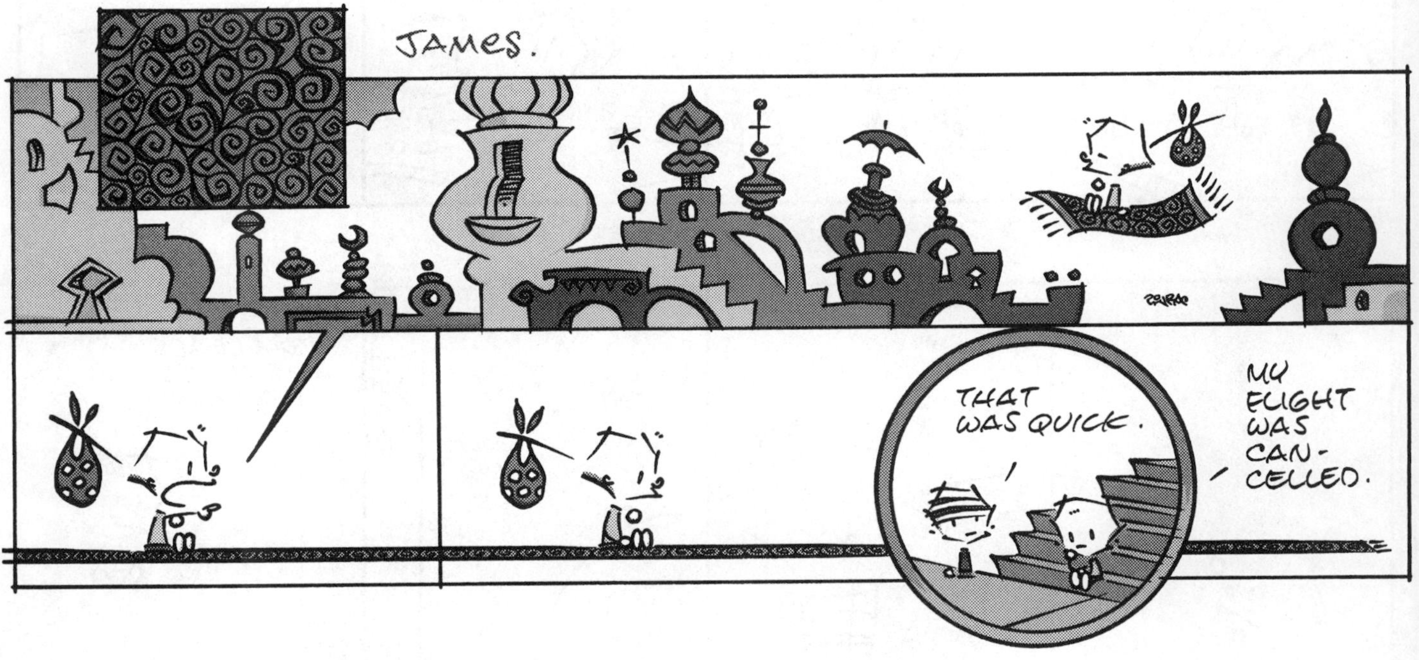
JAMES.
THAT WAS QUICK.
MY FLIGHT WAS CAN-CELLED.

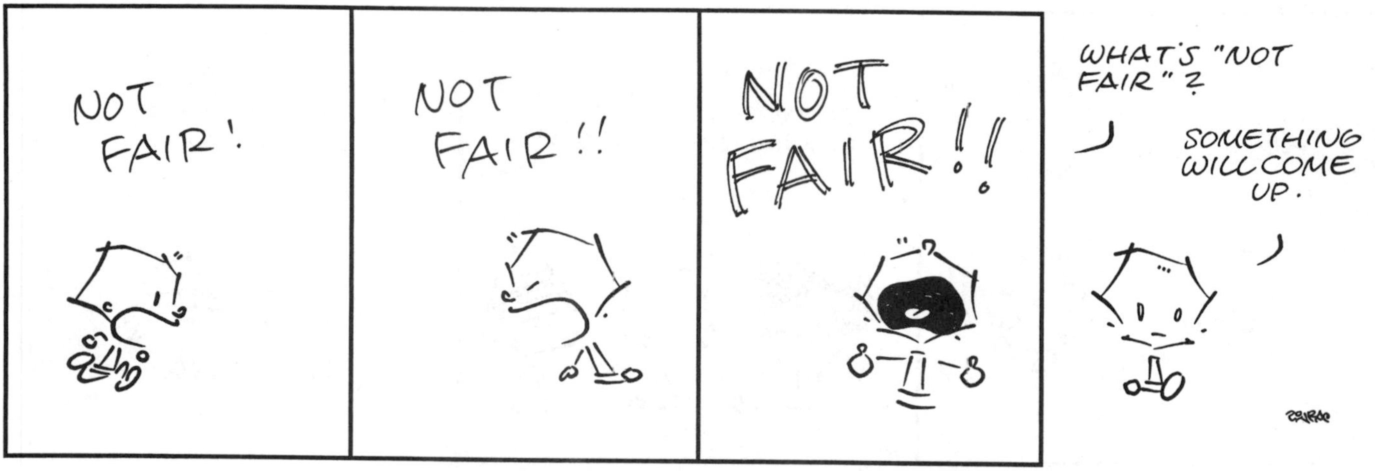
NOT FAIR!
NOT FAIR!!
NOT FAIR!!
WHAT'S "NOT FAIR"?
SOMETHING WILL COME UP.

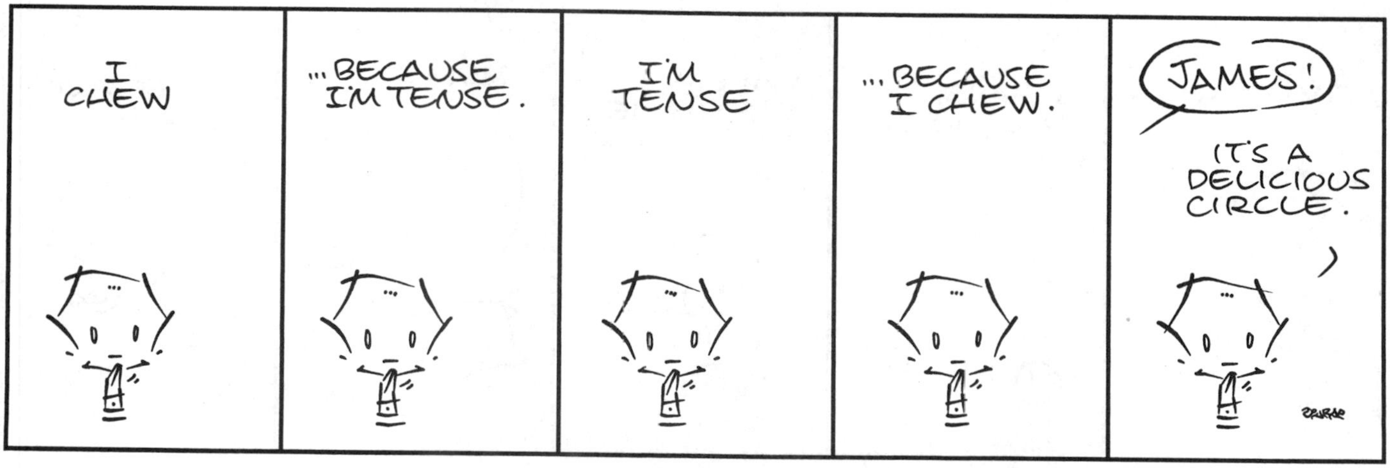
I CHEW
...BECAUSE I'M TENSE.
I'M TENSE
...BECAUSE I CHEW.
JAMES!
IT'S A DELICIOUS CIRCLE.

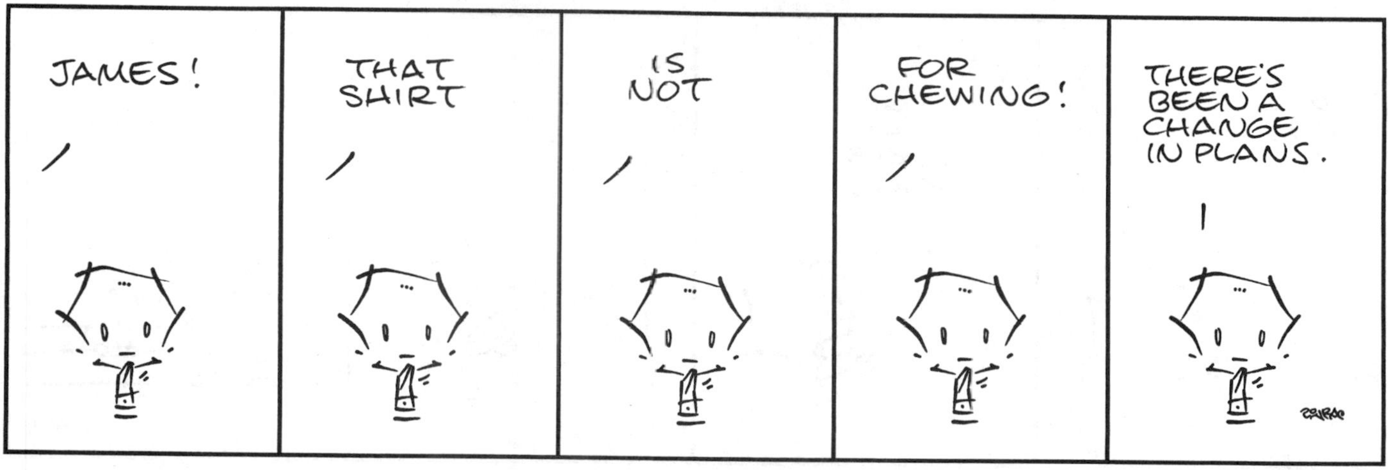
JAMES!
THAT SHIRT
IS NOT
FOR CHEWING!
THERE'S BEEN A CHANGE IN PLANS.

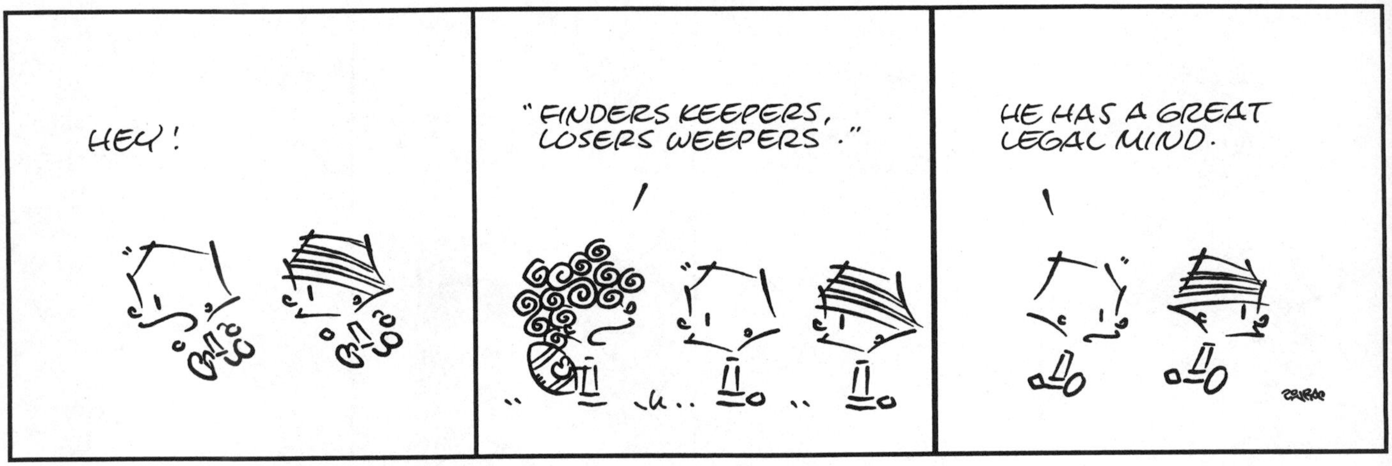
HEY!
"FINDERS KEEPERS, LOSERS WEEPERS."
HE HAS A GREAT LEGAL MIND.

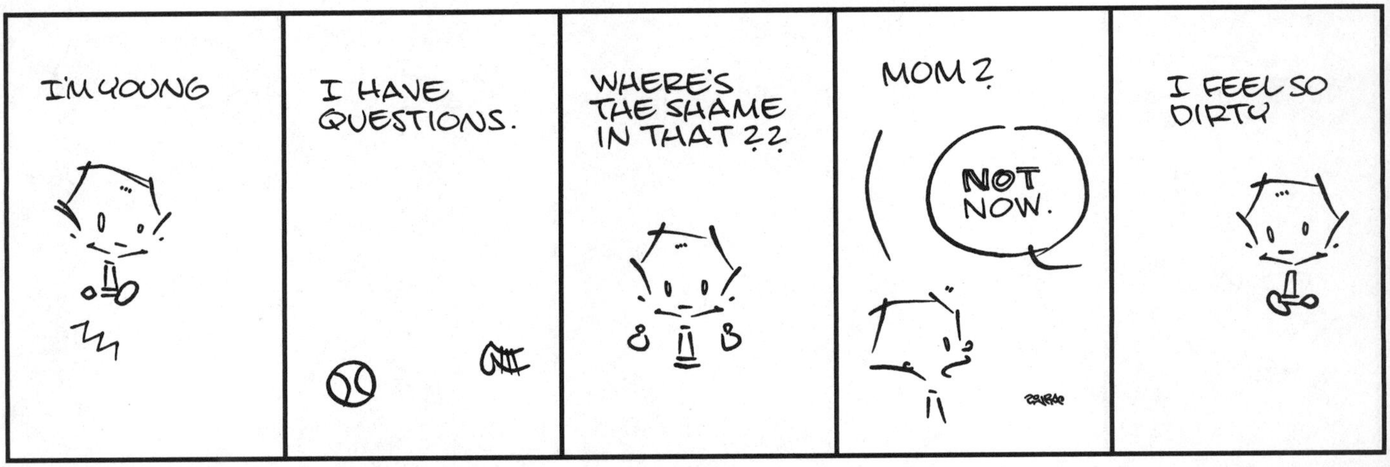
I'M YOUNG
I HAVE QUESTIONS.
WHERE'S THE SHAME IN THAT??
MOM?
NOT NOW.
I FEEL SO DIRTY

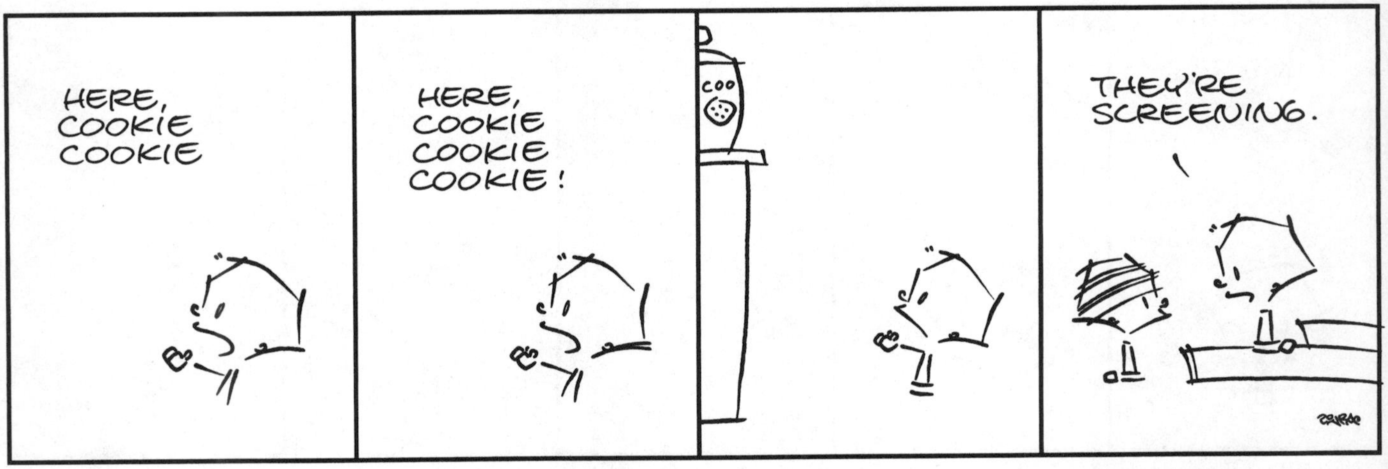
HERE, COOKIE COOKIE
HERE, COOKIE COOKIE COOKIE!
COO
THEY'RE SCREENING.

JAMES.

"CHANGE IS GOOD."

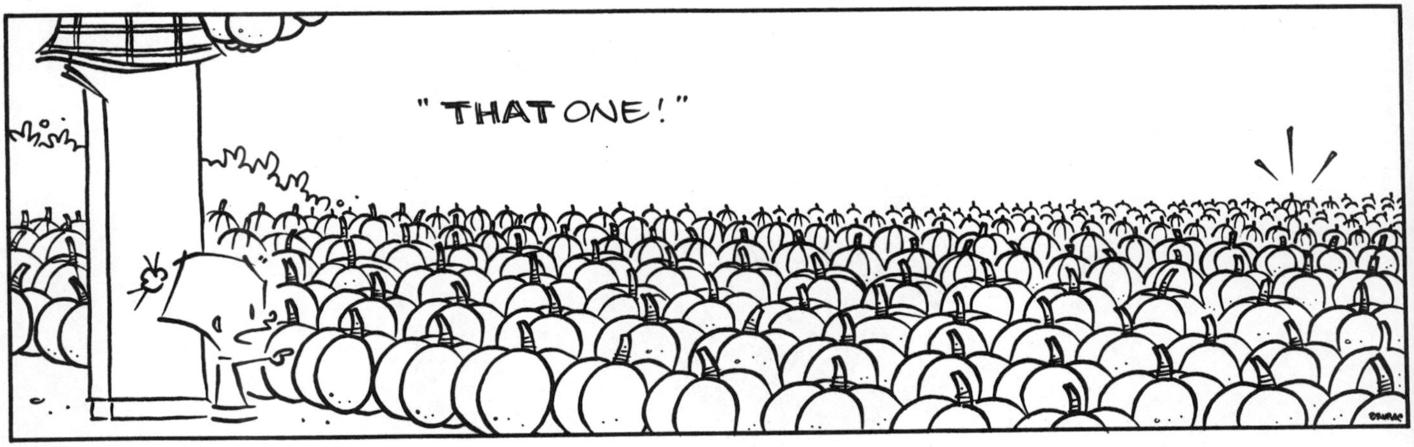
"THAT ONE!"

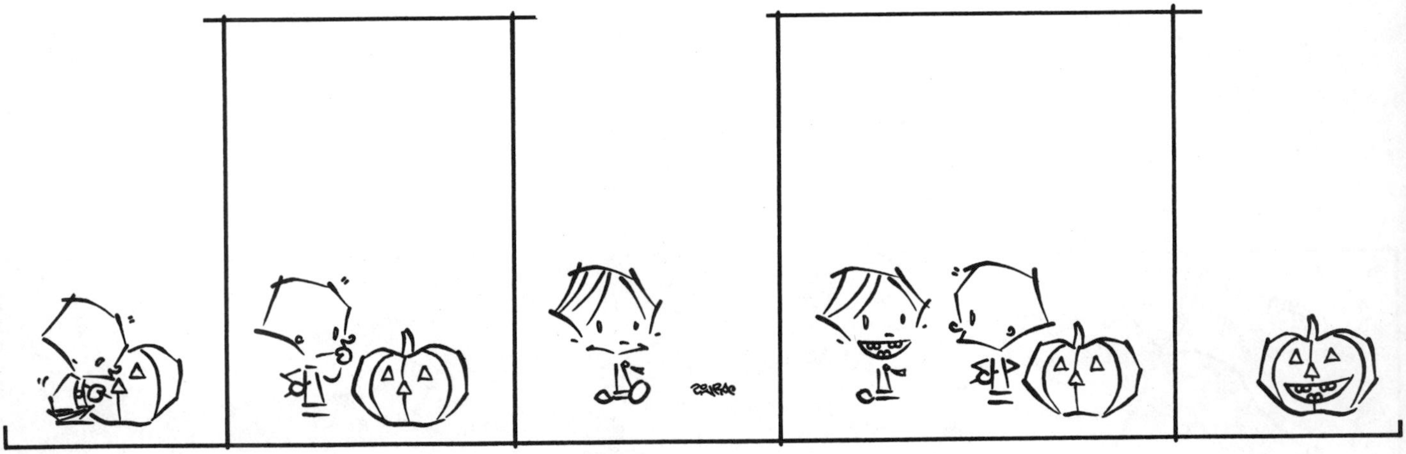

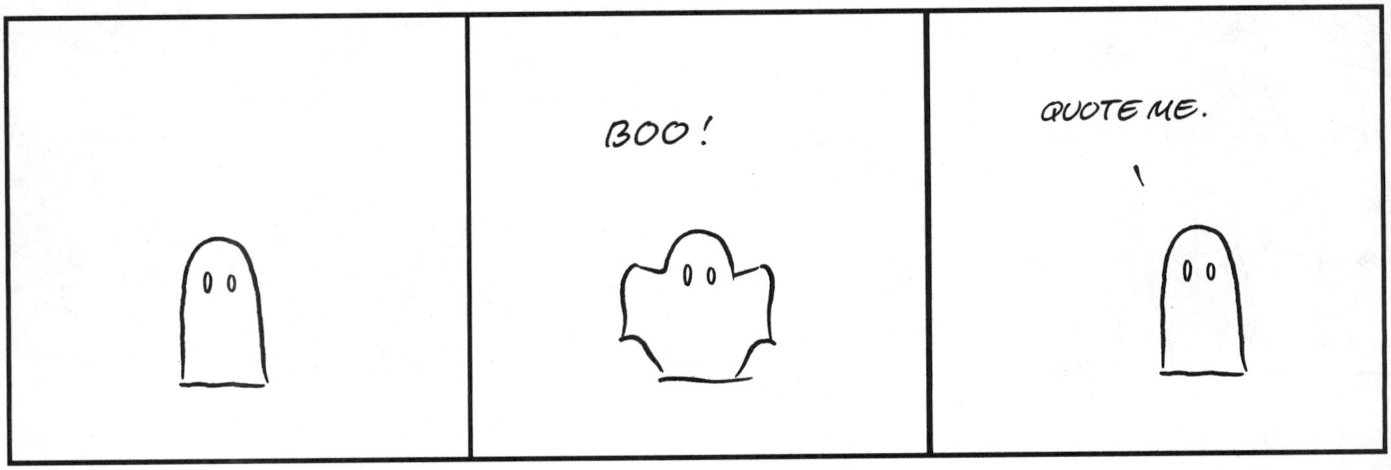
BOO!
QUOTE ME.

JAMES.

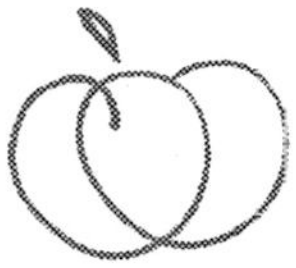

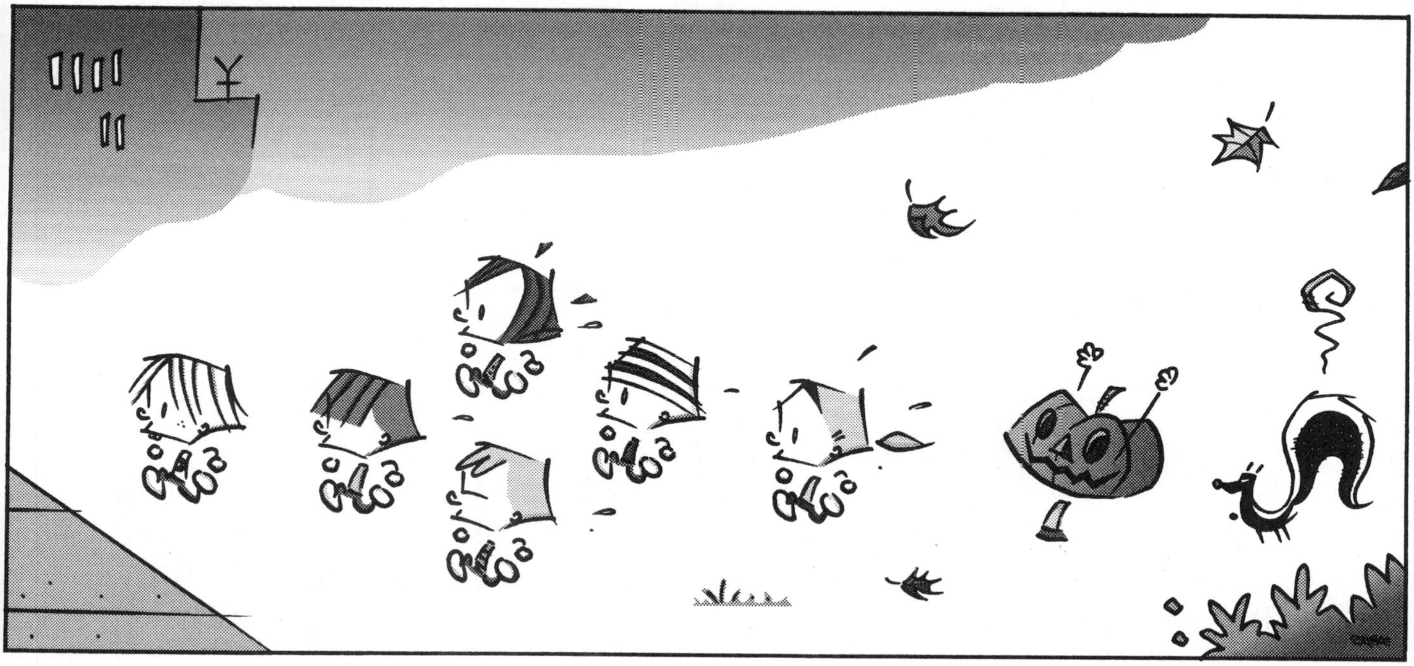

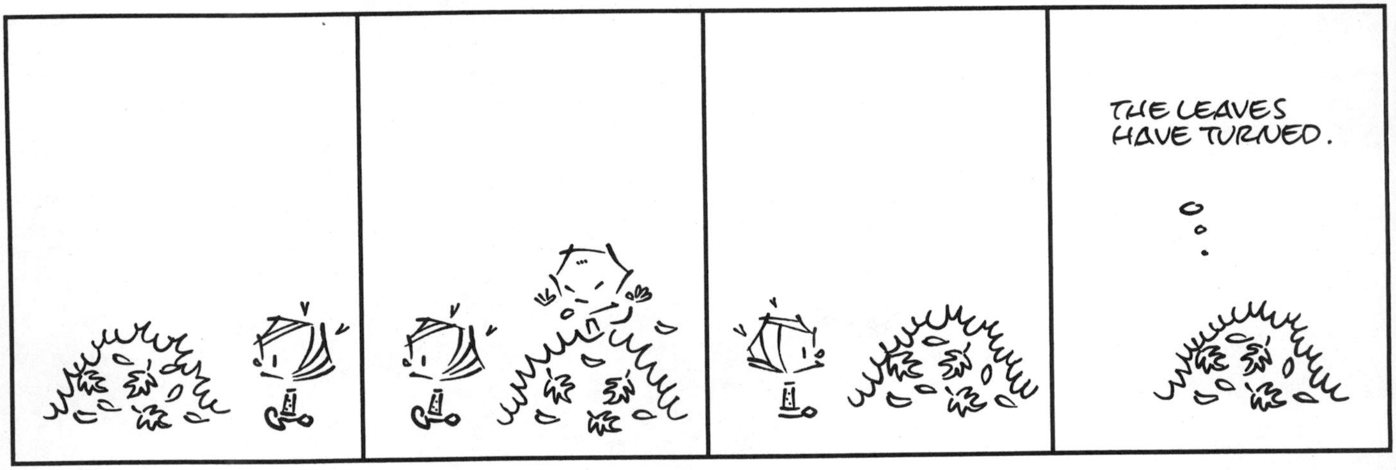
THE LEAVES HAVE TURNED.

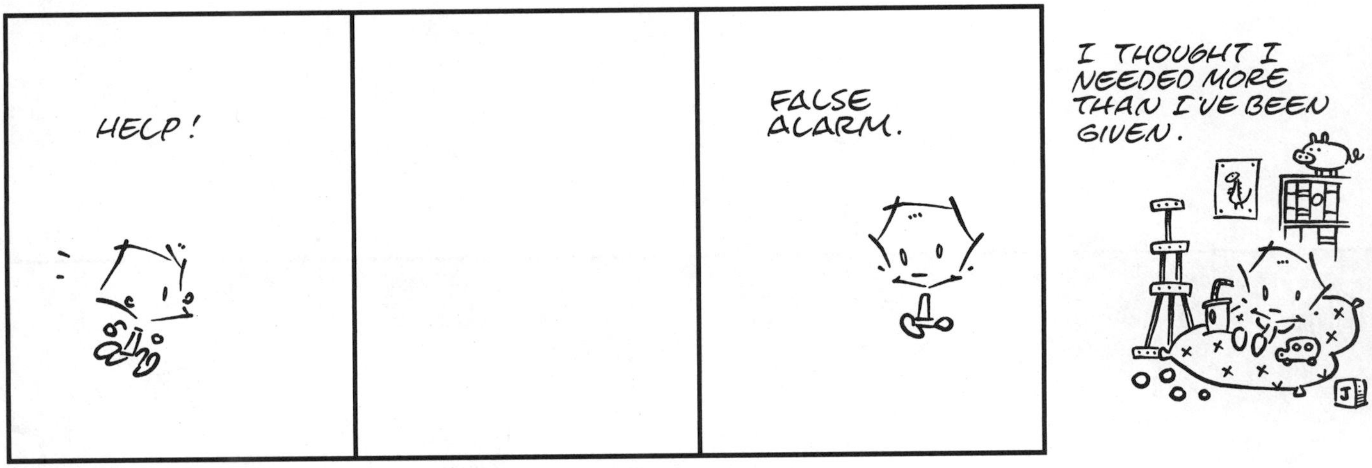
HELP!
FALSE ALARM.
I THOUGHT I NEEDED MORE THAN I'VE BEEN GIVEN.

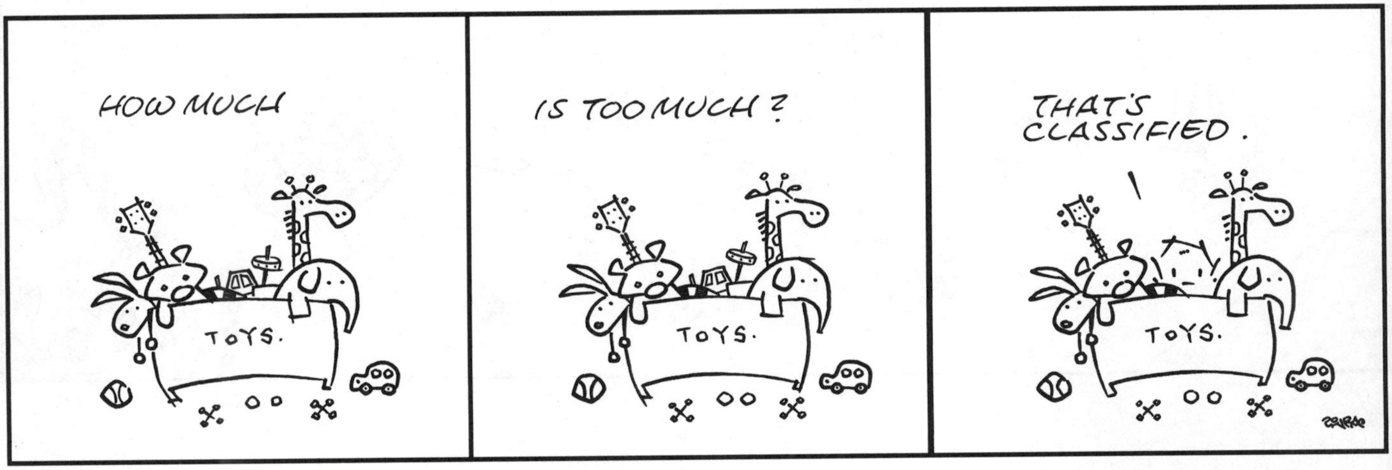
HOW MUCH
IS TOO MUCH?
THAT'S CLASSIFIED.
TOYS.
TOYS.
TOYS.

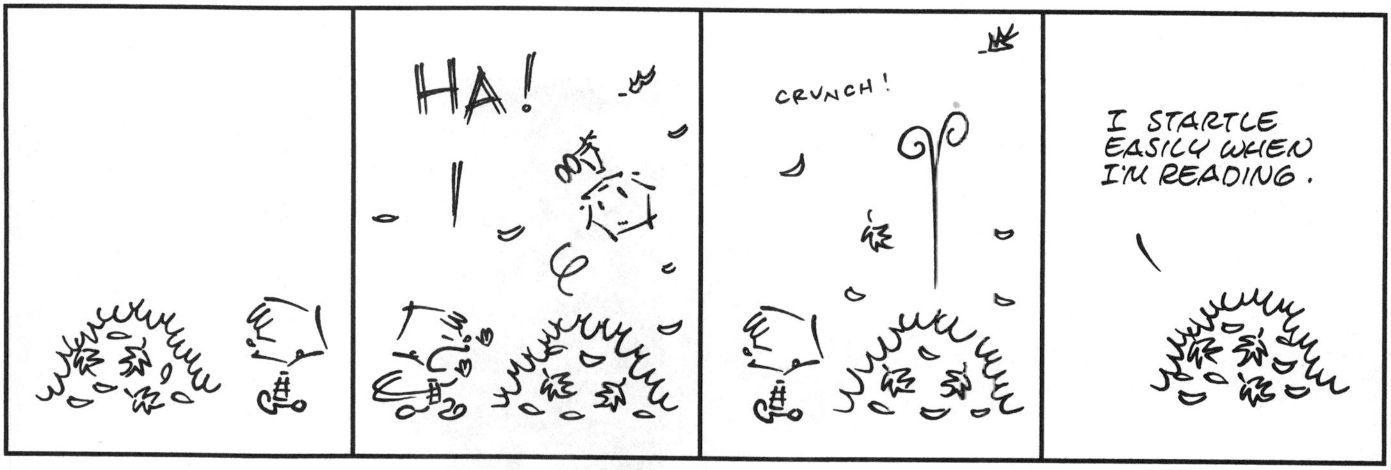
HA!
CRUNCH!
I STARTLE EASILY WHEN I'M READING.

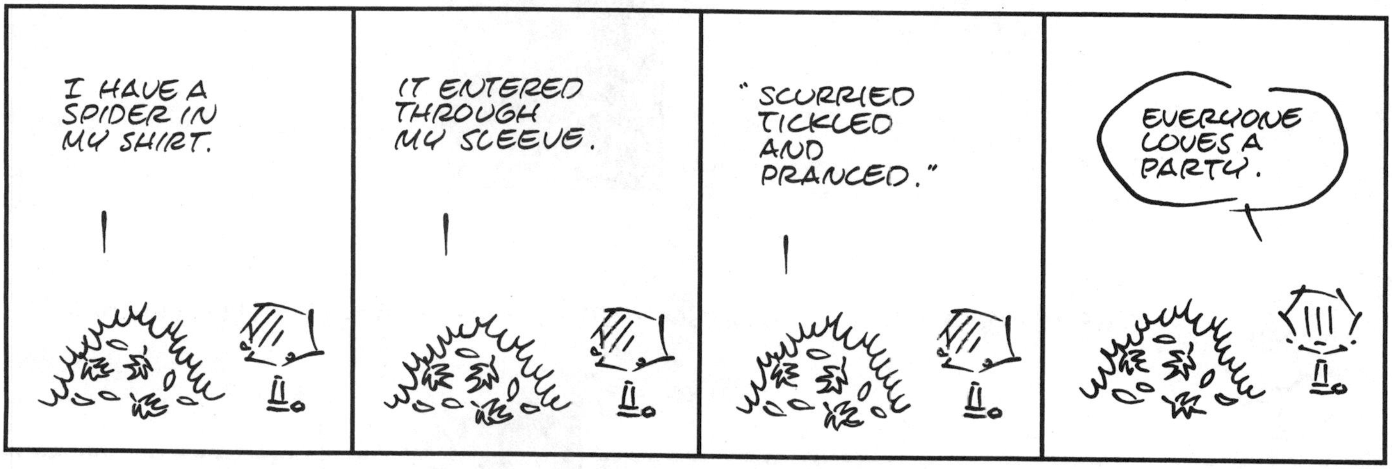
I HAVE A SPIDER IN MY SHIRT.
IT ENTERED THROUGH MY SLEEVE.
"SCURRIED TICKLED AND PRANCED."
EVERYONE LOVES A PARTY.

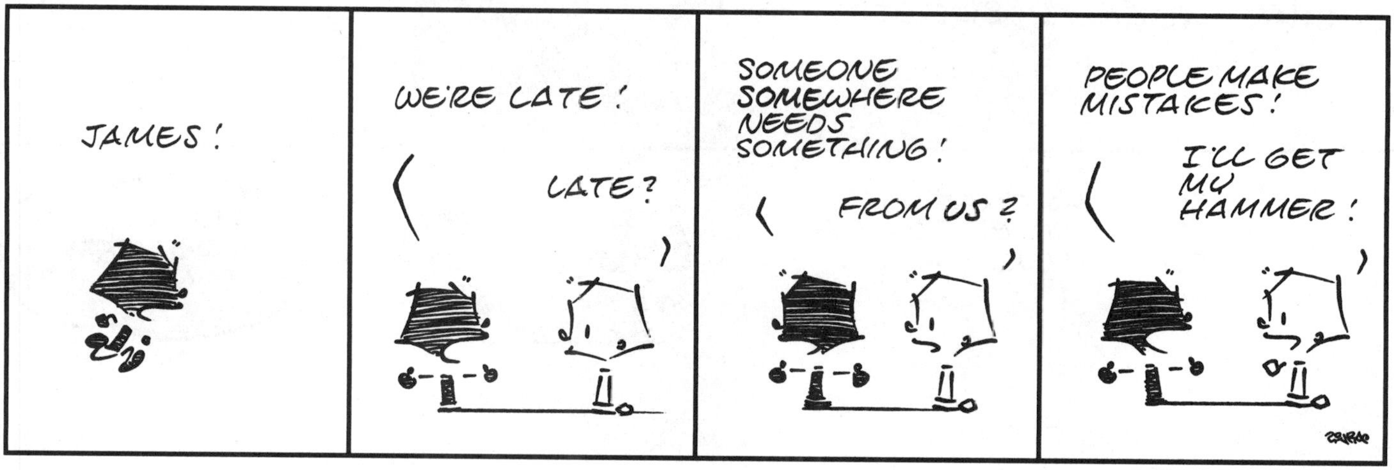
JAMES!
WE'RE LATE!
LATE?
SOMEONE SOMEWHERE NEEDS SOMETHING!
FROM US?
PEOPLE MAKE MISTAKES!
I'LL GET MY HAMMER!

JAMES.

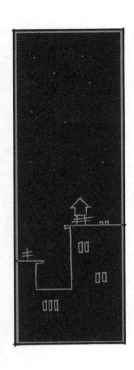

 THIS·IS·WHAT·MY·VOICE·SOUNDS·LIKE·WHEN·I·SIIIIIIIING!

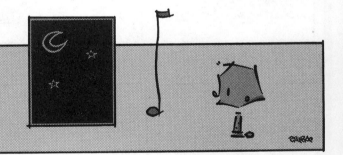

THIS·IS·WHAT·MY·VOICE·SOUNDS·
LIKE·WHEN·I·SLEEEEEEP!

SHE SAYS THAT LIKE
IT'S SUPPOSED TO MEAN
SOMETHING TO ME.

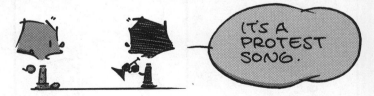

IT'S A PROTEST SONG.

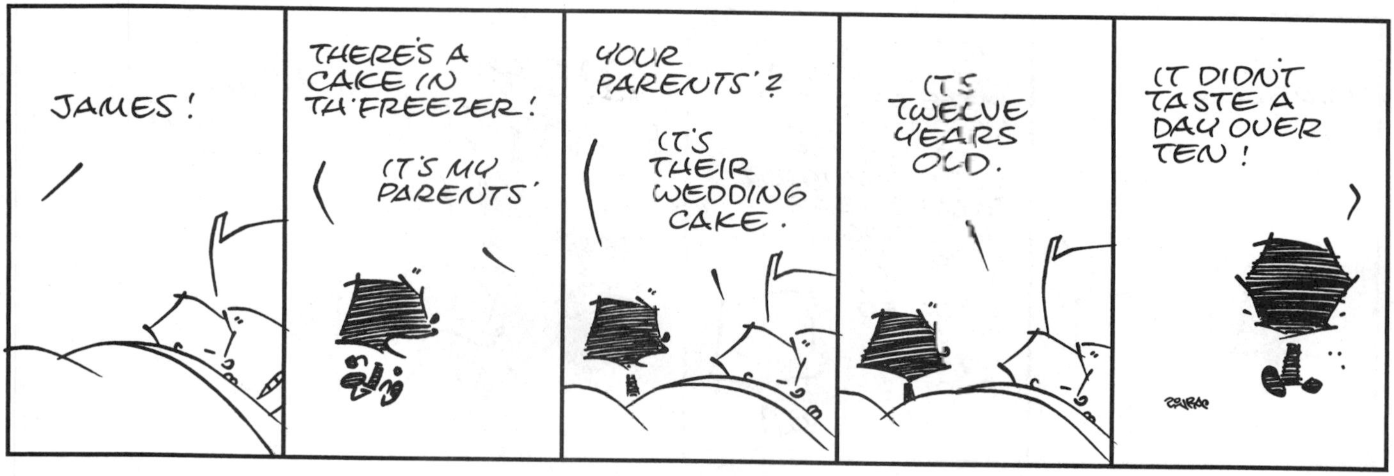
JAMES!
THERE'S A CAKE IN TH' FREEZER!
IT'S MY PARENTS'
YOUR PARENTS'?
IT'S THEIR WEDDING CAKE.
IT'S TWELVE YEARS OLD.
IT DIDN'T TASTE A DAY OVER TEN!

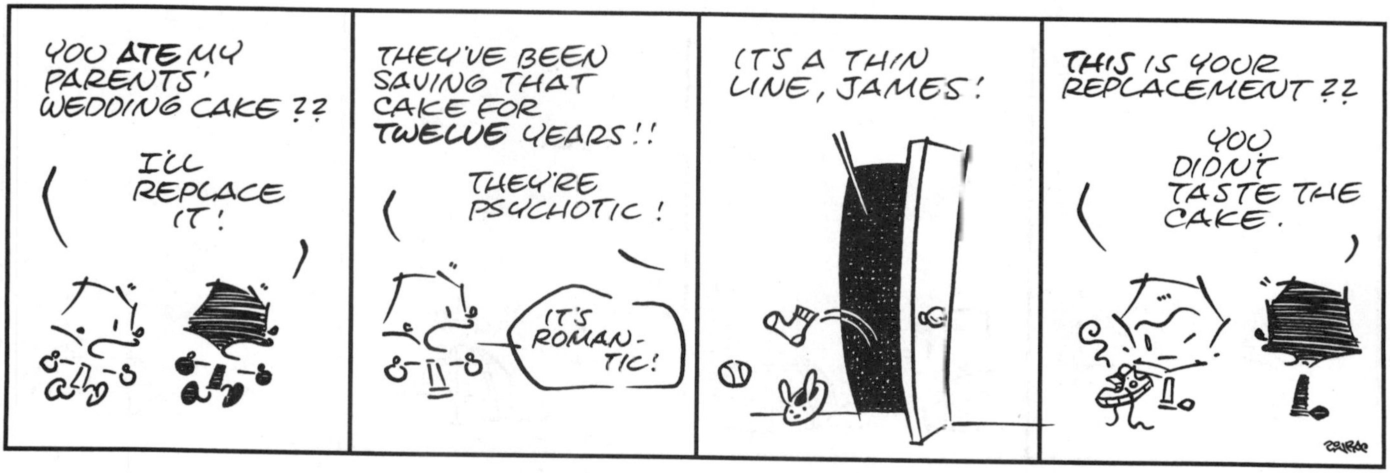
YOU **ATE** MY PARENTS' WEDDING CAKE??
I'LL REPLACE IT!
THEY'VE BEEN SAVING THAT CAKE FOR **TWELVE** YEARS!!
THEY'RE PSYCHOTIC!
IT'S ROMANTIC!
IT'S A THIN LINE, JAMES!
THIS IS YOUR REPLACEMENT??
YOU DIDN'T TASTE THE CAKE.

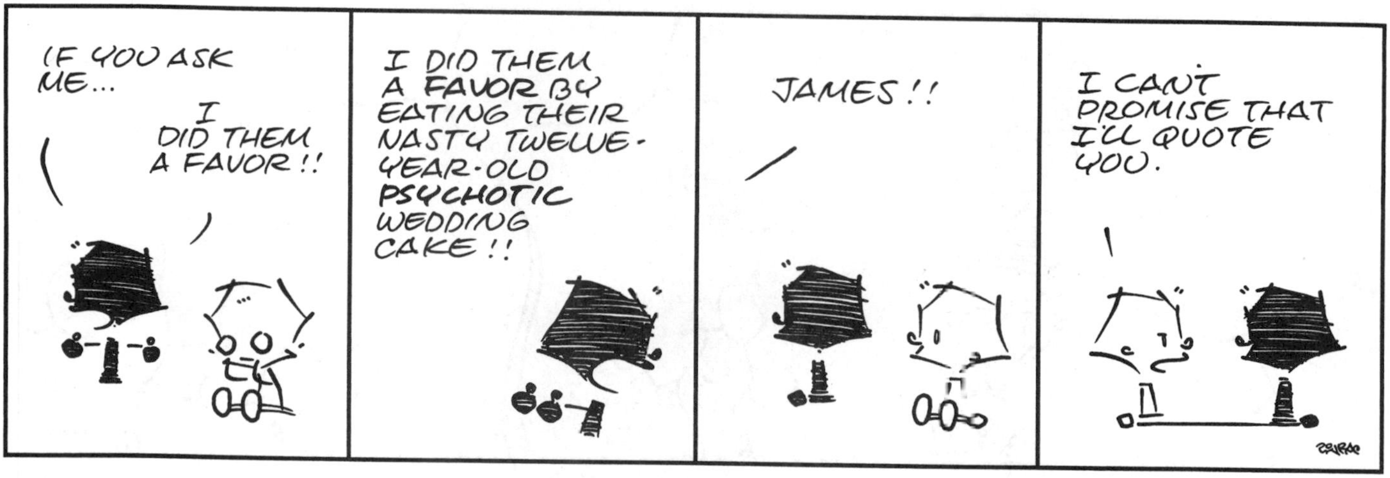
IF YOU ASK ME...
I DID THEM A FAVOR!!
I DID THEM A **FAVOR** BY EATING THEIR NASTY TWELVE-YEAR-OLD **PSYCHOTIC** WEDDING CAKE!!
JAMES!!
I CAN'T PROMISE THAT I'LL QUOTE YOU.

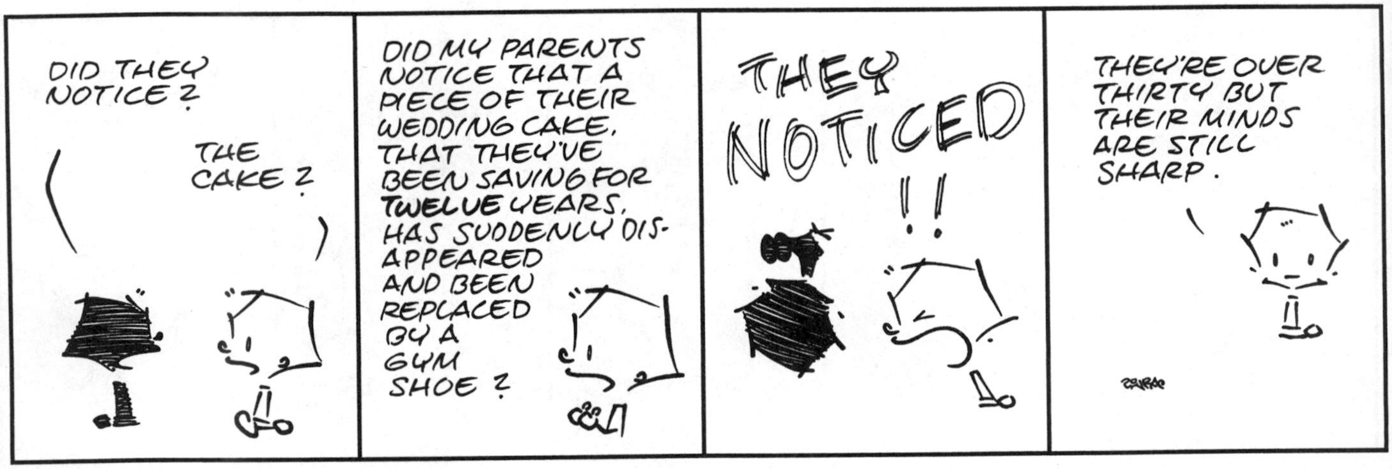
DID THEY NOTICE ?
THE CAKE ?
DID MY PARENTS NOTICE THAT A PIECE OF THEIR WEDDING CAKE, THAT THEY'VE BEEN SAVING FOR **TWELVE** YEARS, HAS SUDDENLY DIS-APPEARED AND BEEN REPLACED BY A GYM SHOE ?
THEY NOTICED
!!
THEY'RE OVER THIRTY BUT THEIR MINDS ARE STILL SHARP.

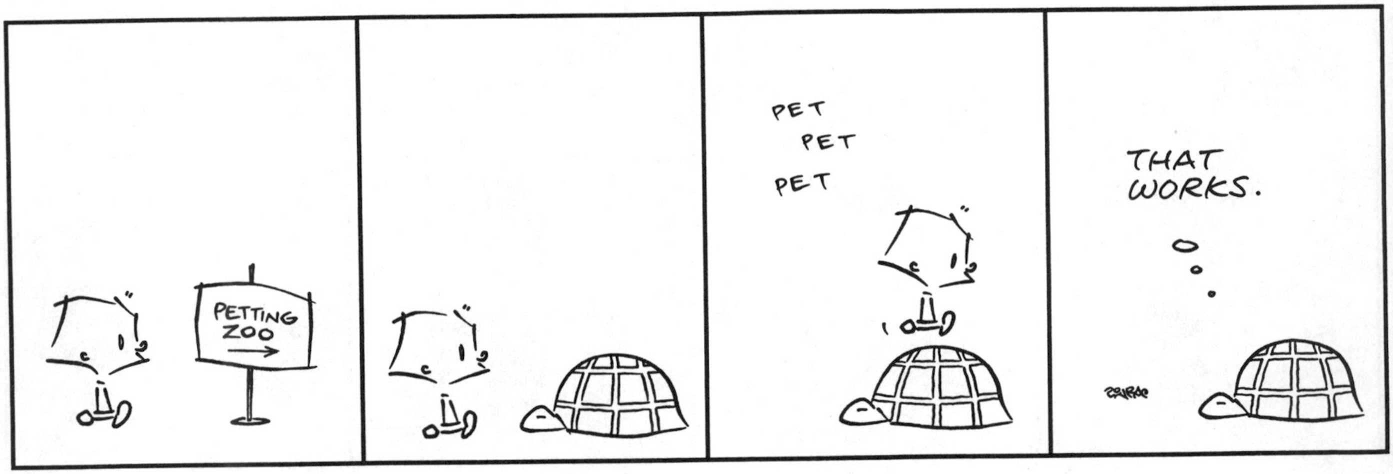
PETTING ZOO
PET PET PET
THAT WORKS.

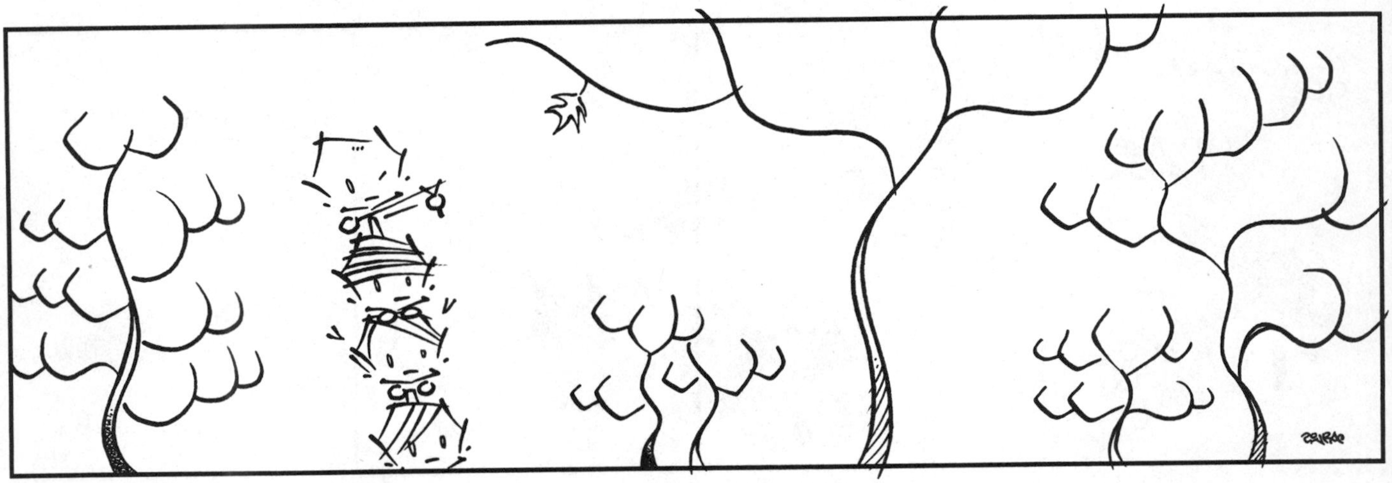

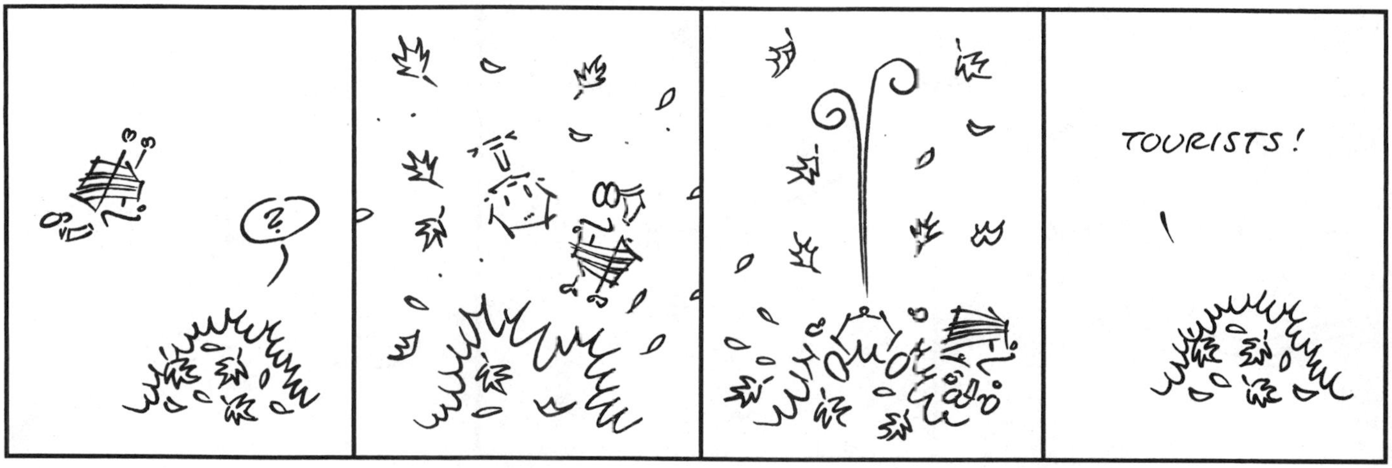
?
TOURISTS!

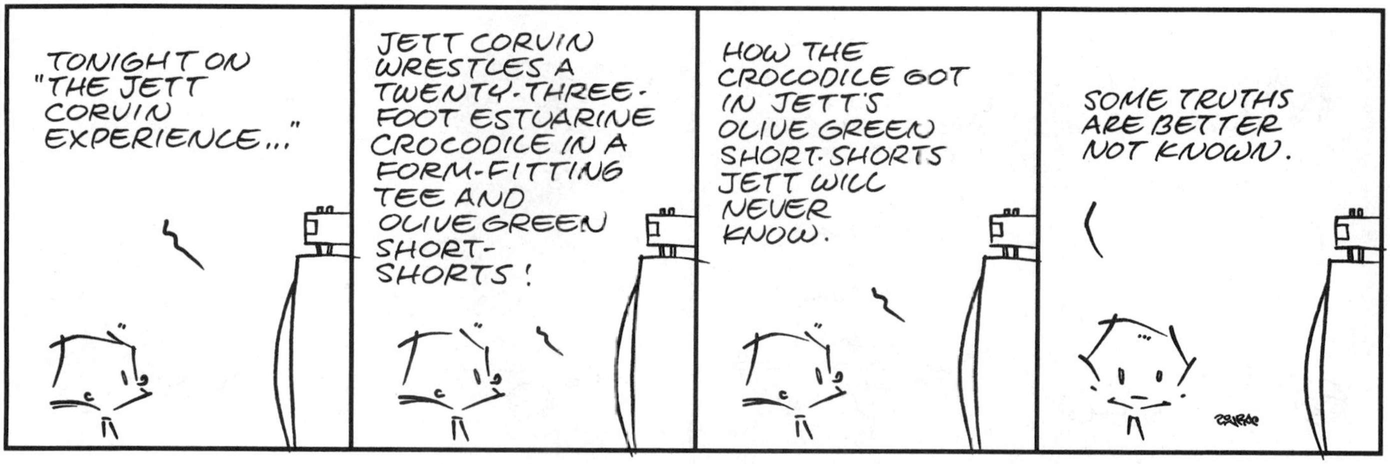
TONIGHT ON "THE JETT CORVIN EXPERIENCE..."
JETT CORVIN WRESTLES A TWENTY-THREE-FOOT ESTUARINE CROCODILE IN A FORM-FITTING TEE AND OLIVE GREEN SHORT-SHORTS!
HOW THE CROCODILE GOT IN JETT'S OLIVE GREEN SHORT-SHORTS JETT WILL NEVER KNOW.
SOME TRUTHS ARE BETTER NOT KNOWN.

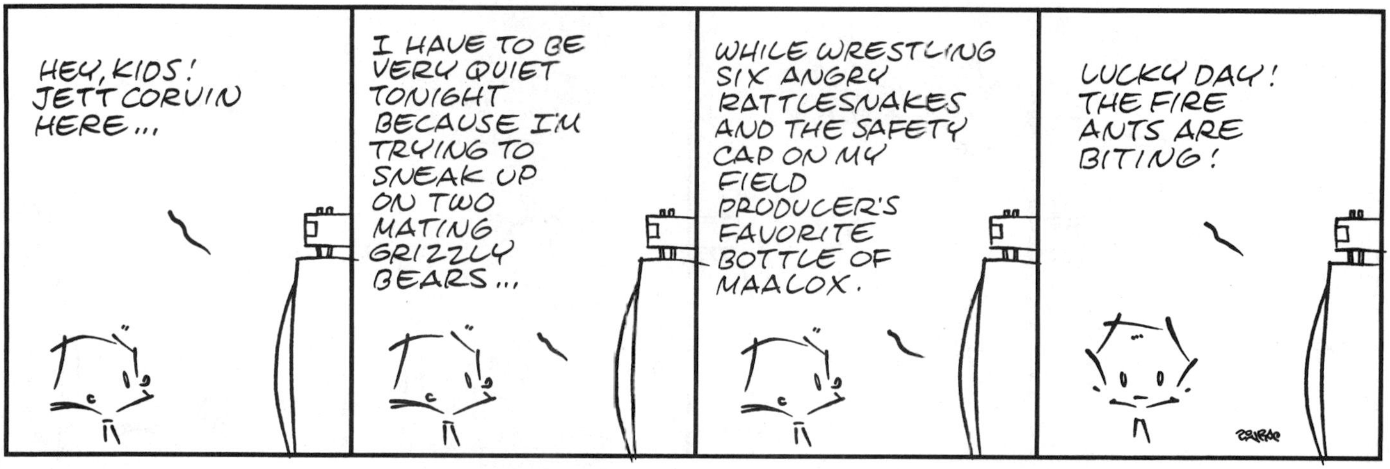
HEY, KIDS! JETT CORVIN HERE...
I HAVE TO BE VERY QUIET TONIGHT BECAUSE I'M TRYING TO SNEAK UP ON TWO MATING GRIZZLY BEARS...
WHILE WRESTLING SIX ANGRY RATTLESNAKES AND THE SAFETY CAP ON MY FIELD PRODUCER'S FAVORITE BOTTLE OF MAALOX.
LUCKY DAY! THE FIRE ANTS ARE BITING!

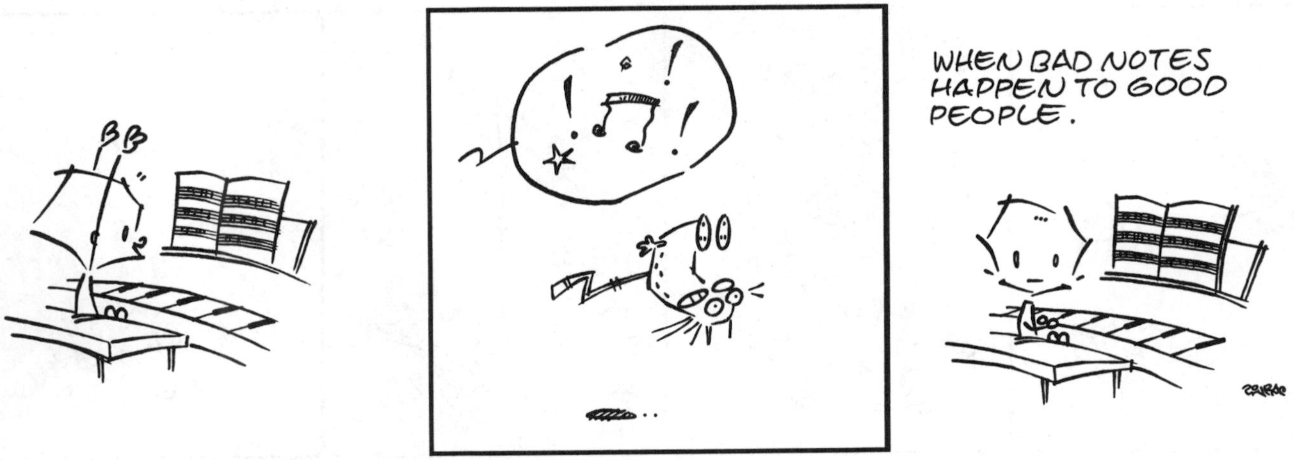
BB
WHEN BAD NOTES HAPPEN TO GOOD PEOPLE.

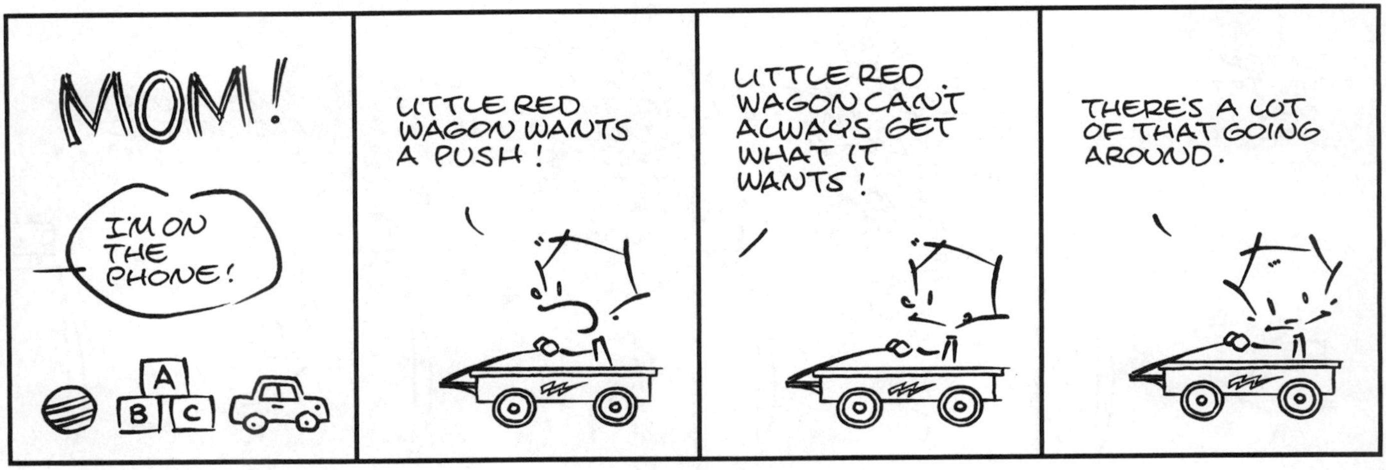
MOM!
I'M ON THE PHONE!
A
B
C
LITTLE RED WAGON WANTS A PUSH!
LITTLE RED WAGON CAN'T ALWAYS GET WHAT IT WANTS!
THERE'S A LOT OF THAT GOING AROUND.

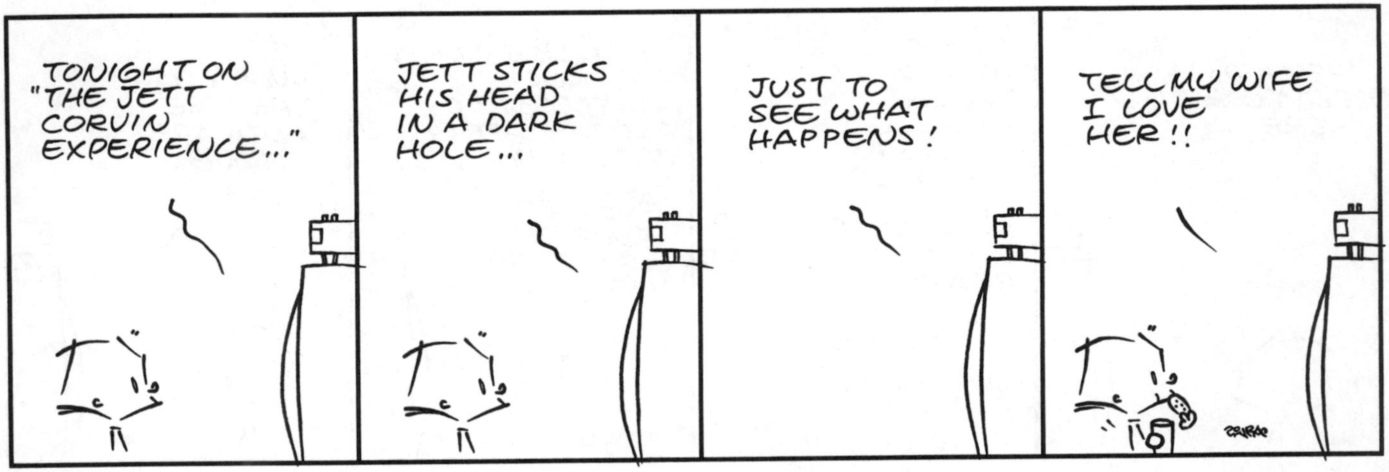
TONIGHT ON "THE JETT CORVIN EXPERIENCE..."
JETT STICKS HIS HEAD IN A DARK HOLE...
JUST TO SEE WHAT HAPPENS!
TELL MY WIFE I LOVE HER!!

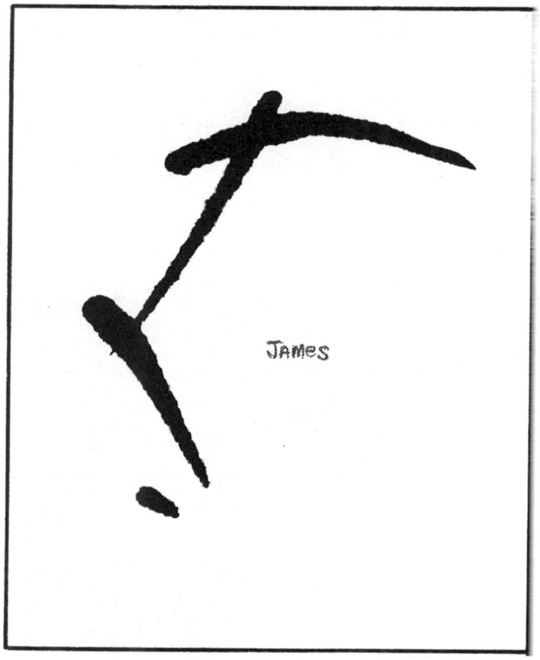
JAMES

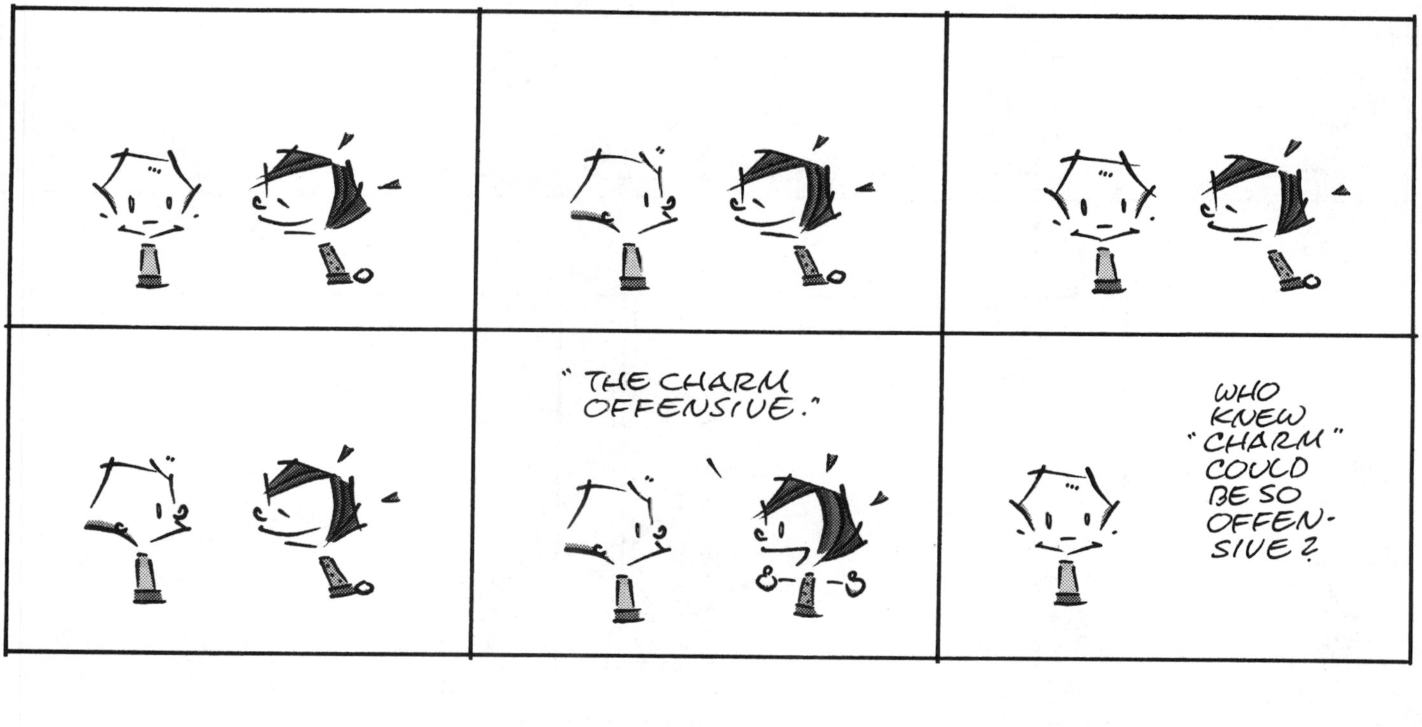
"THE CHARM OFFENSIVE."
WHO KNEW "CHARM" COULD BE SO OFFENSIVE?

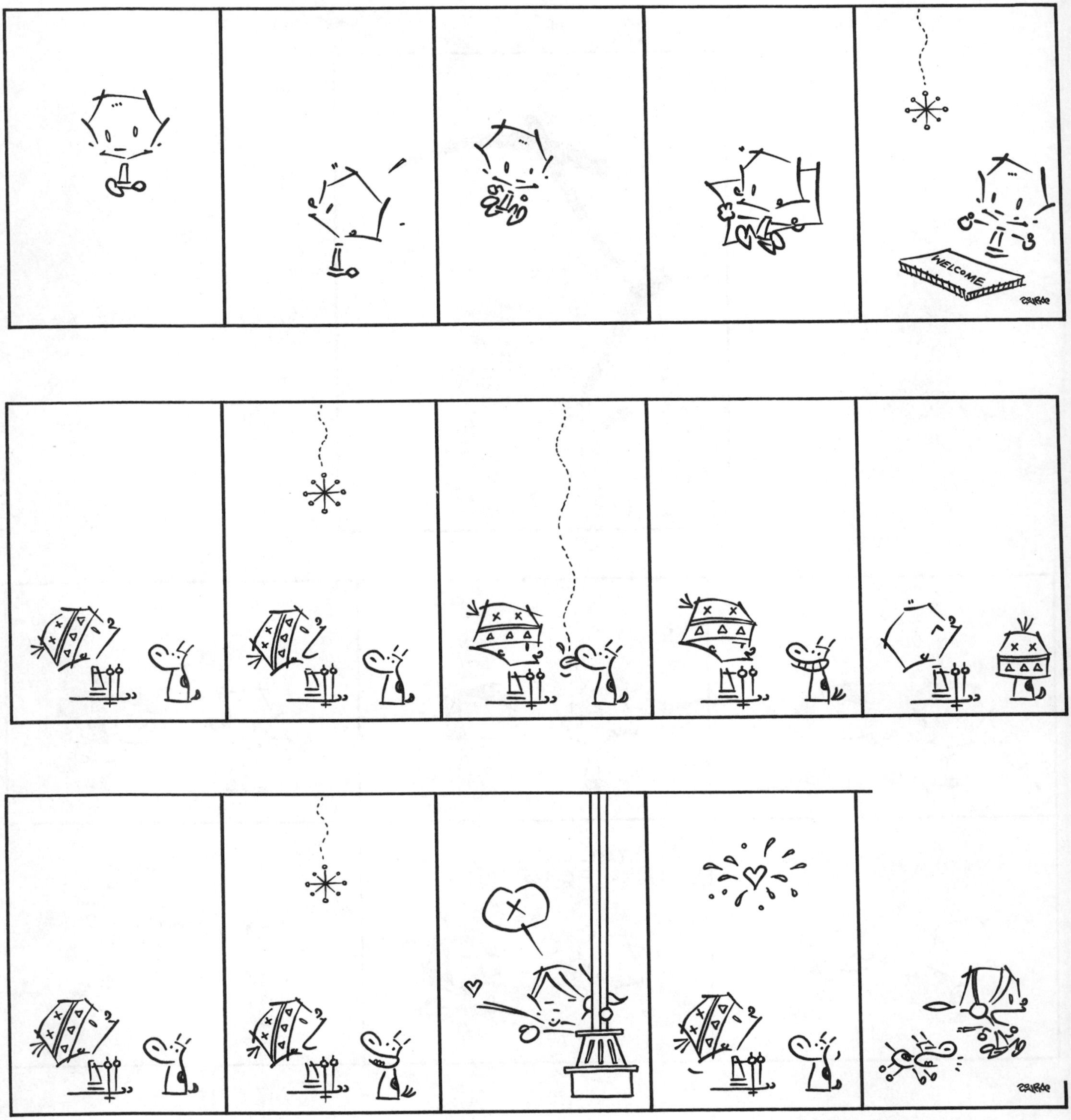
WELCOME

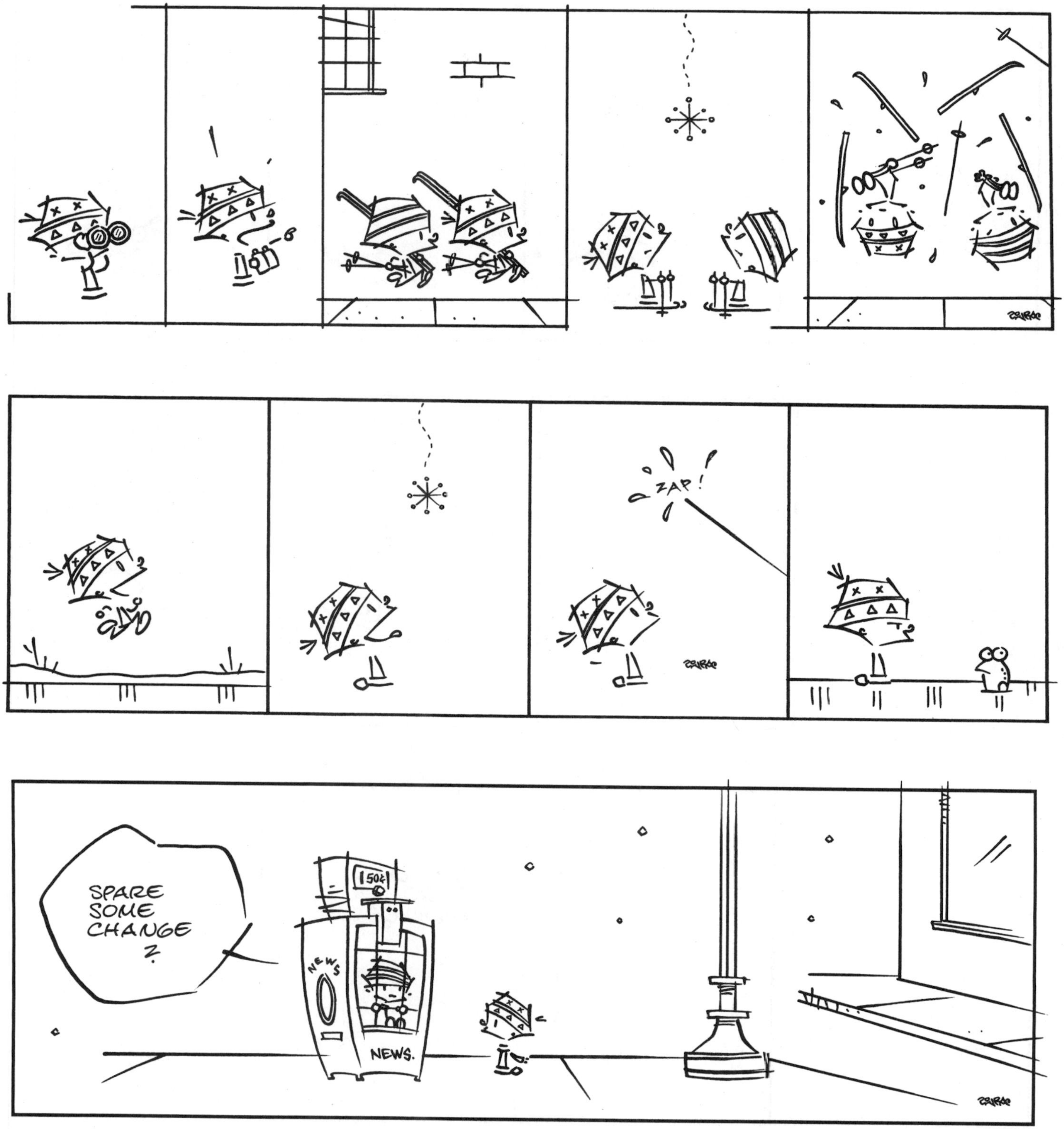
ZAP!
SPARE SOME CHANGE ?
50¢
NEWS
NEWS.

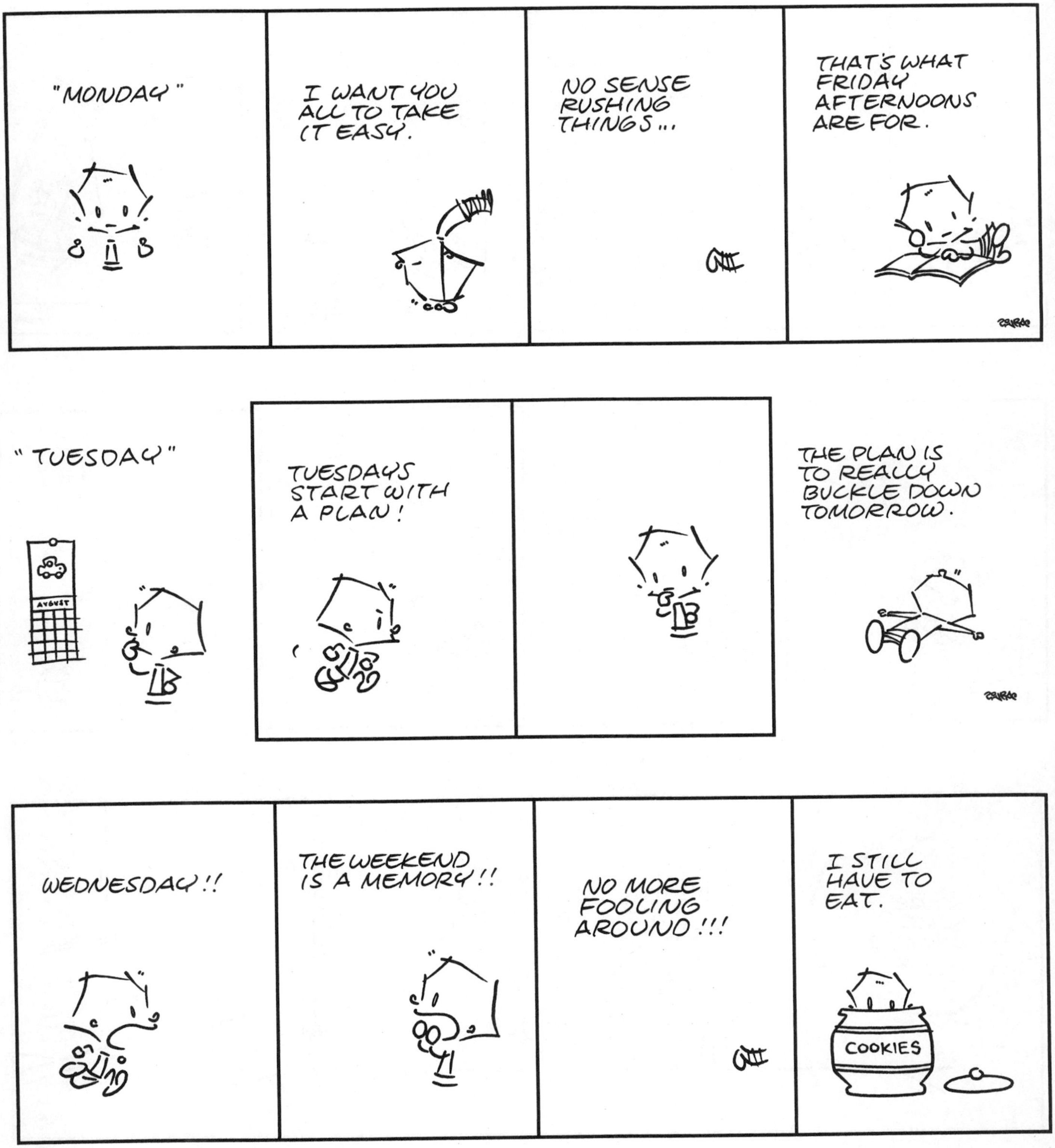
"MONDAY"
I WANT YOU ALL TO TAKE IT EASY.
NO SENSE RUSHING THINGS...
THAT'S WHAT FRIDAY AFTERNOONS ARE FOR.
"TUESDAY"
AUGUST
TUESDAYS START WITH A PLAN!
THE PLAN IS TO REALLY BUCKLE DOWN TOMORROW.
WEDNESDAY!!
THE WEEKEND IS A MEMORY!!
NO MORE FOOLING AROUND!!!
I STILL HAVE TO EAT.
COOKIES

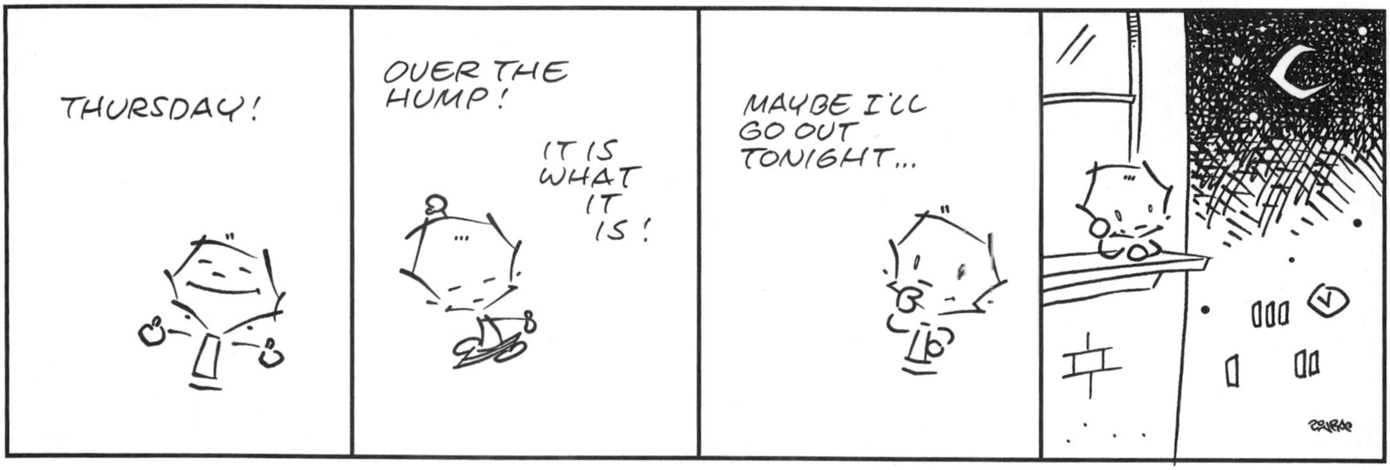
THURSDAY!
OVER THE HUMP!
IT IS WHAT IT IS!
MAYBE I'LL GO OUT TONIGHT...

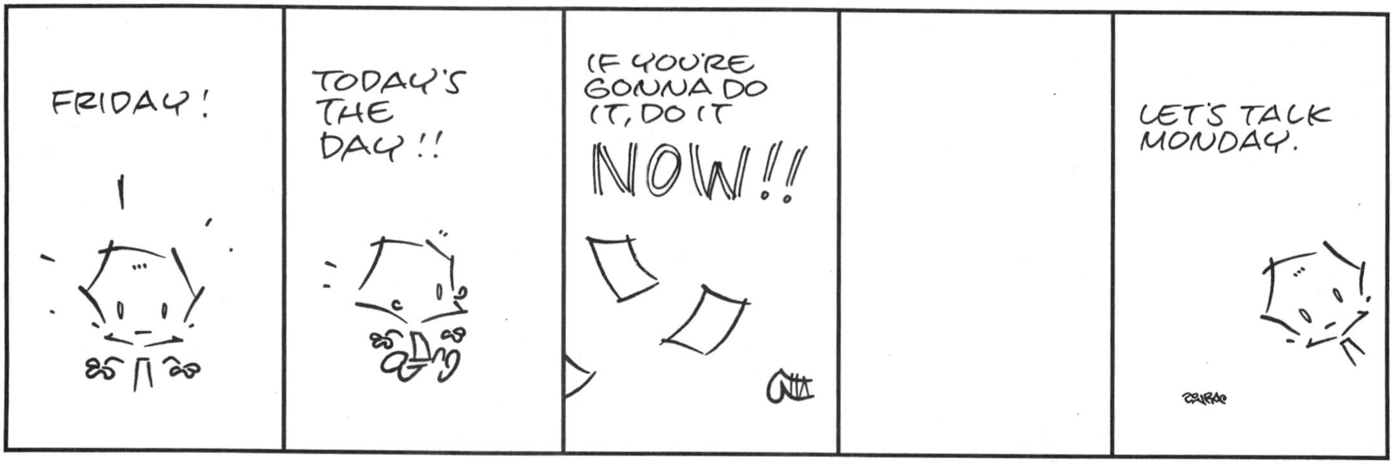
FRIDAY!
TODAY'S THE DAY!!
IF YOU'RE GONNA DO IT, DO IT
NOW!!
LET'S TALK MONDAY.

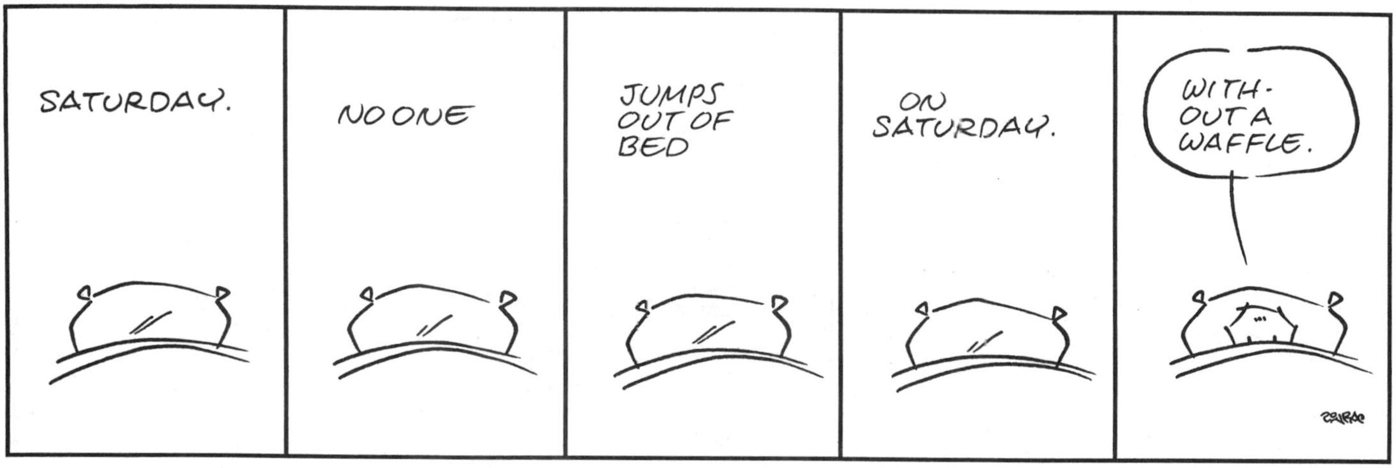
SATURDAY.
NO ONE
JUMPS OUT OF BED
ON SATURDAY.
WITH-OUT A WAFFLE.

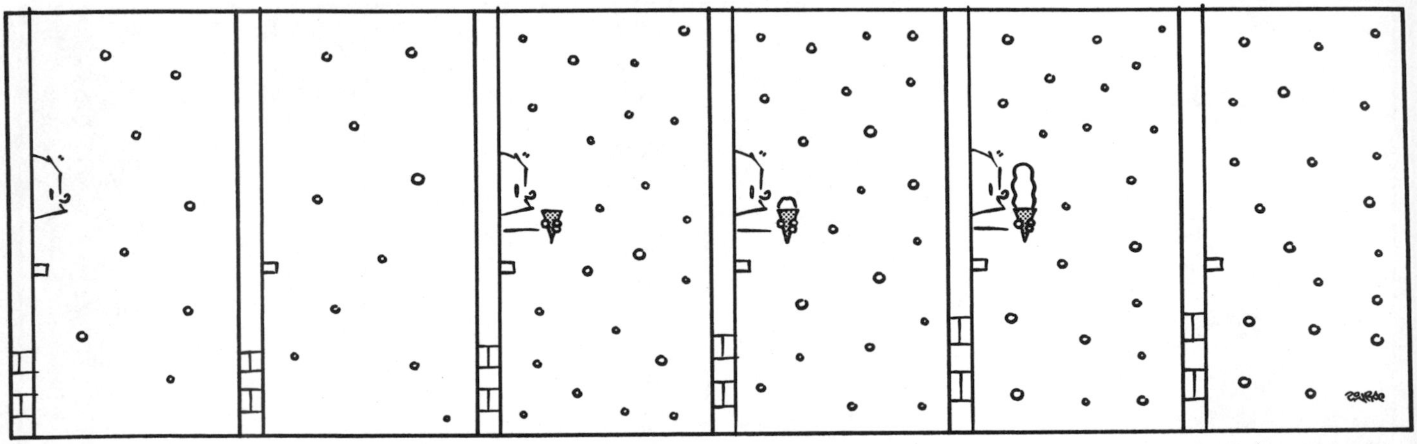

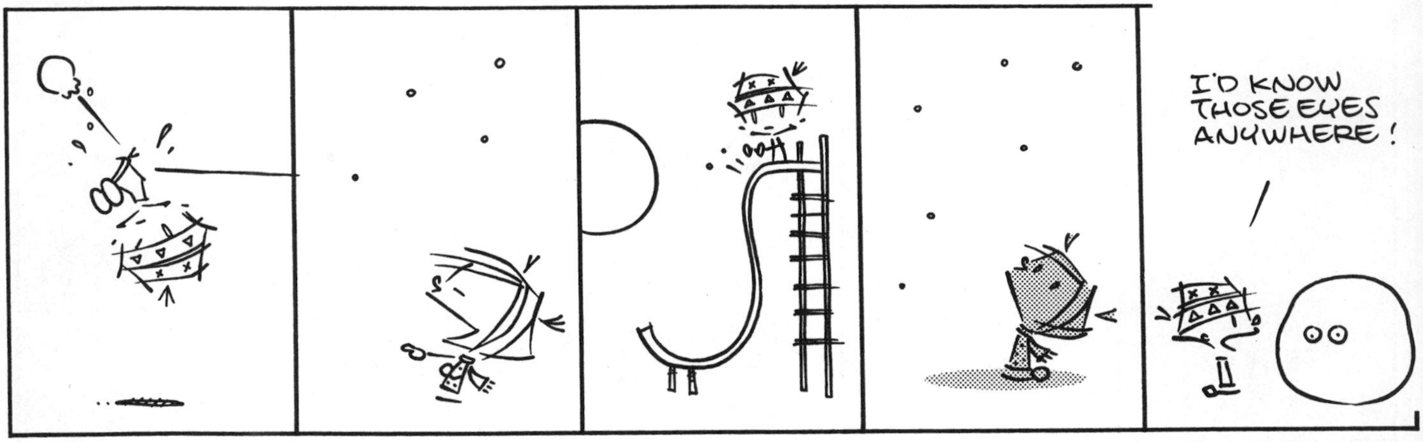
I'D KNOW THOSE EYES ANYWHERE!

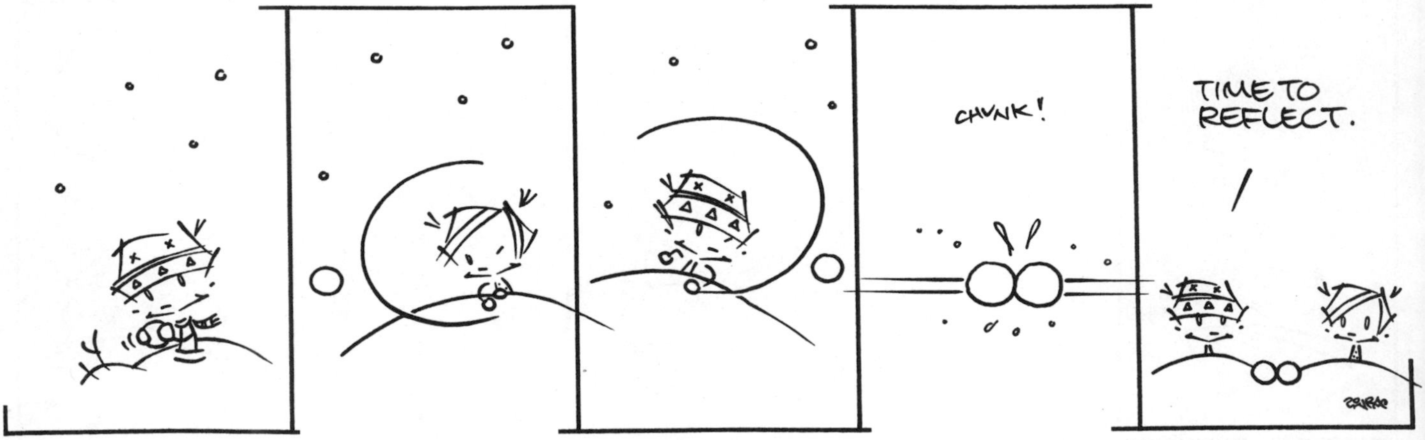
CHUNK!
TIME TO REFLECT.

JAMES!
by MARK

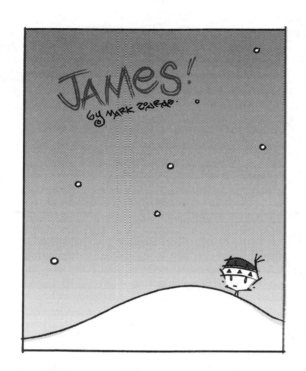

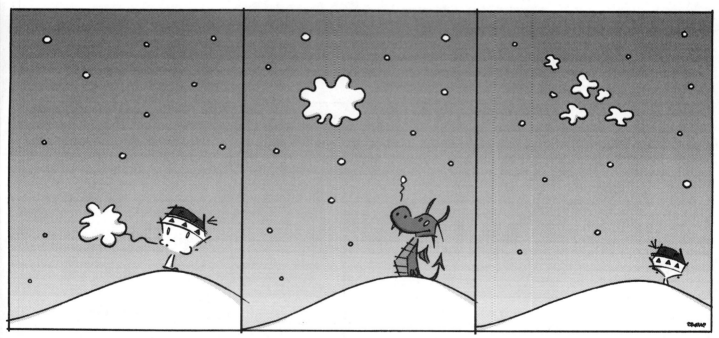

ARE WE THERE YET?

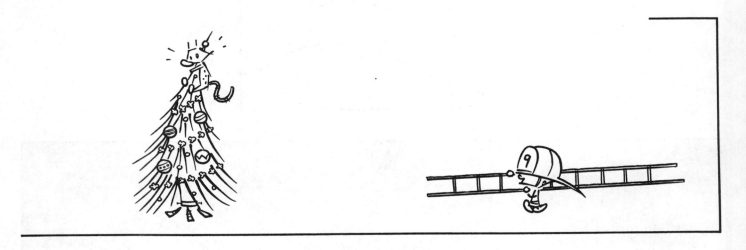

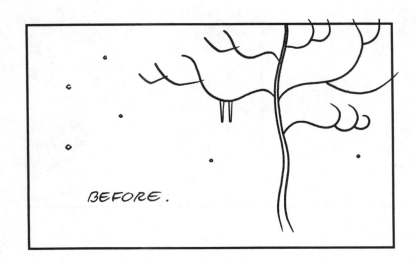

BEFORE.

AFTER.

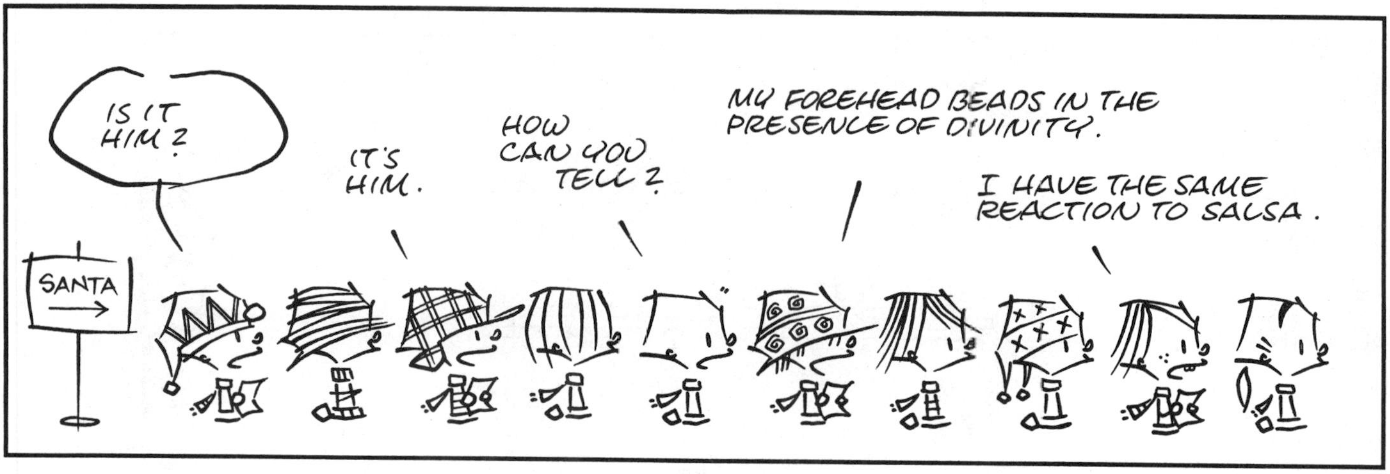
SANTA
IS IT HIM?
IT'S HIM.
HOW CAN YOU TELL?
MY FOREHEAD BEADS IN THE PRESENCE OF DIVINITY.
I HAVE THE SAME REACTION TO SALSA.

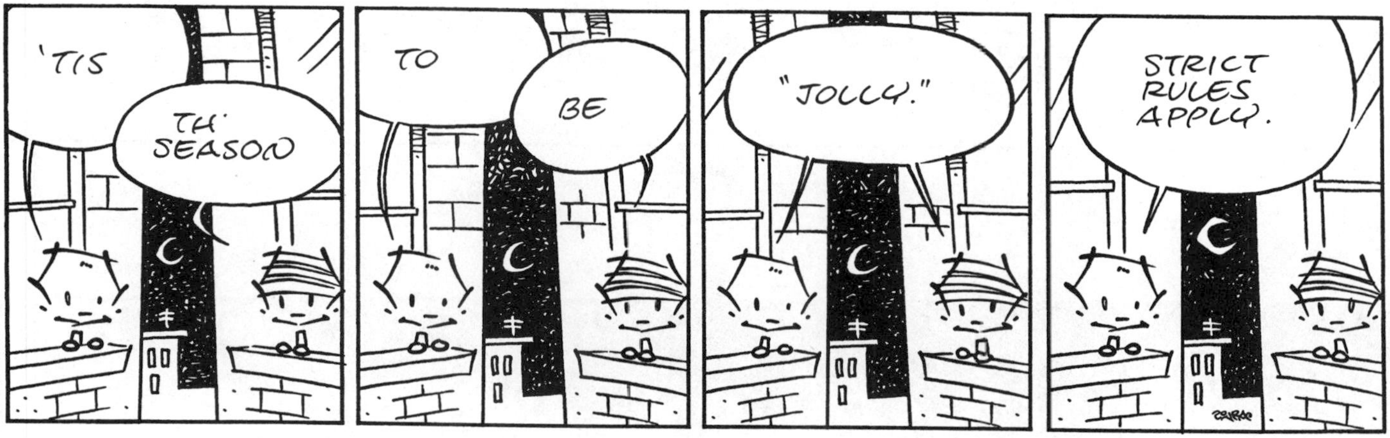
'TIS
TH' SEASON
TO
BE
"JOLLY."
STRICT RULES APPLY.

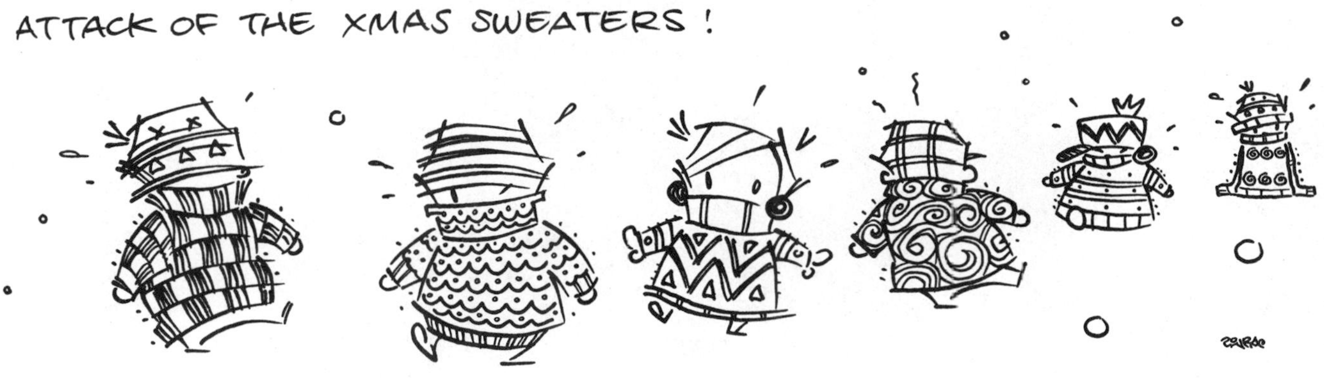
ATTACK OF THE XMAS SWEATERS!

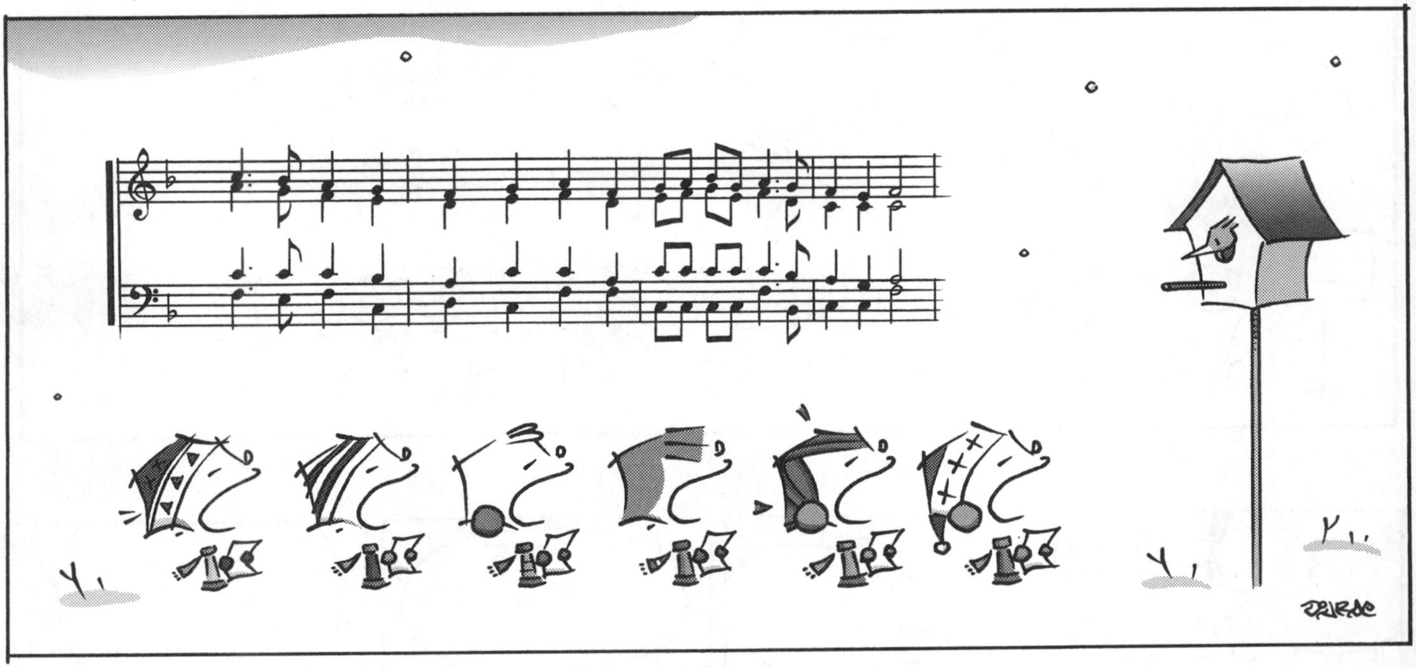
DRUBAC

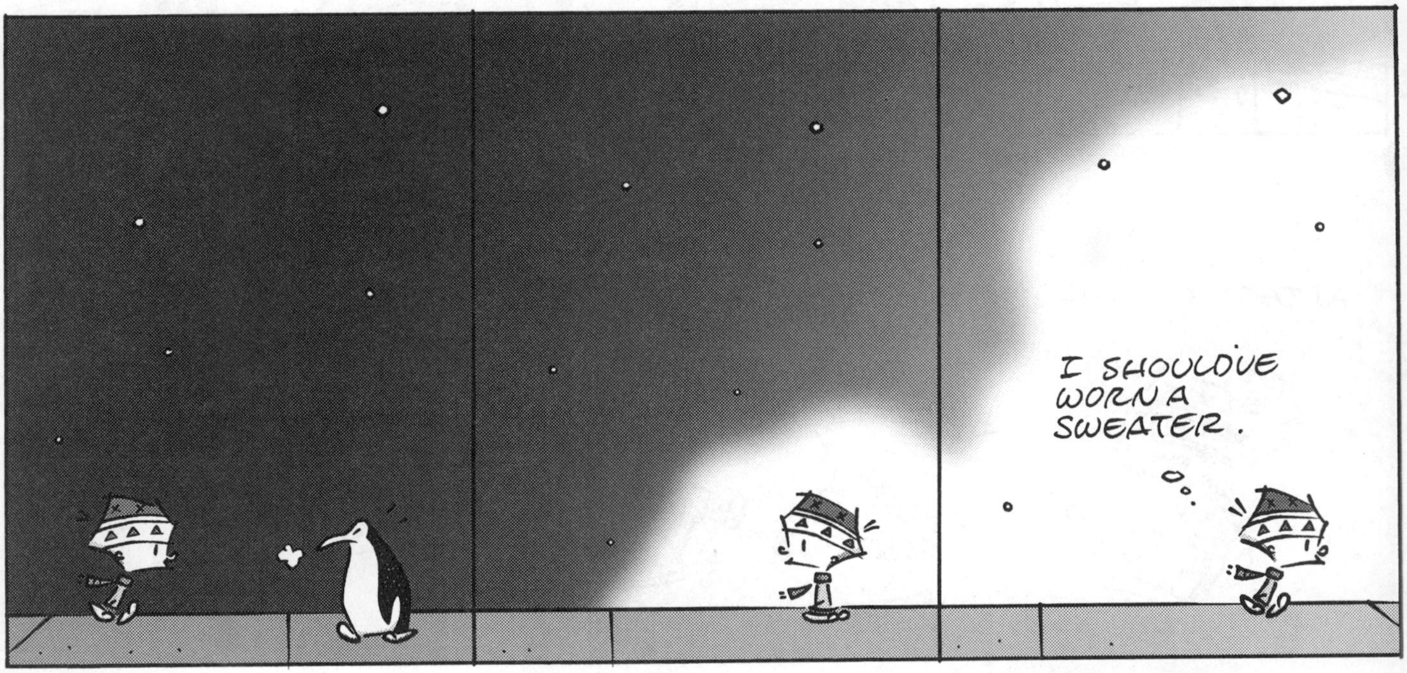
I SHOULDVE WORN A SWEATER.

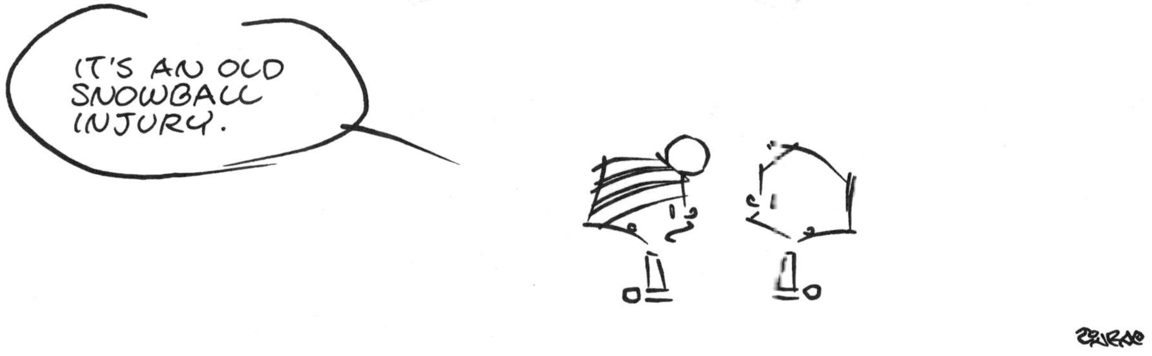
IT'S AN OLD SNOWBALL INJURY.

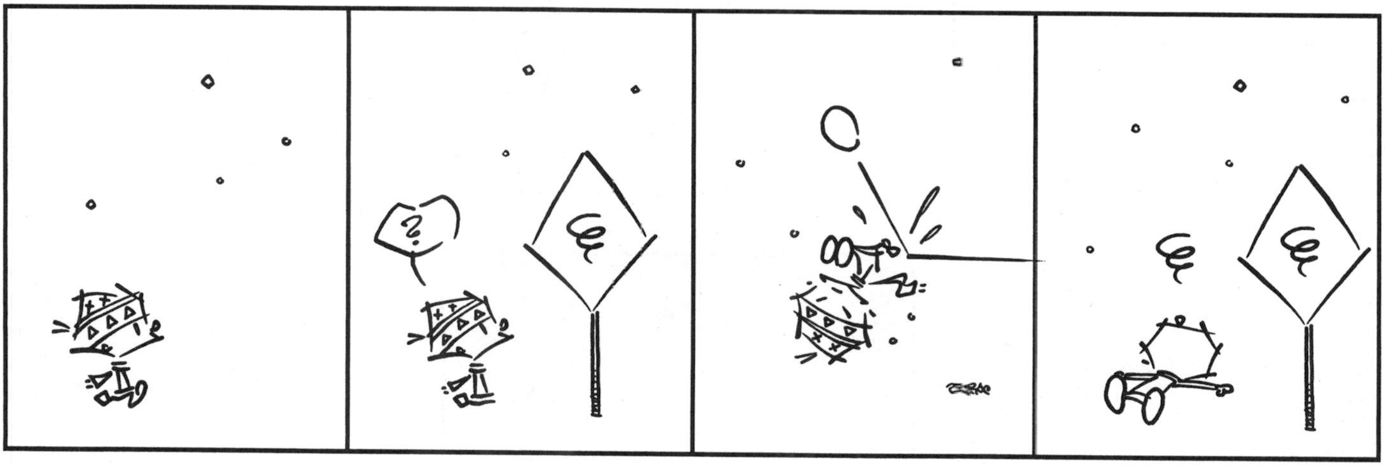

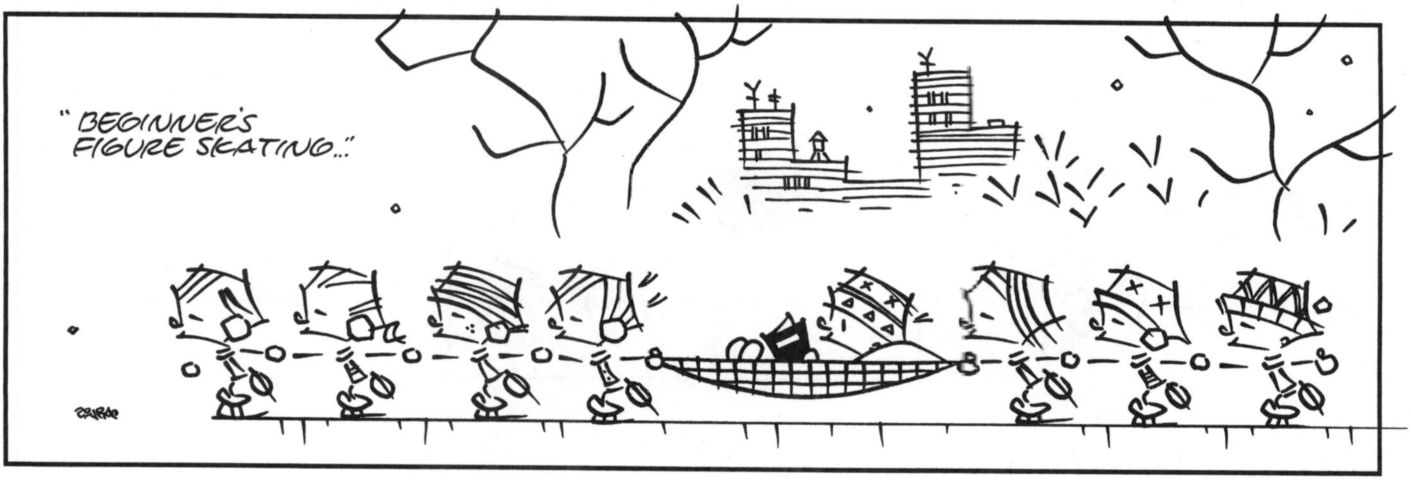
"BEGINNER'S FIGURE SKATING..."

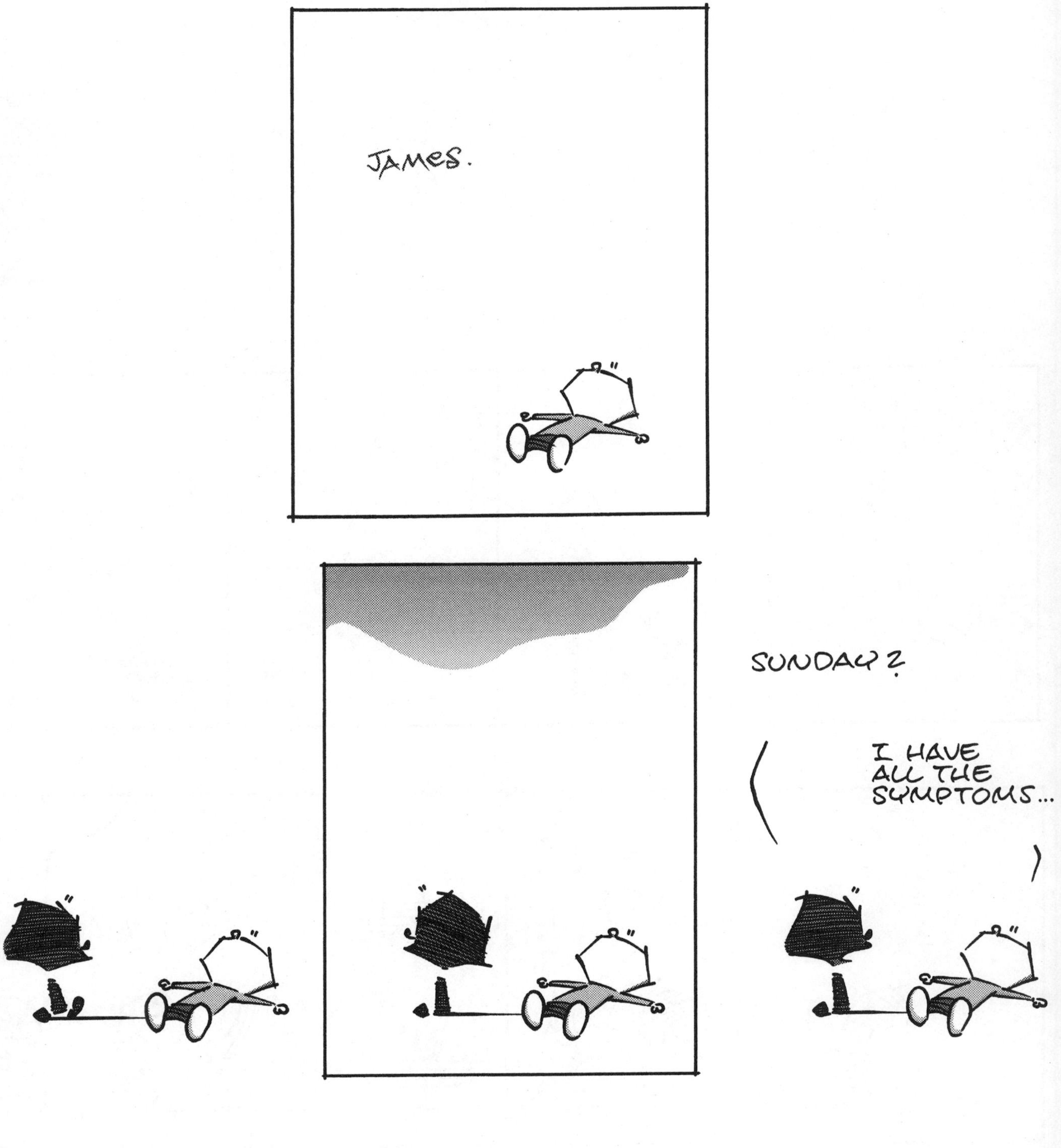
JAMES.
SUNDAY?
I HAVE ALL THE SYMPTOMS...

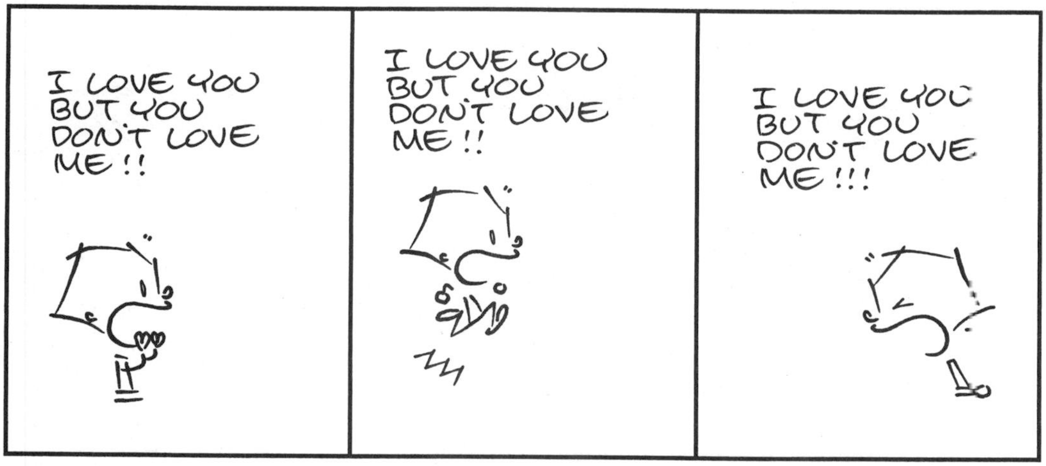
I LOVE YOU BUT YOU DON'T LOVE ME!!
I LOVE YOU BUT YOU DON'T LOVE ME!!
I LOVE YOU BUT YOU DON'T LOVE ME!!!
IT'S MAKING ME WACKY!

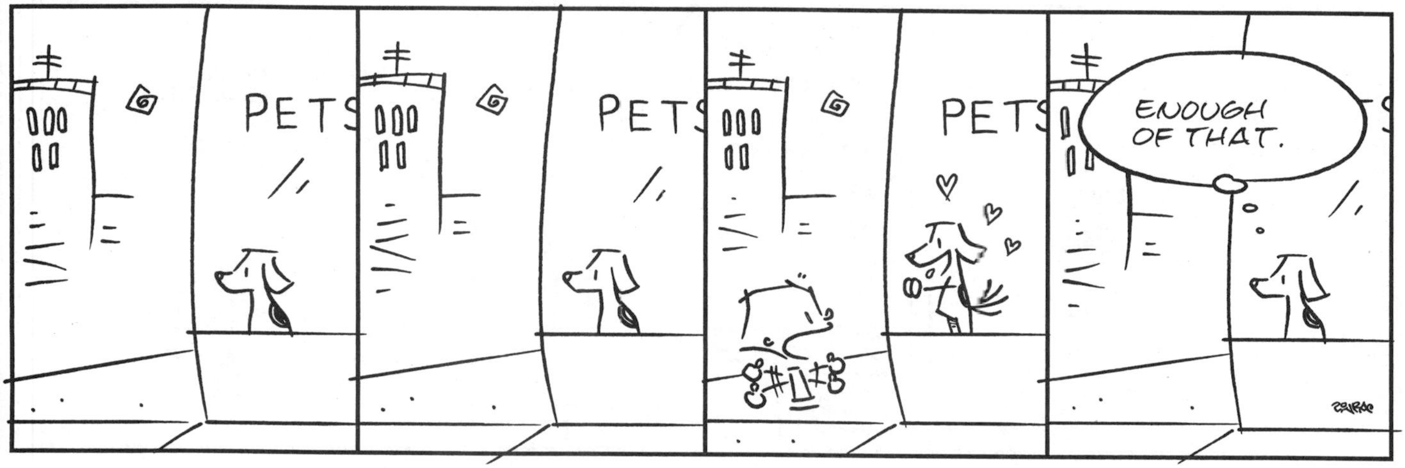
PETS
PETS
PETS
ENOUGH OF THAT.

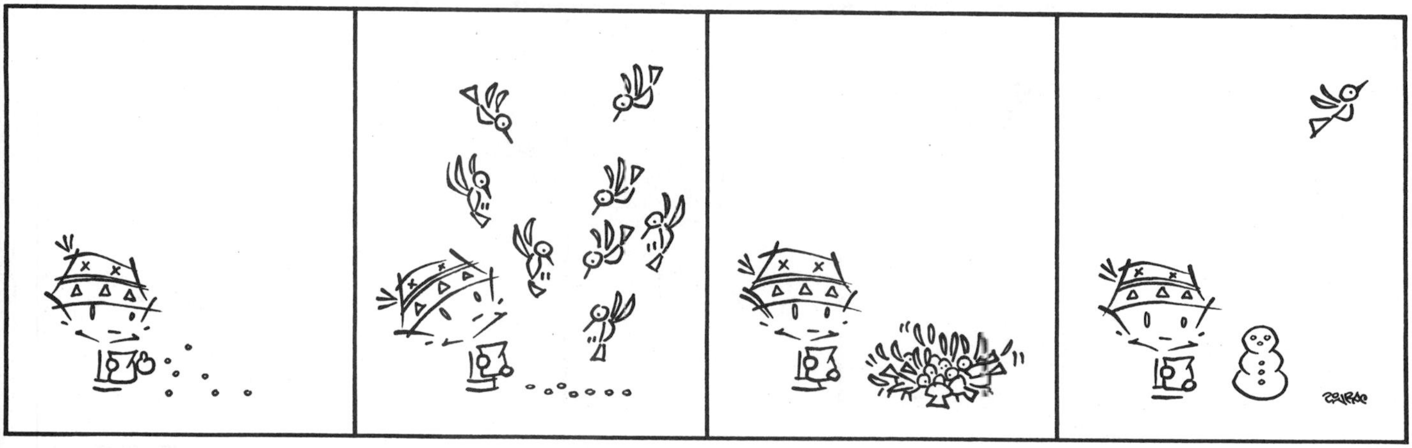

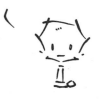

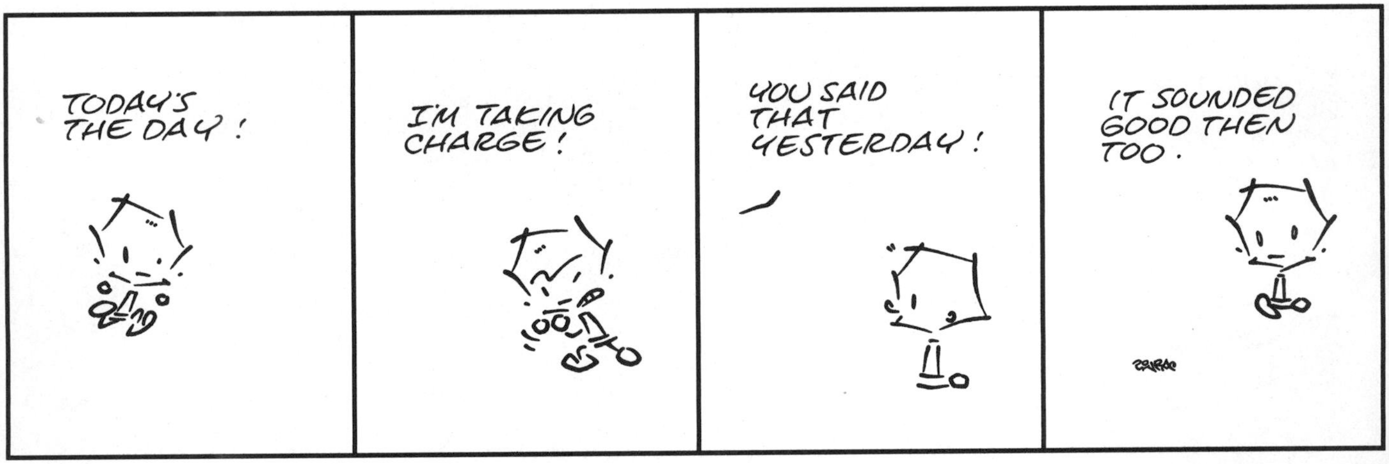
TODAY'S THE DAY!
I'M TAKING CHARGE!
YOU SAID THAT YESTERDAY!
IT SOUNDED GOOD THEN TOO.

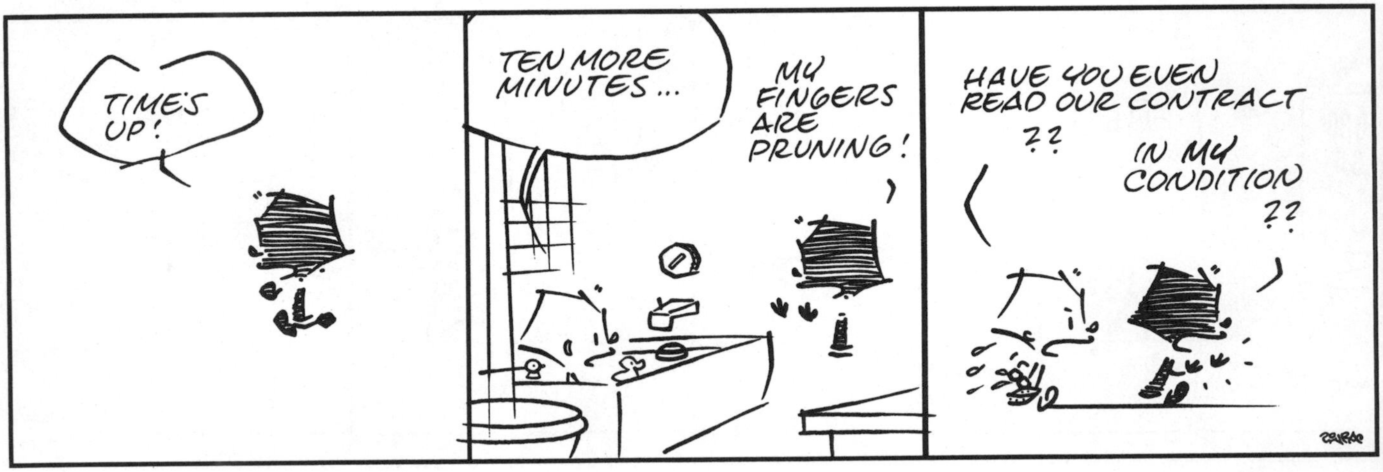
TIME'S UP!
TEN MORE MINUTES...
MY FINGERS ARE PRUNING!
HAVE YOU EVEN READ OUR CONTRACT
??
IN MY CONDITION
??

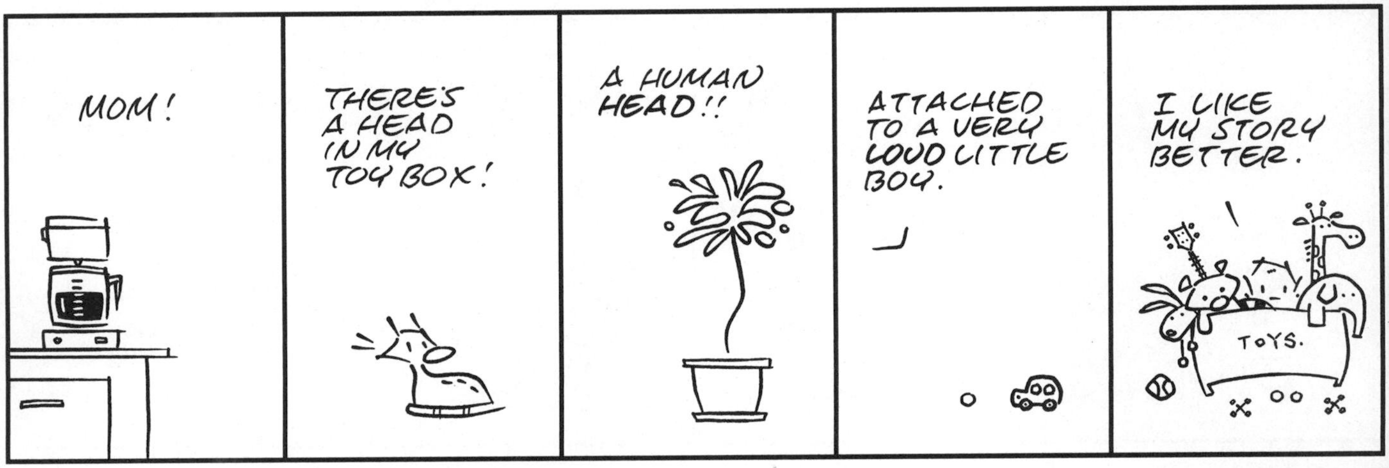
MOM!
THERE'S A HEAD IN MY TOY BOX!
A HUMAN HEAD!!
ATTACHED TO A VERY LOUD LITTLE BOY.
I LIKE MY STORY BETTER.
TOYS.

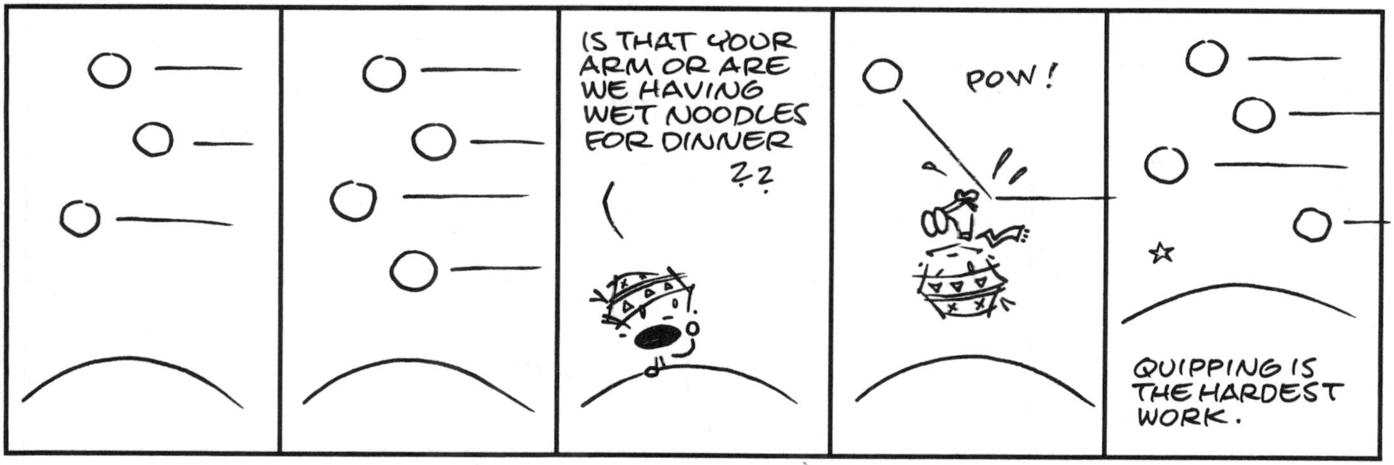
IS THAT YOUR ARM OR ARE WE HAVING WET NOODLES FOR DINNER
ZZ
POW!
QUIPPING IS THE HARDEST WORK.

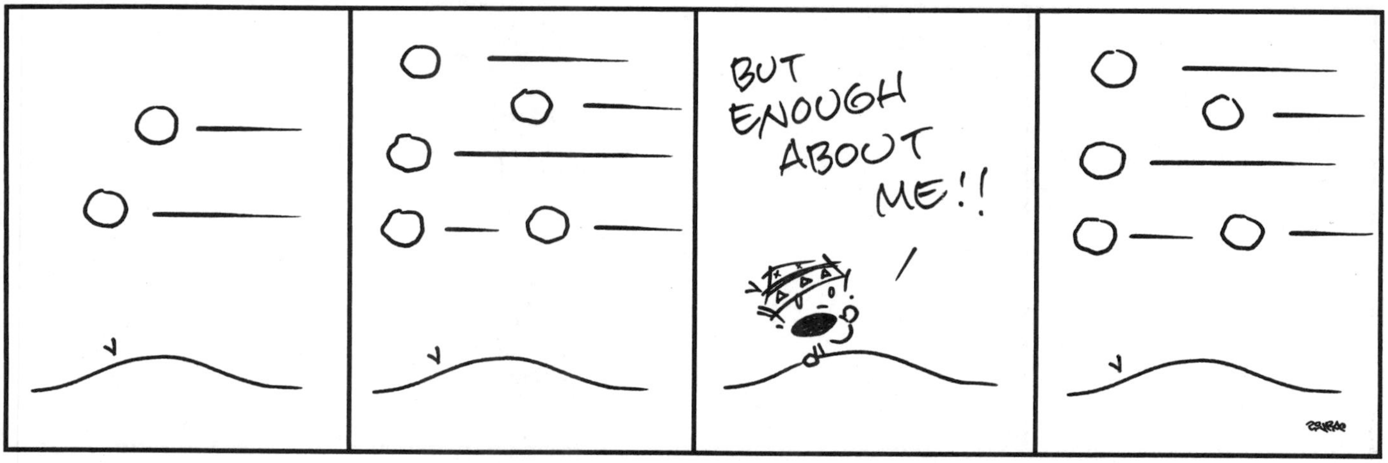
BUT ENOUGH ABOUT ME!!

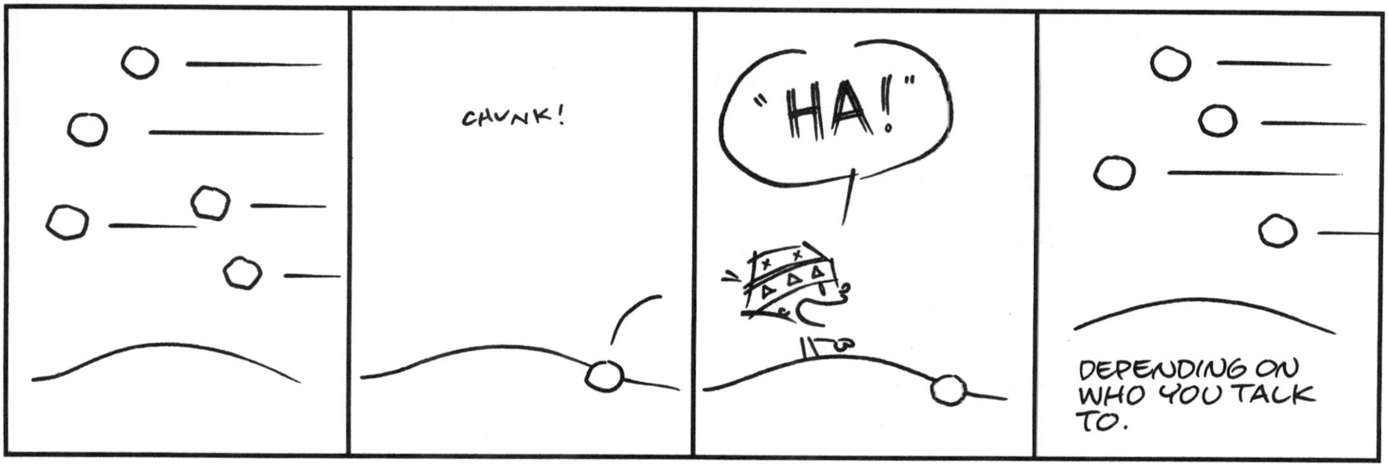
CHUNK!
"HA!"
DEPENDING ON WHO YOU TALK TO.

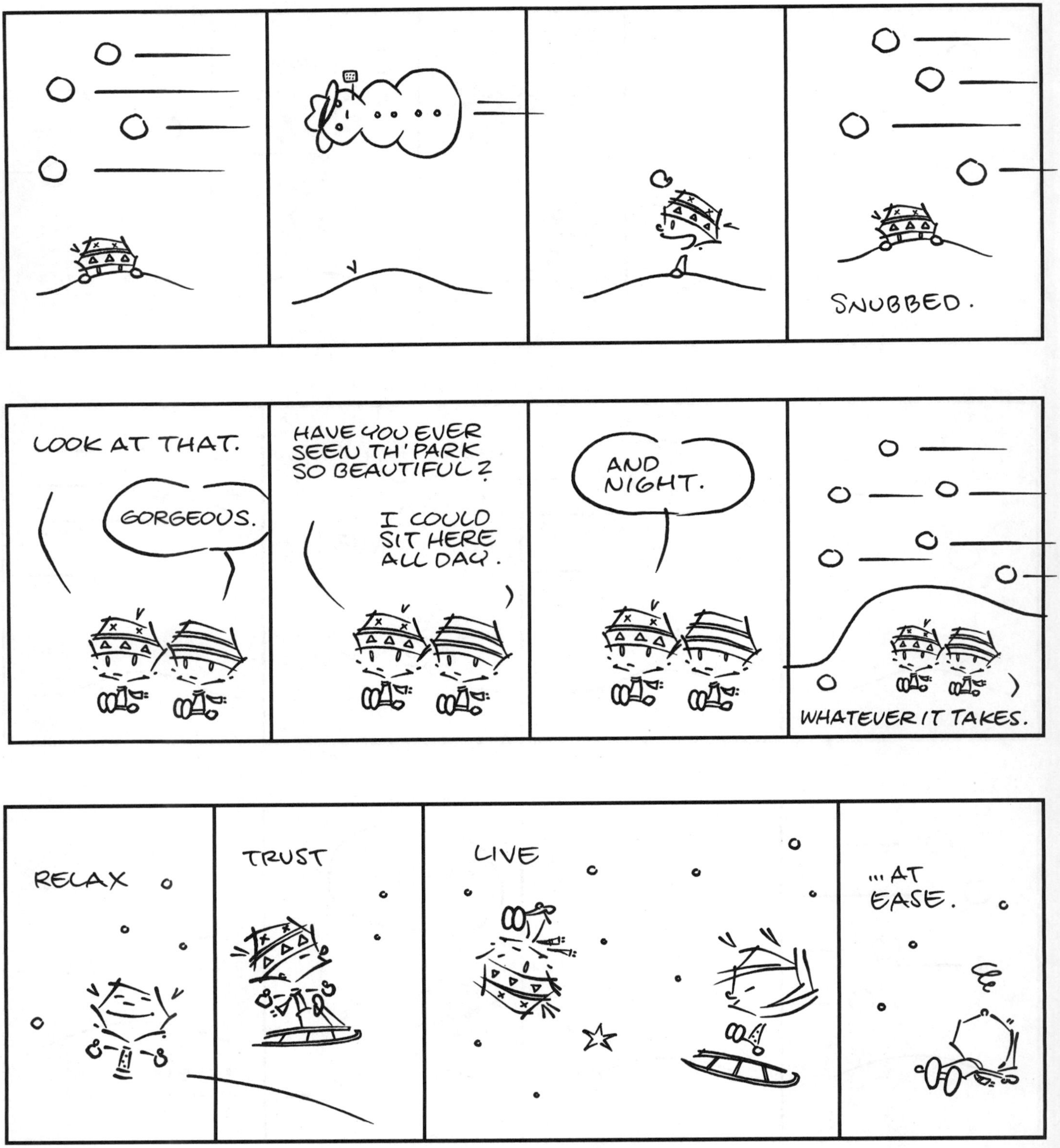
SNUBBED.
LOOK AT THAT.
GORGEOUS.
HAVE YOU EVER SEEN TH' PARK SO BEAUTIFUL?
I COULD SIT HERE ALL DAY.
AND NIGHT.
WHATEVER IT TAKES.
RELAX
TRUST
LIVE
...AT EASE.

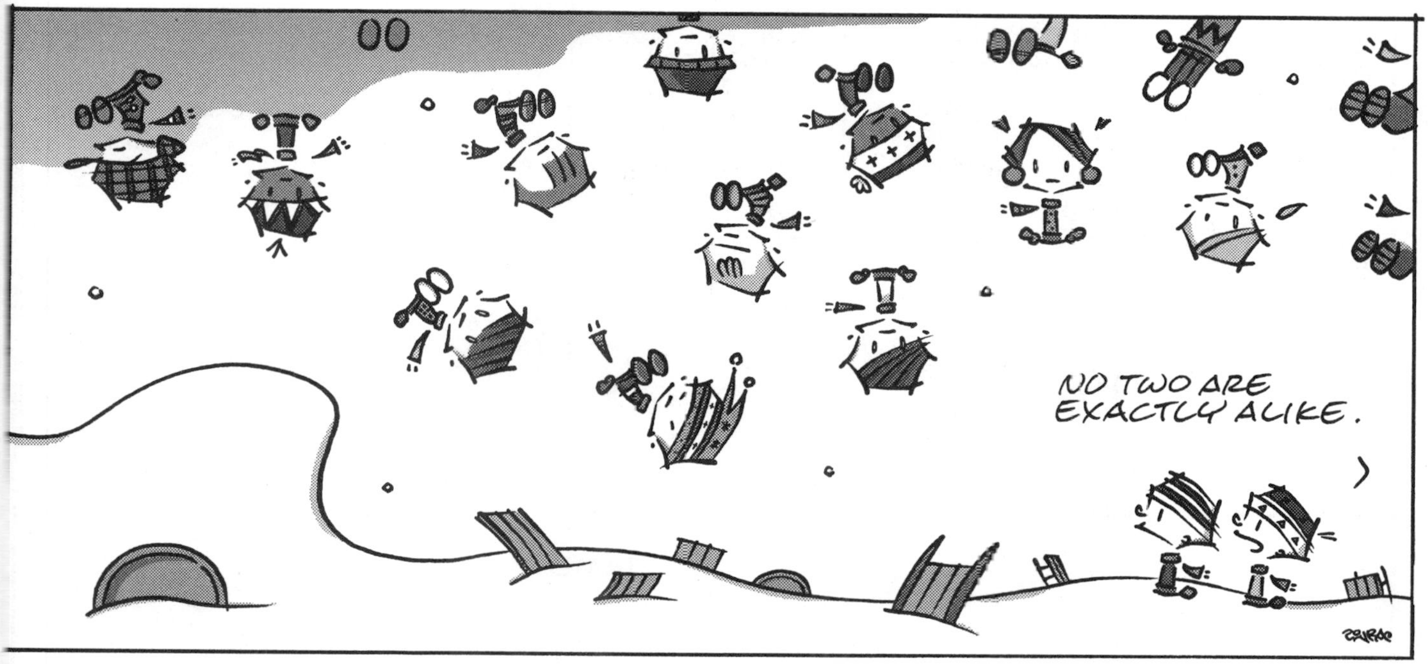
NO TWO ARE
EXACTLY ALIKE.

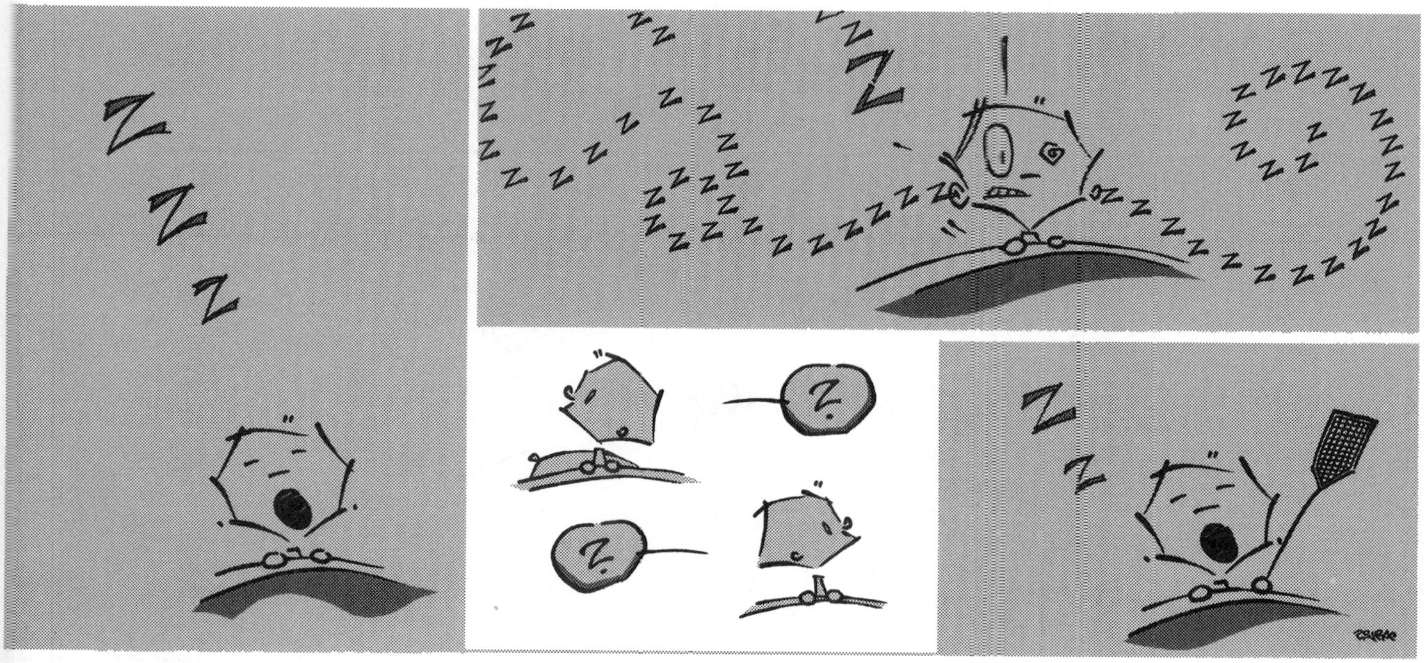

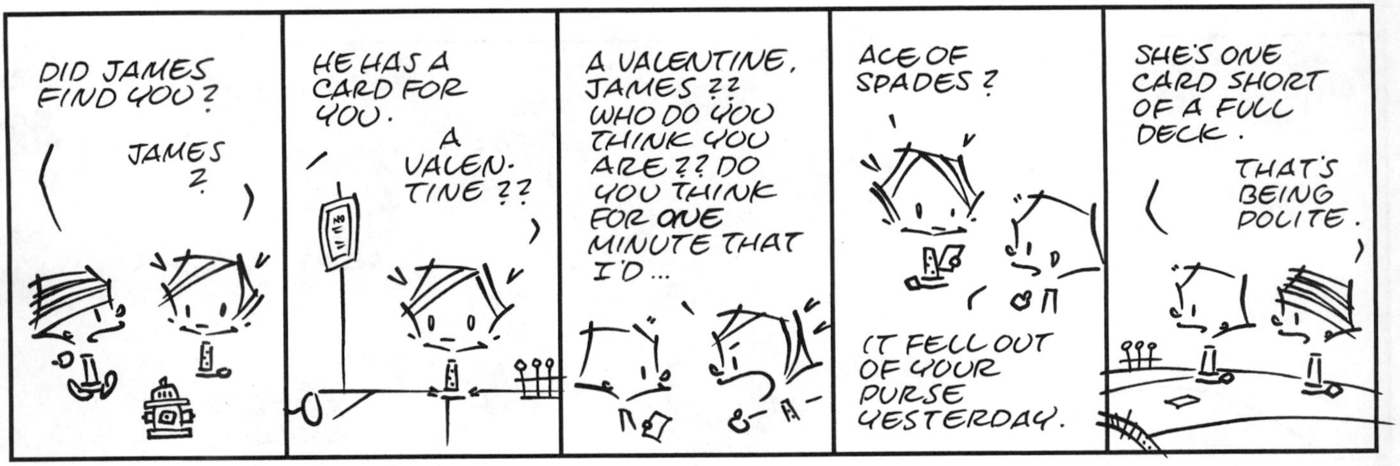
DID JAMES FIND YOU?
JAMES?
HE HAS A CARD FOR YOU.
A VALENTINE??
A VALENTINE, JAMES?? WHO DO YOU THINK YOU ARE?? DO YOU THINK FOR ONE MINUTE THAT I'D...
ACE OF SPADES?
IT FELL OUT OF YOUR PURSE YESTERDAY.
SHE'S ONE CARD SHORT OF A FULL DECK.
THAT'S BEING POLITE.

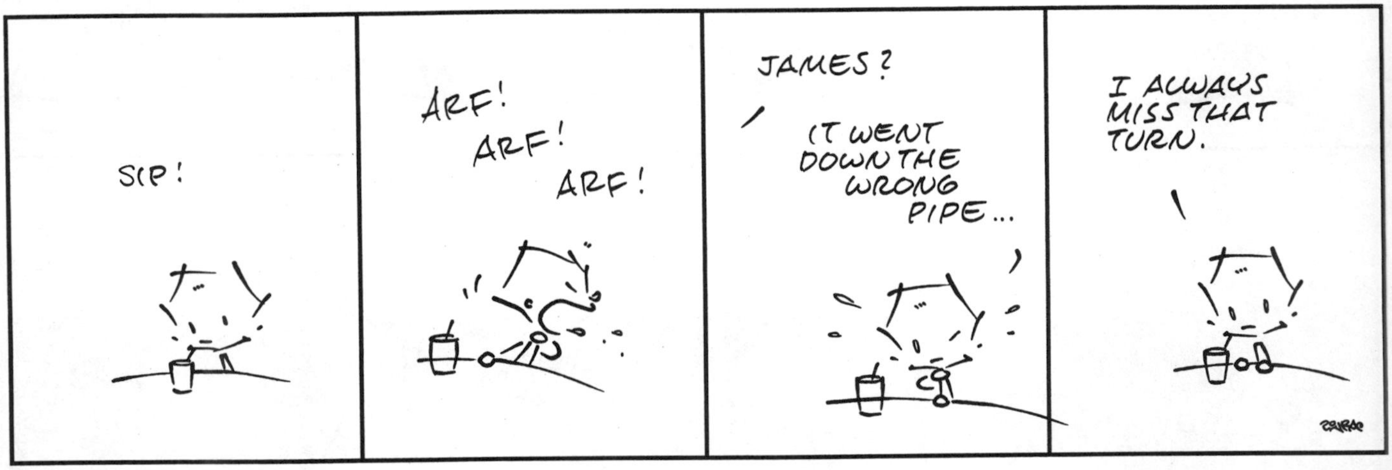
SIP!
ARF!
ARF!
ARF!
JAMES?
IT WENT DOWN THE WRONG PIPE...
I ALWAYS MISS THAT TURN.

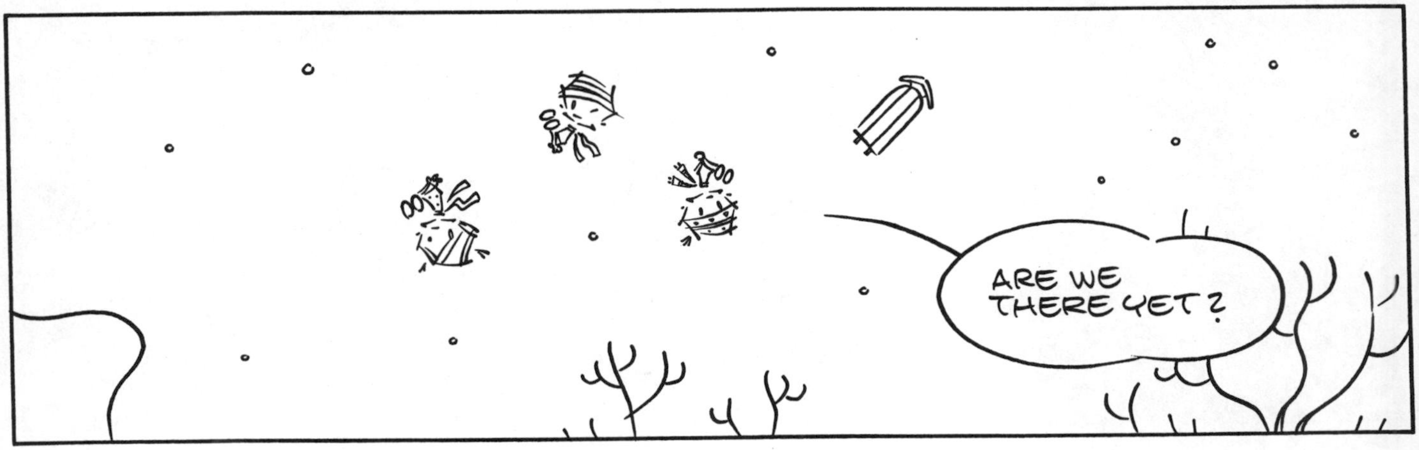
ARE WE THERE YET?

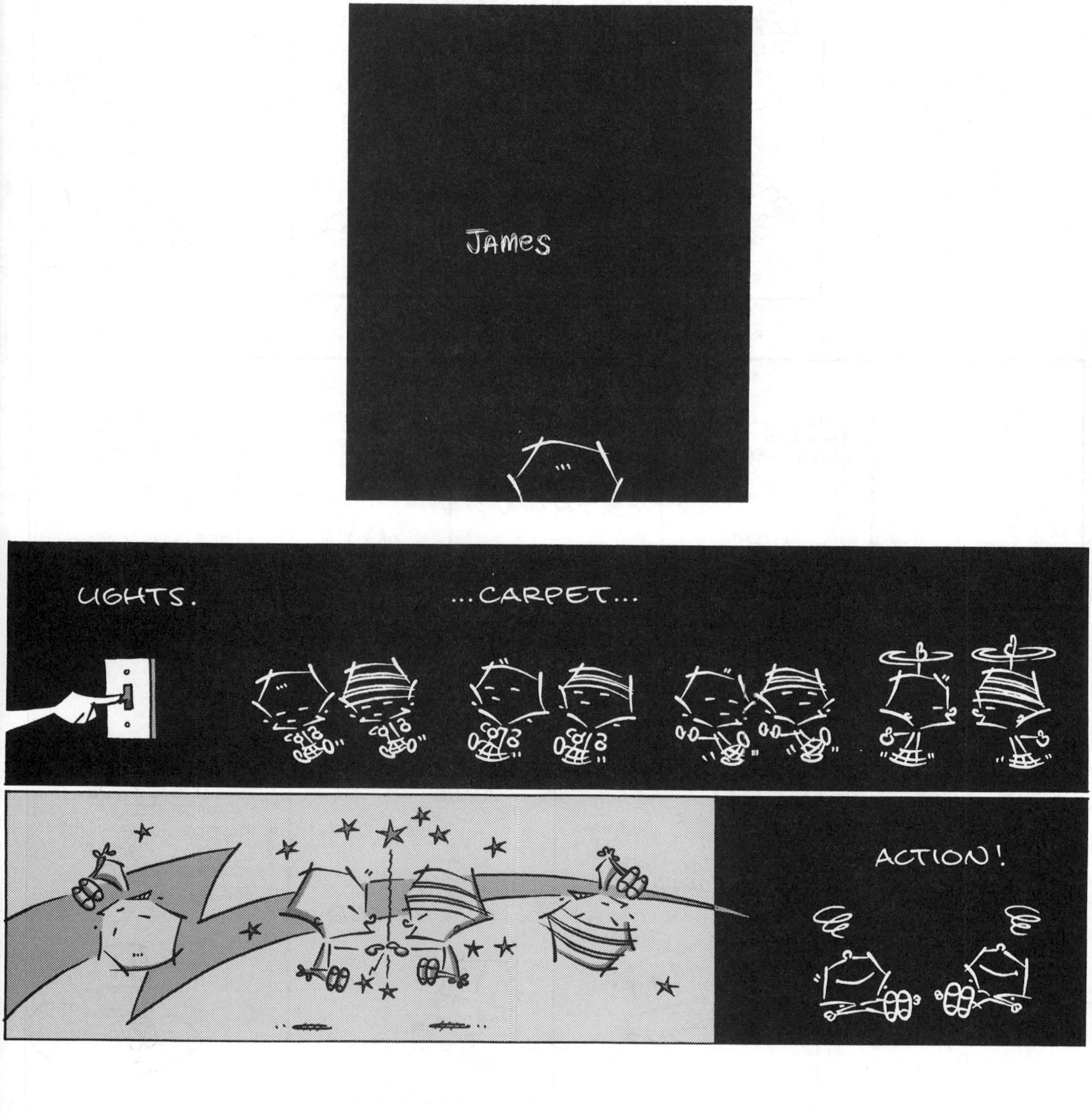
JAMES
LIGHTS.
...CARPET...
ACTION!

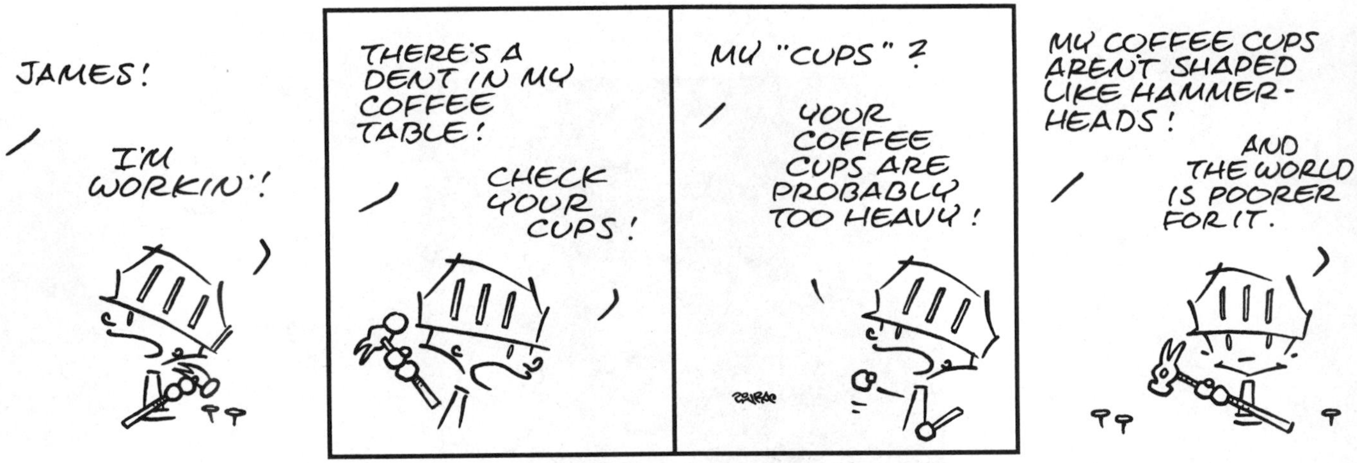
JAMES!
I'M WORKIN'!
THERE'S A DENT IN MY COFFEE TABLE!
CHECK YOUR CUPS!
MY "CUPS"?
YOUR COFFEE CUPS ARE PROBABLY TOO HEAVY!
MY COFFEE CUPS AREN'T SHAPED LIKE HAMMER-HEADS!
AND THE WORLD IS POORER FOR IT.

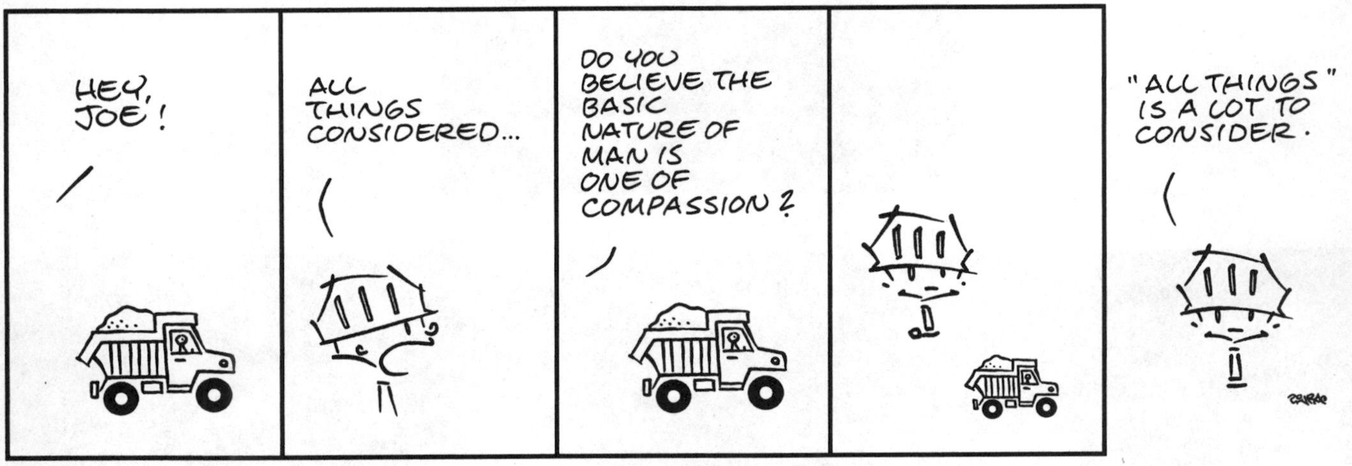
HEY, JOE!
ALL THINGS CONSIDERED...
DO YOU BELIEVE THE BASIC NATURE OF MAN IS ONE OF COMPASSION?
"ALL THINGS" IS A LOT TO CONSIDER.

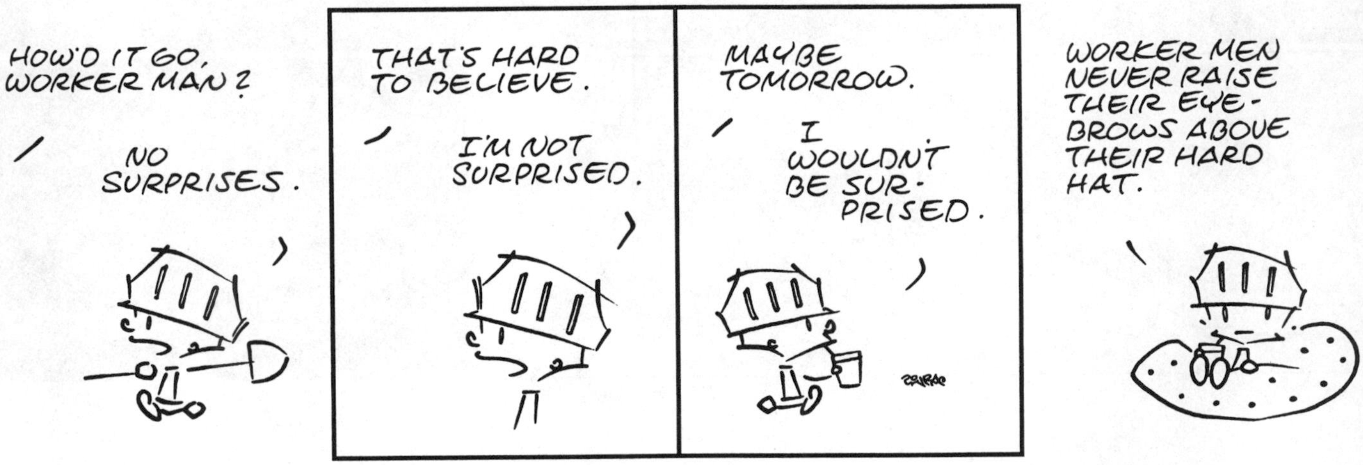
HOW'D IT GO, WORKER MAN?
NO SURPRISES.
THAT'S HARD TO BELIEVE.
I'M NOT SURPRISED.
MAYBE TOMORROW.
I WOULDN'T BE SUR-PRISED.
WORKER MEN NEVER RAISE THEIR EYE-BROWS ABOVE THEIR HARD HAT.

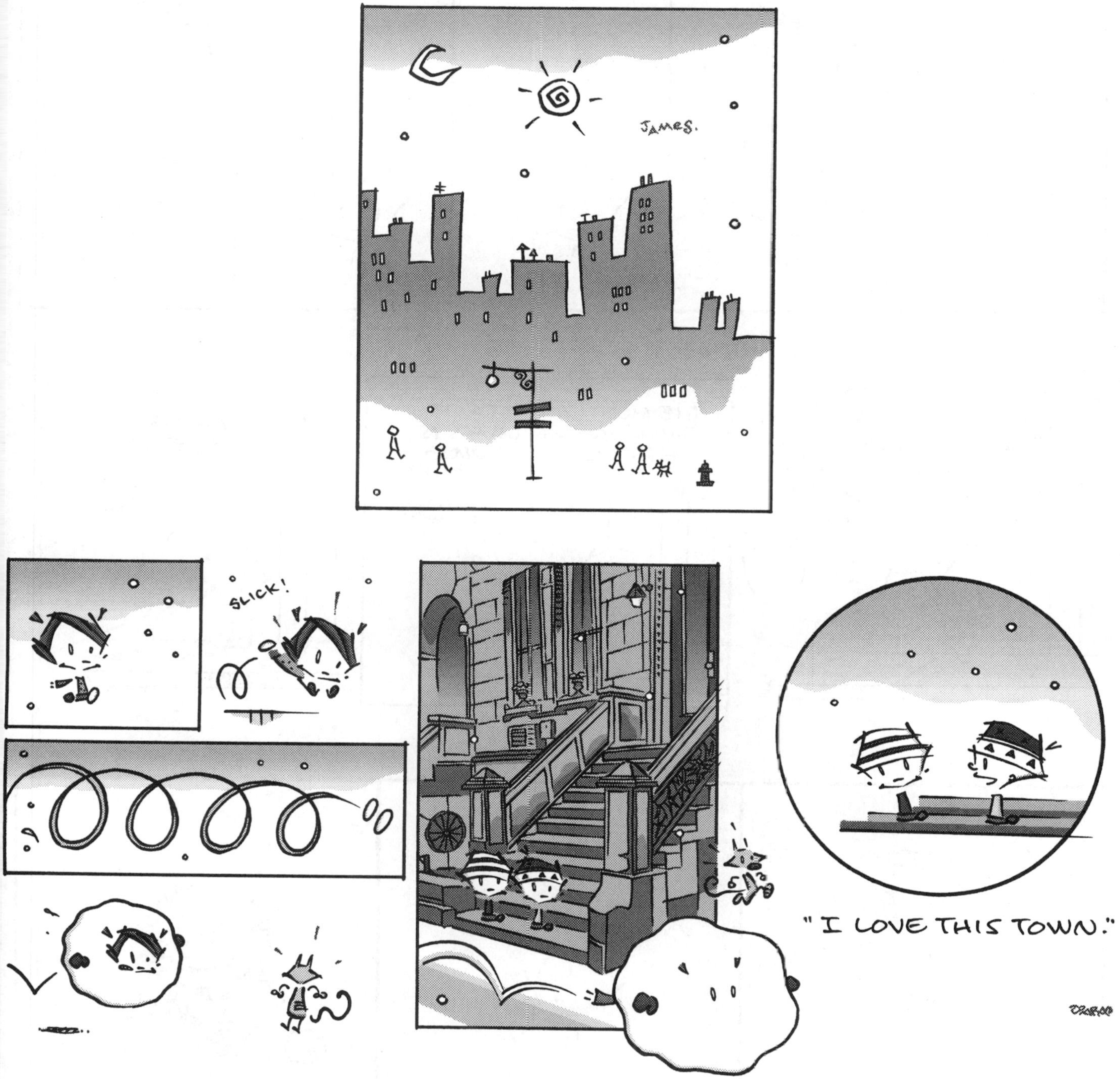
JAMES.
SLICK!
"I LOVE THIS TOWN."

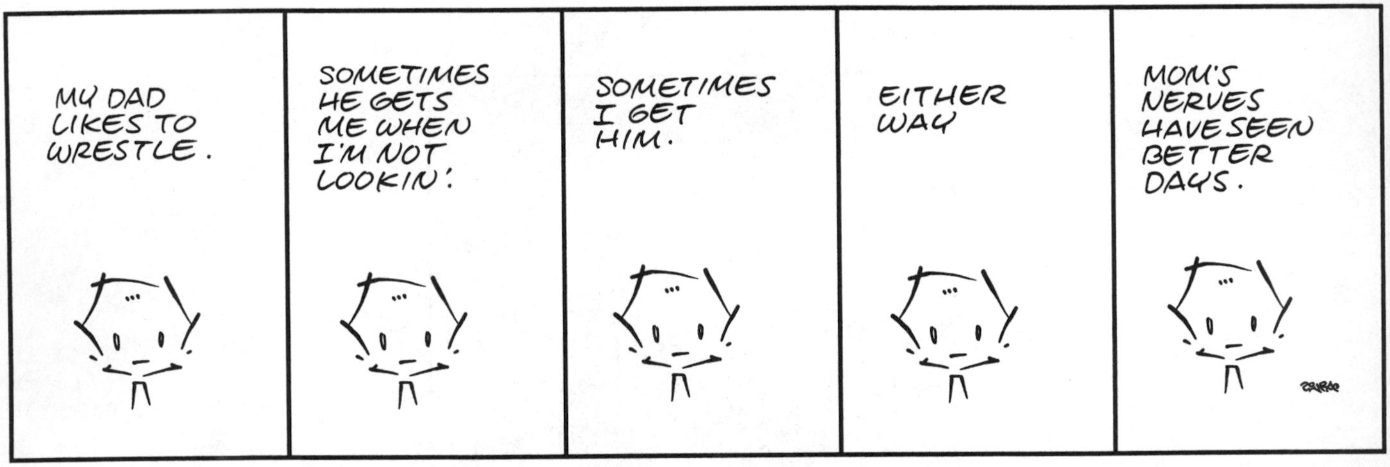
MY DAD LIKES TO WRESTLE.
SOMETIMES HE GETS ME WHEN I'M NOT LOOKIN'.
SOMETIMES I GET HIM.
EITHER WAY
MOM'S NERVES HAVE SEEN BETTER DAYS.

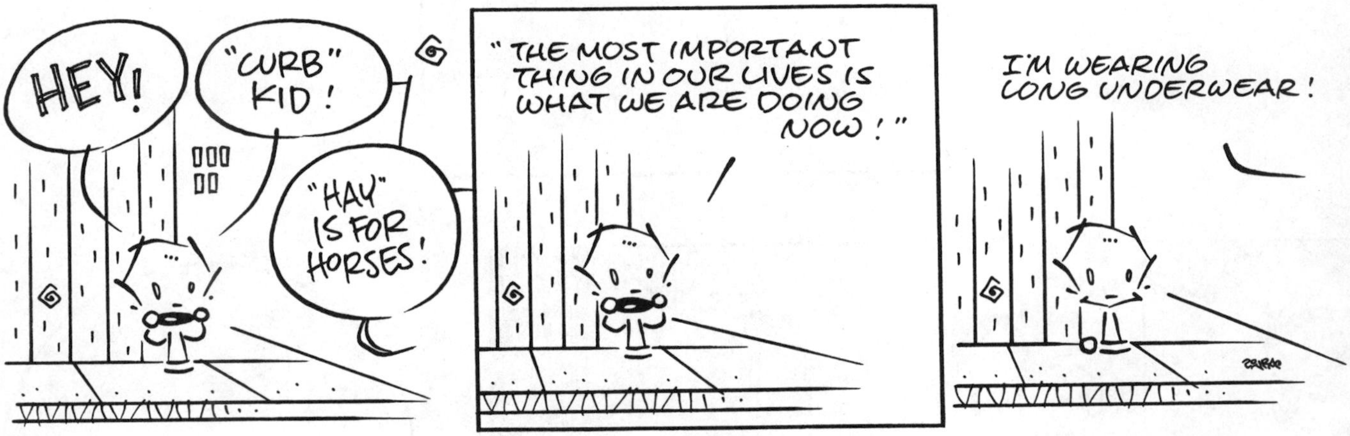
HEY!
"CURB" KID!
"HAY" IS FOR HORSES!
"THE MOST IMPORTANT THING IN OUR LIVES IS WHAT WE ARE DOING NOW!"
I'M WEARING LONG UNDERWEAR!

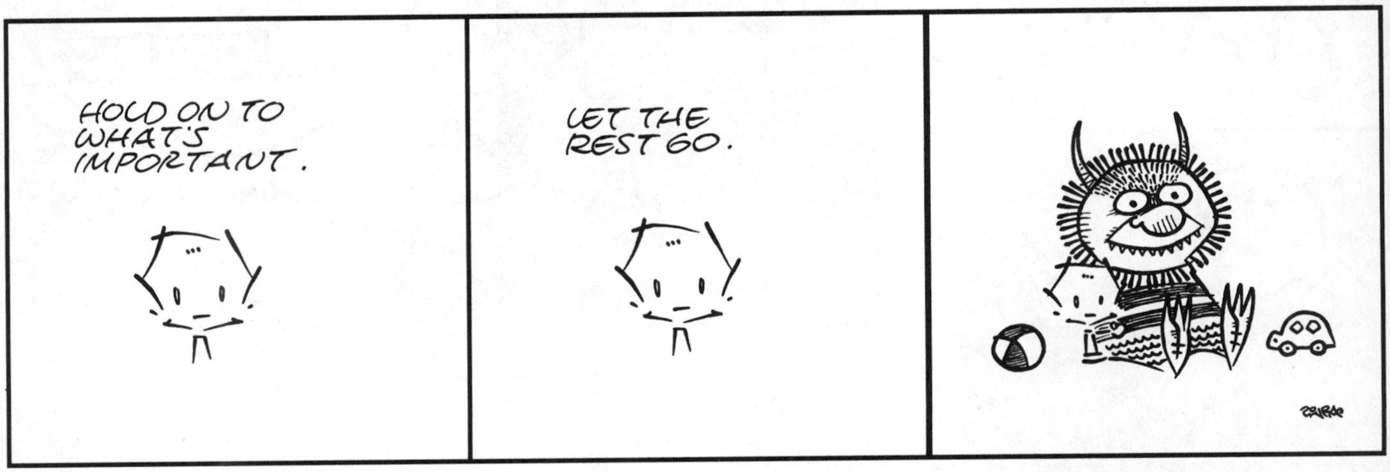
HOLD ON TO WHAT'S IMPORTANT.
LET THE REST GO.

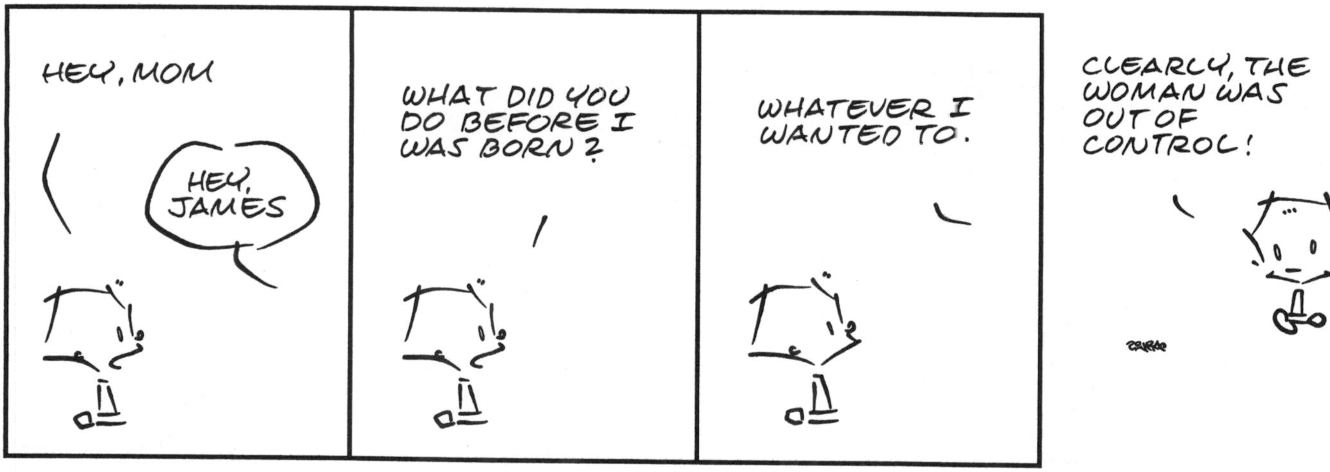
HEY, MOM
HEY, JAMES
WHAT DID YOU DO BEFORE I WAS BORN?
WHATEVER I WANTED TO.
CLEARLY, THE WOMAN WAS OUT OF CONTROL!

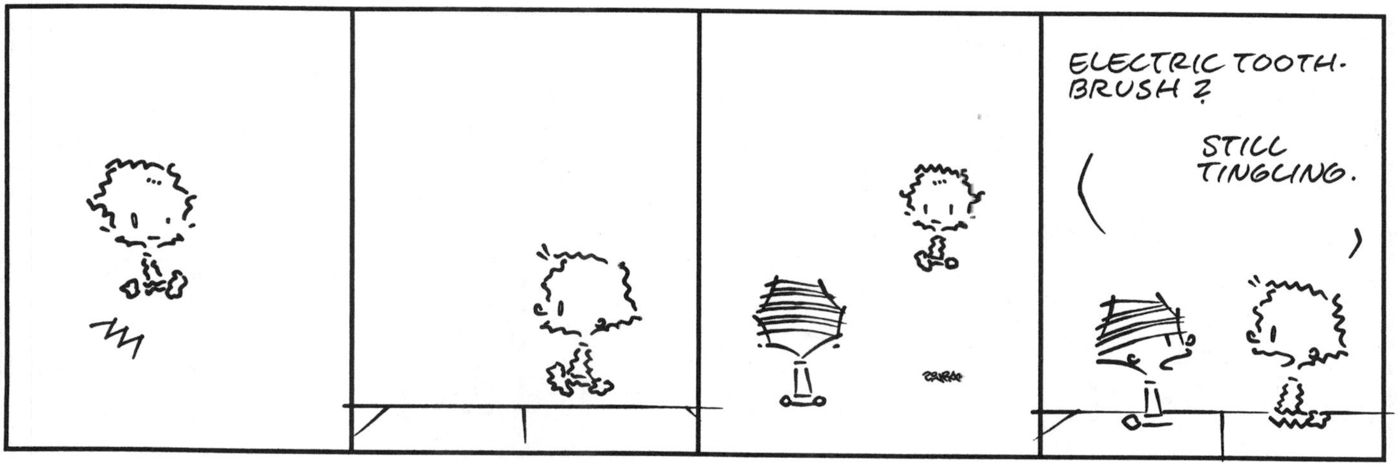
ELECTRIC TOOTH-BRUSH?
STILL TINGLING.

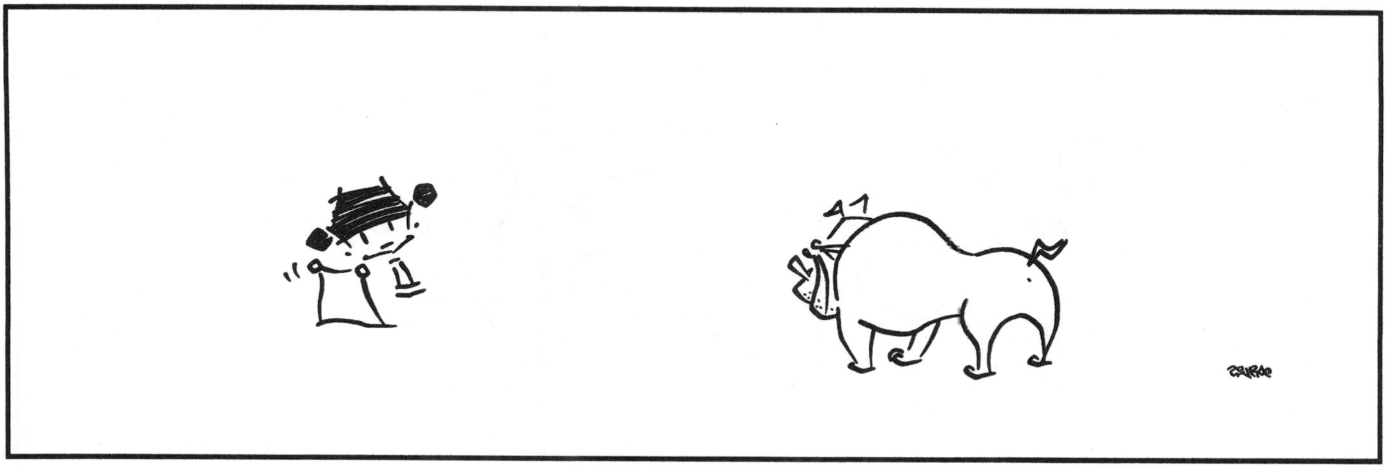

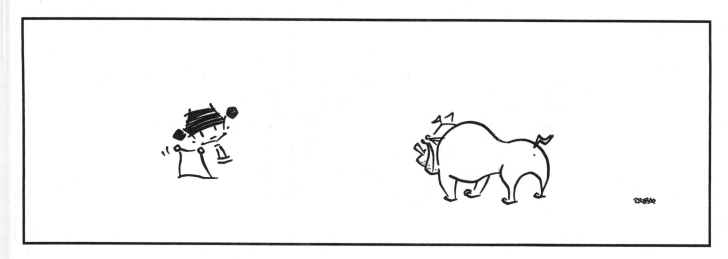

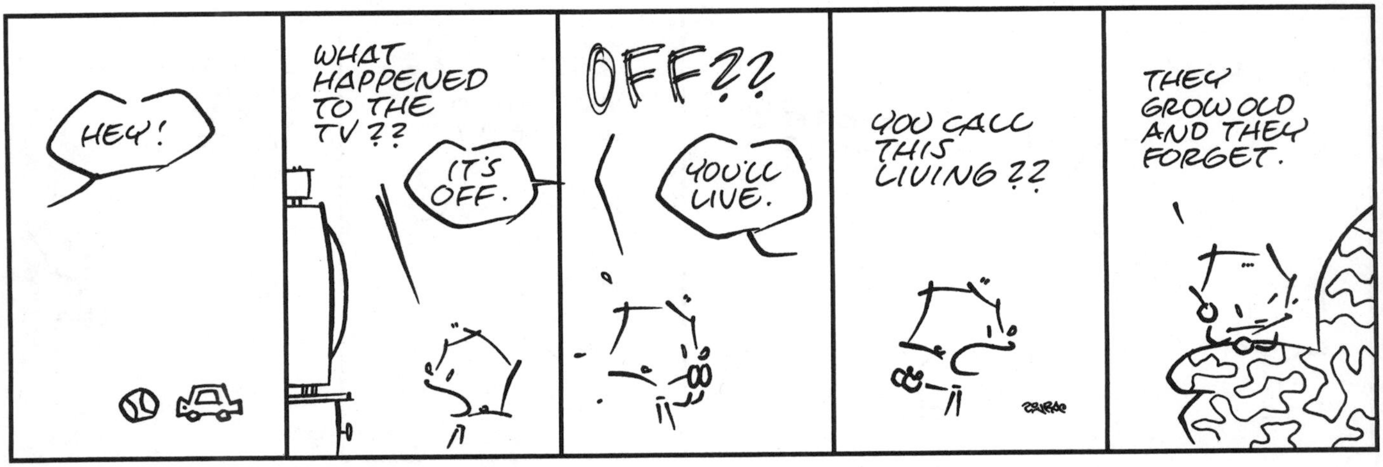
HEY!
WHAT HAPPENED TO THE TV??
IT'S OFF.
OFF??
YOU'LL LIVE.
YOU CALL THIS LIVING??
THEY GROW OLD AND THEY FORGET.

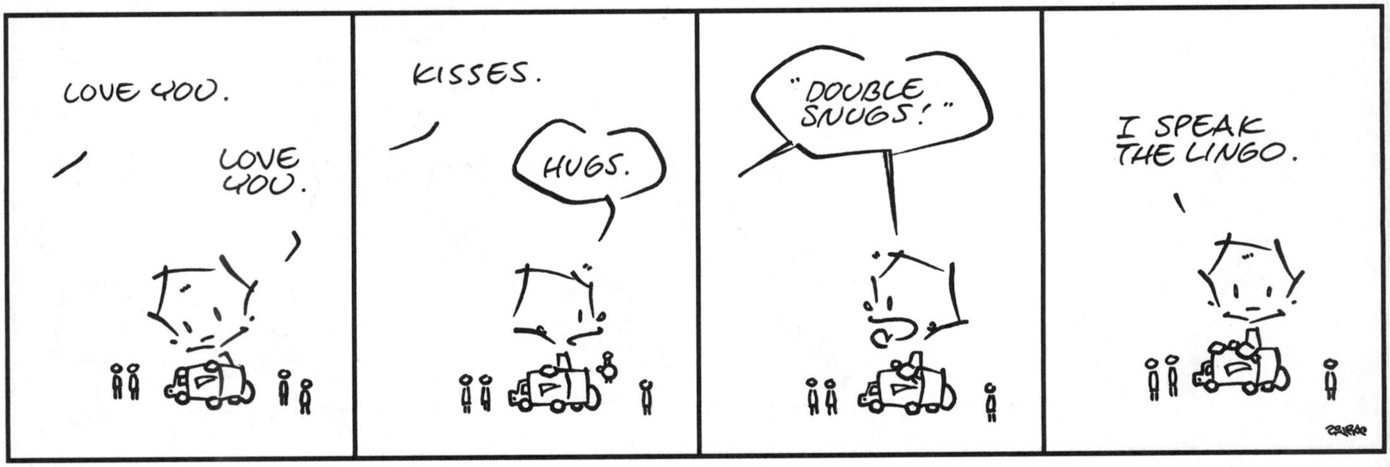
LOVE YOU.
LOVE YOU.
KISSES.
HUGS.
"DOUBLE SNUGS!"
I SPEAK THE LINGO.

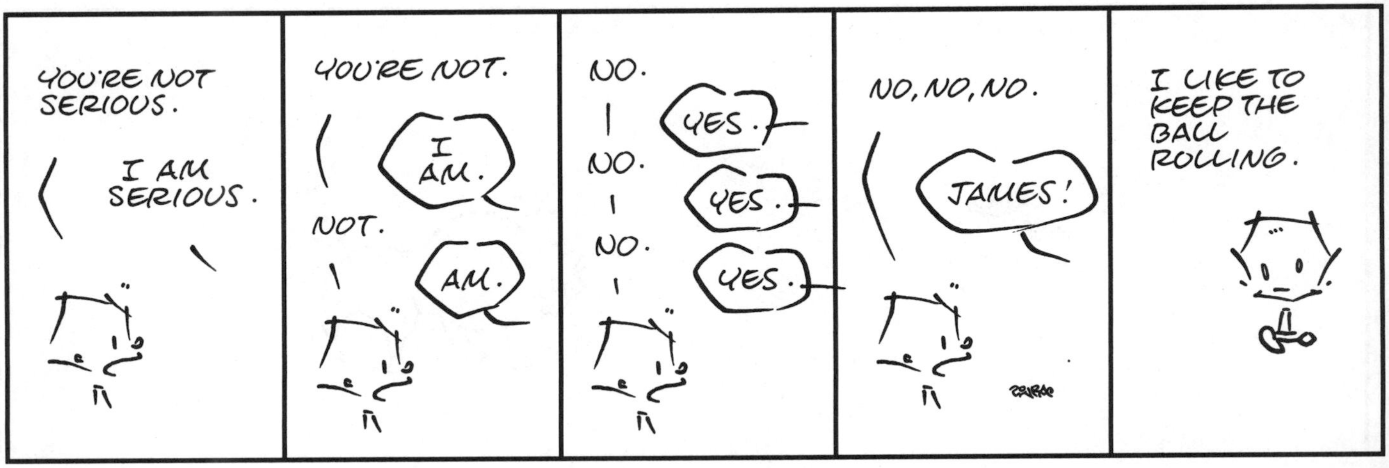
YOU'RE NOT SERIOUS.
I AM SERIOUS.
YOU'RE NOT.
I AM.
NOT.
AM.
NO.
YES.
NO.
YES.
NO.
YES.
NO, NO, NO.
JAMES!
I LIKE TO KEEP THE BALL ROLLING.

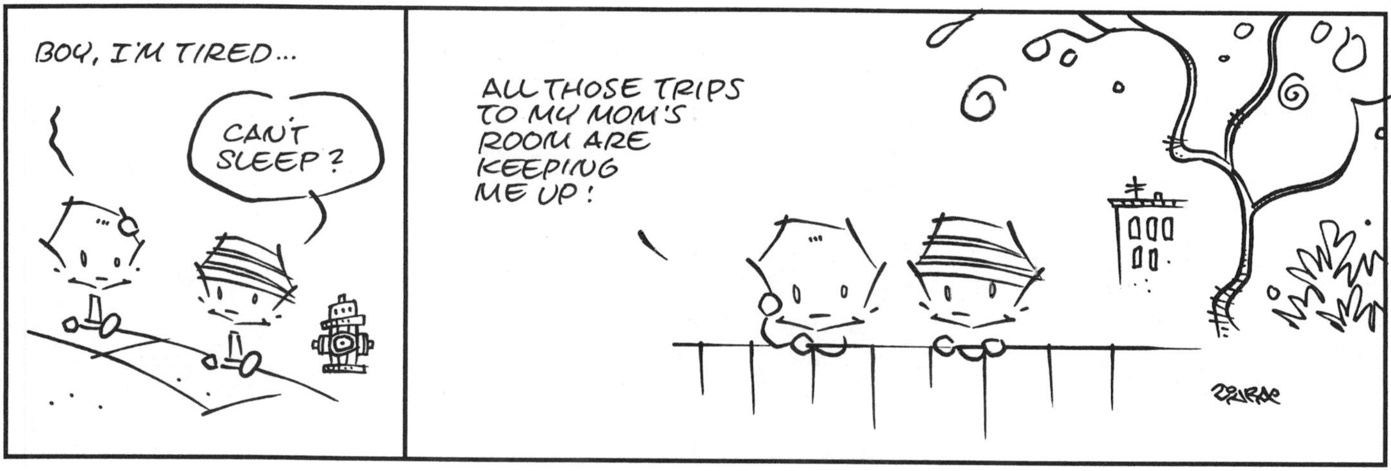
BOY, I'M TIRED...
CAN'T SLEEP?
ALL THOSE TRIPS TO MY MOM'S ROOM ARE KEEPING ME UP!

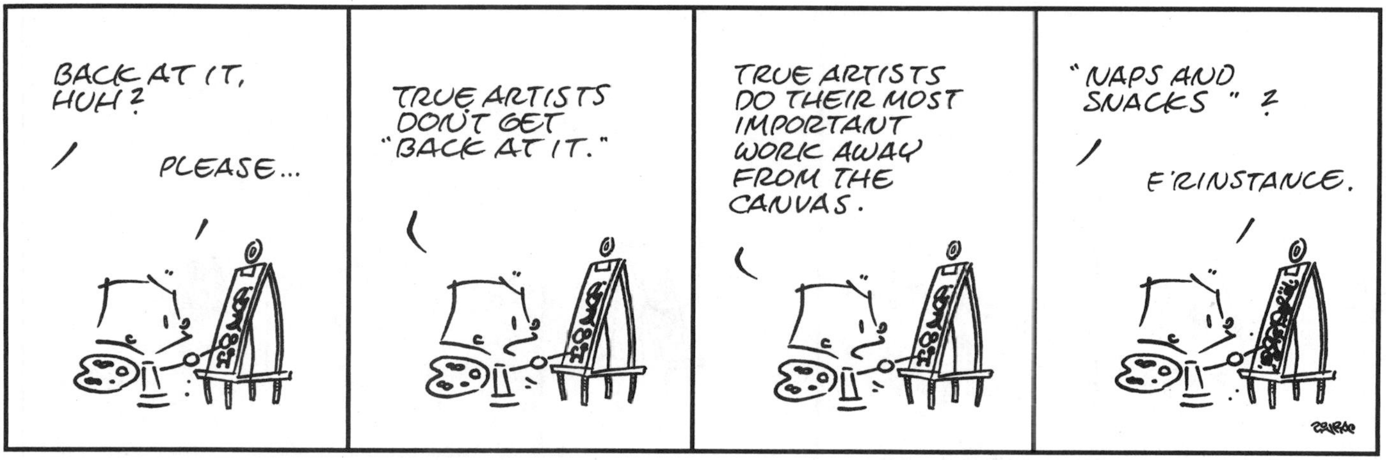
BACK AT IT, HUH?
PLEASE...
TRUE ARTISTS DON'T GET "BACK AT IT."
TRUE ARTISTS DO THEIR MOST IMPORTANT WORK AWAY FROM THE CANVAS.
"NAPS AND SNACKS"?
F'RINSTANCE.

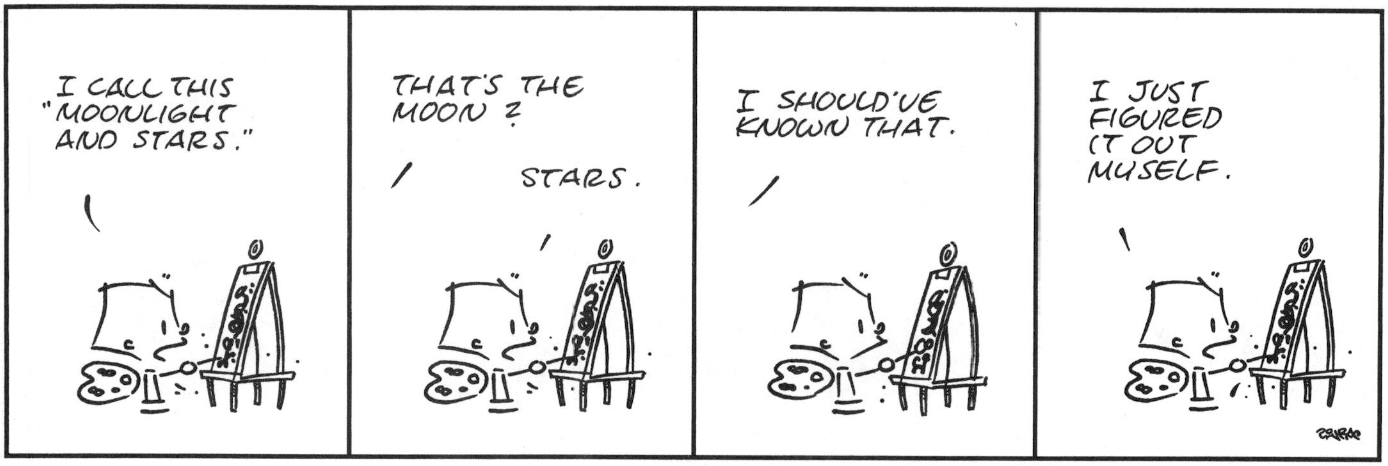
I CALL THIS "MOONLIGHT AND STARS."
THAT'S THE MOON?
STARS.
I SHOULD'VE KNOWN THAT.
I JUST FIGURED IT OUT MYSELF.

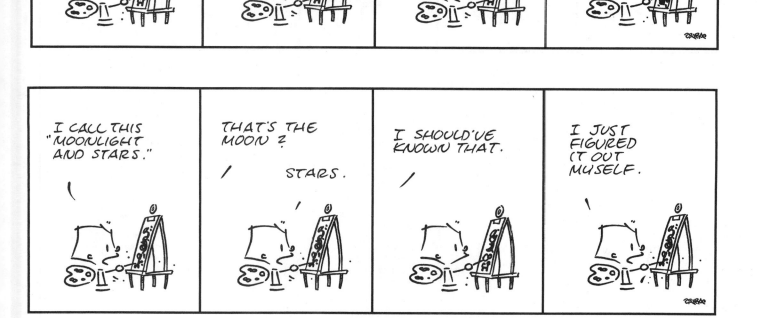

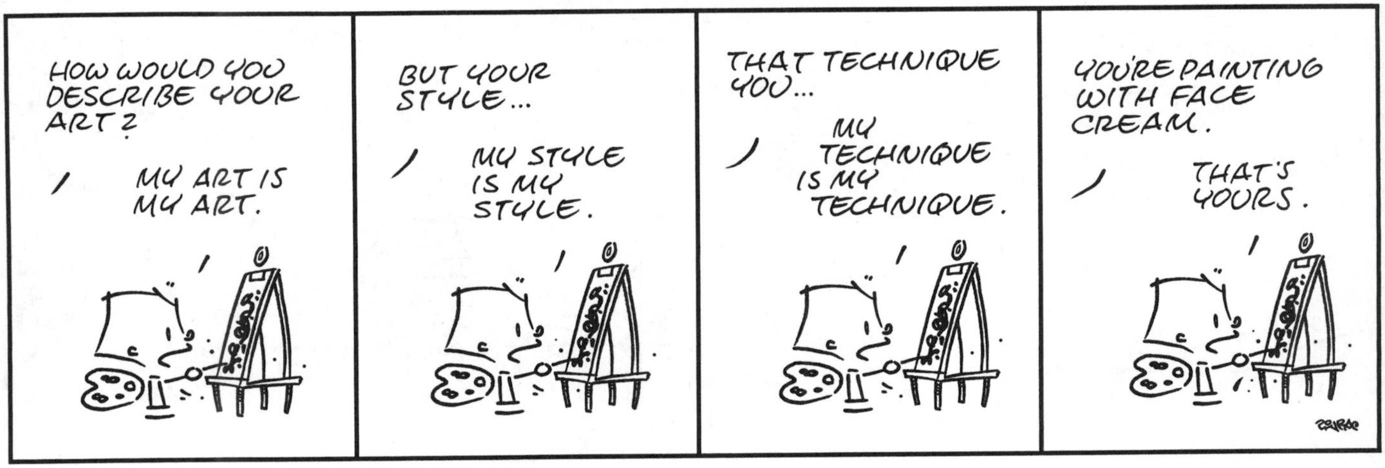
HOW WOULD YOU DESCRIBE YOUR ART?
MY ART IS MY ART.
BUT YOUR STYLE...
MY STYLE IS MY STYLE.
THAT TECHNIQUE YOU...
MY TECHNIQUE IS MY TECHNIQUE.
YOU'RE PAINTING WITH FACE CREAM.
THAT'S YOURS.

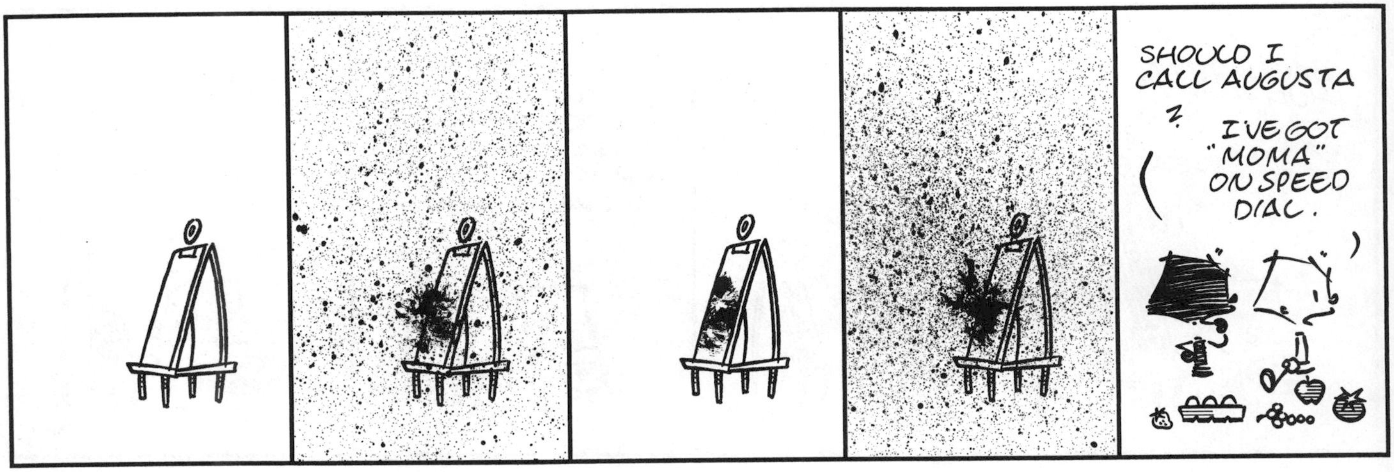
SHOULD I CALL AUGUSTA?
I'VE GOT "MOMA" ON SPEED DIAL.

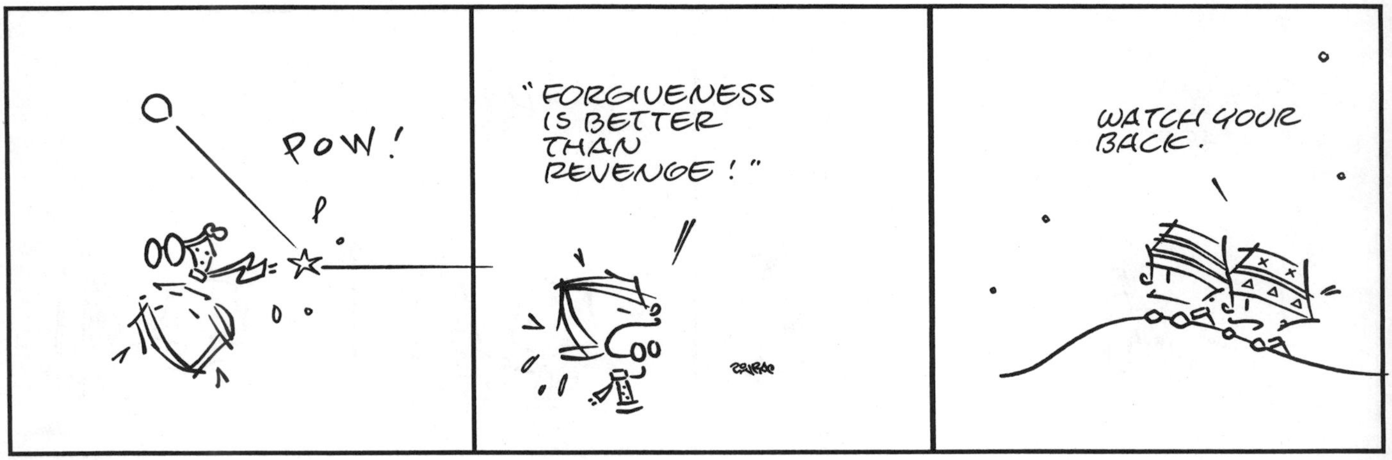
POW!
"FORGIVENESS IS BETTER THAN REVENGE!"
WATCH YOUR BACK.

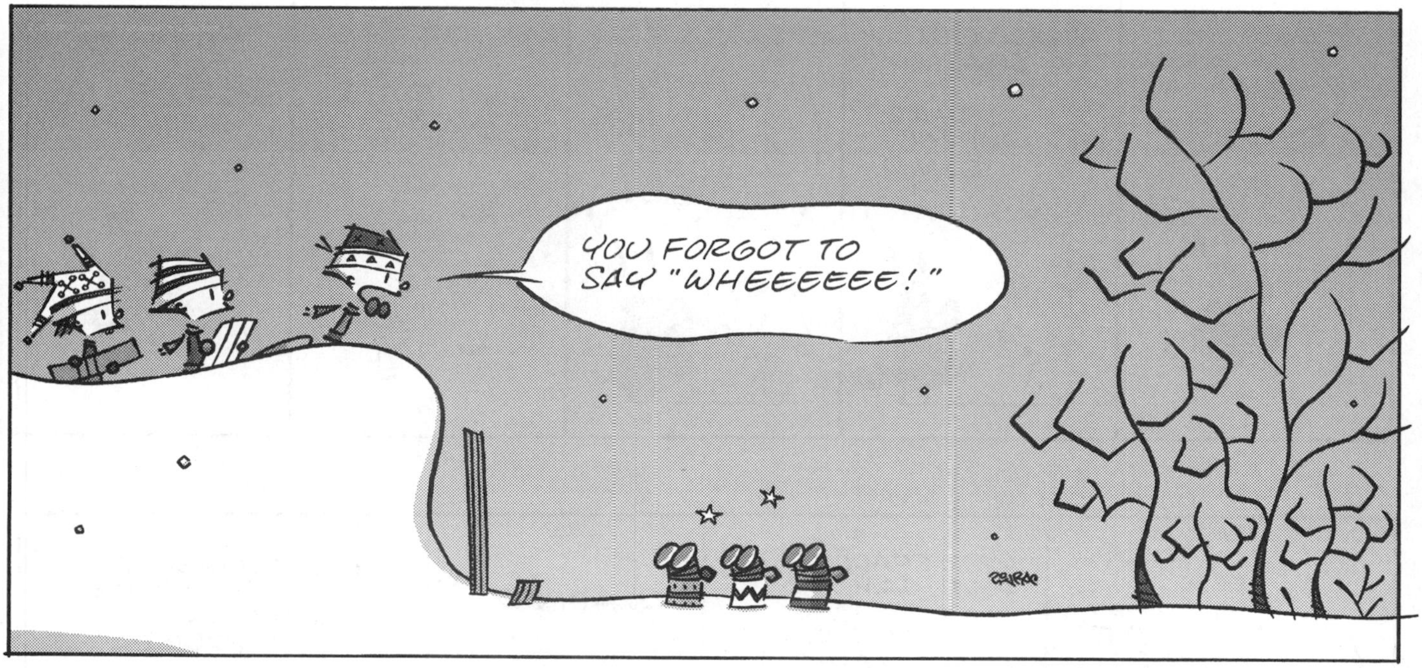
YOU FORGOT TO
SAY "WHEEEEEEE!"

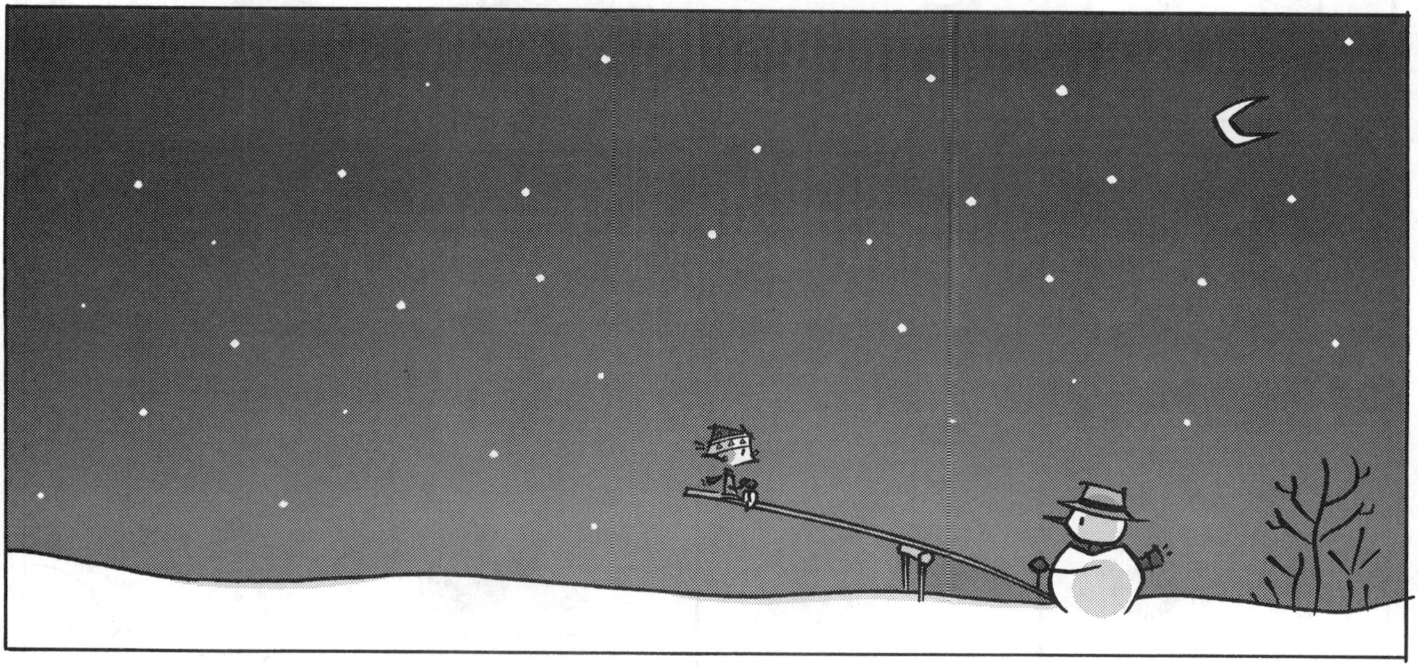

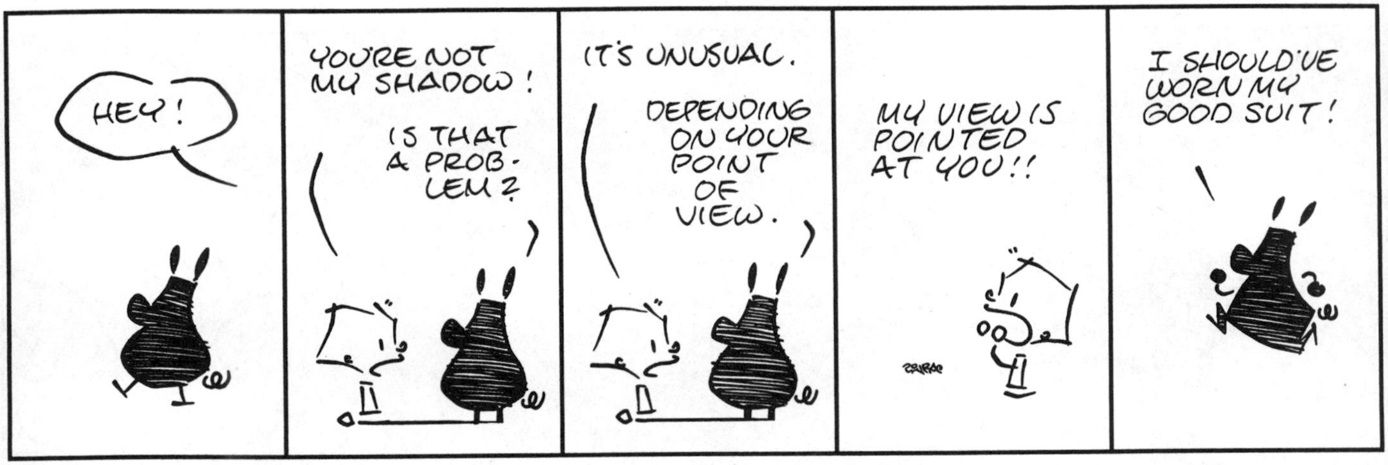
HEY!
YOU'RE NOT MY SHADOW!
IS THAT A PROB-LEM?
IT'S UNUSUAL.
DEPENDING ON YOUR POINT OF VIEW.
MY VIEW IS POINTED AT YOU!!
I SHOULD'VE WORN MY GOOD SUIT!

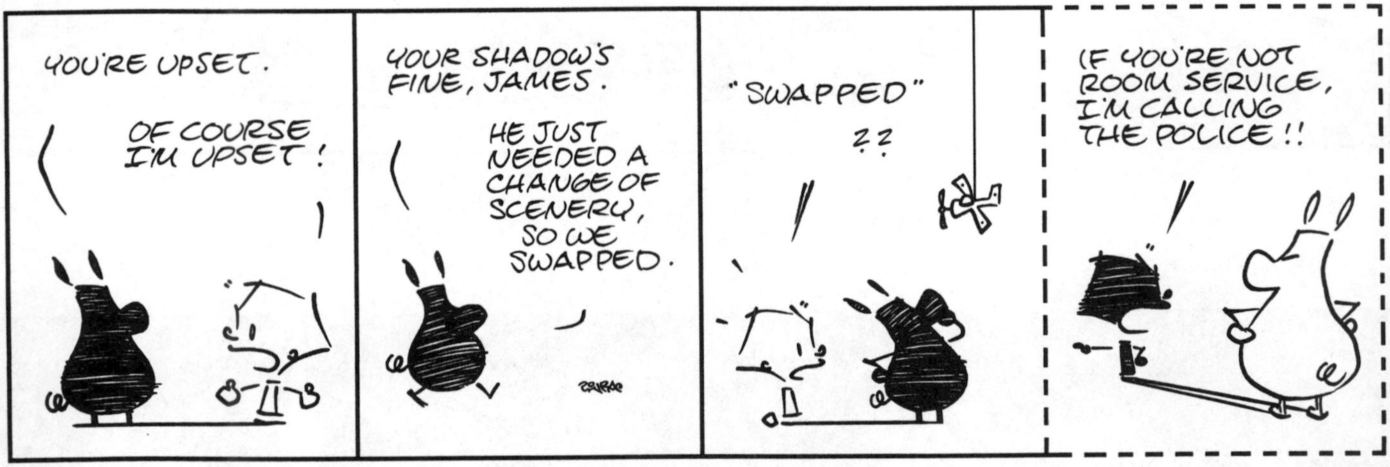
YOU'RE UPSET.
OF COURSE I'M UPSET!
YOUR SHADOW'S FINE, JAMES.
HE JUST NEEDED A CHANGE OF SCENERY, SO WE SWAPPED.
"SWAPPED"
??
IF YOU'RE NOT ROOM SERVICE, I'M CALLING THE POLICE!!

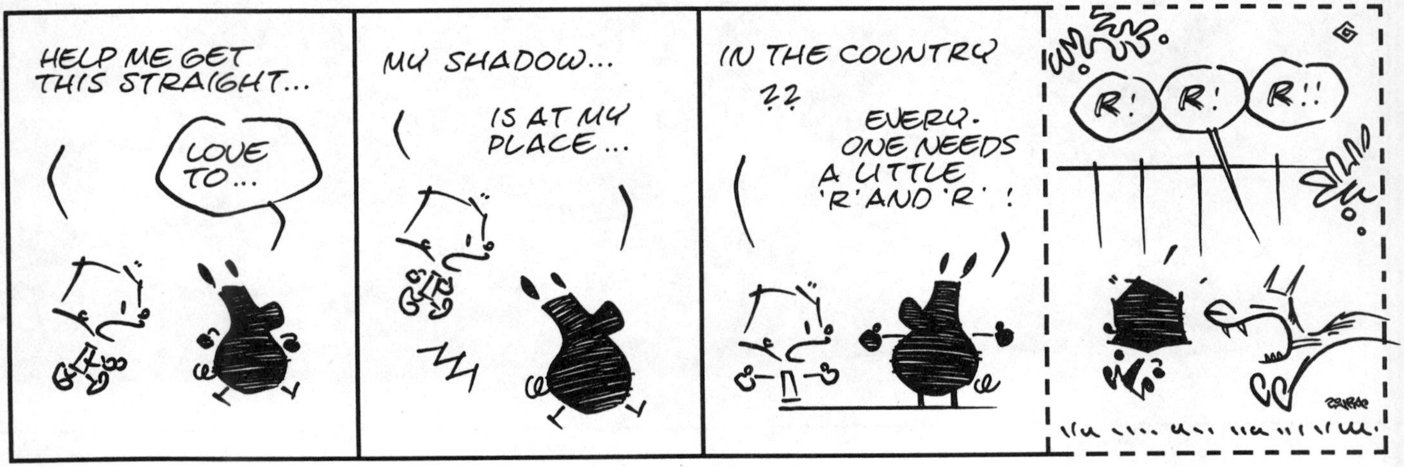
HELP ME GET THIS STRAIGHT...
LOVE TO...
MY SHADOW...
IS AT MY PLACE...
IN THE COUNTRY
??
EVERY-ONE NEEDS A LITTLE 'R' AND 'R'!
R!
R!
R!!

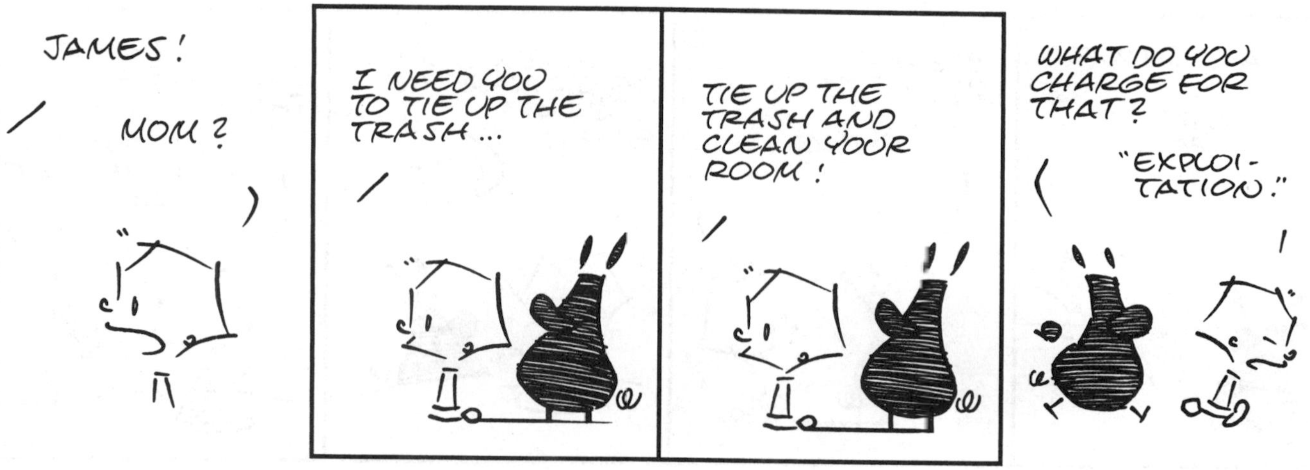
JAMES!
MOM?
I NEED YOU TO TIE UP THE TRASH...
TIE UP THE TRASH AND CLEAN YOUR ROOM!
WHAT DO YOU CHARGE FOR THAT?
"EXPLOITATION."

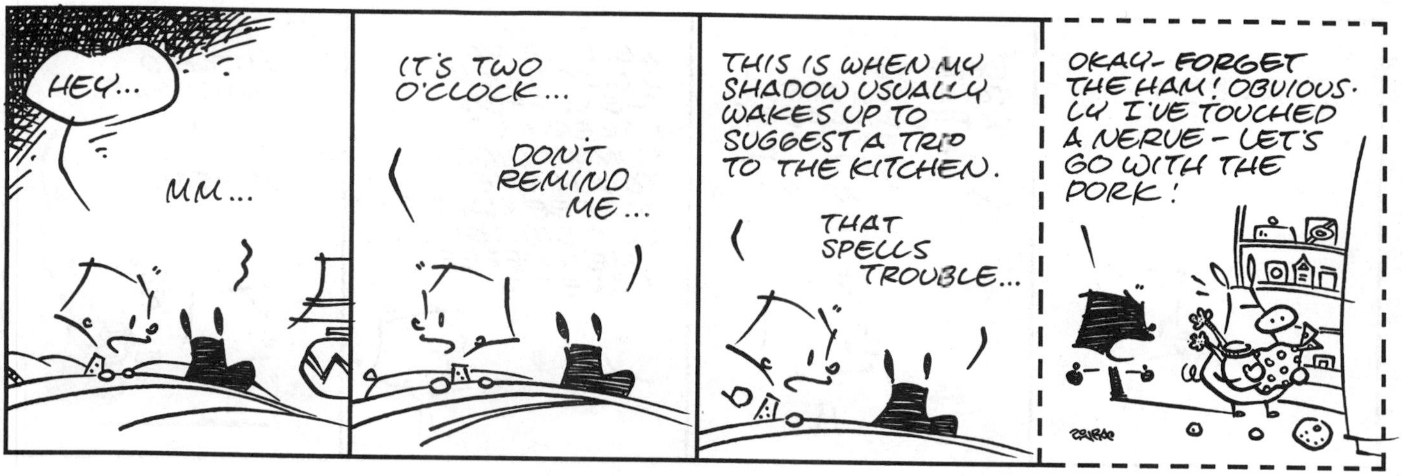
HEY...
MM...
IT'S TWO O'CLOCK...
DON'T REMIND ME...
THIS IS WHEN MY SHADOW USUALLY WAKES UP TO SUGGEST A TRIP TO THE KITCHEN.
THAT SPELLS TROUBLE...
OKAY- FORGET THE HAM! OBVIOUSLY I'VE TOUCHED A NERVE - LET'S GO WITH THE PORK!

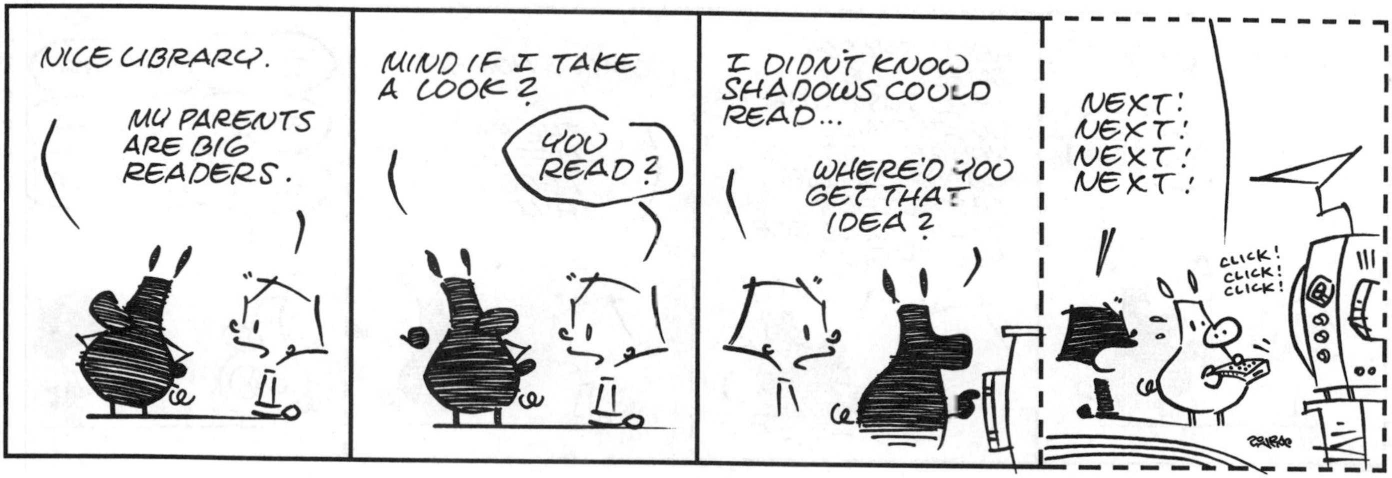
NICE LIBRARY.
MY PARENTS ARE BIG READERS.
MIND IF I TAKE A LOOK?
YOU READ?
I DIDN'T KNOW SHADOWS COULD READ...
WHERE'D YOU GET THAT IDEA?
NEXT! NEXT! NEXT! NEXT!
CLICK! CLICK! CLICK!

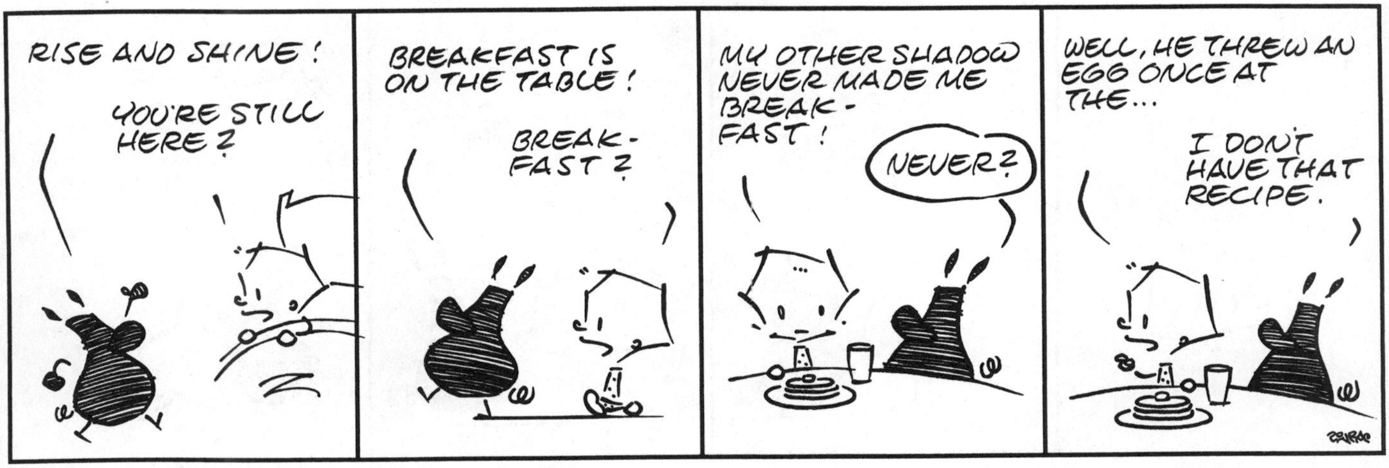
RISE AND SHINE!
YOU'RE STILL HERE?
BREAKFAST IS ON THE TABLE!
BREAK-FAST?
MY OTHER SHADOW NEVER MADE ME BREAK-FAST!
NEVER?
WELL, HE THREW AN EGG ONCE AT THE...
I DON'T HAVE THAT RECIPE.

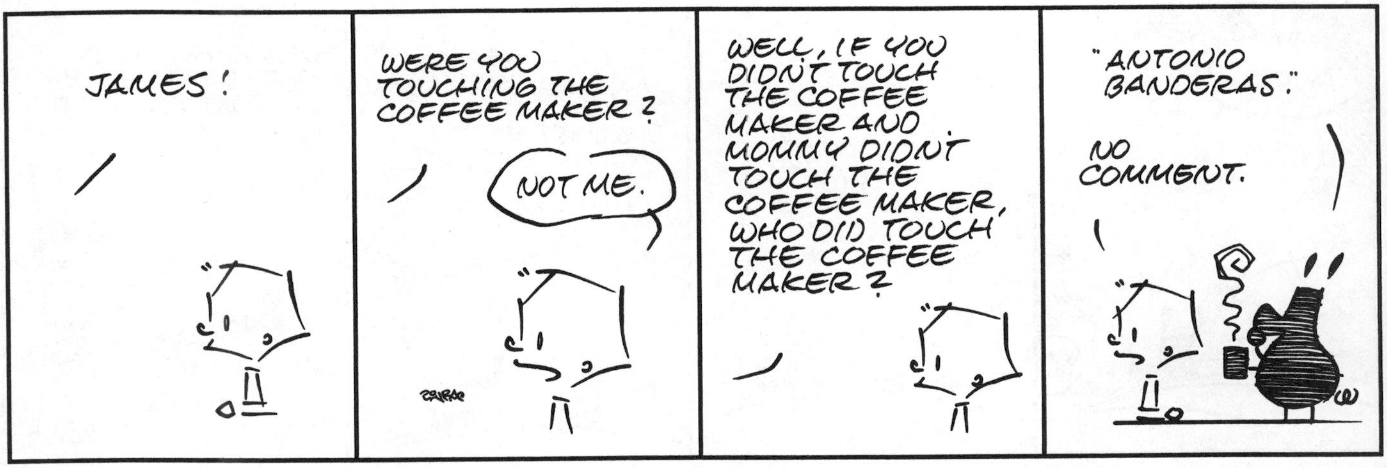
JAMES!
WERE YOU TOUCHING THE COFFEE MAKER?
NOT ME.
WELL, IF YOU DIDN'T TOUCH THE COFFEE MAKER AND MOMMY DIDN'T TOUCH THE COFFEE MAKER, WHO DID TOUCH THE COFFEE MAKER?
"ANTONIO BANDERAS."
NO COMMENT.

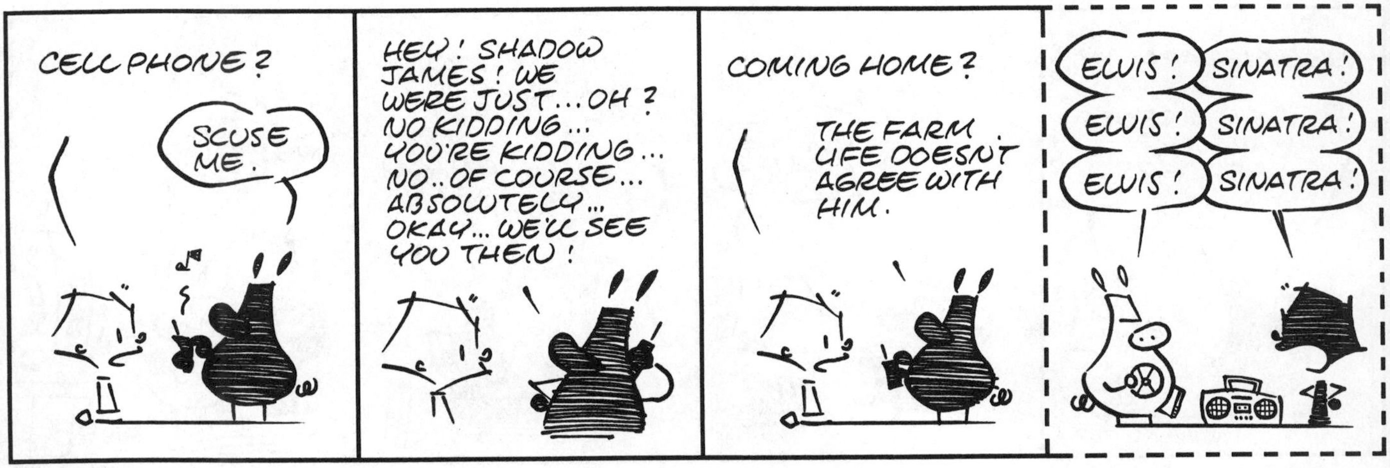
CELL PHONE?
SCUSE ME.
HEY! SHADOW JAMES! WE WERE JUST... OH? NO KIDDING... YOU'RE KIDDING... NO.. OF COURSE... ABSOLUTELY... OKAY... WE'LL SEE YOU THEN!
COMING HOME?
THE FARM LIFE DOESN'T AGREE WITH HIM.
ELVIS!
SINATRA!
ELVIS!
SINATRA!
ELVIS!
SINATRA!

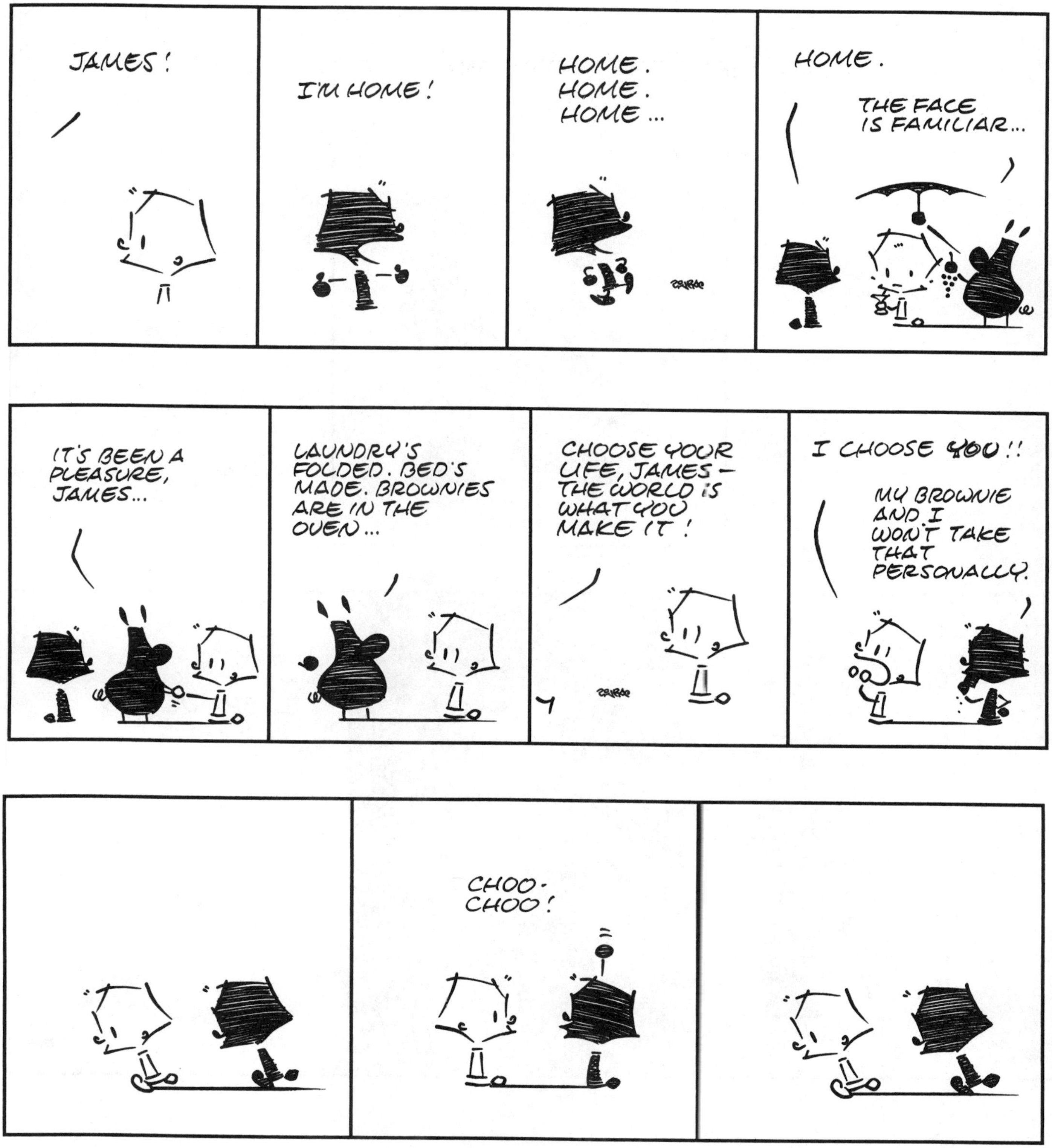
JAMES!
I'M HOME!
HOME. HOME. HOME...
HOME.
THE FACE IS FAMILIAR...
IT'S BEEN A PLEASURE, JAMES...
LAUNDRY'S FOLDED. BED'S MADE. BROWNIES ARE IN THE OVEN...
CHOOSE YOUR LIFE, JAMES – THE WORLD IS WHAT YOU MAKE IT!
I CHOOSE YOU!!
MY BROWNIE AND I WON'T TAKE THAT PERSONALLY.
CHOO-CHOO!

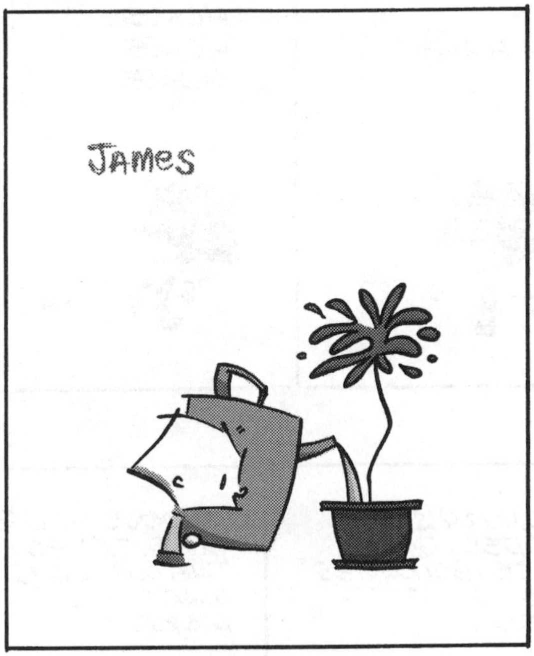
JAMES

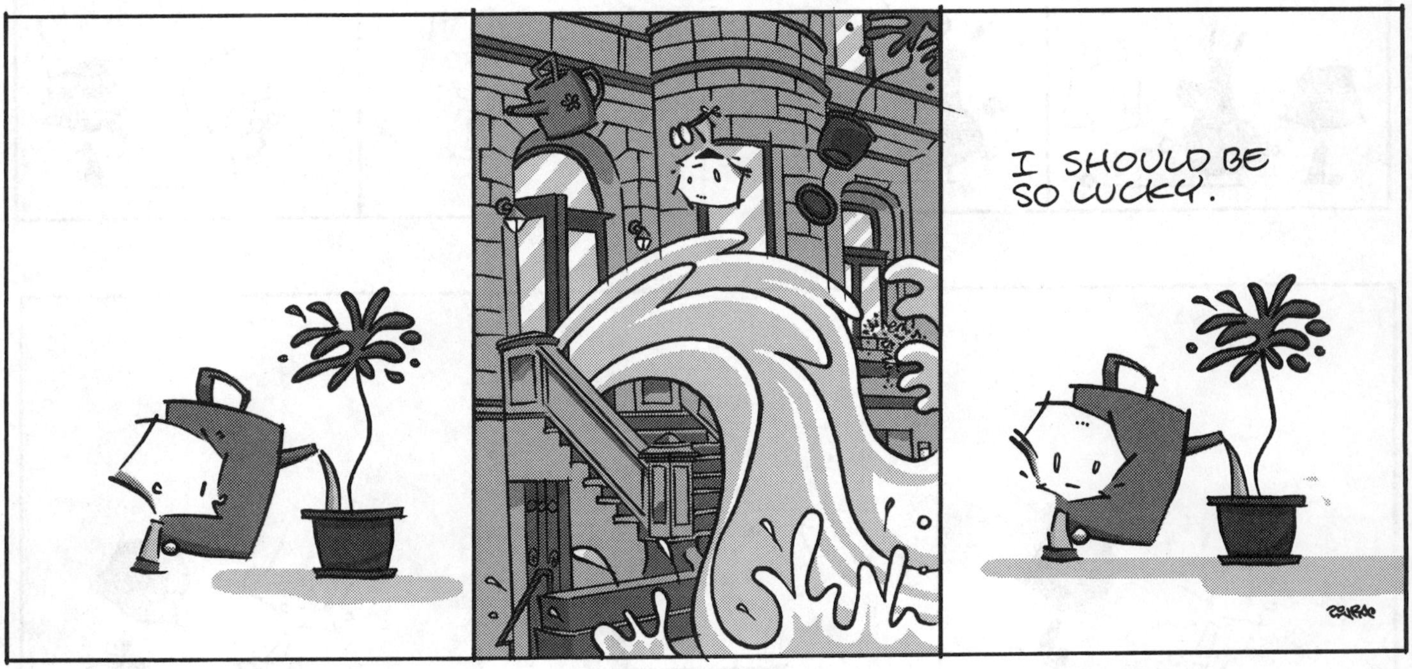
I SHOULD BE SO LUCKY.

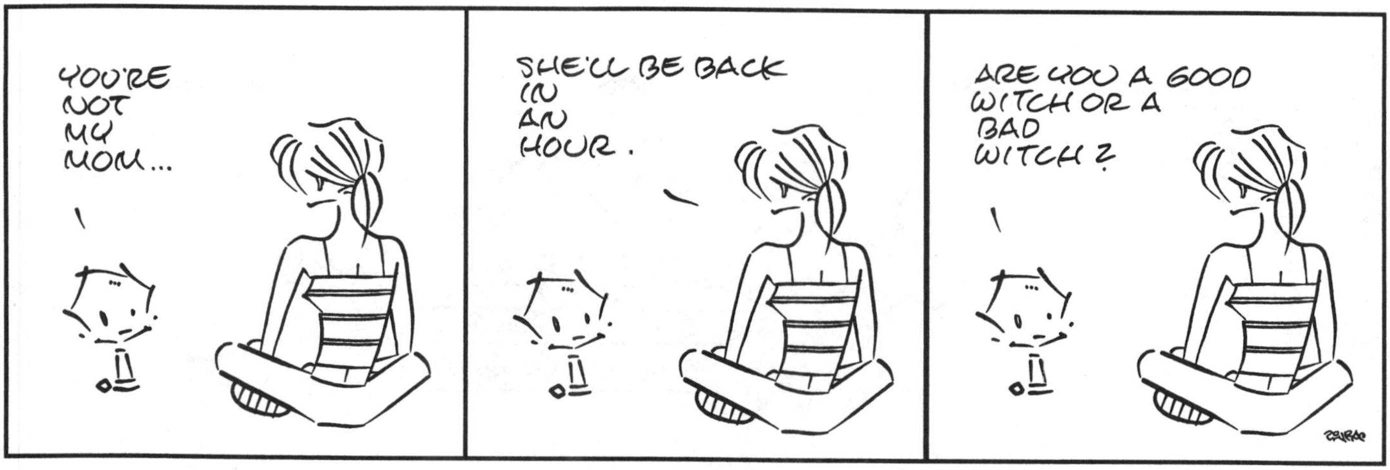
YOU'RE NOT MY MOM...
SHE'LL BE BACK IN AN HOUR.
ARE YOU A GOOD WITCH OR A BAD WITCH ?

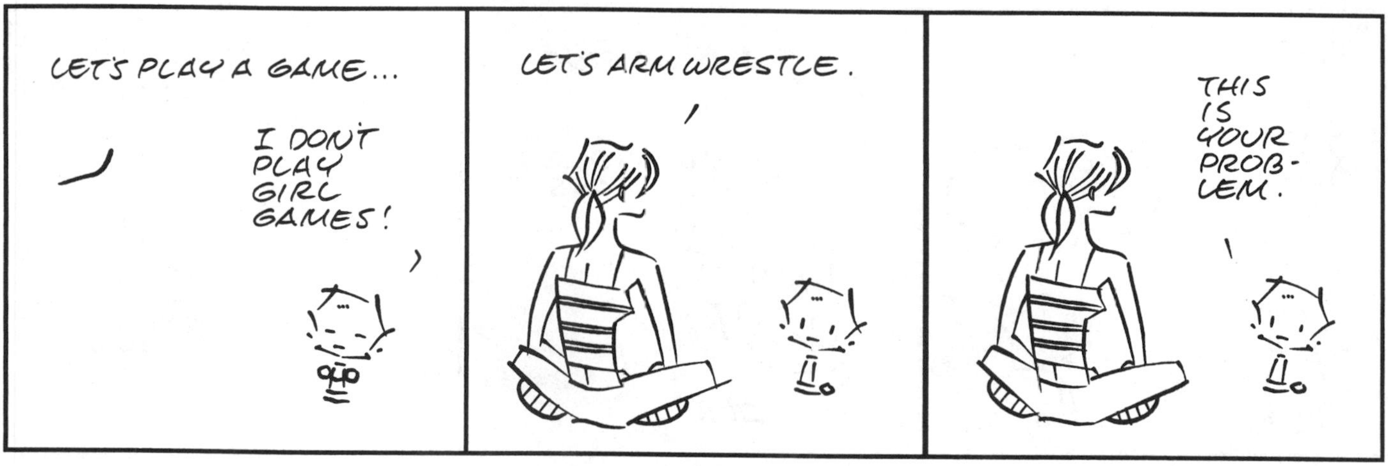
LET'S PLAY A GAME...
I DON'T PLAY GIRL GAMES!
LET'S ARM WRESTLE.
THIS IS YOUR PROB-LEM.

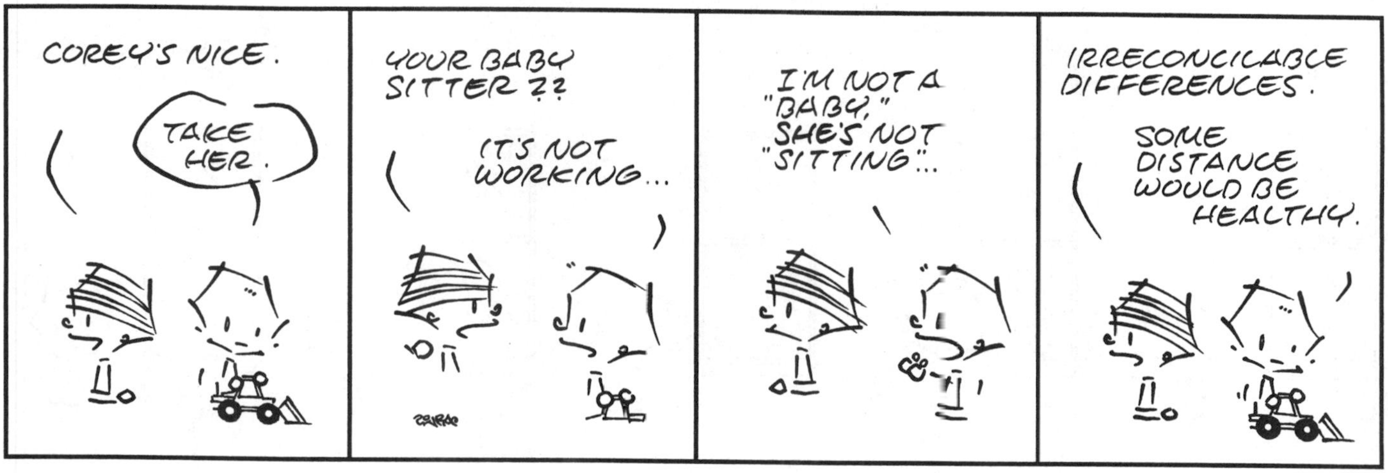
COREY'S NICE.
TAKE HER.
YOUR BABY SITTER ??
IT'S NOT WORKING...
I'M NOT A "BABY," SHE'S NOT "SITTING"...
IRRECONCILABLE DIFFERENCES.
SOME DISTANCE WOULD BE HEALTHY.

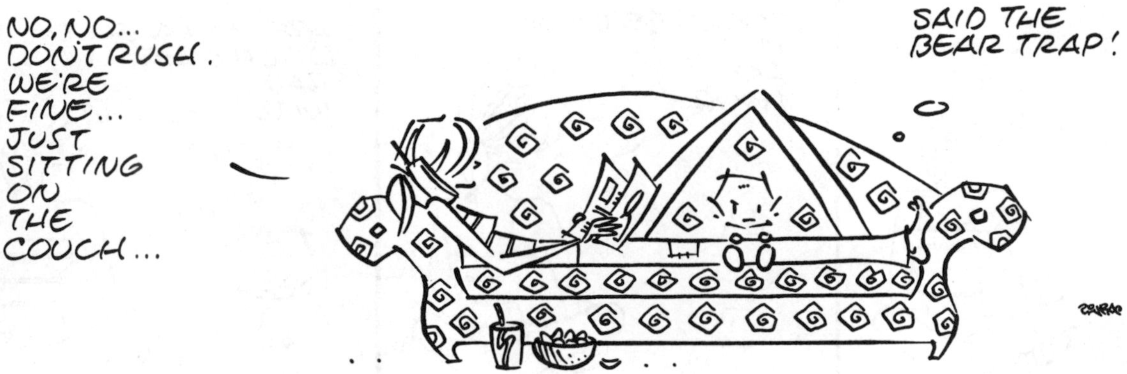
NO, NO... DON'T RUSH. WE'RE FINE... JUST SITTING ON THE COUCH...
SAID THE BEAR TRAP!

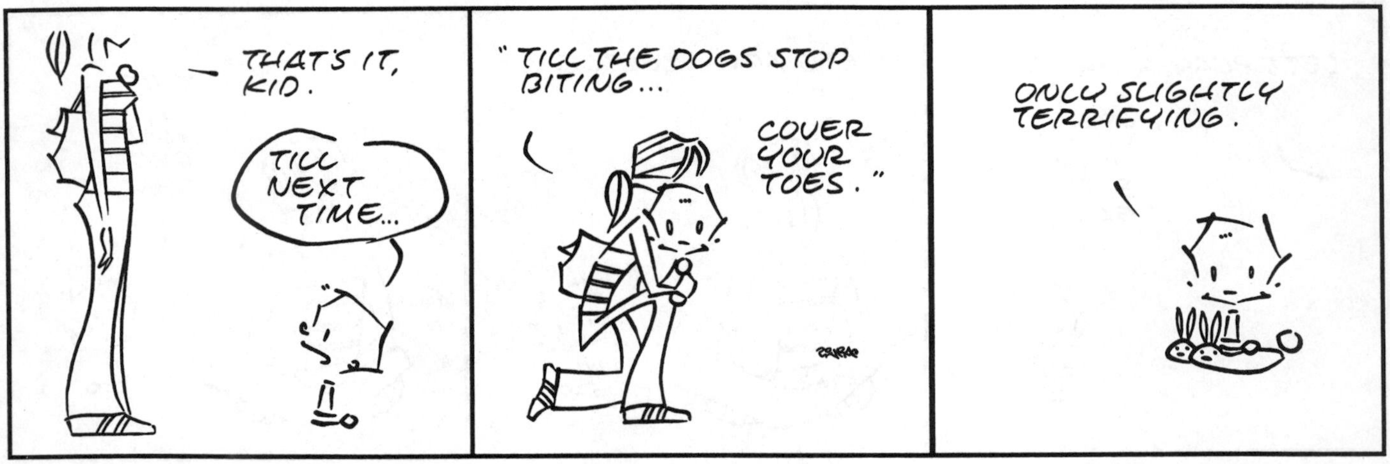
THAT'S IT, KID.
TILL NEXT TIME...
"TILL THE DOGS STOP BITING...
COVER YOUR TOES."
ONLY SLIGHTLY TERRIFYING.

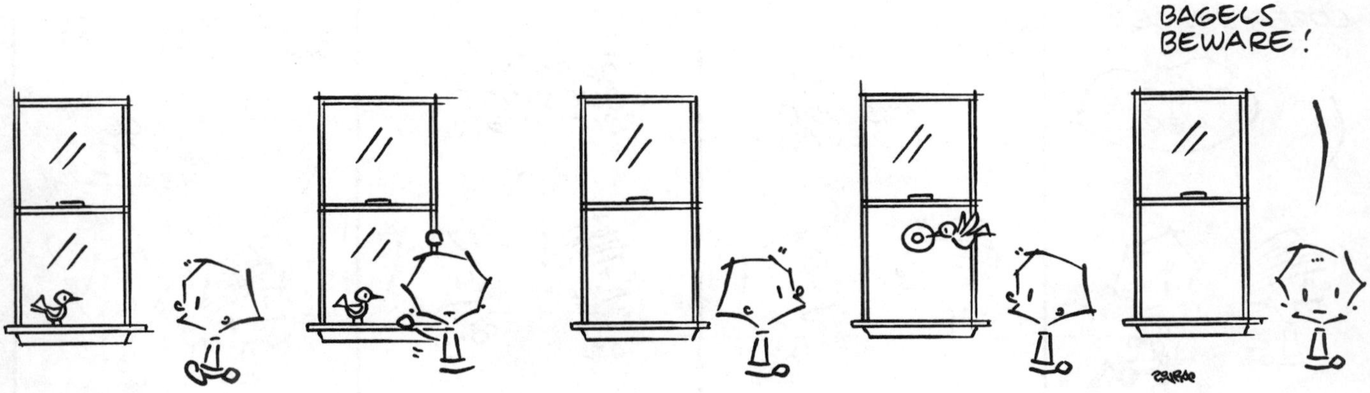
BAGELS BEWARE!

OKAY, JAMES.	JAMES...	DO IT FOR DADDY.	WAVE FOR DADDY!
JAMESY...	JAMES!	I GIVE UP.	WHAT I'D REALLY LIKE TO DO IS DIRECT.

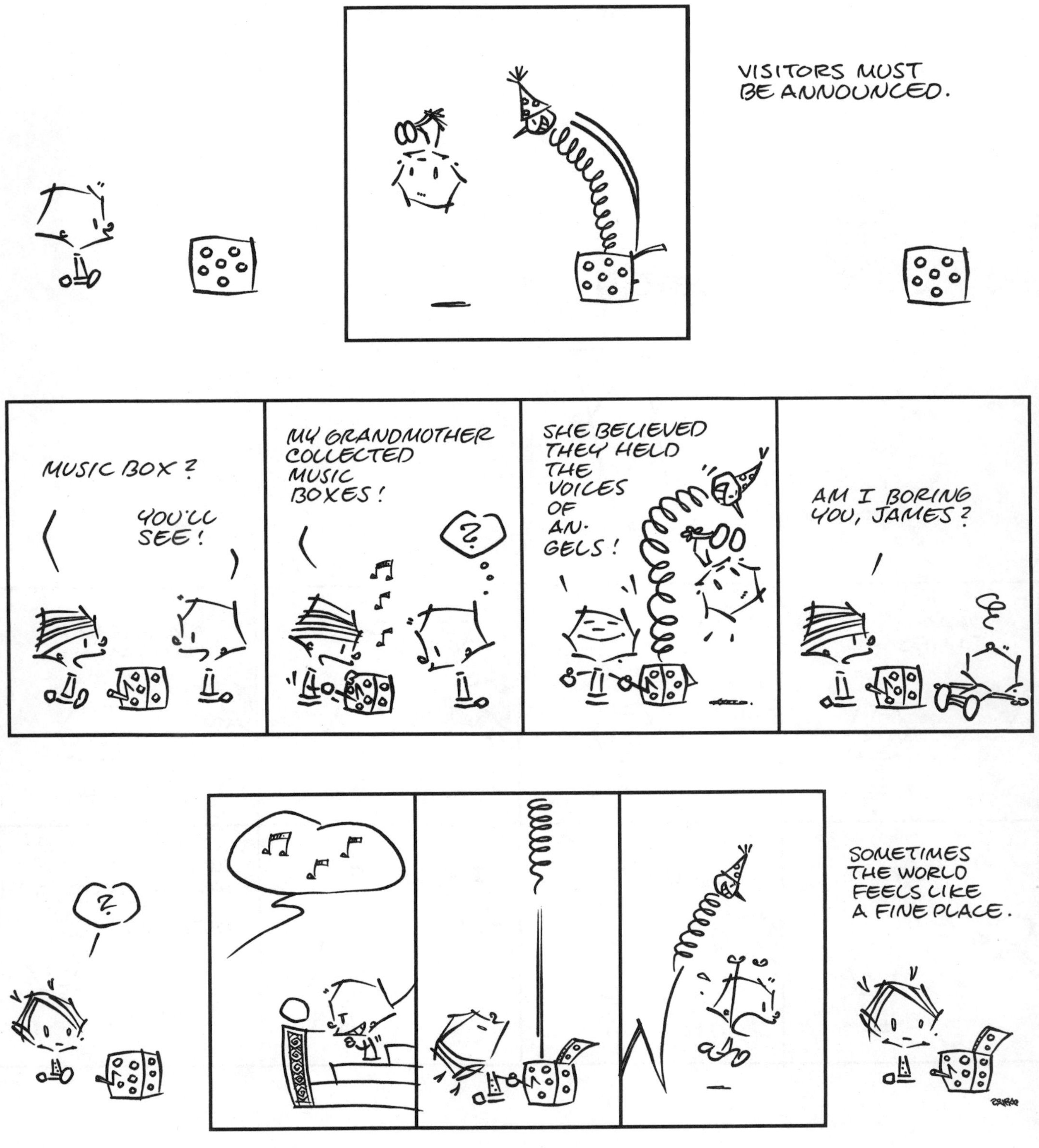
VISITORS MUST BE ANNOUNCED.
MUSIC BOX ?
YOU'LL SEE!
MY GRANDMOTHER COLLECTED MUSIC BOXES!
?
SHE BELIEVED THEY HELD THE VOICES OF AN-GELS!
AM I BORING YOU, JAMES ?
?
SOMETIMES THE WORLD FEELS LIKE A FINE PLACE.

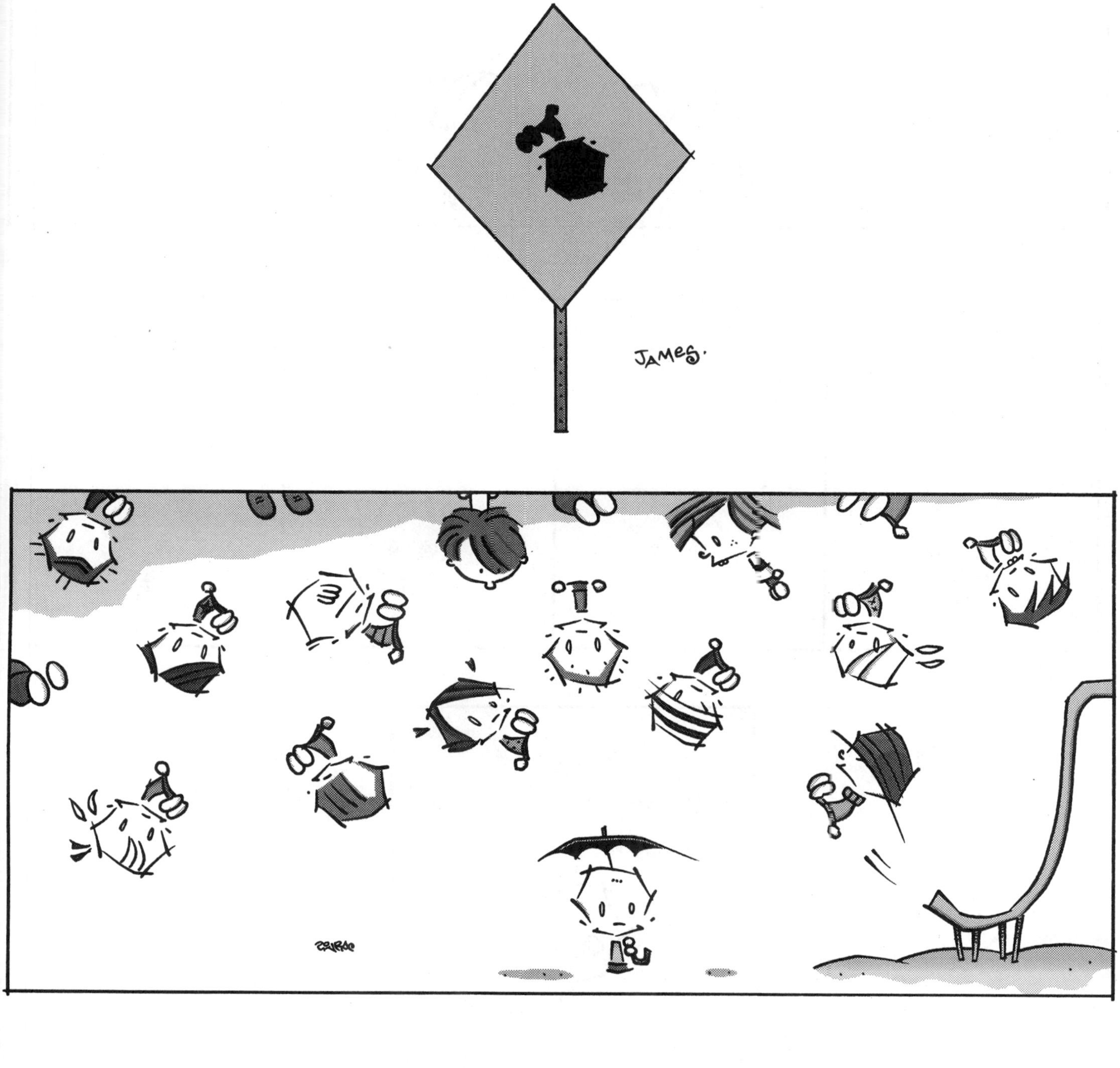
JAMES.

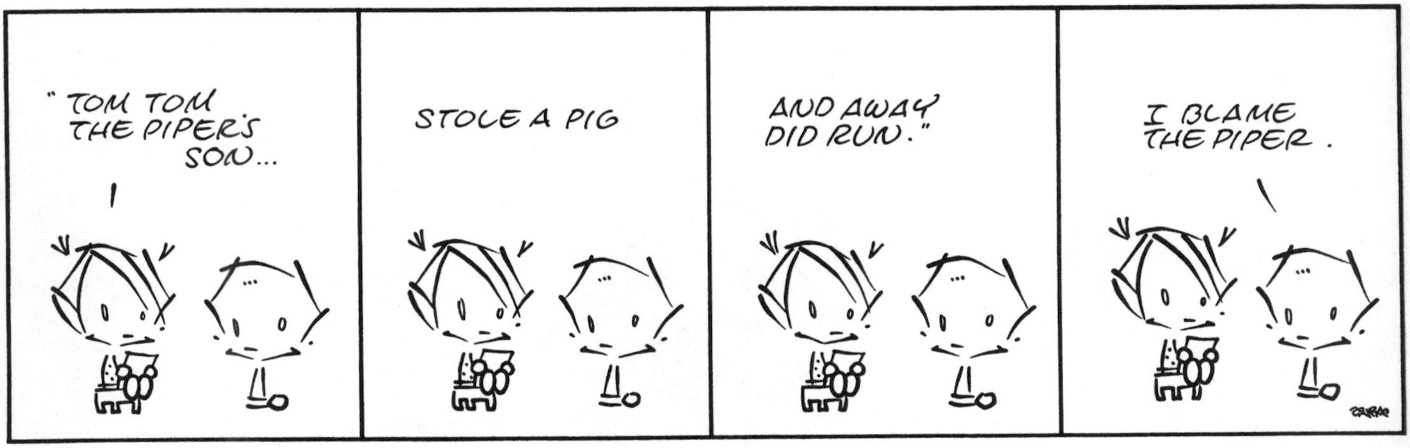
"TOM TOM THE PIPER'S SON...
STOLE A PIG
AND AWAY DID RUN."
I BLAME THE PIPER.

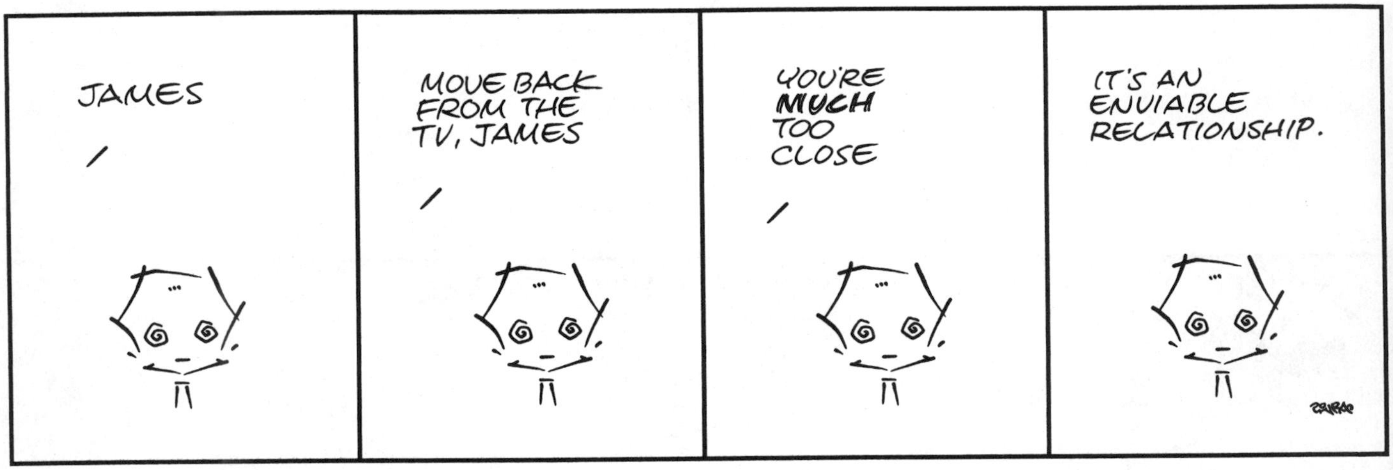
JAMES
MOVE BACK FROM THE TV, JAMES
YOU'RE MUCH TOO CLOSE
IT'S AN ENVIABLE RELATIONSHIP.

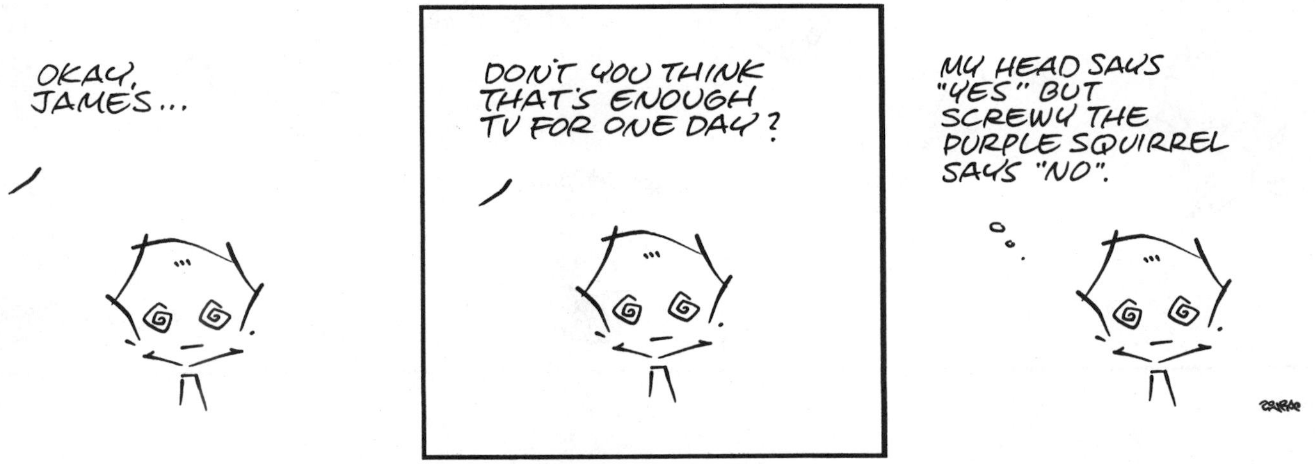
OKAY, JAMES...
DON'T YOU THINK THAT'S ENOUGH TV FOR ONE DAY?
MY HEAD SAYS "YES" BUT SCREWY THE PURPLE SQUIRREL SAYS "NO".

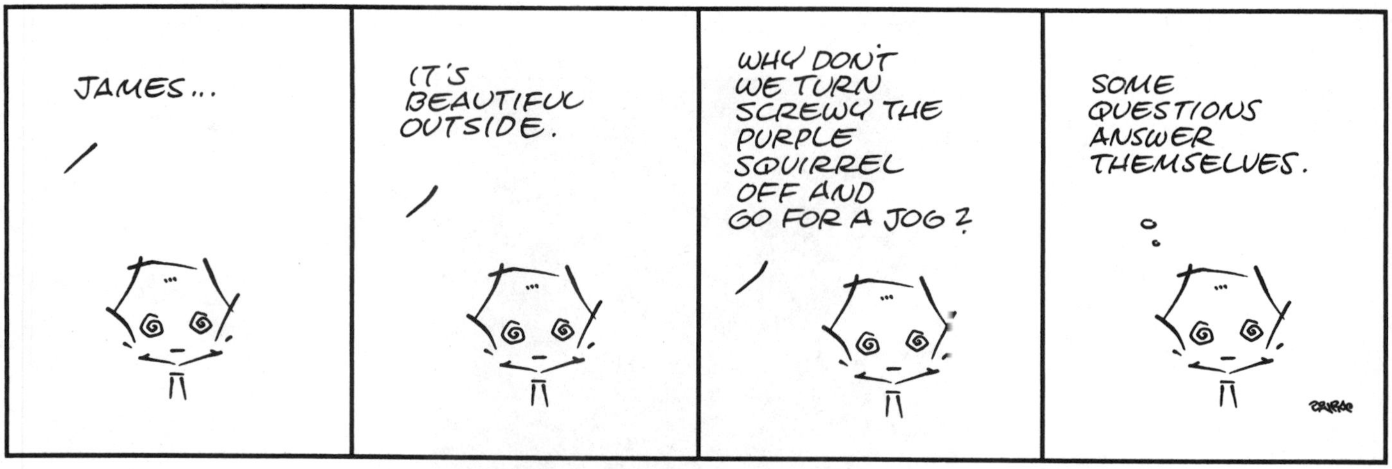
JAMES...
IT'S BEAUTIFUL OUTSIDE.
WHY DON'T WE TURN SCREWY THE PURPLE SQUIRREL OFF AND GO FOR A JOG?
SOME QUESTIONS ANSWER THEMSELVES.

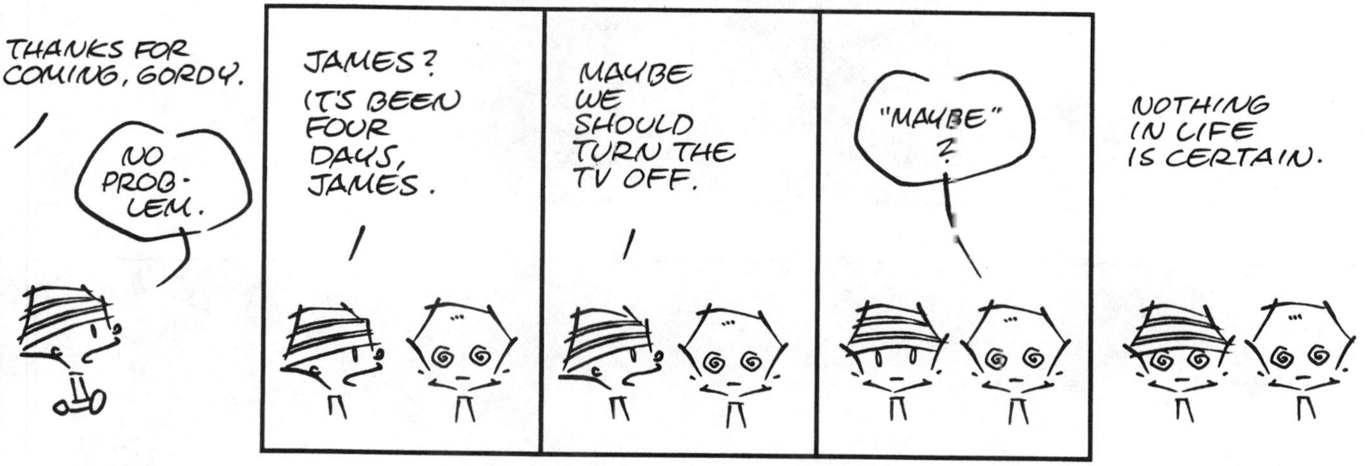
THANKS FOR COMING, GORDY.
NO PROB-LEM.
JAMES?
IT'S BEEN FOUR DAYS, JAMES.
MAYBE WE SHOULD TURN THE TV OFF.
"MAYBE"?
NOTHING IN LIFE IS CERTAIN.

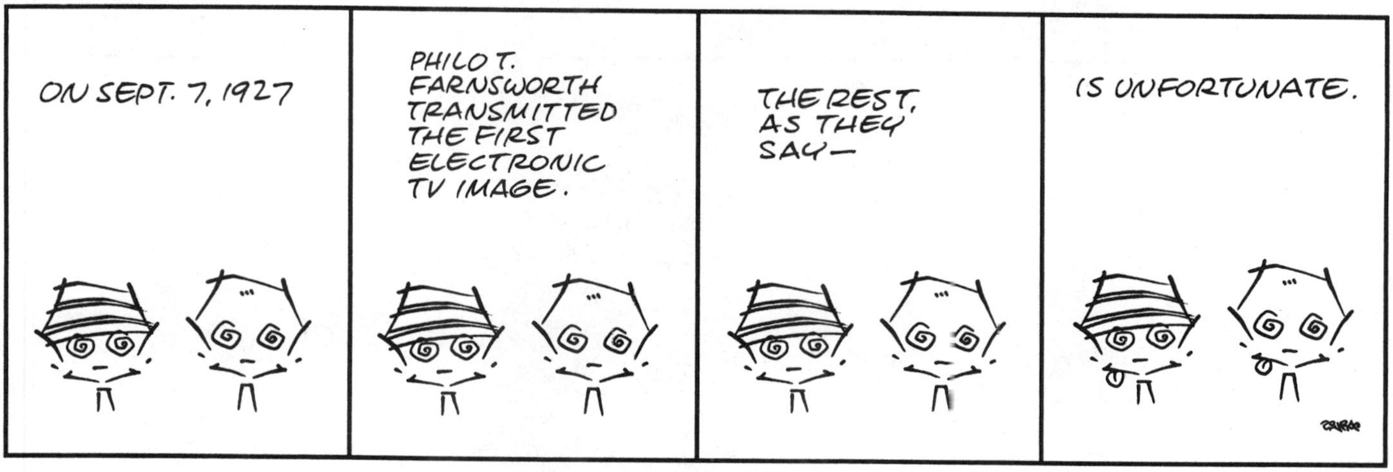
ON SEPT. 7, 1927
PHILO T. FARNSWORTH TRANSMITTED THE FIRST ELECTRONIC TV IMAGE.
THE REST, AS THEY SAY—
IS UNFORTUNATE.

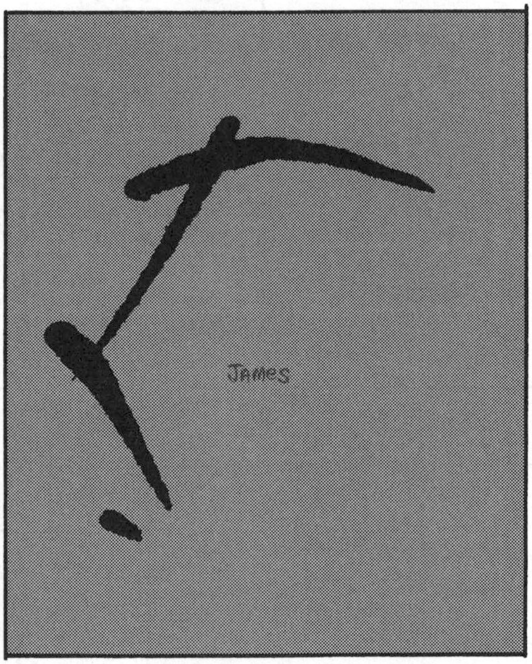
JAMES

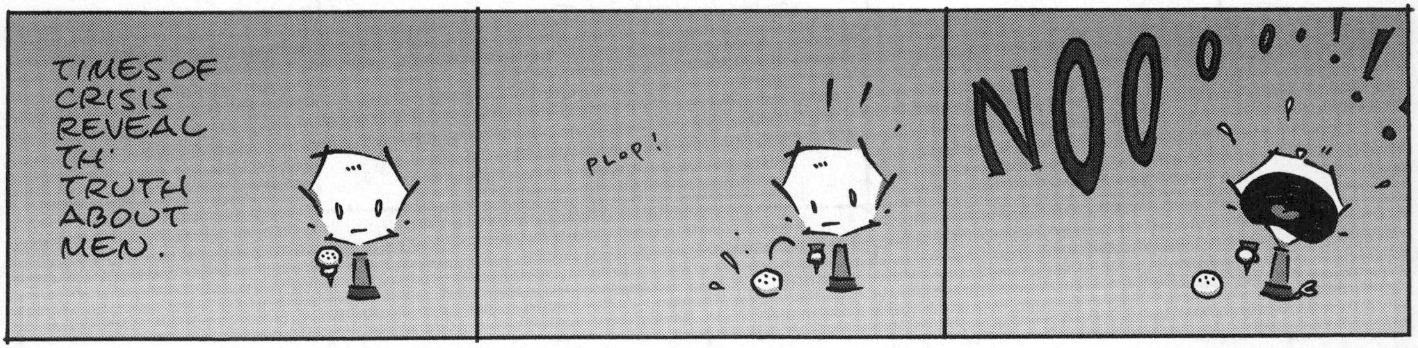
TIMES OF CRISIS REVEAL TH' TRUTH ABOUT MEN.
PLOP!
NOOOO!!

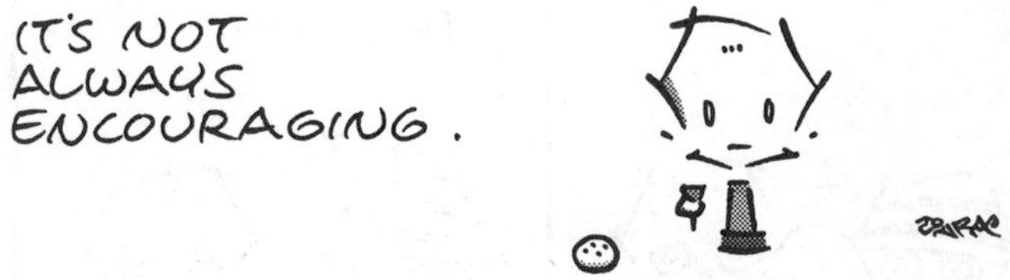
IT'S NOT ALWAYS ENCOURAGING.

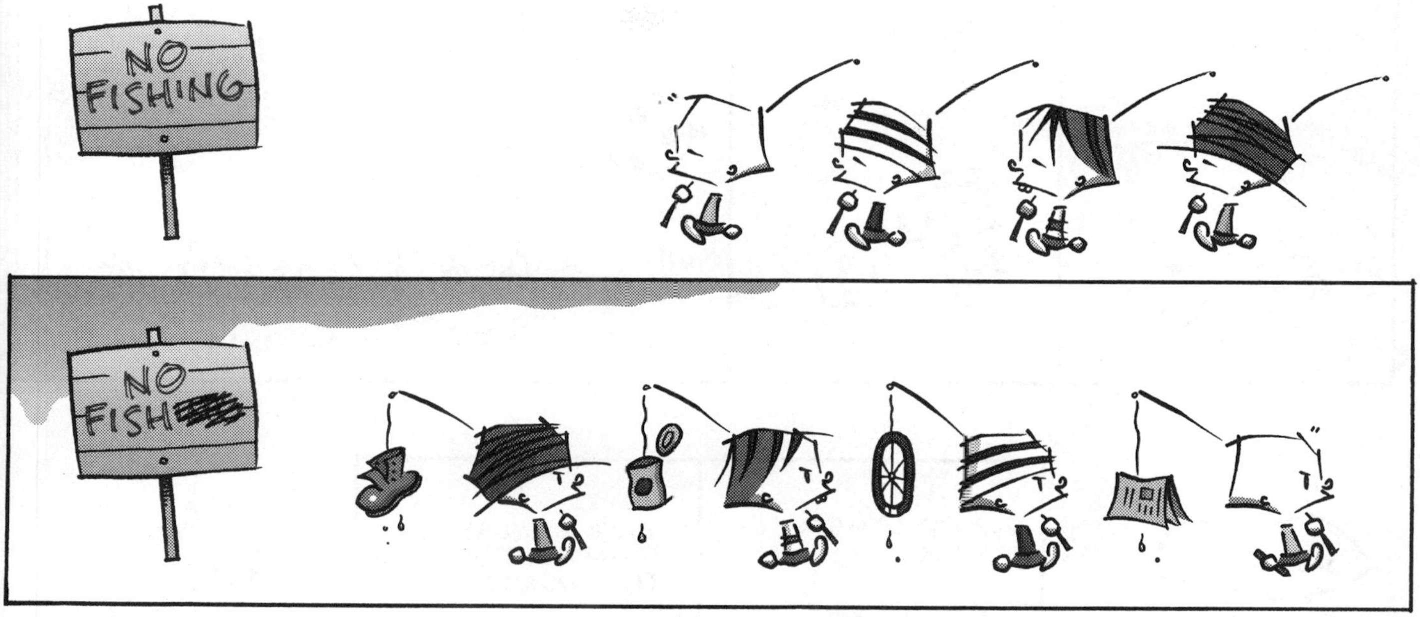
NO FISHING
NO FISH

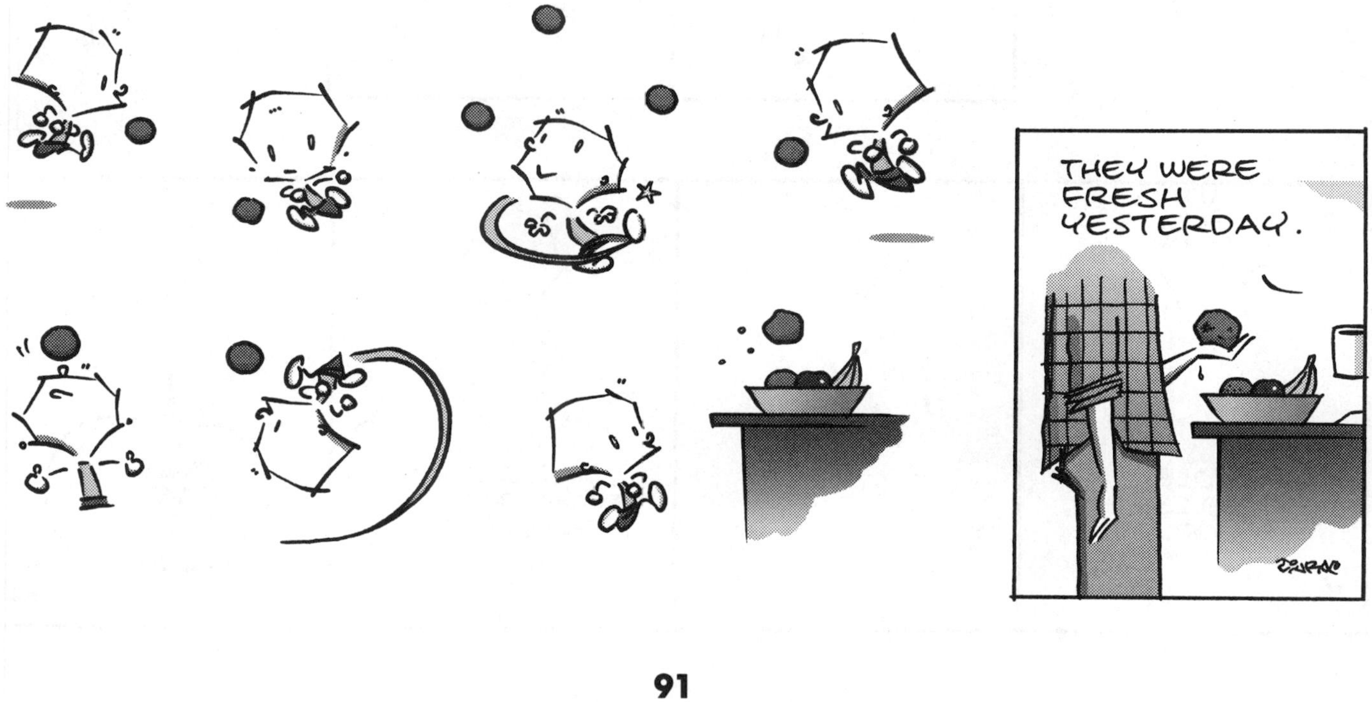
THEY WERE FRESH YESTERDAY.

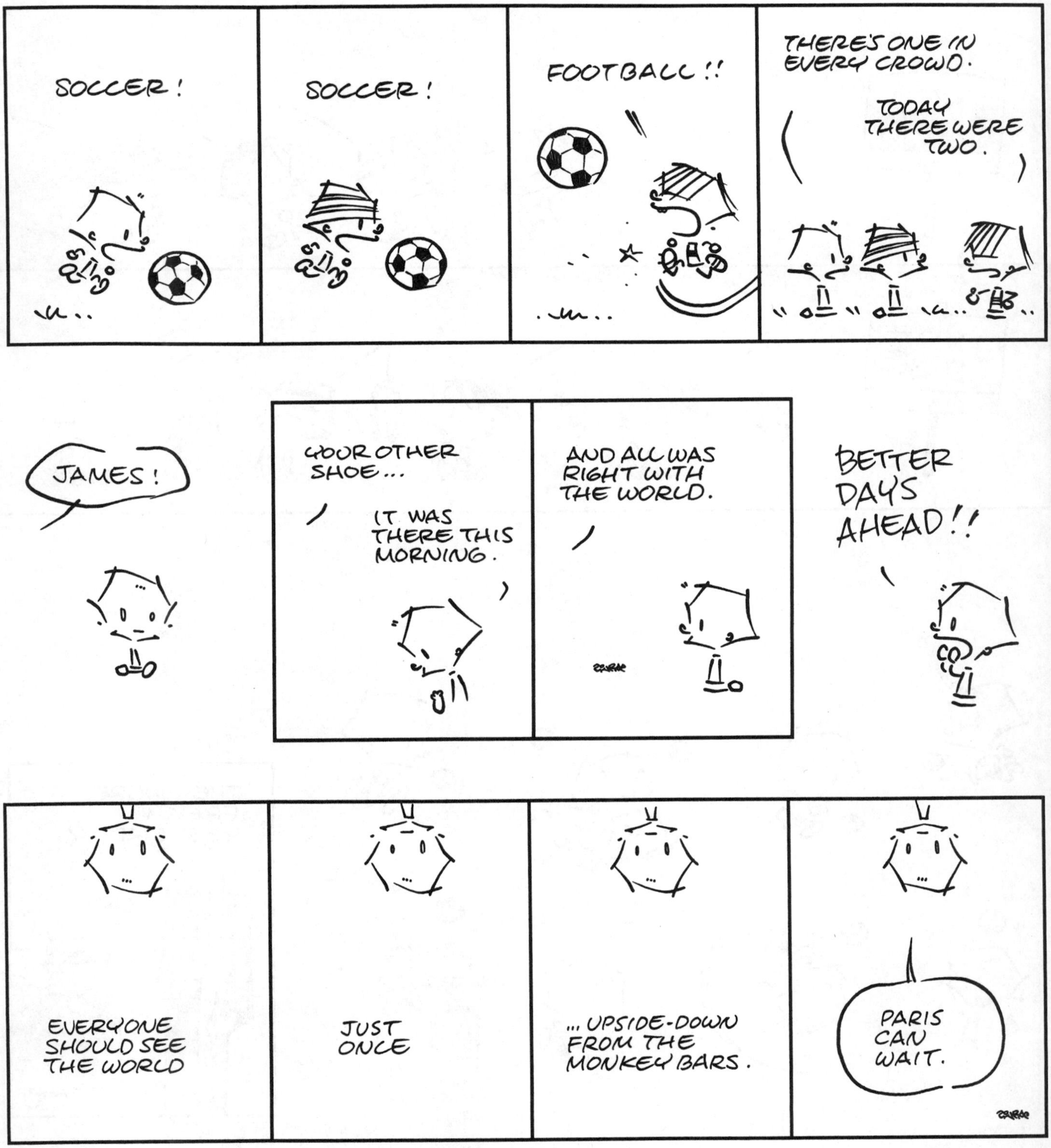
SOCCER!
SOCCER!
FOOTBALL!!
THERE'S ONE IN EVERY CROWD.
TODAY THERE WERE TWO.
JAMES!
YOUR OTHER SHOE...
IT WAS THERE THIS MORNING.
AND ALL WAS RIGHT WITH THE WORLD.
BETTER DAYS AHEAD!!
EVERYONE SHOULD SEE THE WORLD
JUST ONCE
...UPSIDE-DOWN FROM THE MONKEY BARS.
PARIS CAN WAIT.

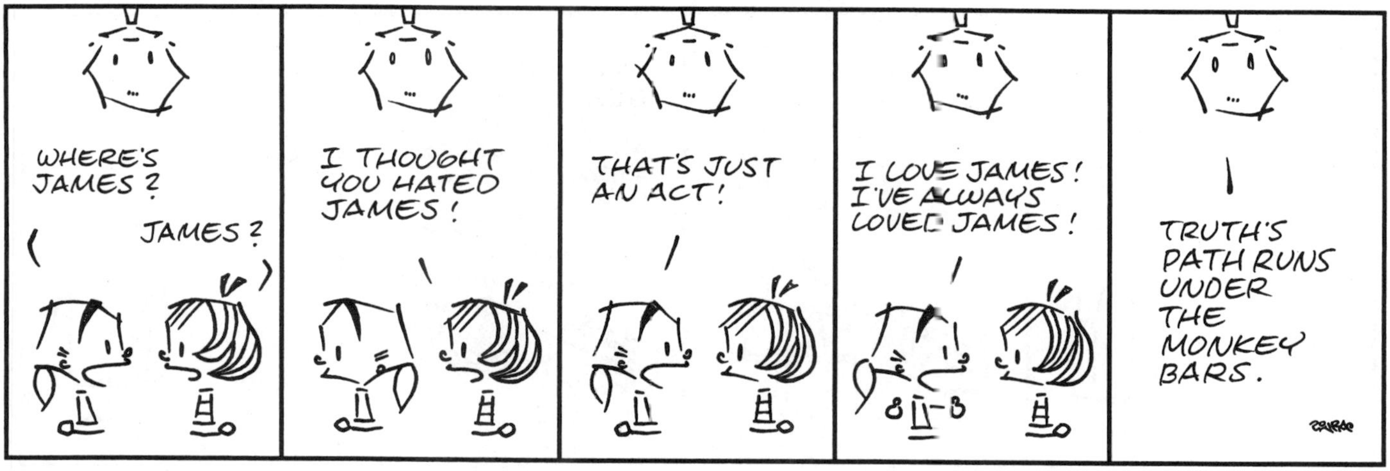
WHERE'S JAMES?
JAMES?
I THOUGHT YOU HATED JAMES!
THAT'S JUST AN ACT!
I LOVE JAMES! I'VE ALWAYS LOVED JAMES!
TRUTH'S PATH RUNS UNDER THE MONKEY BARS.

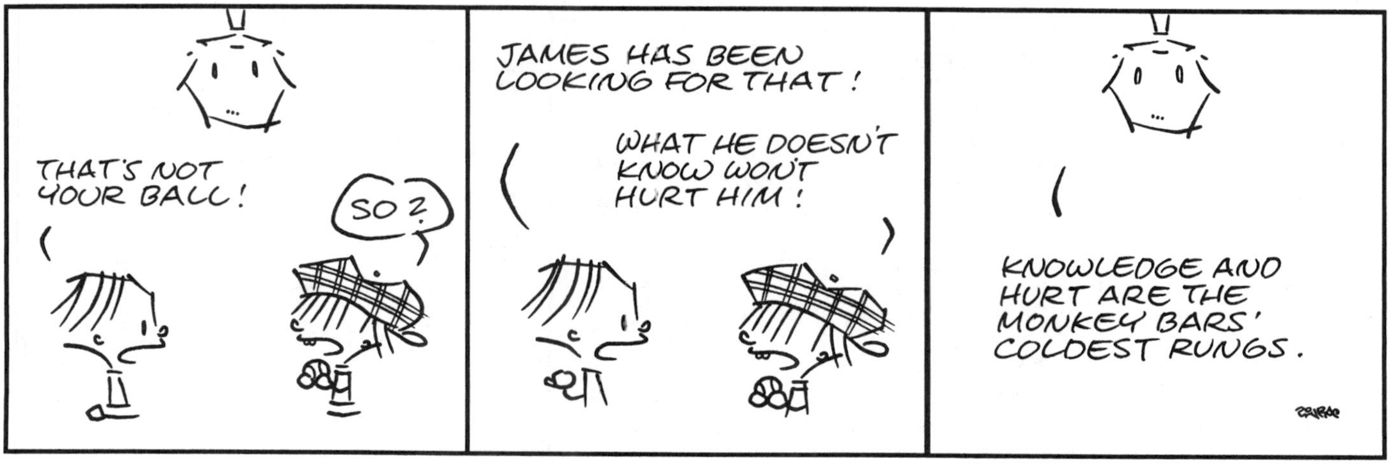
THAT'S NOT YOUR BALL!
SO?
JAMES HAS BEEN LOOKING FOR THAT!
WHAT HE DOESN'T KNOW WON'T HURT HIM!
KNOWLEDGE AND HURT ARE THE MONKEY BARS' COLDEST RUNGS.

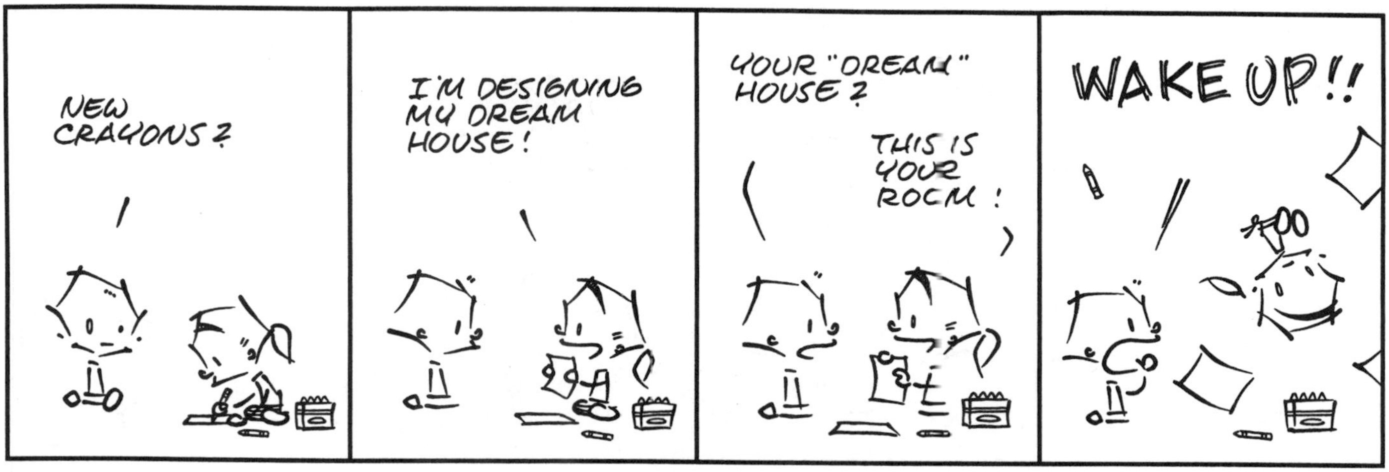
NEW CRAYONS?
I'M DESIGNING MY DREAM HOUSE!
YOUR "DREAM" HOUSE?
THIS IS YOUR ROOM!
WAKE UP!!

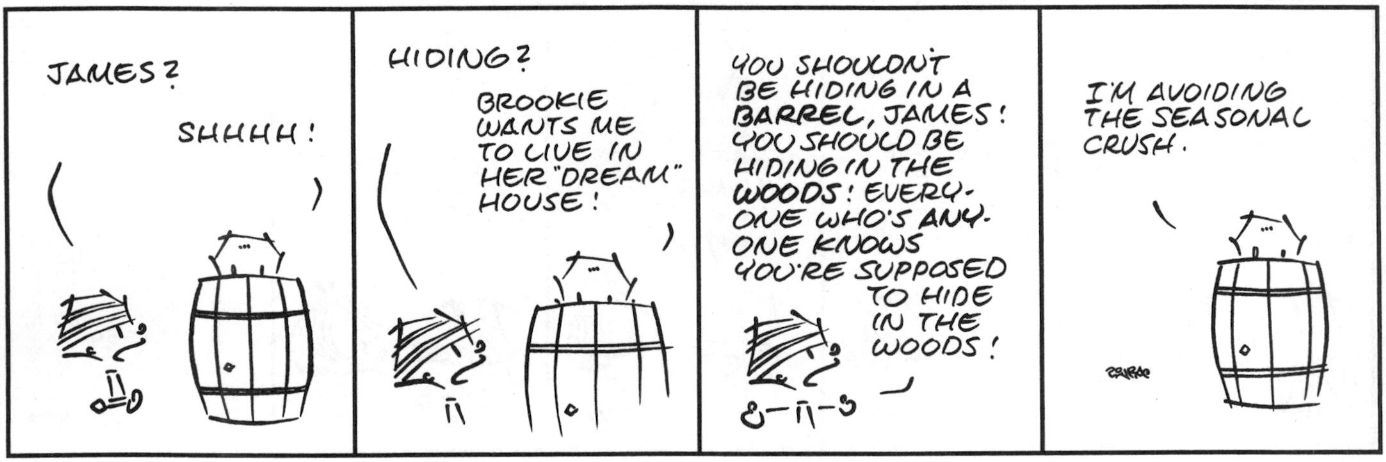
JAMES?
SHHHH!
HIDING?
BROOKIE WANTS ME TO LIVE IN HER "DREAM" HOUSE!
YOU SHOULDN'T BE HIDING IN A BARREL, JAMES! YOU SHOULD BE HIDING IN THE WOODS! EVERYONE WHO'S ANYONE KNOWS YOU'RE SUPPOSED TO HIDE IN THE WOODS!
I'M AVOIDING THE SEASONAL CRUSH.

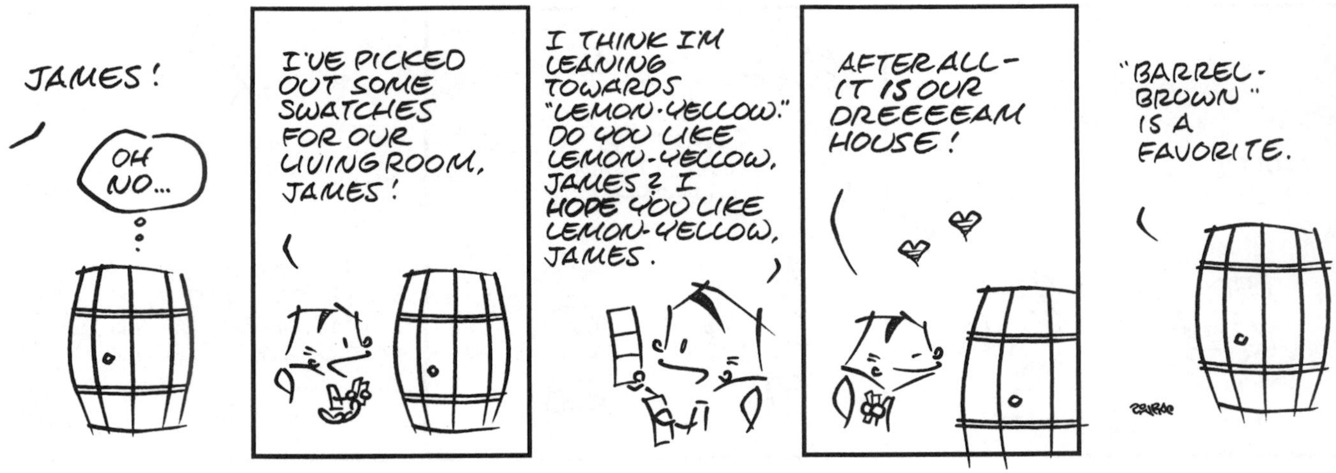
JAMES!
OH NO...
I'VE PICKED OUT SOME SWATCHES FOR OUR LIVING ROOM, JAMES!
I THINK I'M LEANING TOWARDS "LEMON-YELLOW." DO YOU LIKE LEMON-YELLOW, JAMES? I HOPE YOU LIKE LEMON-YELLOW, JAMES.
AFTER ALL - IT IS OUR DREEEEEAM HOUSE!
"BARREL-BROWN" IS A FAVORITE.

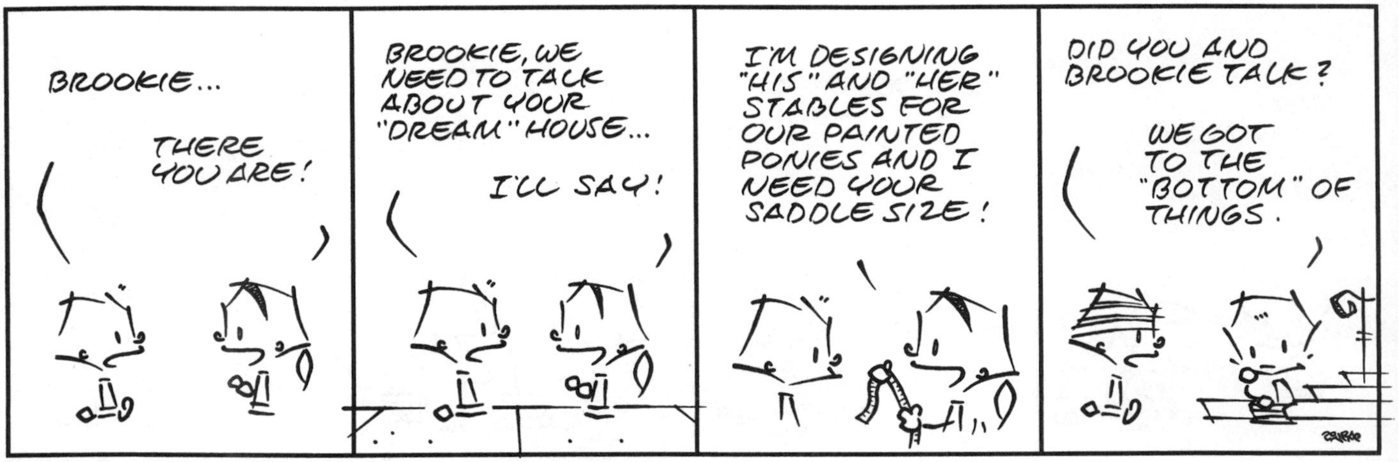
BROOKIE...
THERE YOU ARE!
BROOKIE, WE NEED TO TALK ABOUT YOUR "DREAM" HOUSE...
I'LL SAY!
I'M DESIGNING "HIS" AND "HER" STABLES FOR OUR PAINTED PONIES AND I NEED YOUR SADDLE SIZE!
DID YOU AND BROOKIE TALK?
WE GOT TO THE "BOTTOM" OF THINGS.

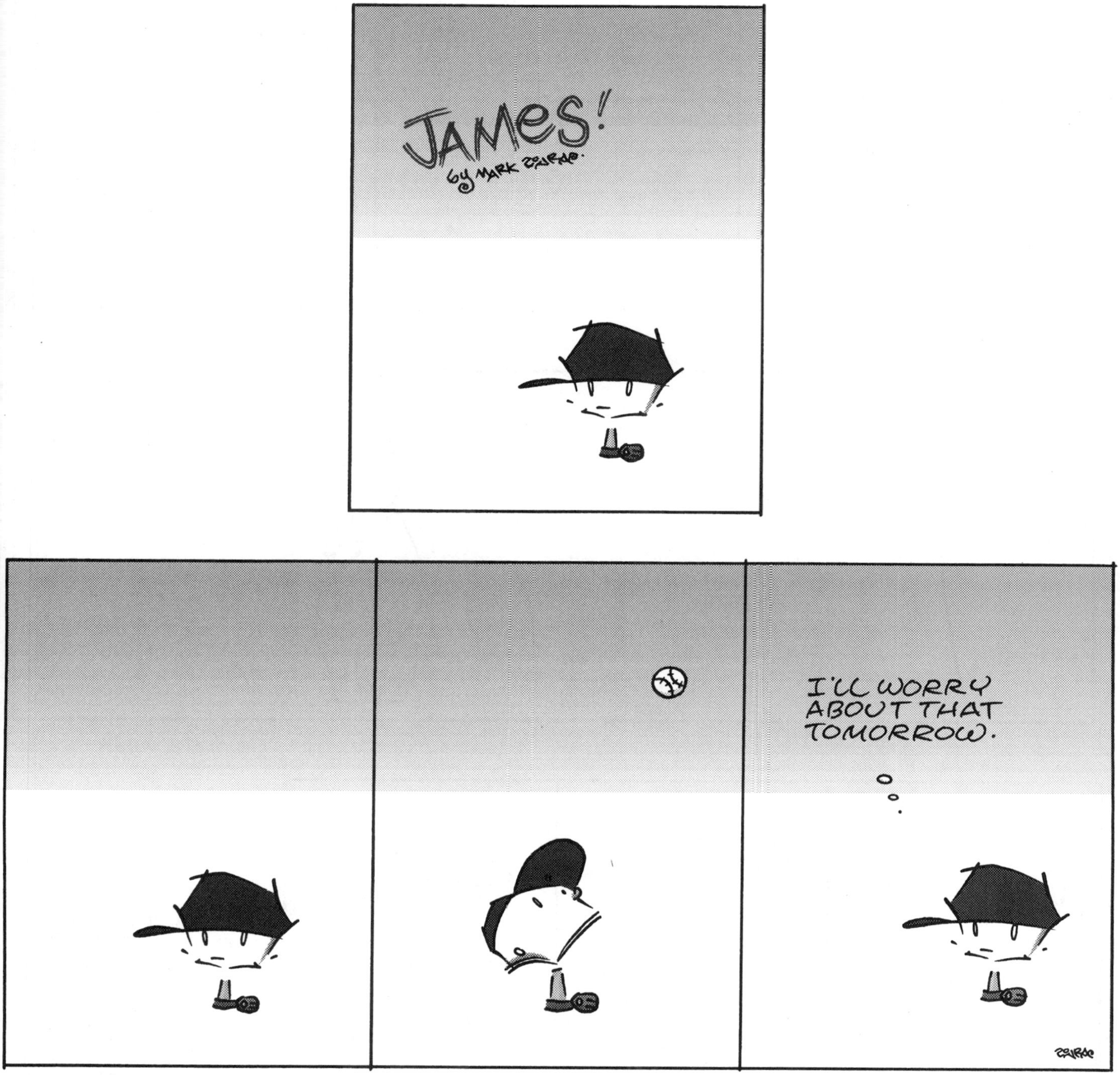
JAMES!
by MARK ZIURDO.
I'LL WORRY ABOUT THAT TOMORROW.
ZIURDO

YEARS PASS.

TH'WORLD TURNS.

WHAT'S IT ALL ABOUT?

PRESENT COMPANY EXCLUDED.

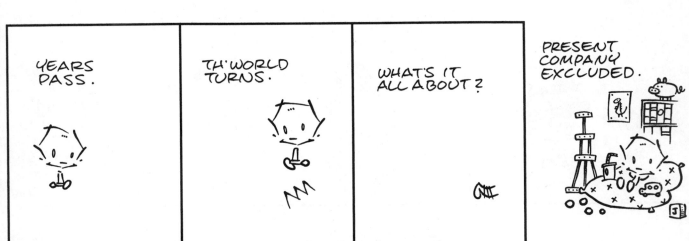

SPIN

AND THE WORLD SPINS WITH YOO!

FROGS BE DANGEROUS!	FIRES BE DANGEROUS!	MEAN DIRTY DRAGONS...	THEY BE DANGER-OUS!!	MY SOURCES HAVE ASSURED ME.

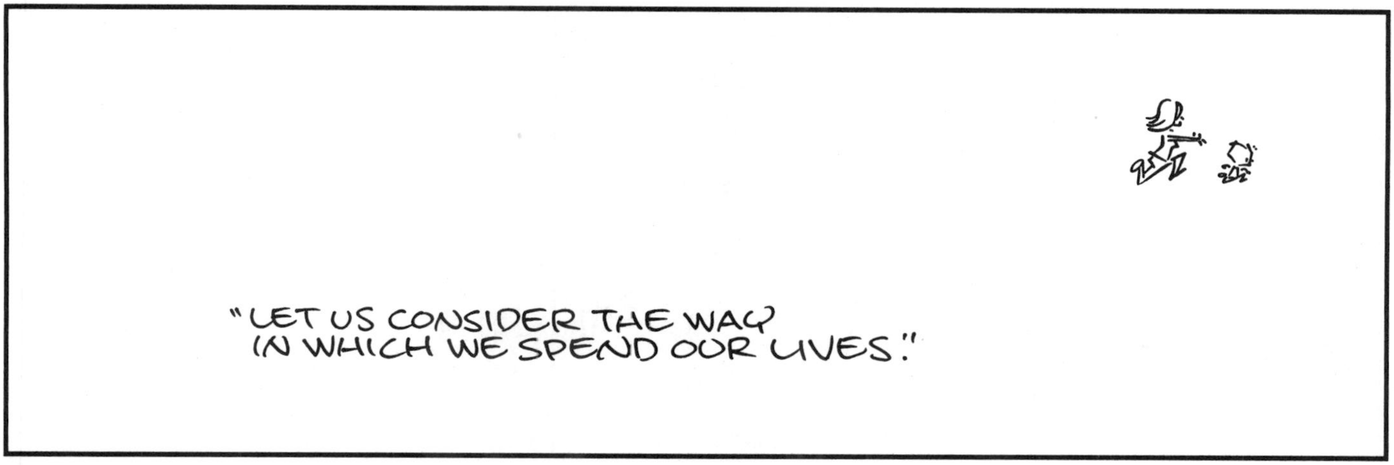

"LET US CONSIDER THE WAY
IN WHICH WE SPEND OUR LIVES."

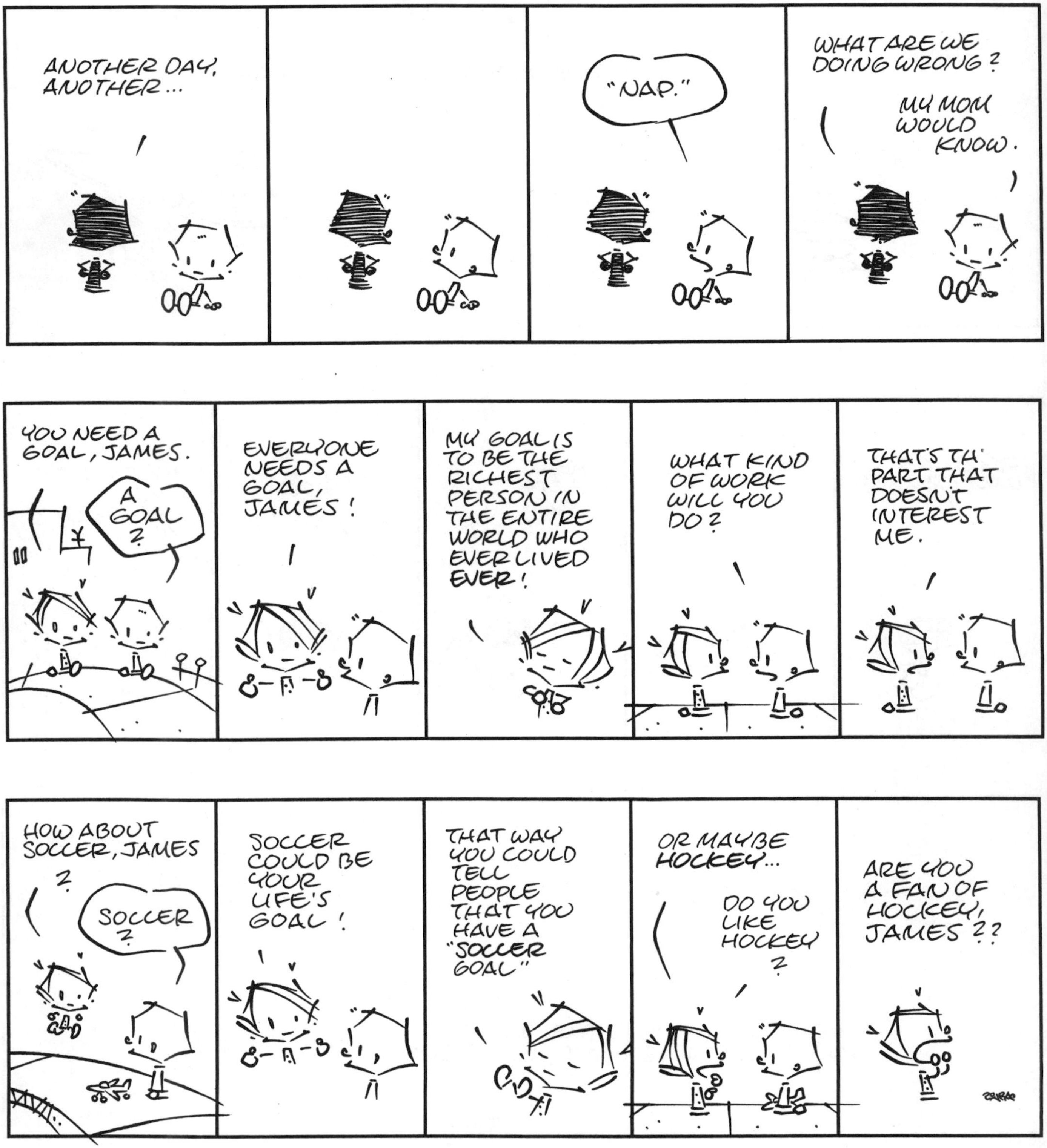
ANOTHER DAY, ANOTHER...
"NAP."
WHAT ARE WE DOING WRONG?
MY MOM WOULD KNOW.
YOU NEED A GOAL, JAMES.
A GOAL?
EVERYONE NEEDS A GOAL, JAMES!
MY GOAL IS TO BE THE RICHEST PERSON IN THE ENTIRE WORLD WHO EVER LIVED EVER!
WHAT KIND OF WORK WILL YOU DO?
THAT'S TH' PART THAT DOESN'T INTEREST ME.
HOW ABOUT SOCCER, JAMES?
SOCCER?
SOCCER COULD BE YOUR LIFE'S GOAL!
THAT WAY YOU COULD TELL PEOPLE THAT YOU HAVE A "SOCCER GOAL"
OR MAYBE HOCKEY...
DO YOU LIKE HOCKEY?
ARE YOU A FAN OF HOCKEY, JAMES??

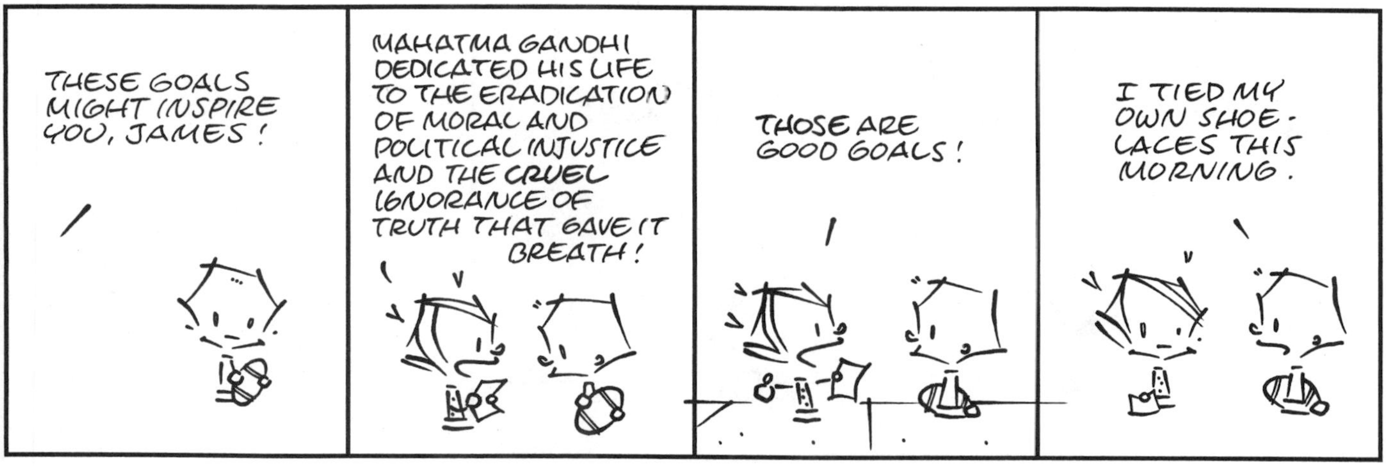
THESE GOALS MIGHT INSPIRE YOU, JAMES!
MAHATMA GANDHI DEDICATED HIS LIFE TO THE ERADICATION OF MORAL AND POLITICAL INJUSTICE AND THE CRUEL IGNORANCE OF TRUTH THAT GAVE IT BREATH!
THOSE ARE GOOD GOALS!
I TIED MY OWN SHOE-LACES THIS MORNING.

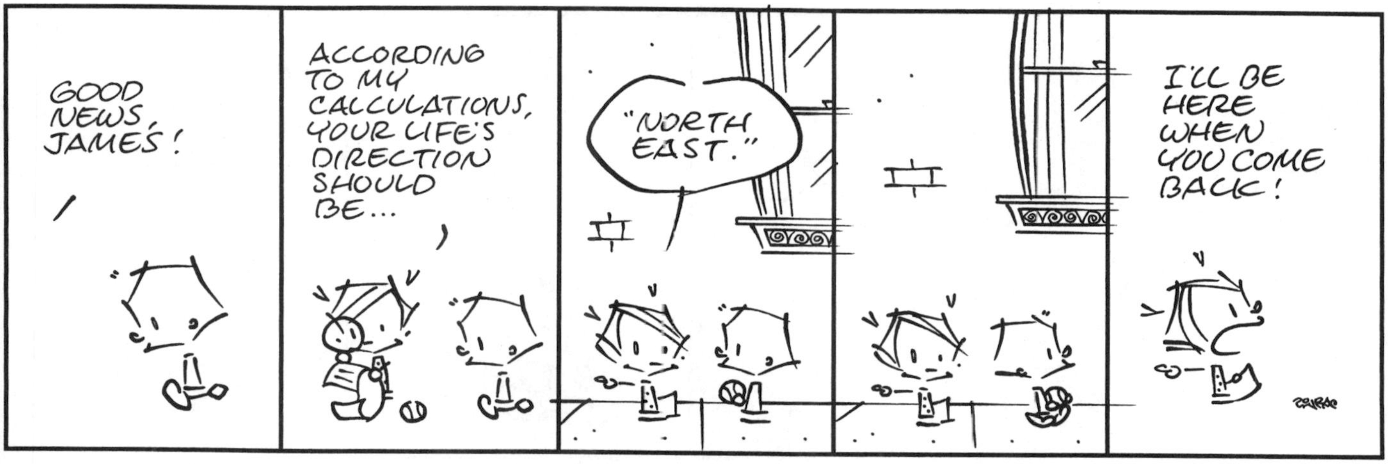
GOOD NEWS, JAMES!
ACCORDING TO MY CALCULATIONS, YOUR LIFE'S DIRECTION SHOULD BE...
"NORTH EAST."
I'LL BE HERE WHEN YOU COME BACK!

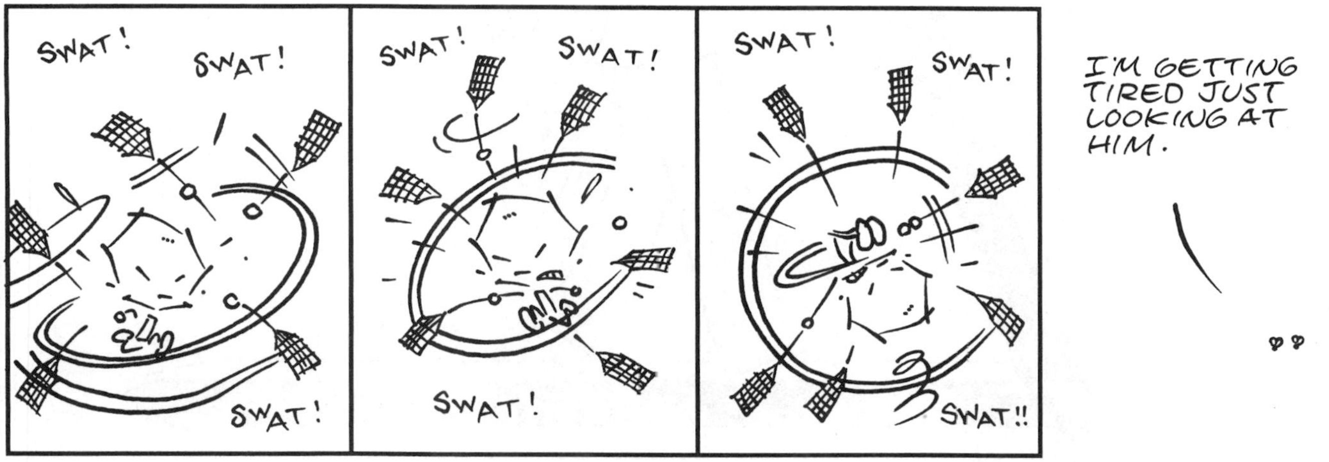
SWAT!
SWAT!
SWAT!
SWAT!
SWAT!
SWAT!
SWAT!
SWAT!
SWAT!!
I'M GETTING TIRED JUST LOOKING AT HIM.

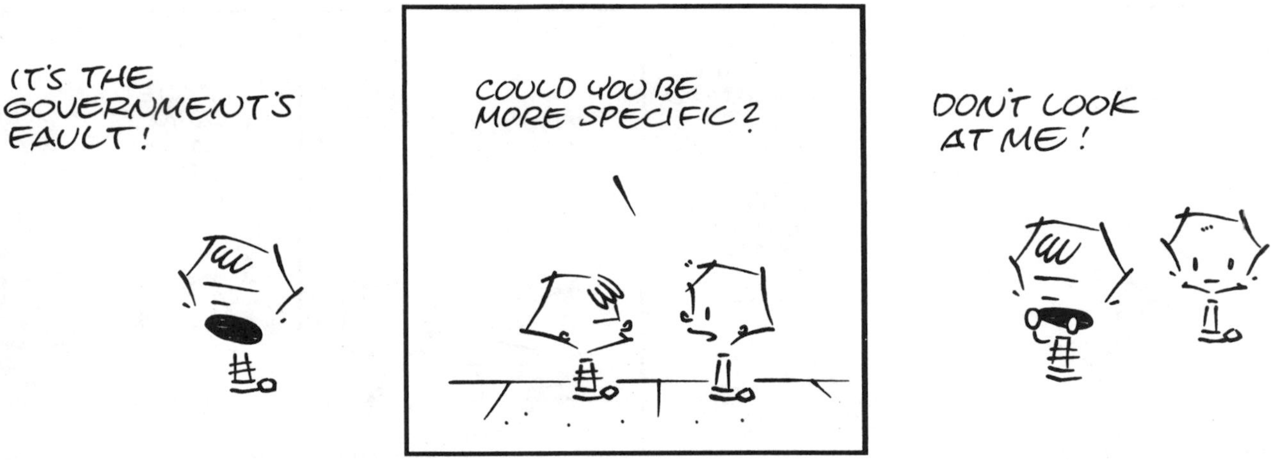
IT'S THE GOVERNMENT'S FAULT!
COULD YOU BE MORE SPECIFIC?
DON'T LOOK AT ME!

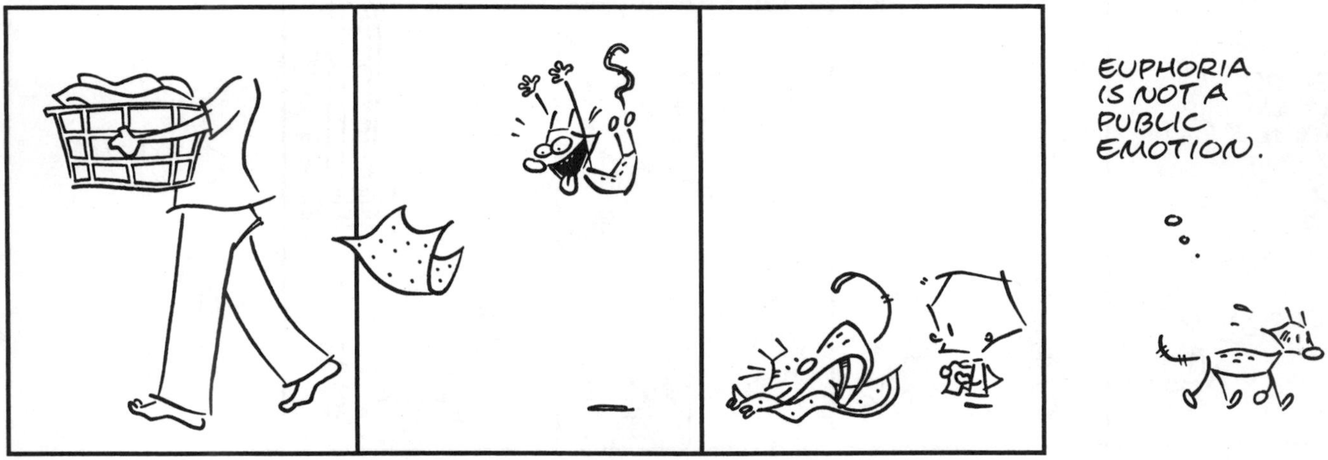
EUPHORIA IS NOT A PUBLIC EMOTION.

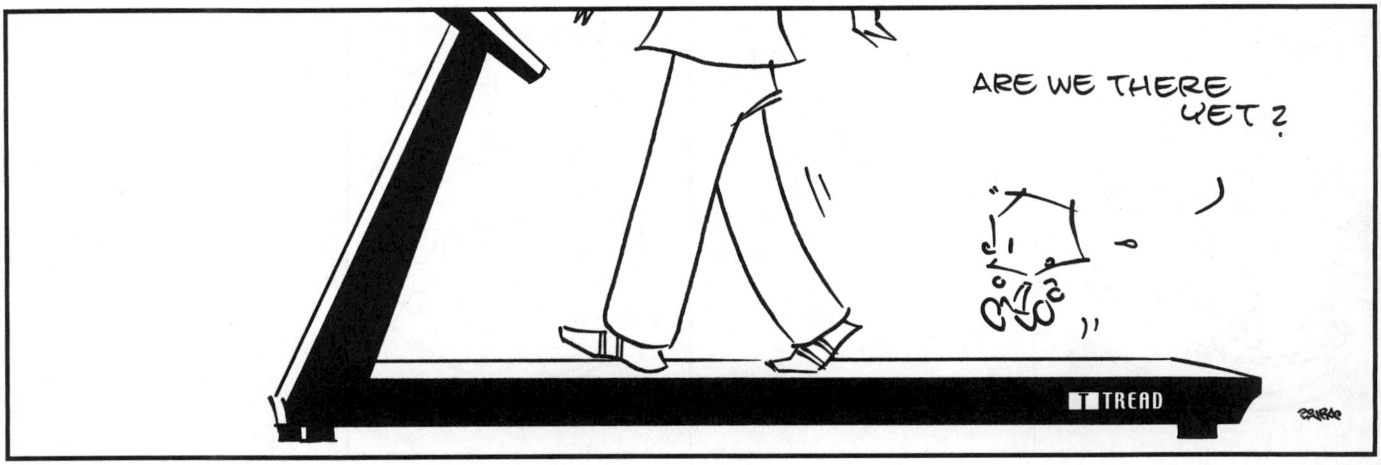
ARE WE THERE YET?
TREAD

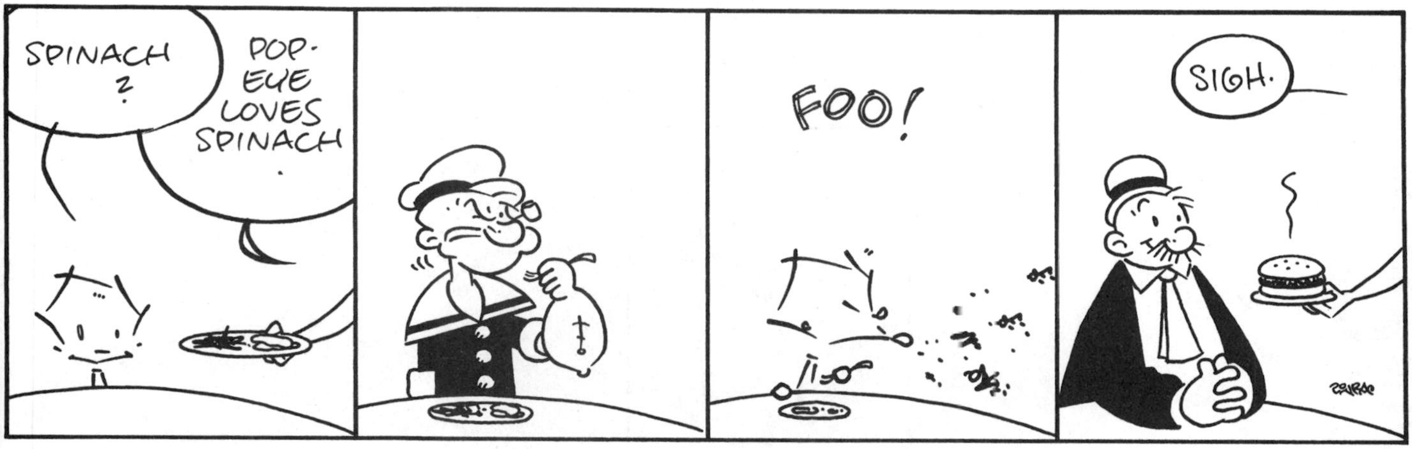
SPINACH?
POP-EYE LOVES SPINACH.
FOO!
SIGH.

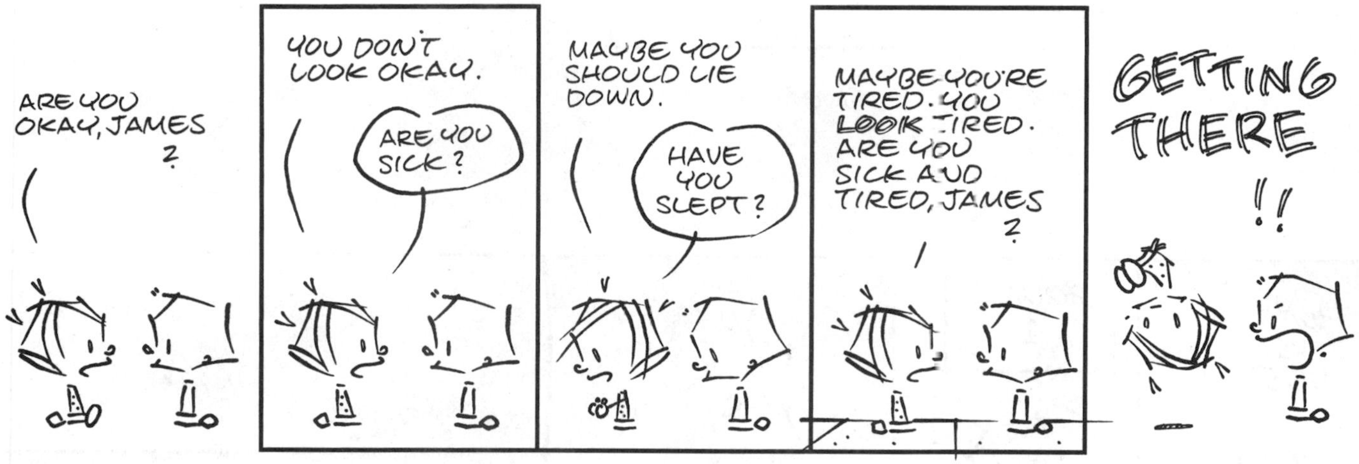
ARE YOU OKAY, JAMES?
YOU DON'T LOOK OKAY.
ARE YOU SICK?
MAYBE YOU SHOULD LIE DOWN.
HAVE YOU SLEPT?
MAYBE YOU'RE TIRED. YOU LOOK TIRED. ARE YOU SICK AND TIRED, JAMES?
GETTING THERE
!!

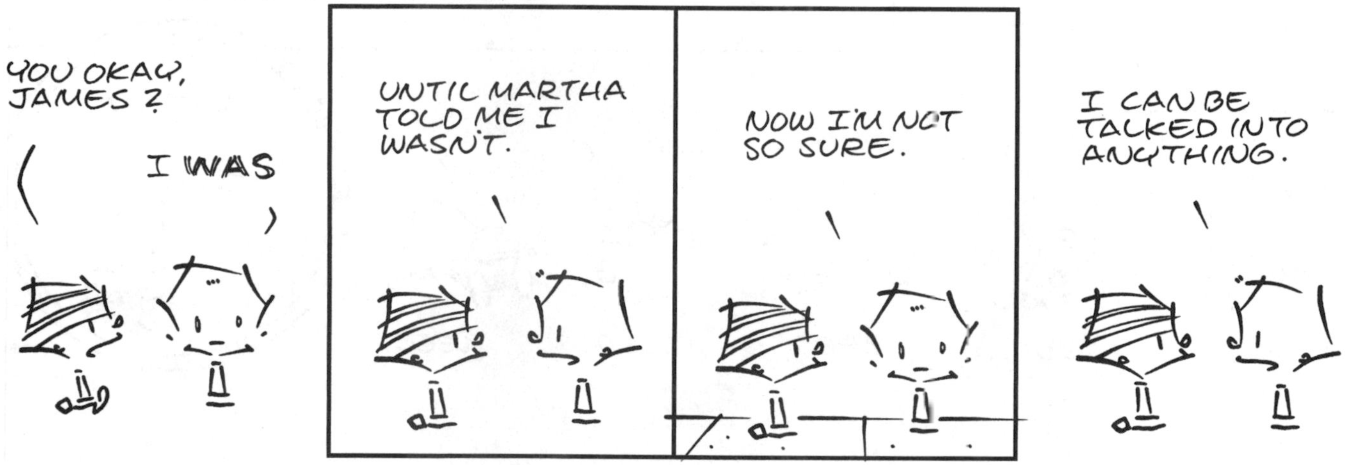
YOU OKAY, JAMES?
I WAS
UNTIL MARTHA TOLD ME I WASN'T.
NOW I'M NOT SO SURE.
I CAN BE TALKED INTO ANYTHING.

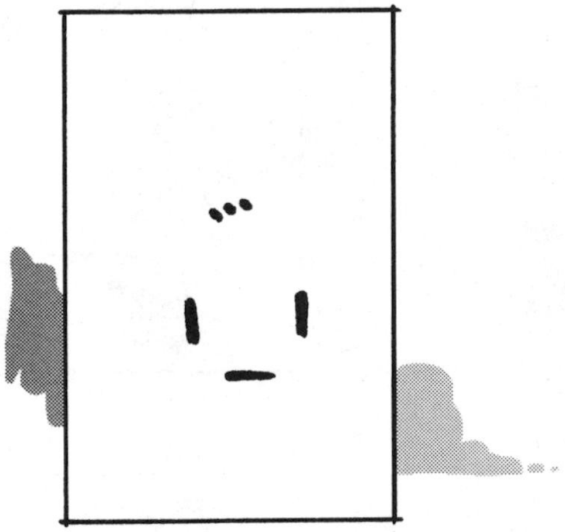

JAMES.

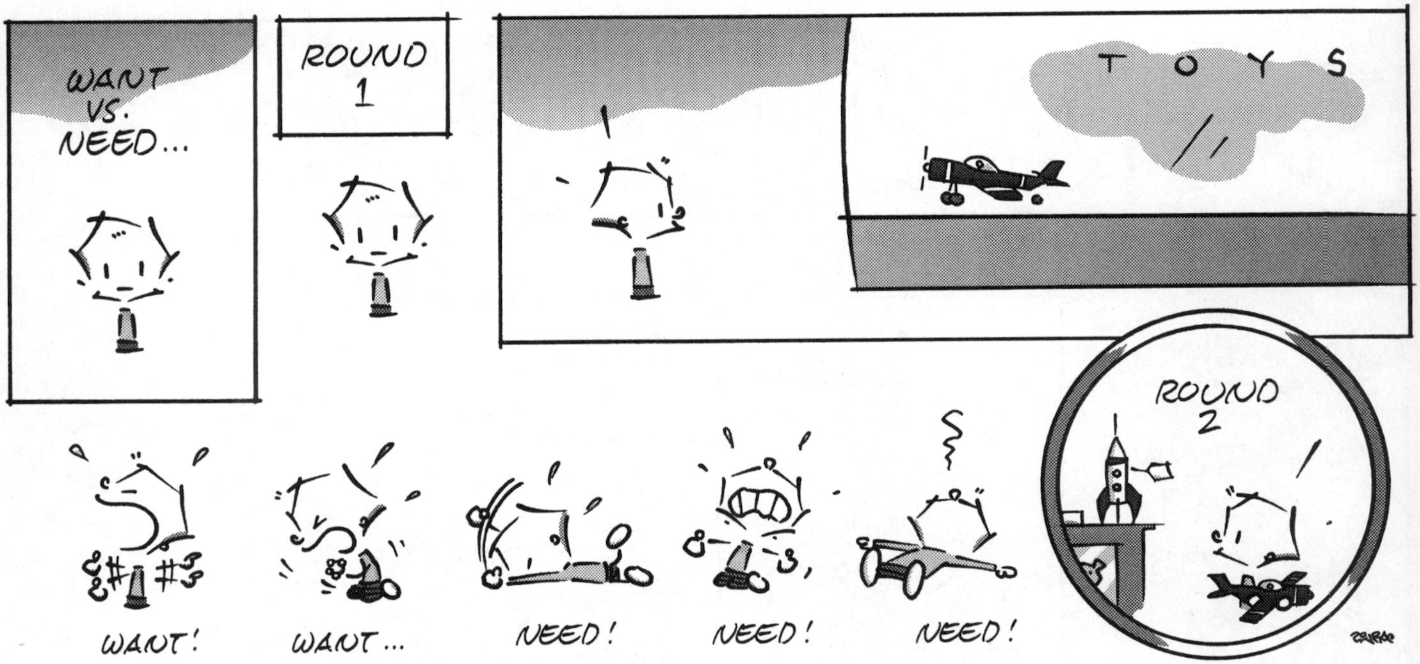
WANT VS. NEED...
ROUND 1
TOYS
WANT!
WANT...
NEED!
NEED!
NEED!
ROUND 2

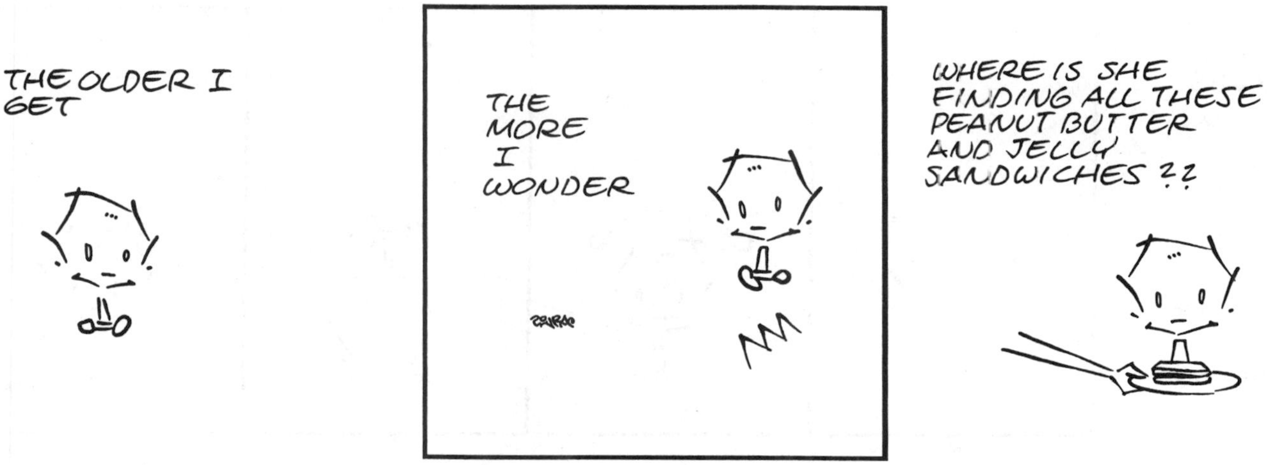
THE OLDER I GET
THE MORE I WONDER
WHERE IS SHE FINDING ALL THESE PEANUT BUTTER AND JELLY SANDWICHES ??

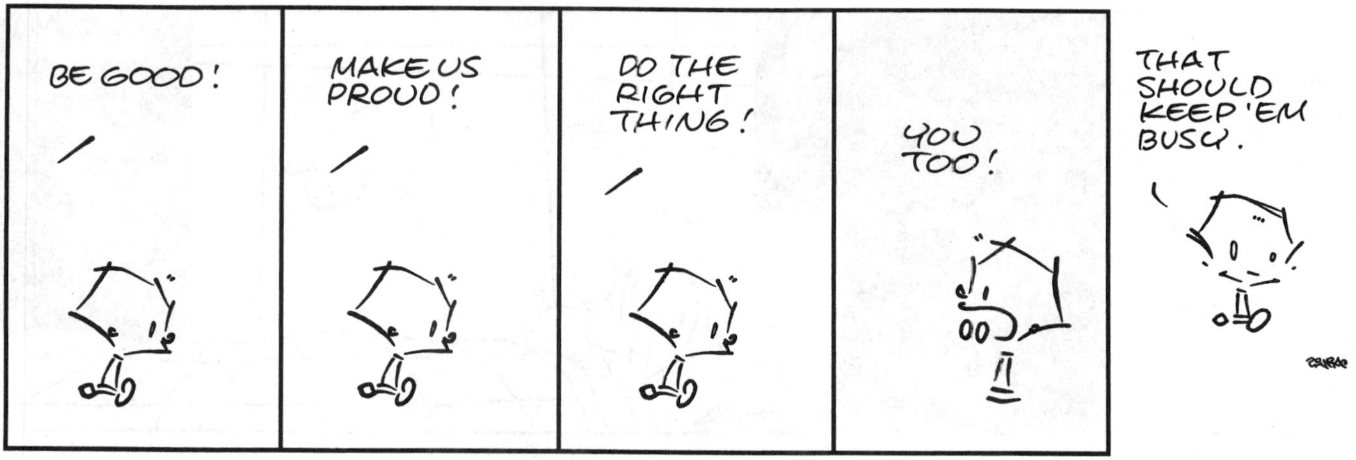
BE GOOD!
MAKE US PROUD!
DO THE RIGHT THING!
YOU TOO!
THAT SHOULD KEEP 'EM BUSY.

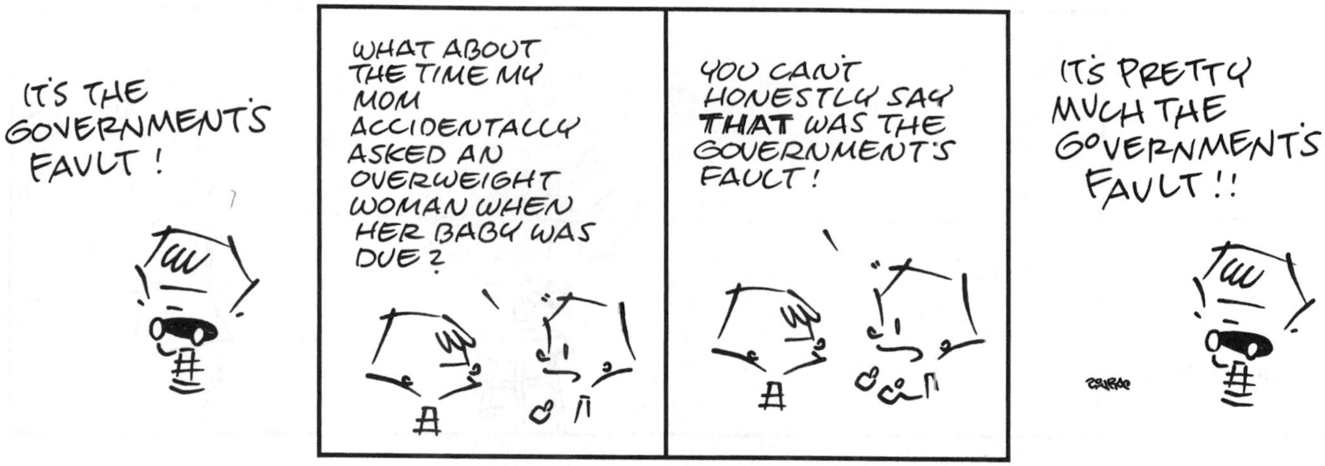
IT'S THE GOVERNMENT'S FAULT!
WHAT ABOUT THE TIME MY MOM ACCIDENTALLY ASKED AN OVERWEIGHT WOMAN WHEN HER BABY WAS DUE?
YOU CAN'T HONESTLY SAY **THAT** WAS THE GOVERNMENT'S FAULT!
IT'S PRETTY MUCH THE GOVERNMENT'S FAULT!!

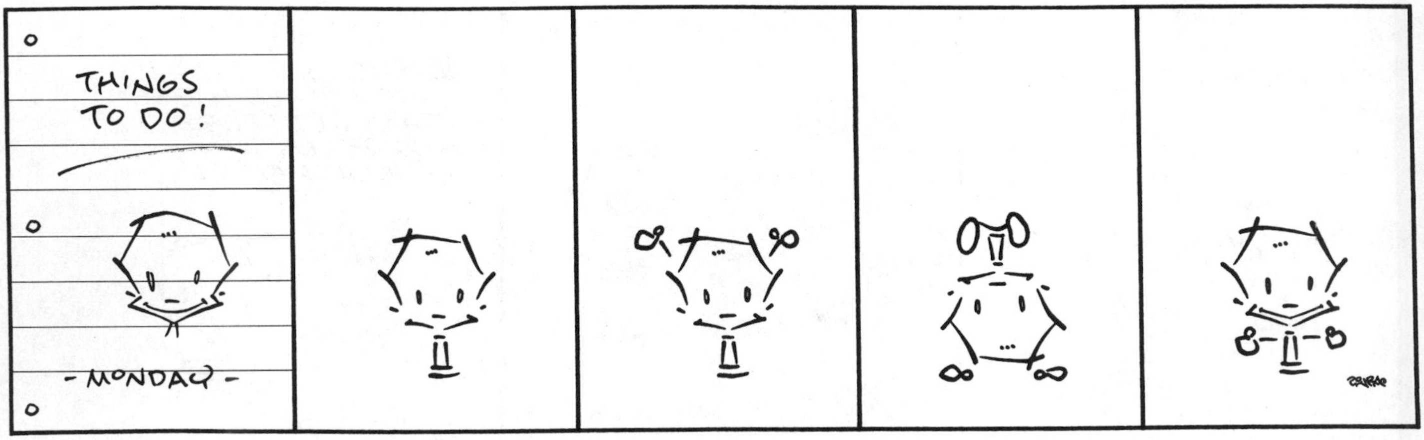
THINGS TO DO!
- MONDAY -

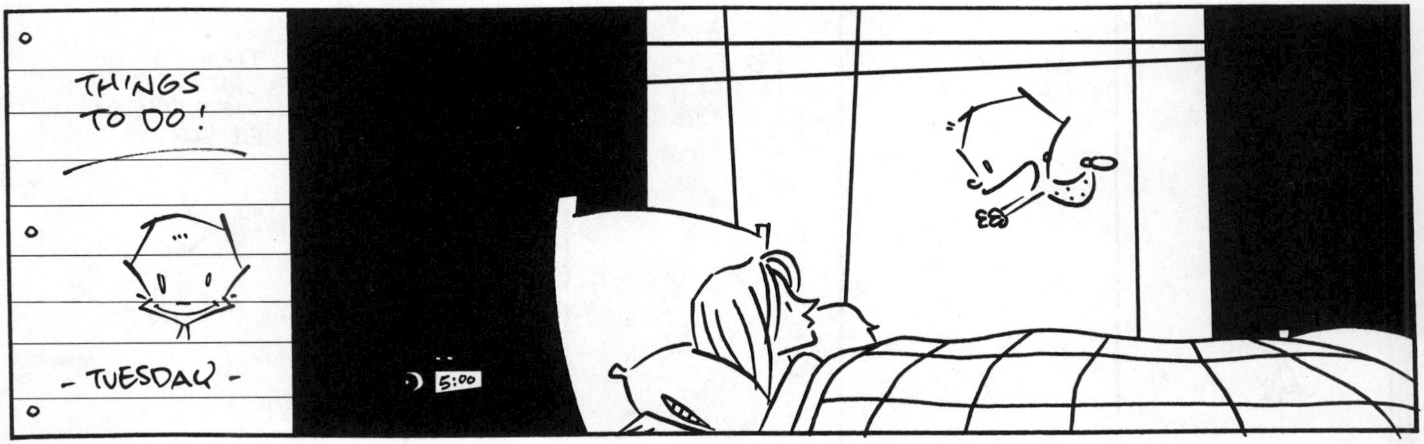
THINGS TO DO!
- TUESDAY -
5:00

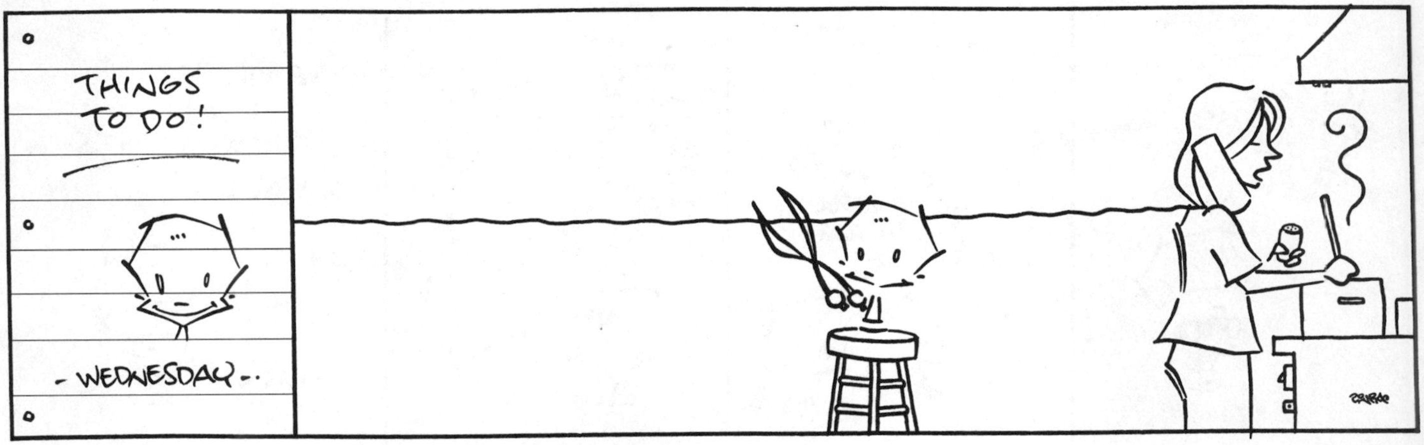
THINGS TO DO!
- WEDNESDAY -

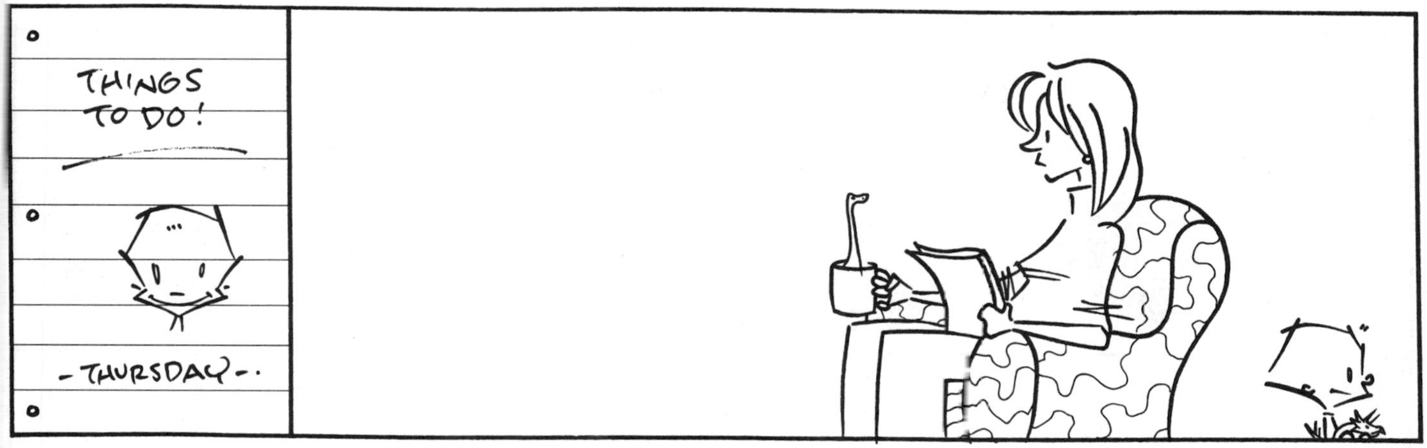
THINGS TO DO!
-THURSDAY-

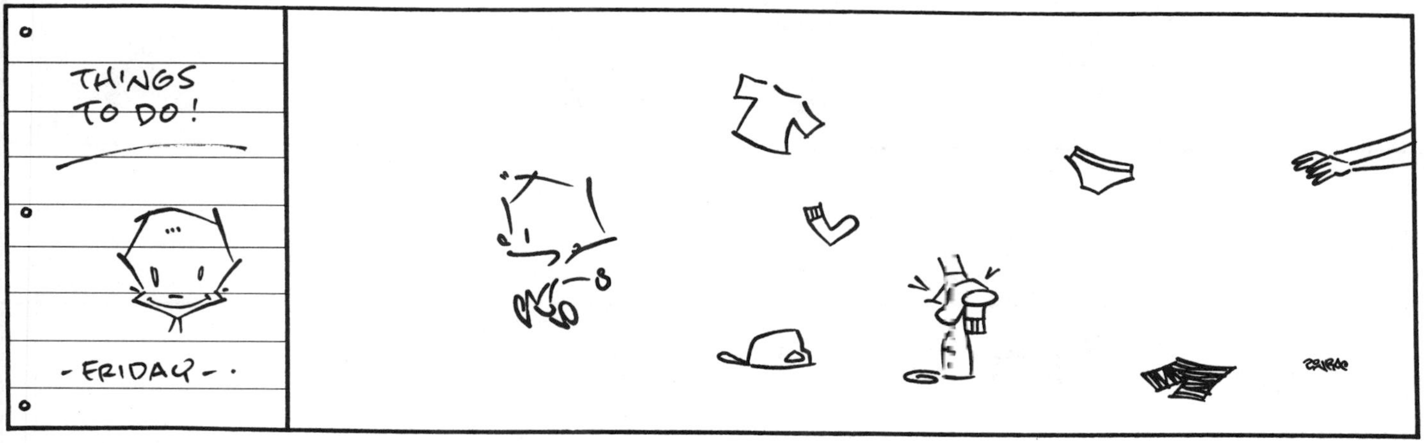
THINGS TO DO!
-FRIDAY-

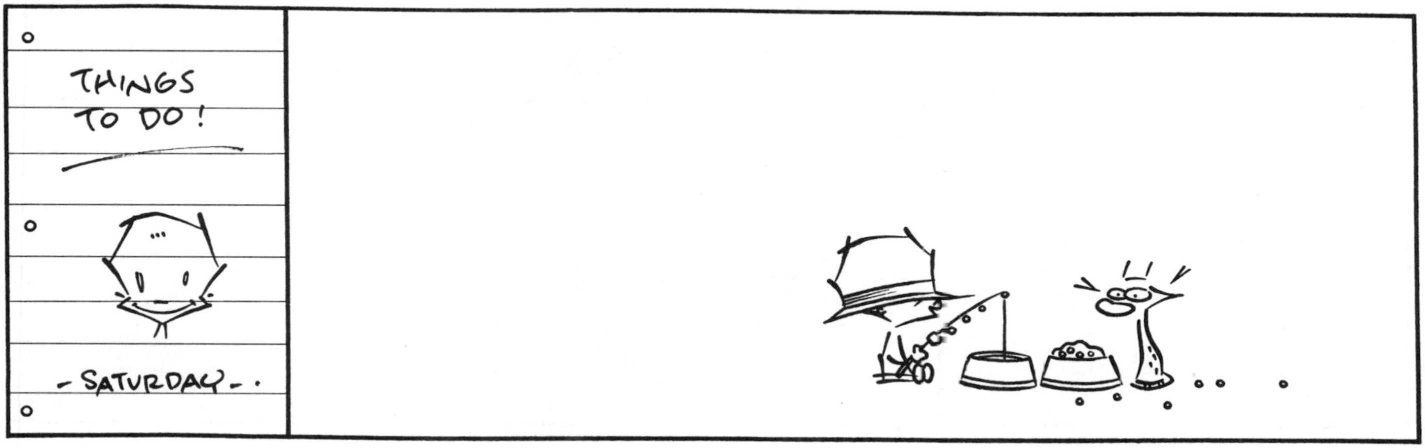
THINGS TO DO!
-SATURDAY-

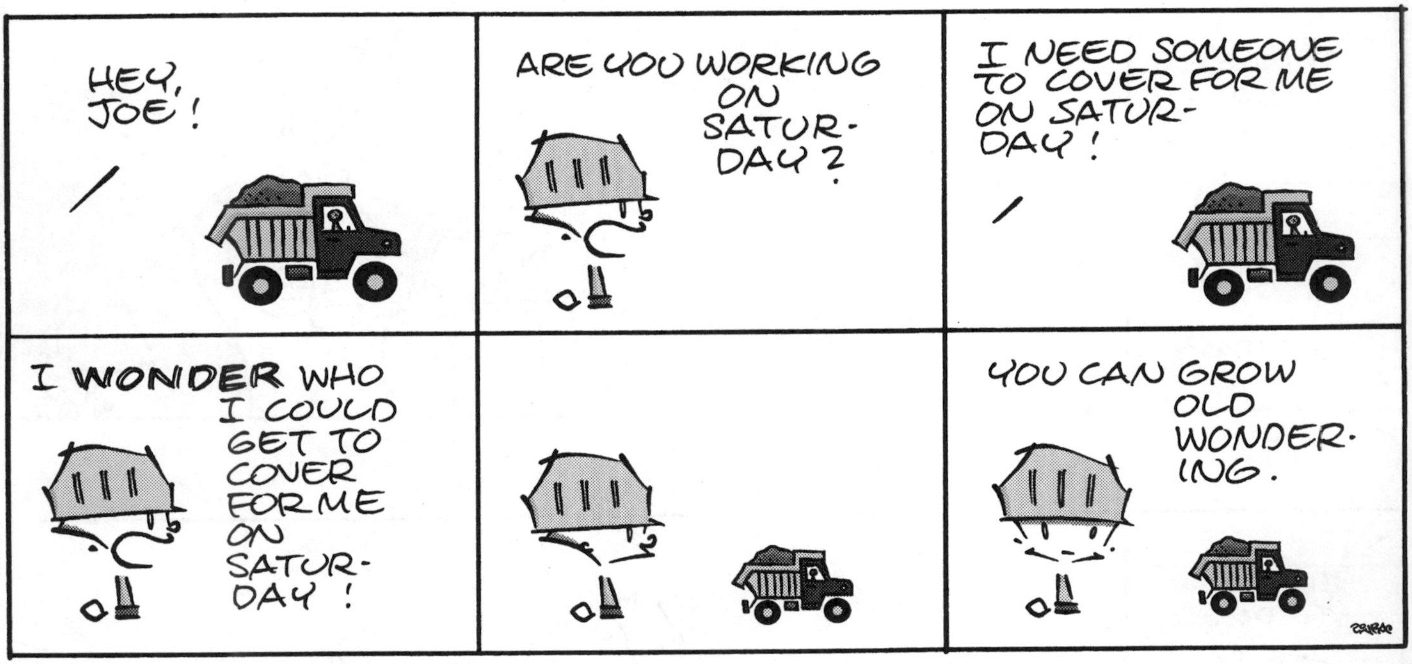
HEY, JOE!
ARE YOU WORKING ON SATURDAY?
I NEED SOMEONE TO COVER FOR ME ON SATURDAY!
I WONDER WHO I COULD GET TO COVER FOR ME ON SATURDAY!
YOU CAN GROW OLD WONDERING.

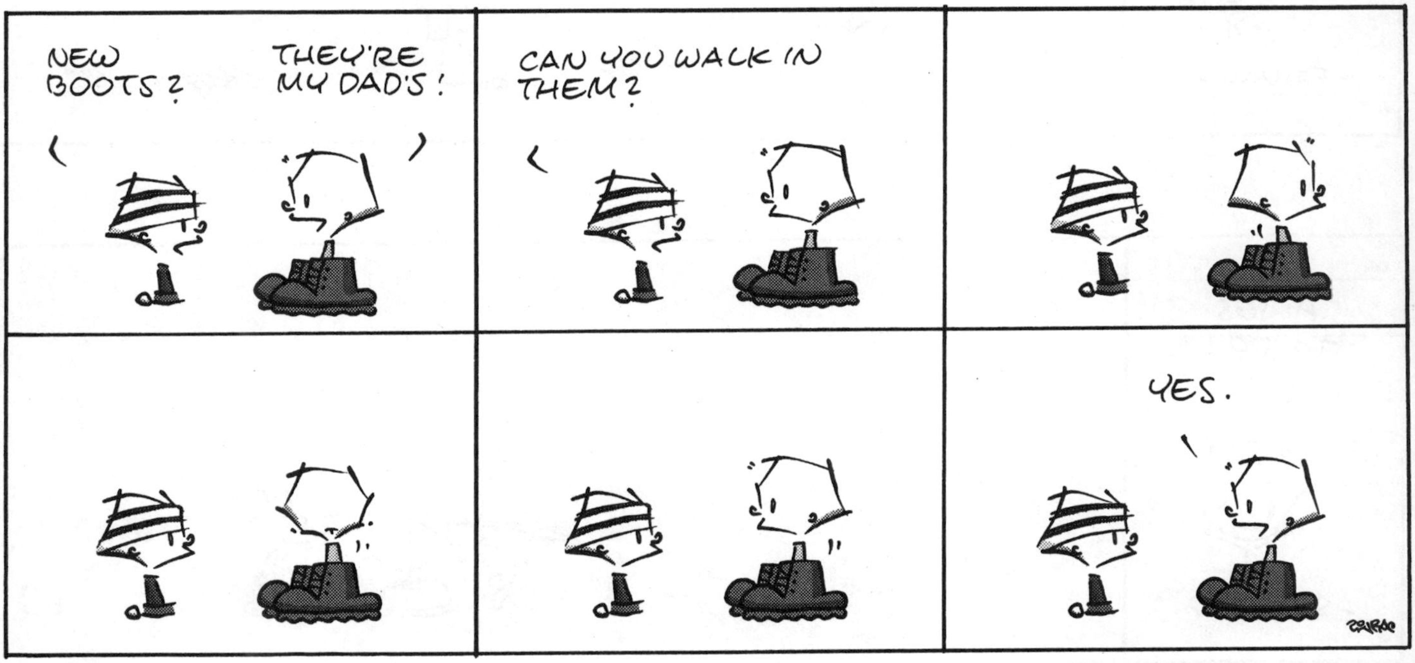
NEW BOOTS?
THEY'RE MY DAD'S!
CAN YOU WALK IN THEM?
YES.

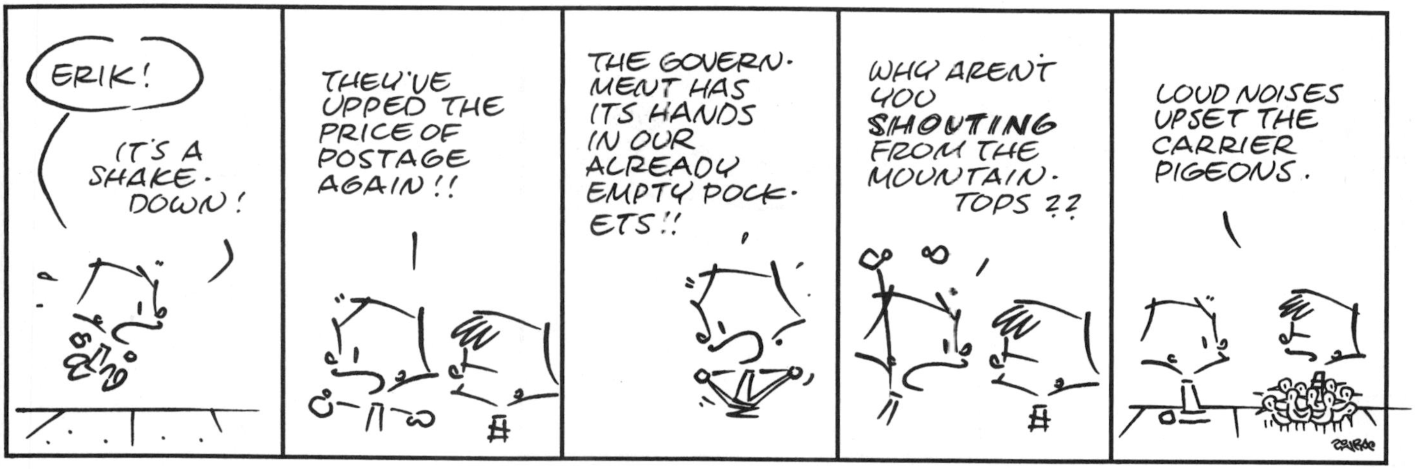
ERIK!
IT'S A SHAKE-DOWN!
THEY'VE UPPED THE PRICE OF POSTAGE AGAIN!!
THE GOVERN-MENT HAS ITS HANDS IN OUR ALREADY EMPTY POCK-ETS!!
WHY AREN'T YOU SHOUTING FROM THE MOUNTAIN-TOPS??
LOUD NOISES UPSET THE CARRIER PIGEONS.

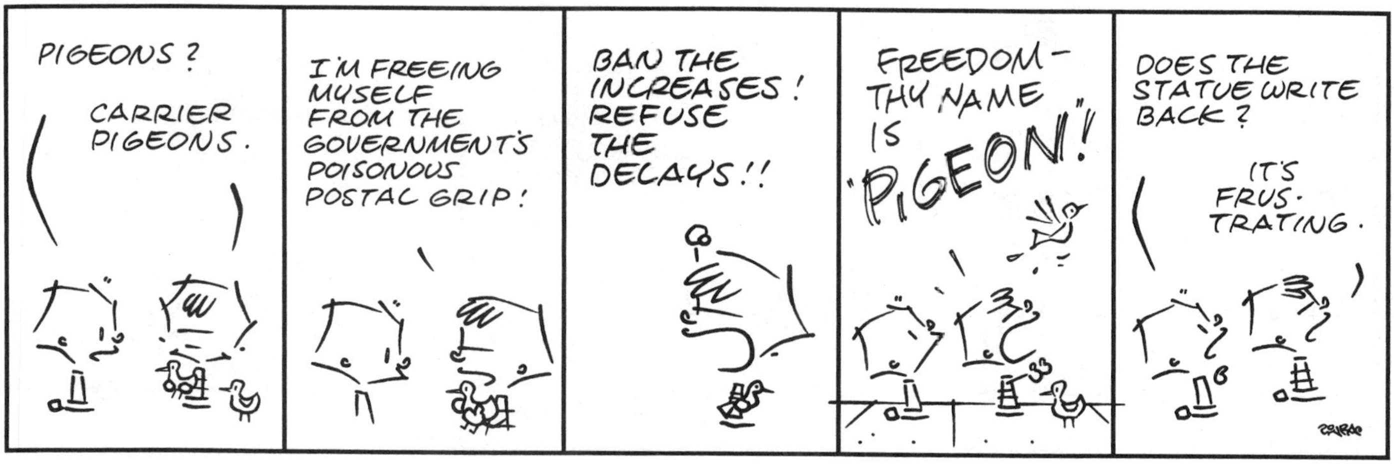
PIGEONS?
CARRIER PIGEONS.
I'M FREEING MYSELF FROM THE GOVERNMENT'S POISONOUS POSTAL GRIP!
BAN THE INCREASES! REFUSE THE DELAYS!!
FREEDOM-THY NAME IS "PIGEON!"
DOES THE STATUE WRITE BACK?
IT'S FRUS-TRATING.

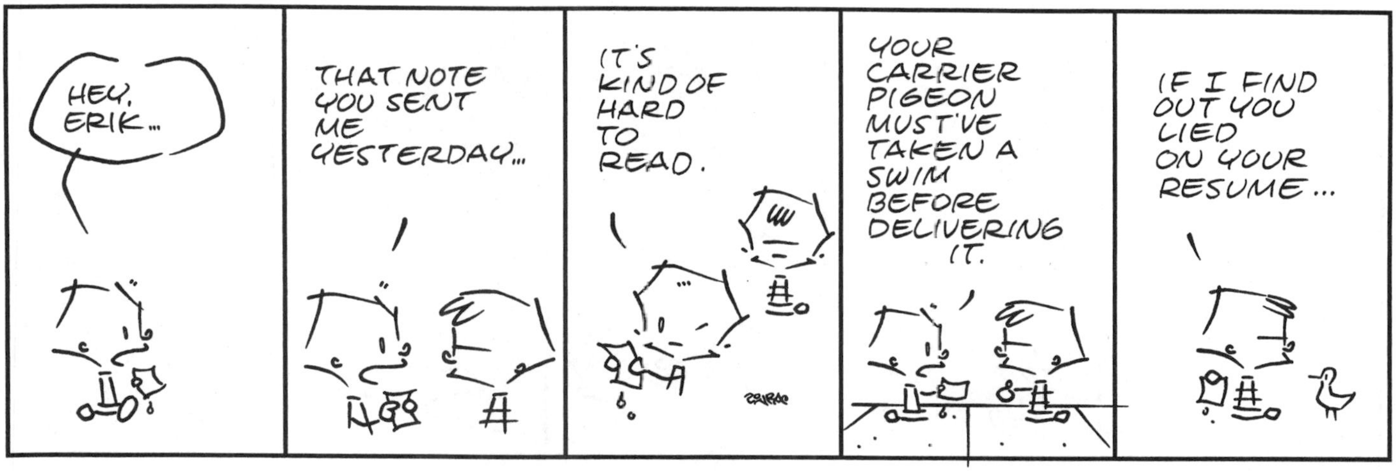
HEY, ERIK...
THAT NOTE YOU SENT ME YESTERDAY...
IT'S KIND OF HARD TO READ.
YOUR CARRIER PIGEON MUST'VE TAKEN A SWIM BEFORE DELIVERING IT.
IF I FIND OUT YOU LIED ON YOUR RESUME...

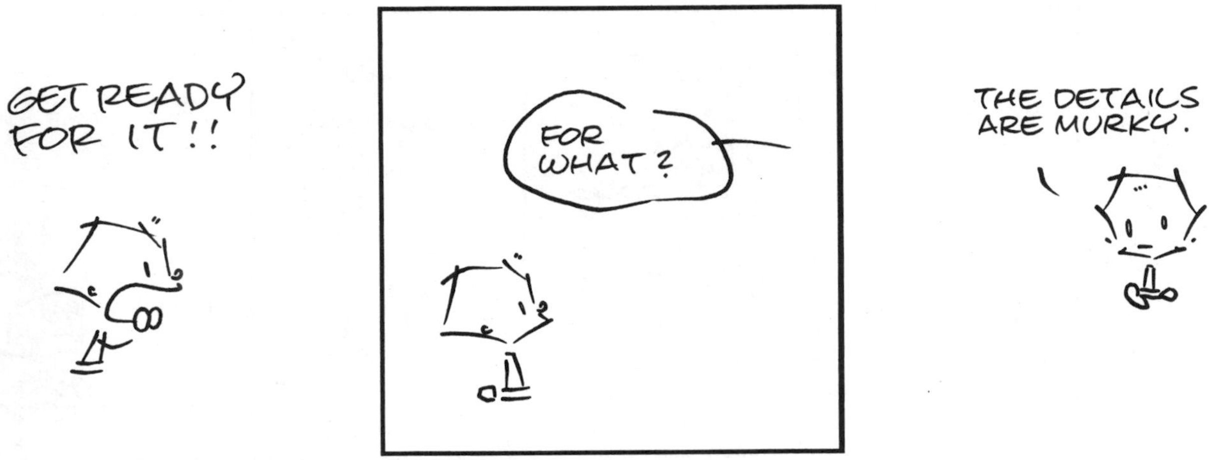
GET READY FOR IT!!
FOR WHAT?
THE DETAILS ARE MURKY.

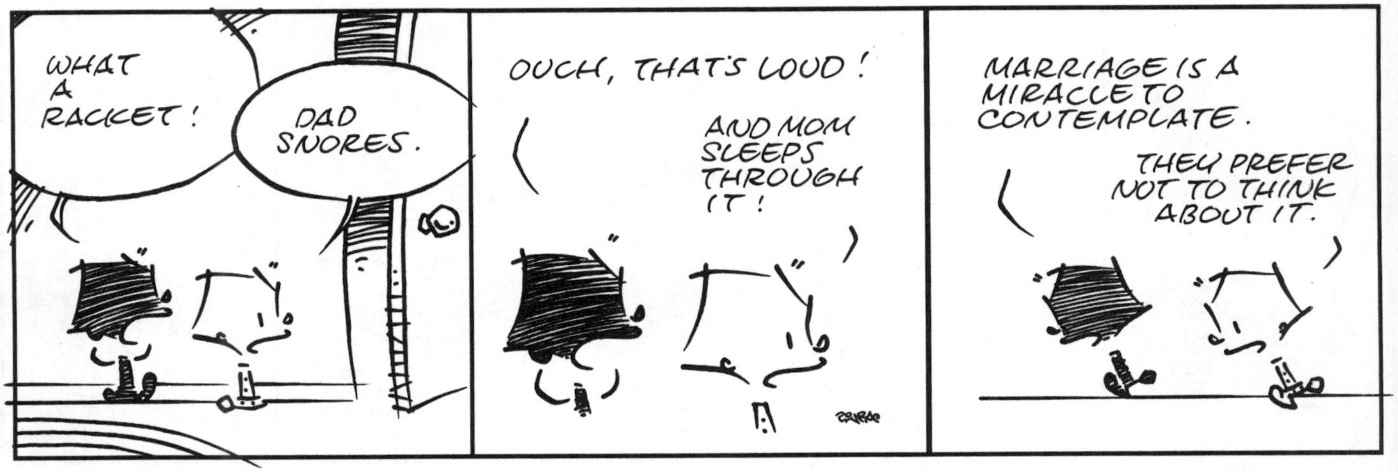
WHAT A RACKET!
DAD SNORES.
OUCH, THAT'S LOUD!
AND MOM SLEEPS THROUGH IT!
MARRIAGE IS A MIRACLE TO CONTEMPLATE.
THEY PREFER NOT TO THINK ABOUT IT.

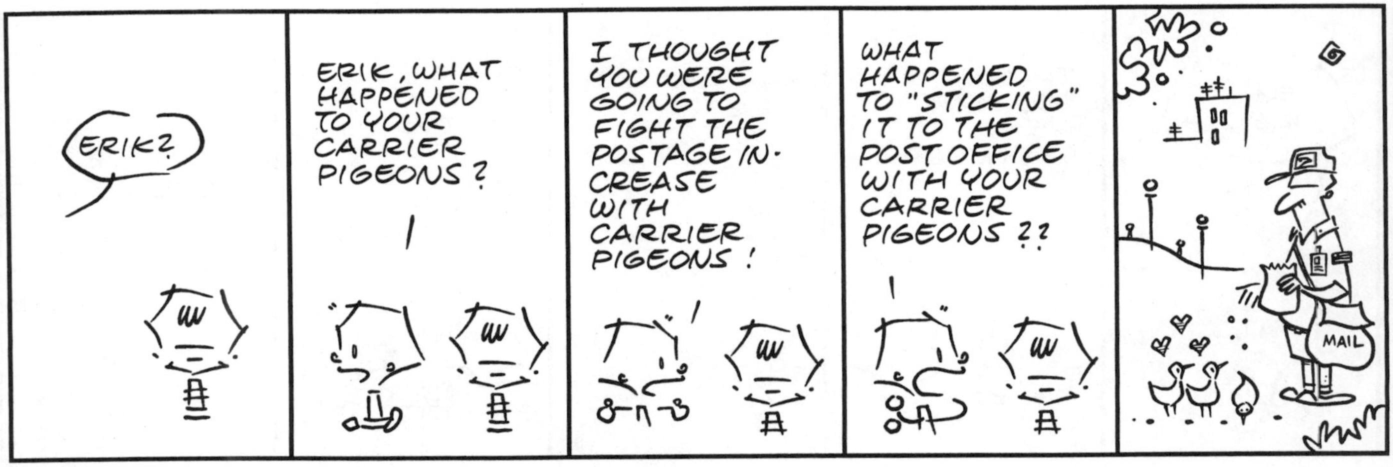
ERIK?
ERIK, WHAT HAPPENED TO YOUR CARRIER PIGEONS?
I THOUGHT YOU WERE GOING TO FIGHT THE POSTAGE IN-CREASE WITH CARRIER PIGEONS!
WHAT HAPPENED TO "STICKING" IT TO THE POST OFFICE WITH YOUR CARRIER PIGEONS??
MAIL

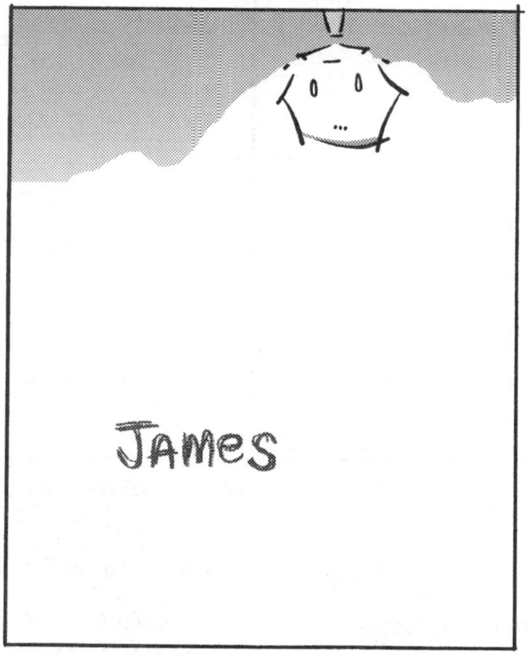
JAMES

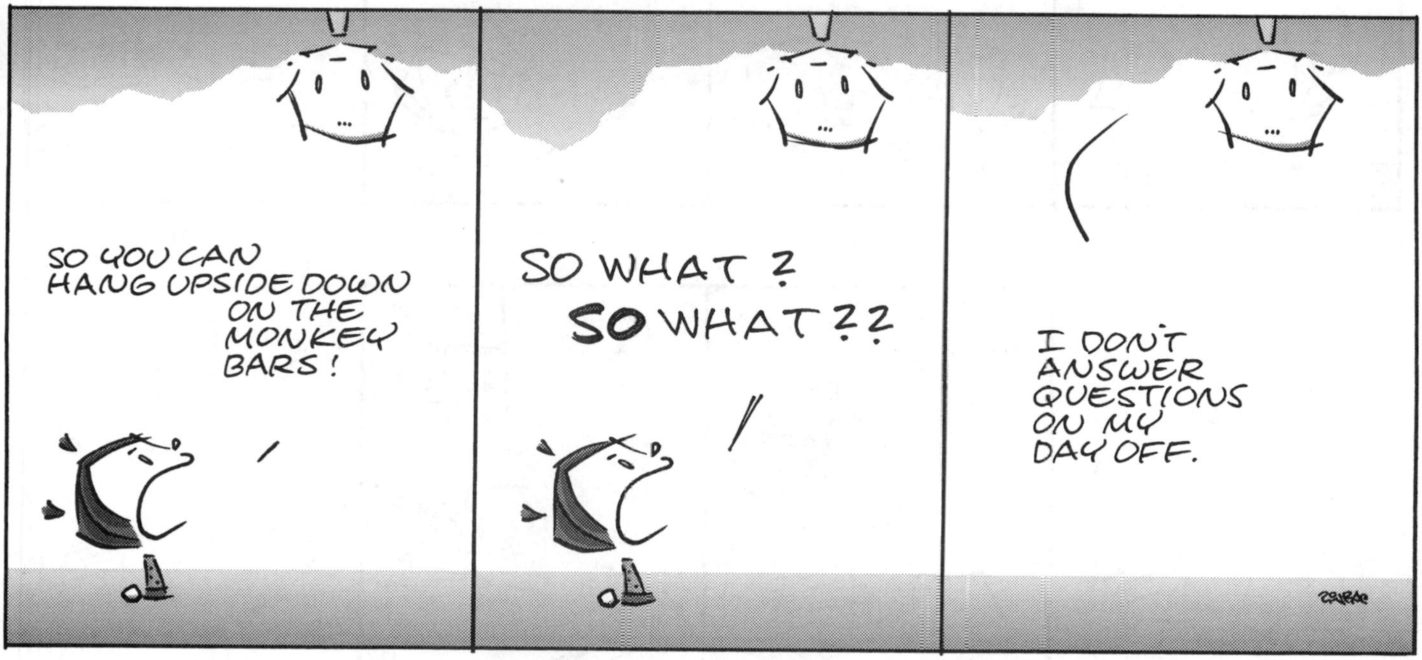
SO YOU CAN HANG UPSIDE DOWN ON THE MONKEY BARS!
SO WHAT? SO WHAT??
I DON'T ANSWER QUESTIONS ON MY DAY OFF.

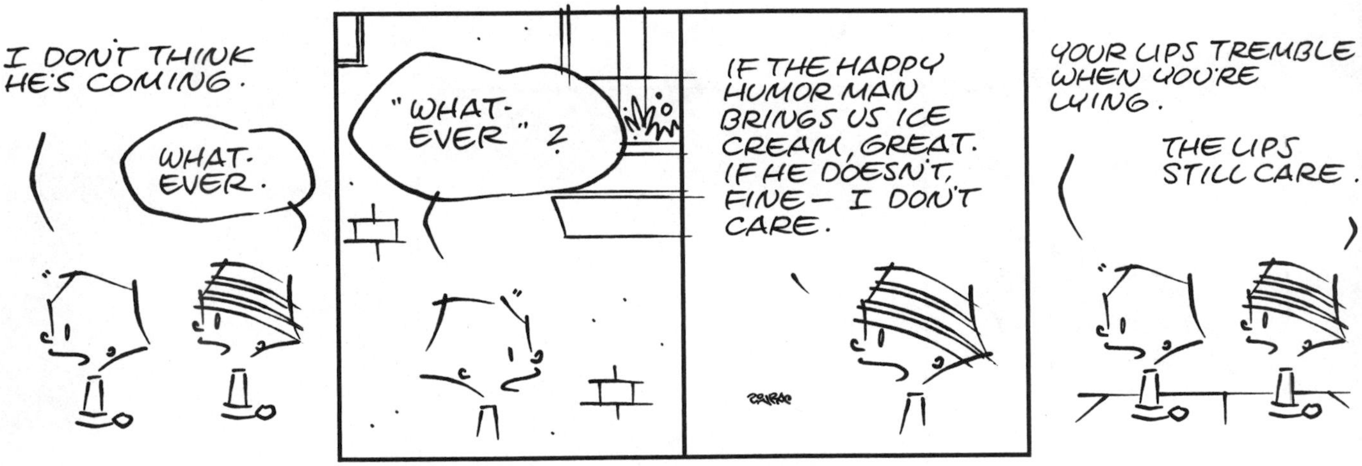
I DON'T THINK HE'S COMING.
WHAT-EVER.
"WHAT-EVER"?
IF THE HAPPY HUMOR MAN BRINGS US ICE CREAM, GREAT. IF HE DOESN'T, FINE— I DON'T CARE.
YOUR LIPS TREMBLE WHEN YOU'RE LYING.
THE LIPS STILL CARE.

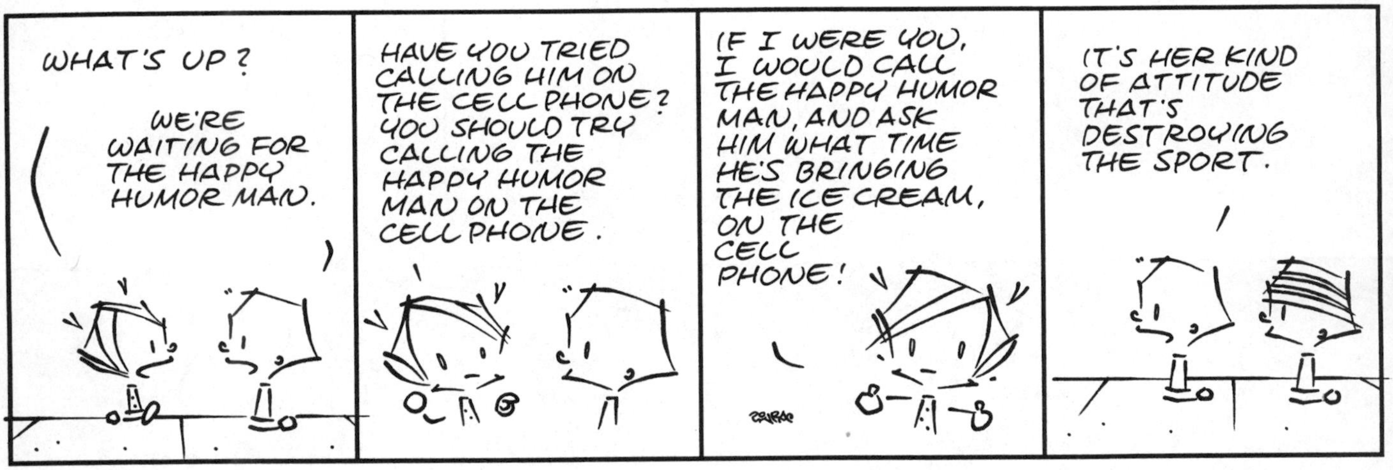
WHAT'S UP?
WE'RE WAITING FOR THE HAPPY HUMOR MAN.
HAVE YOU TRIED CALLING HIM ON THE CELL PHONE? YOU SHOULD TRY CALLING THE HAPPY HUMOR MAN ON THE CELL PHONE.
IF I WERE YOU, I WOULD CALL THE HAPPY HUMOR MAN, AND ASK HIM WHAT TIME HE'S BRINGING THE ICE CREAM, ON THE CELL PHONE!
IT'S HER KIND OF ATTITUDE THAT'S DESTROYING THE SPORT.

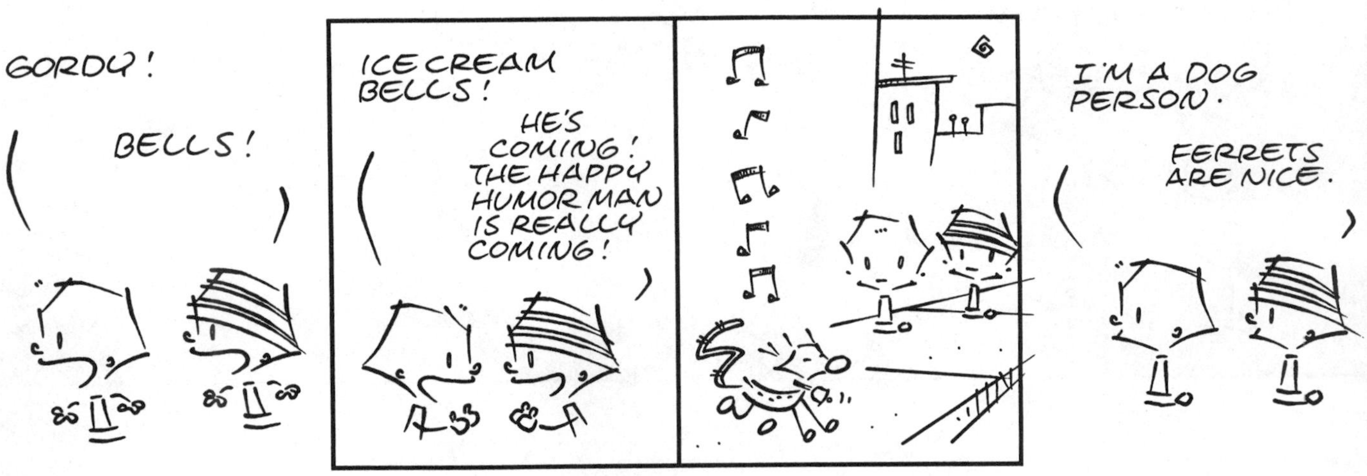
GORDY!
BELLS!
ICE CREAM BELLS!
HE'S COMING! THE HAPPY HUMOR MAN IS REALLY COMING!
I'M A DOG PERSON.
FERRETS ARE NICE.

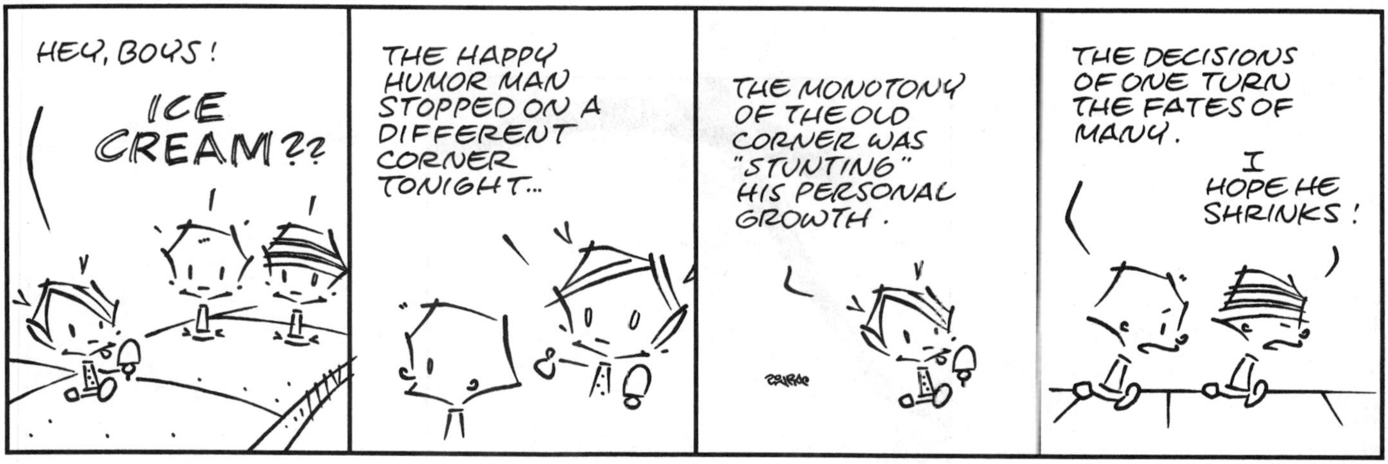
HEY, BOYS!
ICE CREAM??
THE HAPPY HUMOR MAN STOPPED ON A DIFFERENT CORNER TONIGHT...
THE MONOTONY OF THE OLD CORNER WAS "STUNTING" HIS PERSONAL GROWTH.
THE DECISIONS OF ONE TURN THE FATES OF MANY.
I HOPE HE SHRINKS!

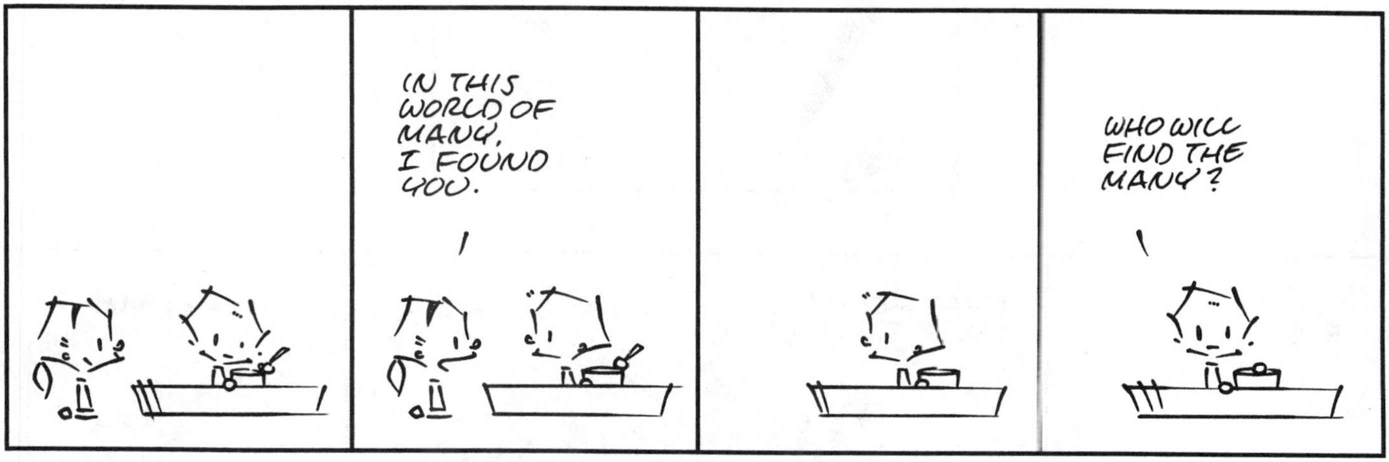
IN THIS WORLD OF MANY, I FOUND YOU.
WHO WILL FIND THE MANY?

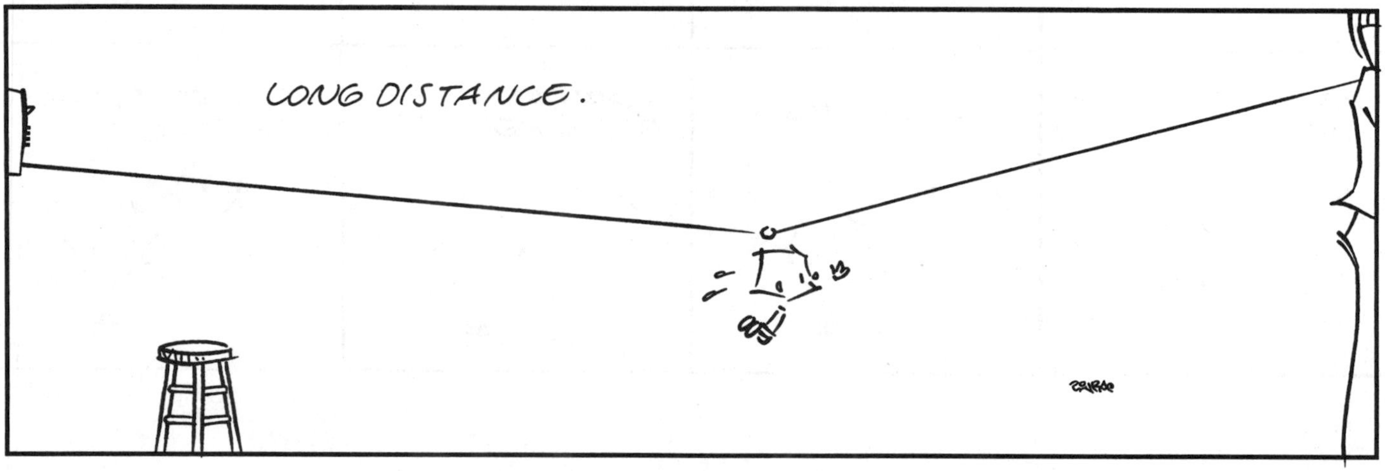
LONG DISTANCE.

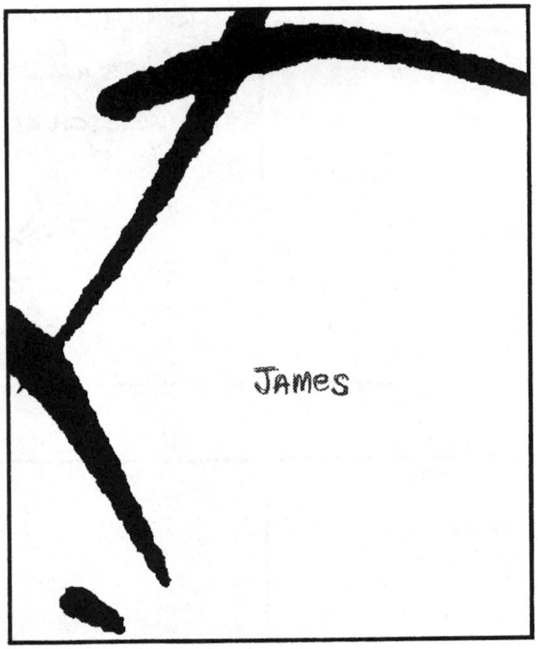
JAMES

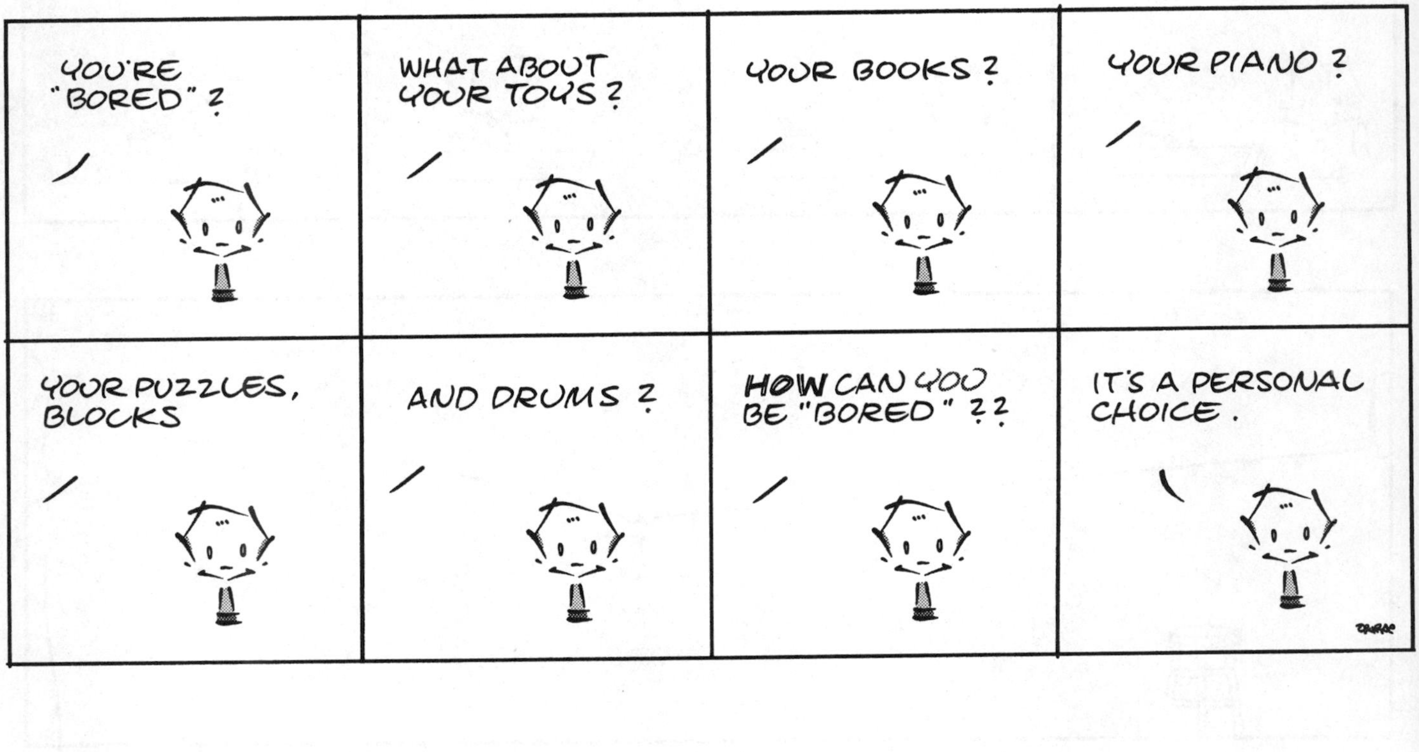
YOU'RE "BORED"?
WHAT ABOUT YOUR TOYS?
YOUR BOOKS?
YOUR PIANO?
YOUR PUZZLES, BLOCKS
AND DRUMS?
HOW CAN YOU BE "BORED"??
IT'S A PERSONAL CHOICE.

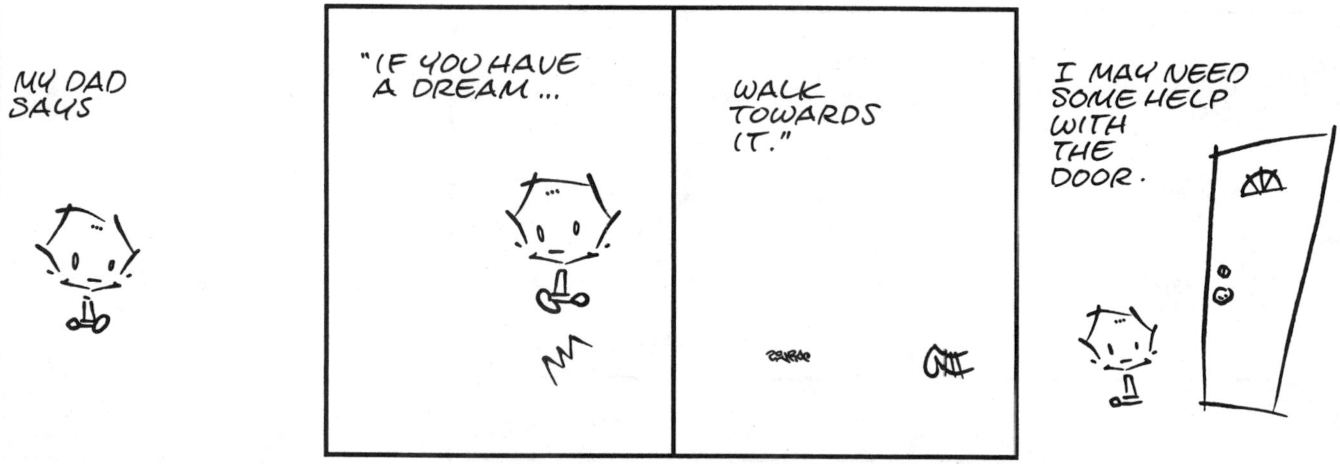
MY DAD SAYS
"IF YOU HAVE A DREAM...
WALK TOWARDS IT."
I MAY NEED SOME HELP WITH THE DOOR.

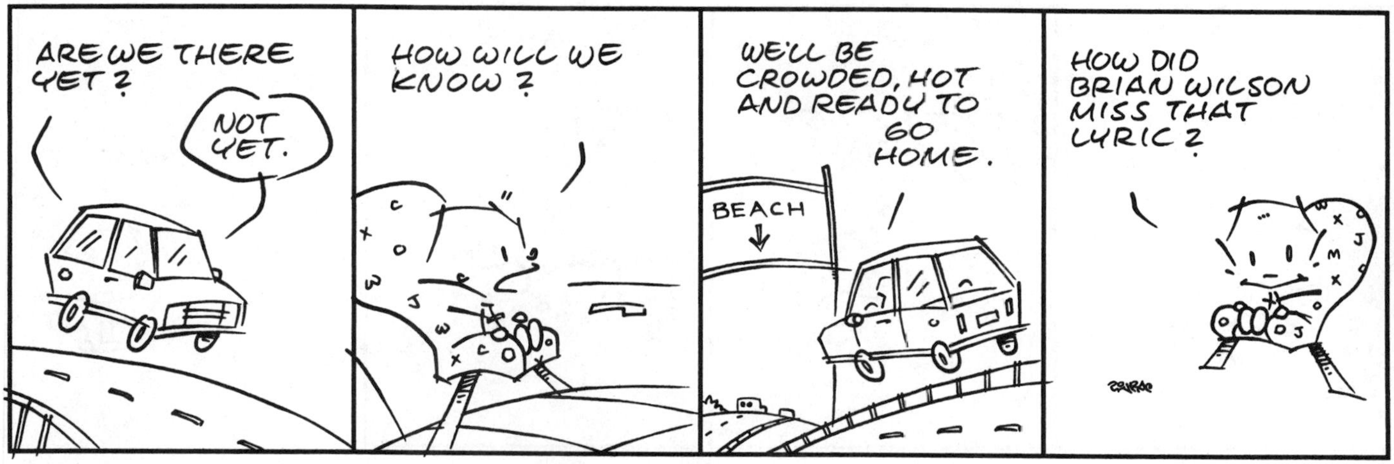
ARE WE THERE YET?
NOT YET.
HOW WILL WE KNOW?
WE'LL BE CROWDED, HOT AND READY TO GO HOME.
BEACH
HOW DID BRIAN WILSON MISS THAT LYRIC?

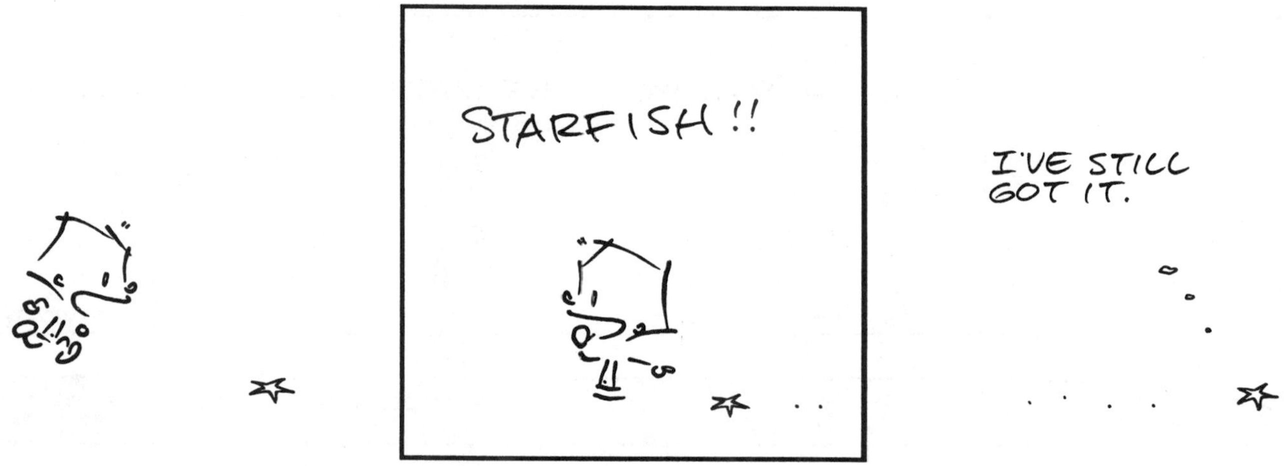
STARFISH!!
I'VE STILL GOT IT.

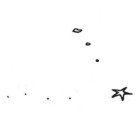

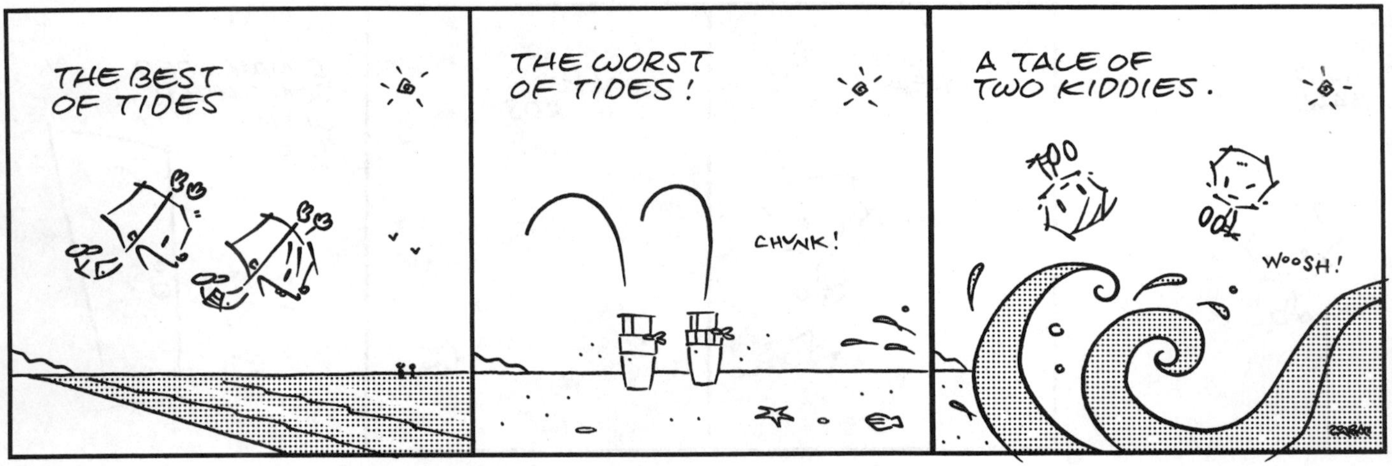
THE BEST OF TIDES
THE WORST OF TIDES!
CHUNK!
A TALE OF TWO KIDDIES.
WOOSH!

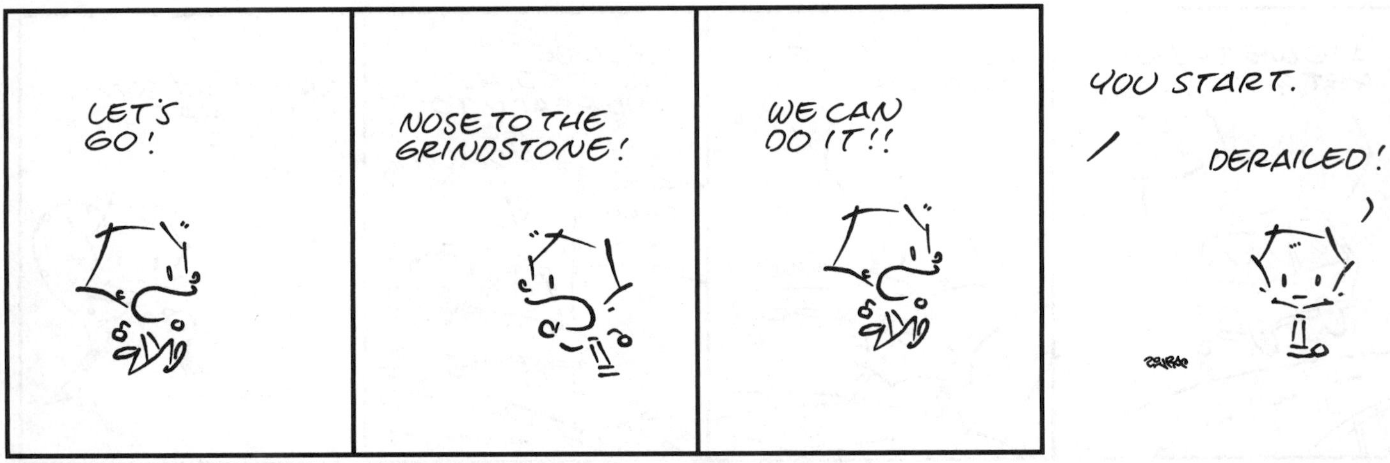
LET'S GO!
NOSE TO THE GRINDSTONE!
WE CAN DO IT!!
YOU START.
DERAILED!

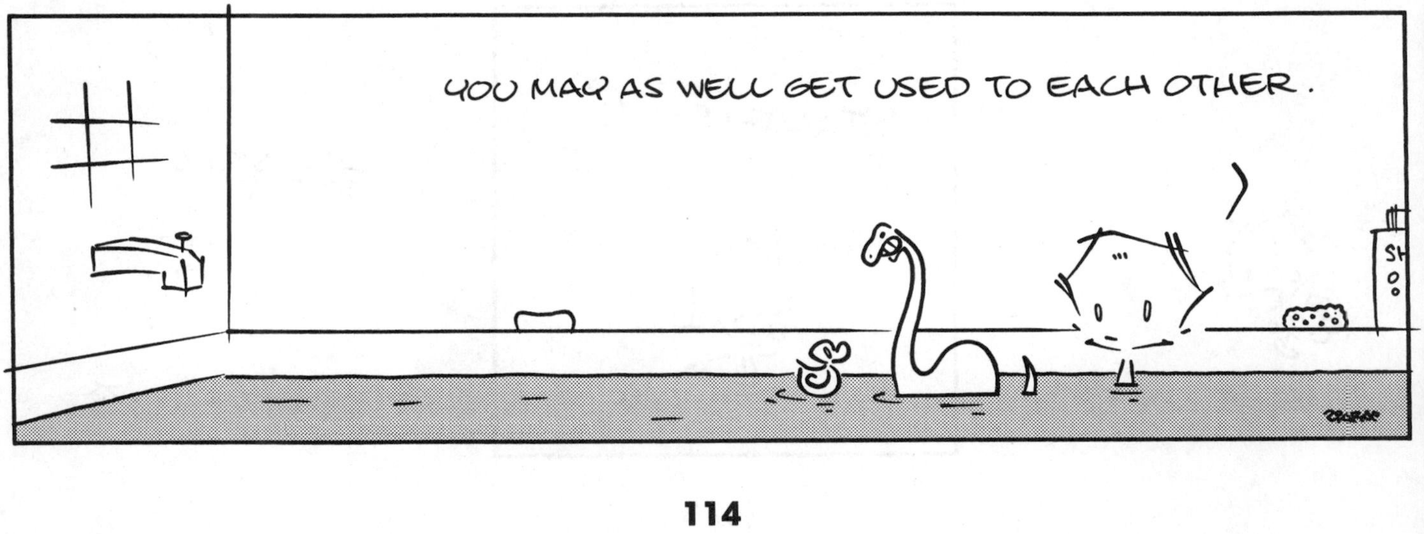
YOU MAY AS WELL GET USED TO EACH OTHER.

JAMES

AGAIN WITH THE MONKEY BARS ?? WHAT ARE YOU — TRYING TO MAKE THE REST OF US LOOK BAD ?

TRYING TO SET SOME KIND OF AN UPSIDE DOWN **WORLD** RECORD ?? IS THAT WHAT YOU'RE TRYING TO DO, JAMES ? IS IT ?? SHAME ON YOU, JAMES ! **SHAME** ON YOU !!!

IF MY LEGS CAN SLEEP THROUGH THAT, THEY CAN SLEEP THROUGH ANYTHING.

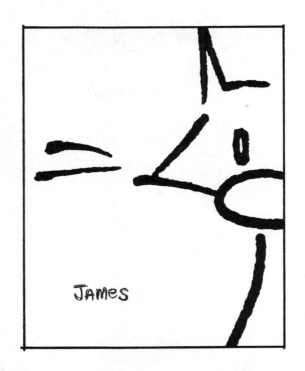

JAMES

SUMMERTIME

AND

THE

LIVIN'

IS

"SEEDY."

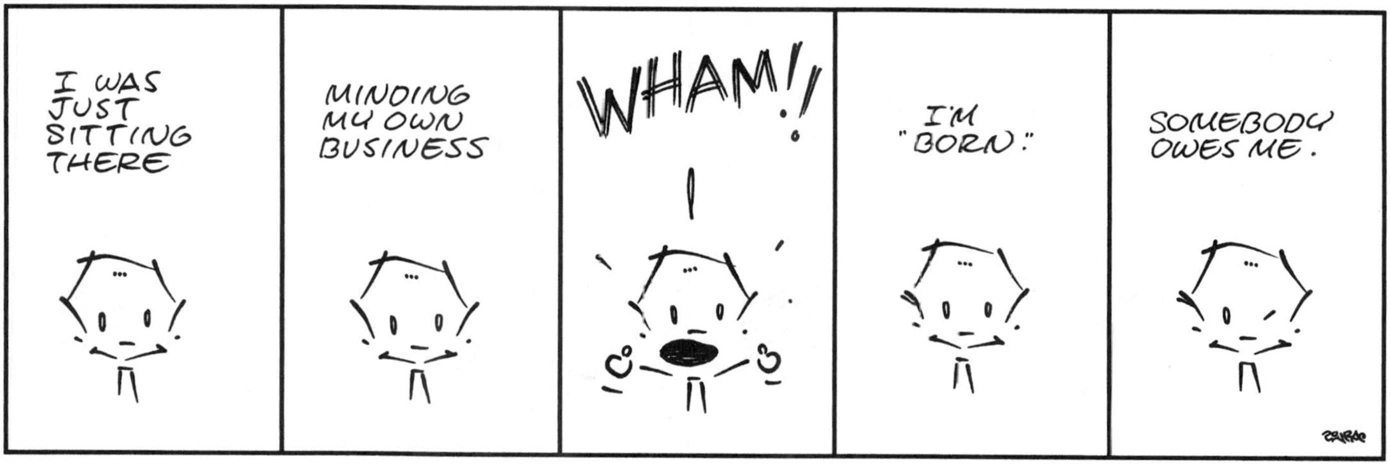
I WAS JUST SITTING THERE
MINDING MY OWN BUSINESS
WHAM!!
I'M "BORN."
SOMEBODY OWES ME.

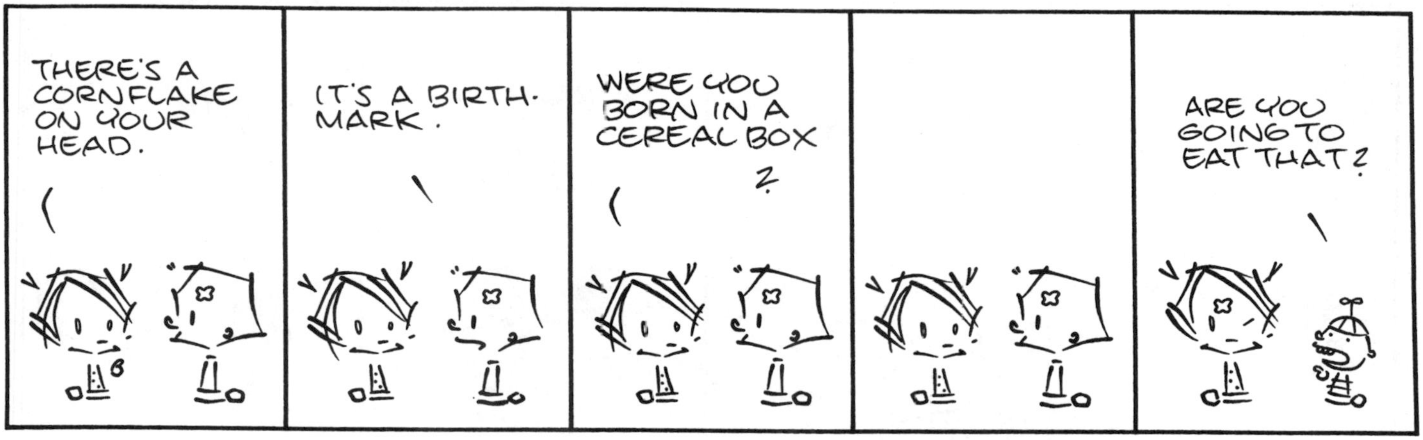
THERE'S A CORNFLAKE ON YOUR HEAD.
IT'S A BIRTH-MARK.
WERE YOU BORN IN A CEREAL BOX?
ARE YOU GOING TO EAT THAT?

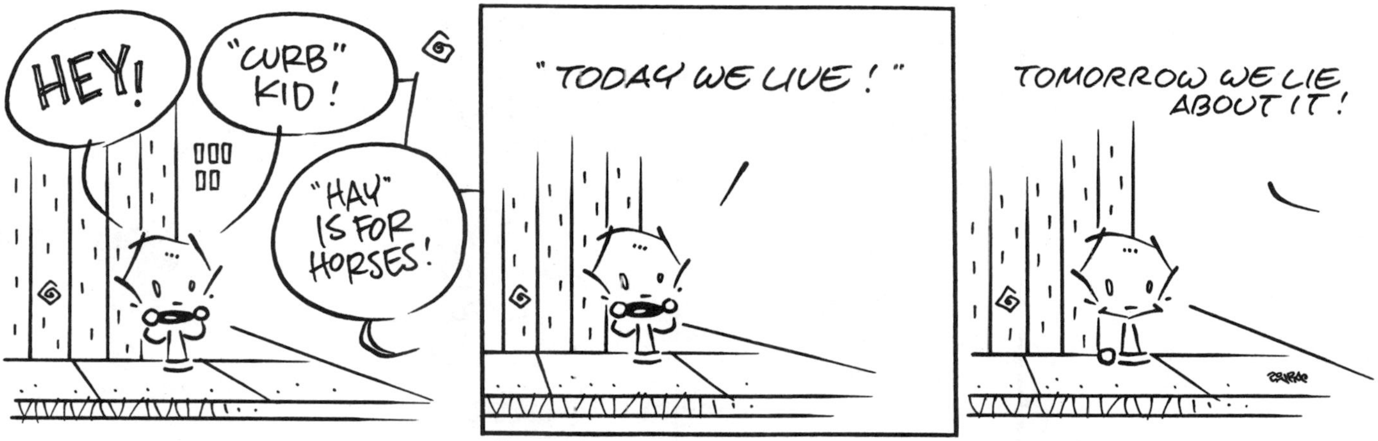
HEY!
"CURB" KID!
"HAY" IS FOR HORSES!
"TODAY WE LIVE!"
TOMORROW WE LIE ABOUT IT!

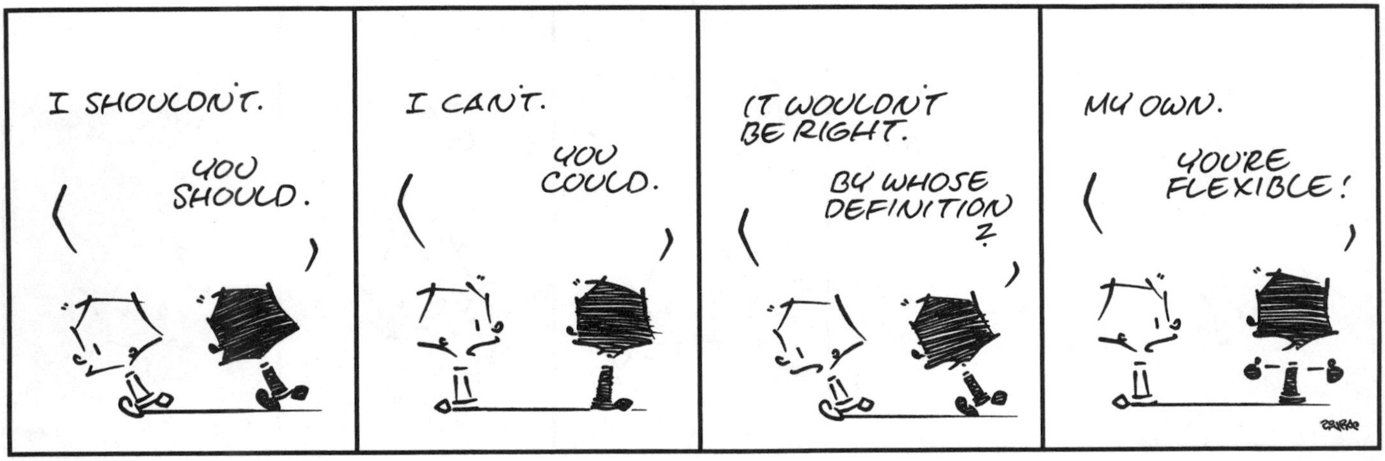
I SHOULDN'T.
YOU SHOULD.
I CAN'T.
YOU COULD.
IT WOULDN'T BE RIGHT.
BY WHOSE DEFINITION?
MY OWN.
YOU'RE FLEXIBLE!

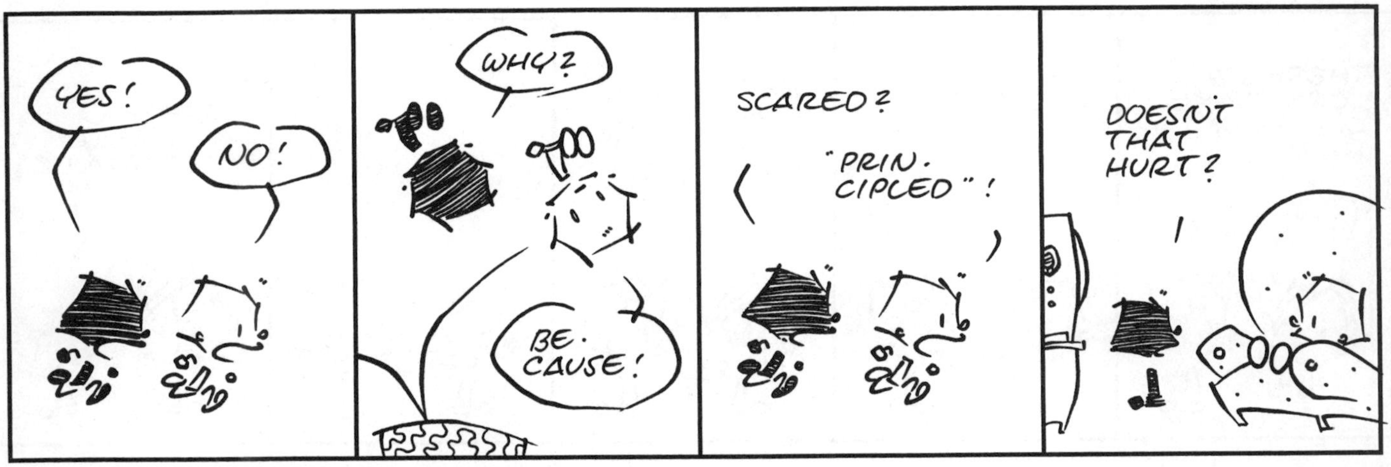
YES!
NO!
WHY?
BE-CAUSE!
SCARED?
"PRIN-CIPLED"!
DOESN'T THAT HURT?

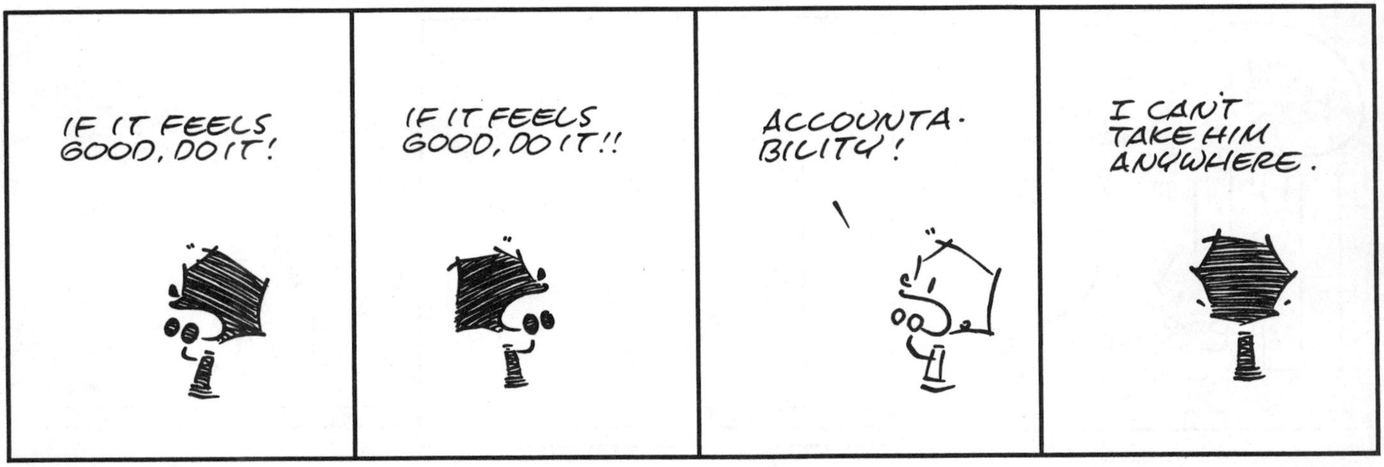
IF IT FEELS GOOD, DO IT!
IF IT FEELS GOOD, DO IT!!
ACCOUNTA-BILITY!
I CAN'T TAKE HIM ANYWHERE.

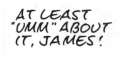
AT LEAST "UMM" ABOUT IT, JAMES!

I'VE MADE MY DECISION.

JAMES!

UMMMMMMMMMMM

"NO."

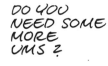
DO YOU NEED SOME MORE UMS?

WHAT IF WE DO?

WHAT IF WE DON'T?

WHAT IF WE DO?

WHAT IF, WE DON'T?

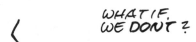

WE'RE GETTING A LOT DONE TODAY.

A SOLUTION WOULD ONLY COMPLICATE THINGS.

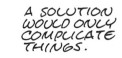

"THE CHEESE STANDS ALONE.

THE CHEESE STANDS ALONE.

HI-HO, THE DERRY-O...

THE CHEESE STANDS ALONE."

I LOVE A SURPRISE ENDING.

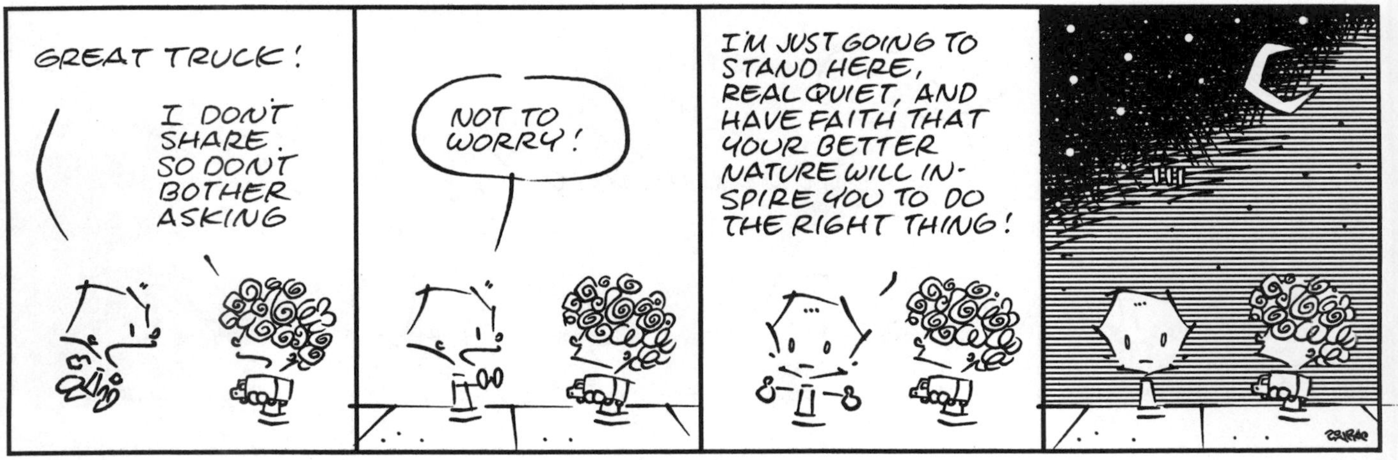
GREAT TRUCK!
I DON'T SHARE. SO DON'T BOTHER ASKING
NOT TO WORRY!
I'M JUST GOING TO STAND HERE, REAL QUIET, AND HAVE FAITH THAT YOUR BETTER NATURE WILL IN-SPIRE YOU TO DO THE RIGHT THING!

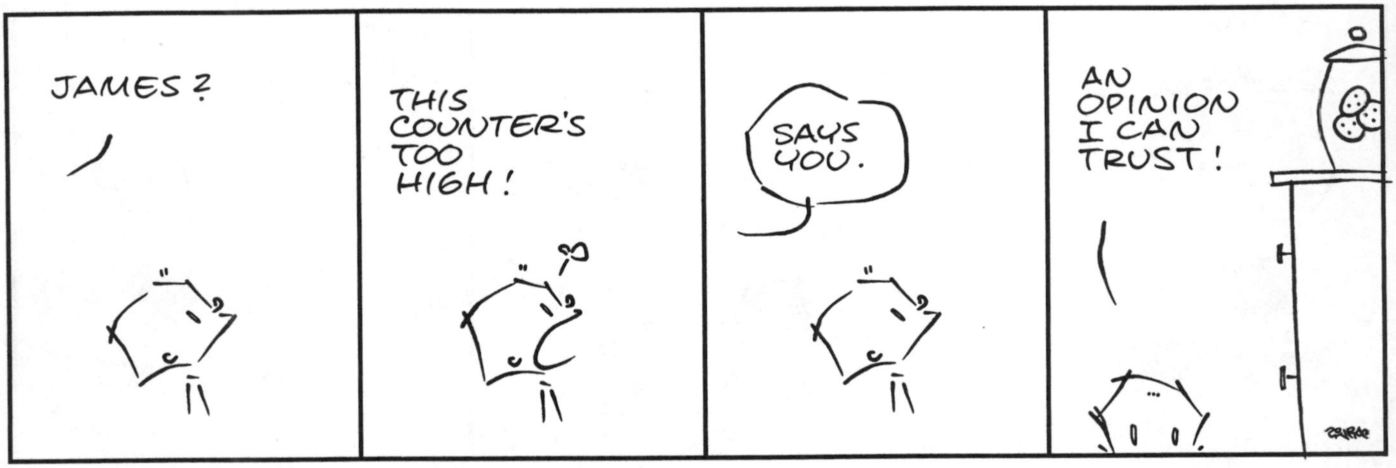
JAMES?
THIS COUNTER'S TOO HIGH!
SAYS YOU.
AN OPINION I CAN TRUST!

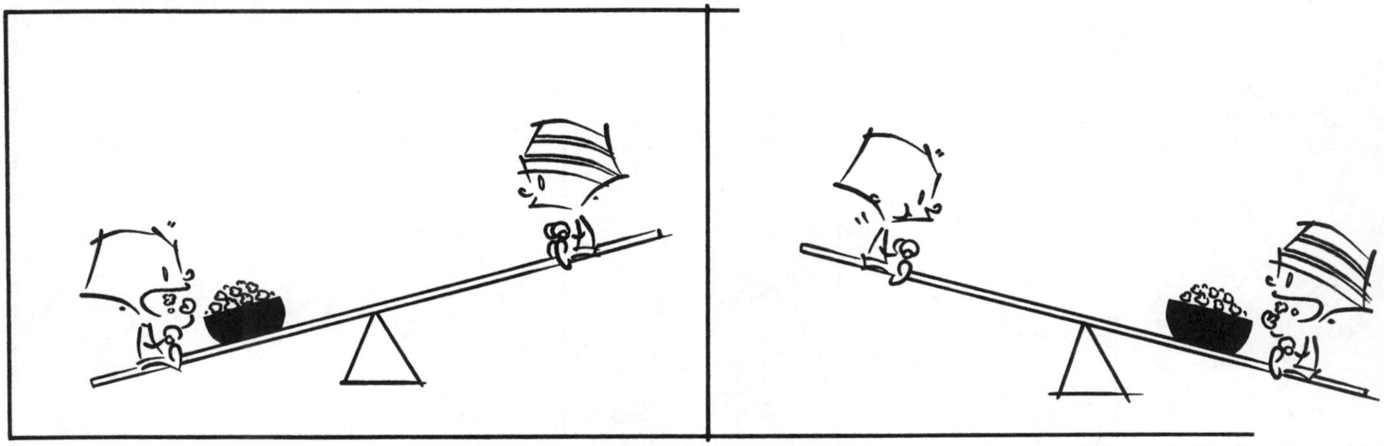

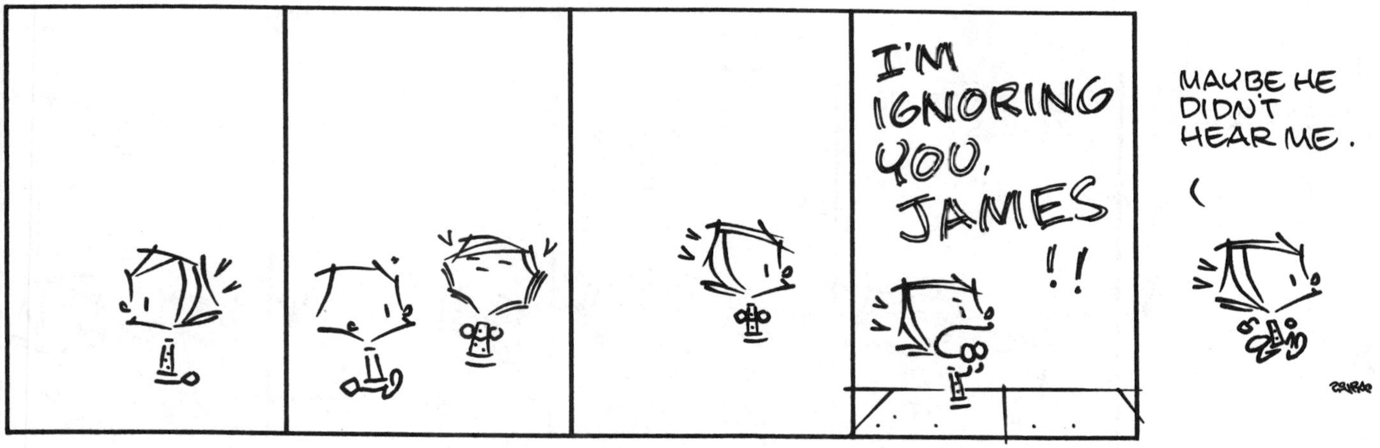
I'M IGNORING YOU, JAMES !!
MAYBE HE DIDN'T HEAR ME.

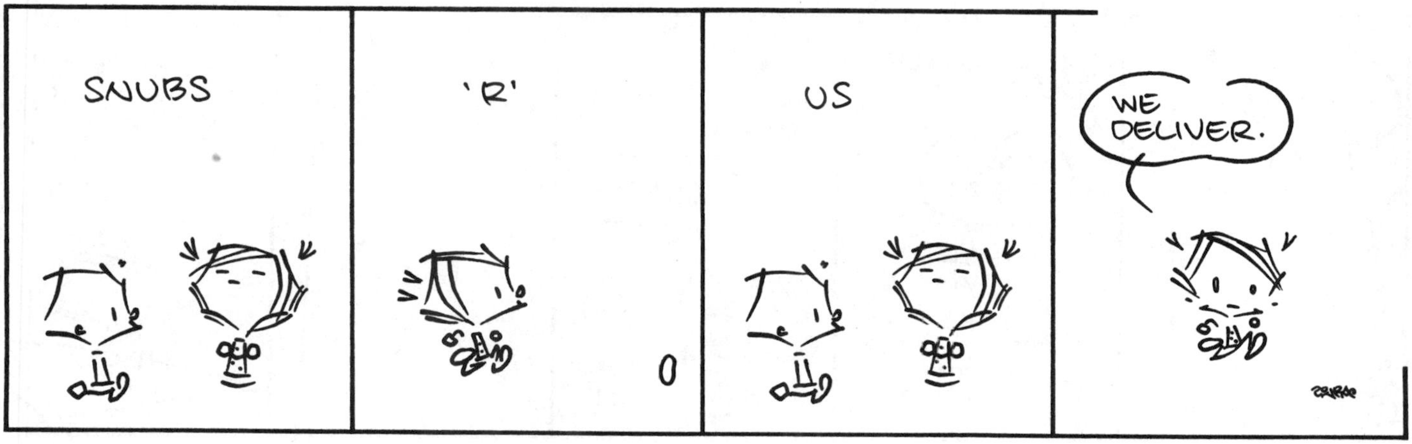
SNUBS
'R'
US
WE DELIVER.

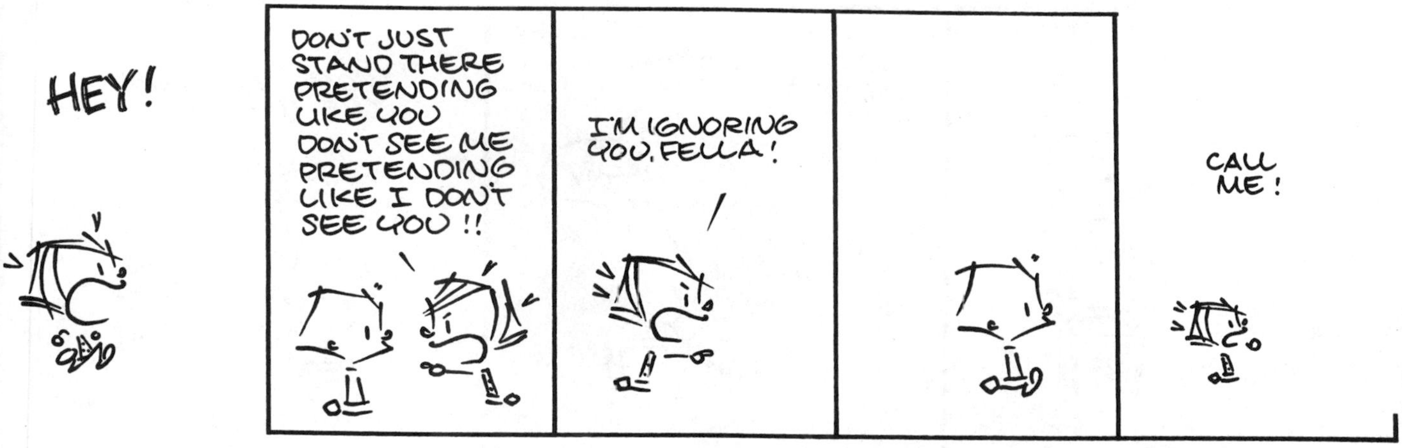
HEY!
DON'T JUST STAND THERE PRETENDING LIKE YOU DON'T SEE ME PRETENDING LIKE I DON'T SEE YOU !!
I'M IGNORING YOU, FELLA!
CALL ME!

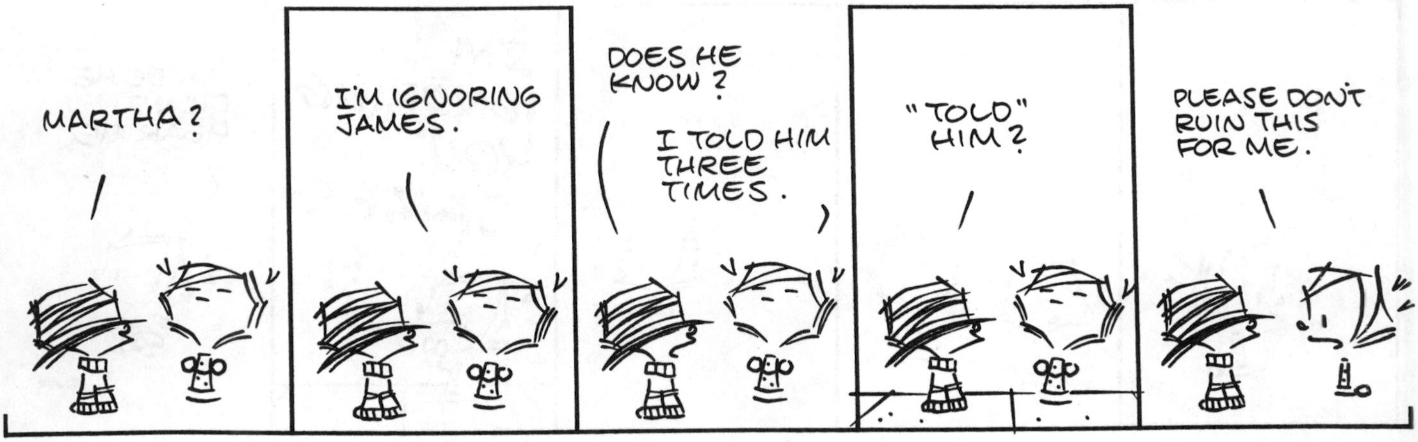
MARTHA?
I'M IGNORING JAMES.
DOES HE KNOW?
I TOLD HIM THREE TIMES.
"TOLD" HIM?
PLEASE DON'T RUIN THIS FOR ME.

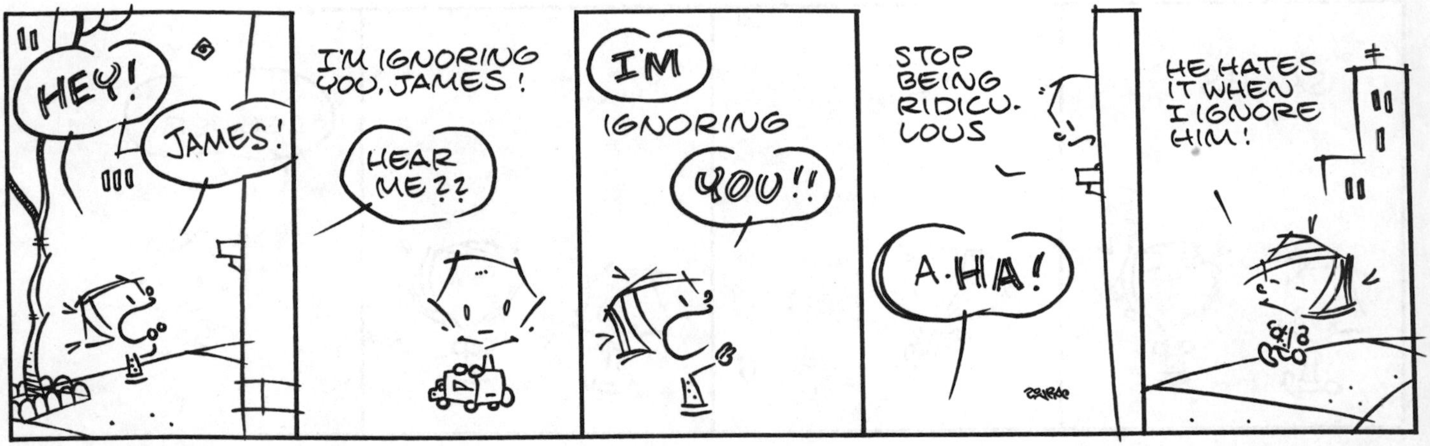
HEY!
JAMES!
I'M IGNORING YOU, JAMES!
HEAR ME??
I'M
IGNORING
YOU!!
STOP BEING RIDICU-LOUS
A-HA!
HE HATES IT WHEN I IGNORE HIM!

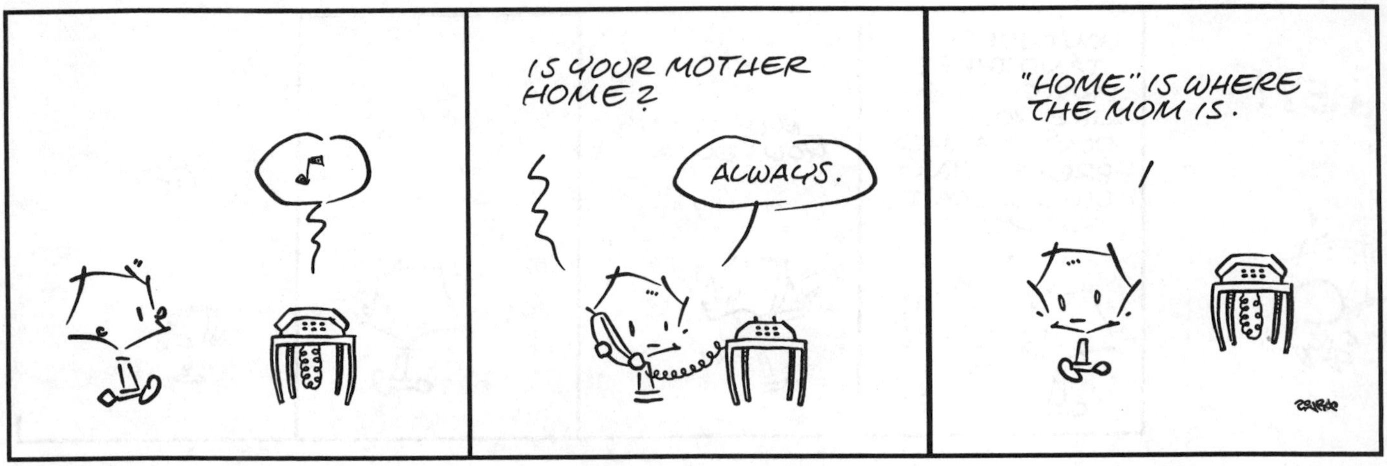
IS YOUR MOTHER HOME?
ALWAYS.
"HOME" IS WHERE THE MOM IS.

U
T B D F R
J C
A M e S
Z I G H P V
N K L W
O Q
X Y

MULTIPLE CHOICE!

WHO, ME??
Ⓐ
YES.
Ⓑ
NO!
Ⓒ ALL OF THE ABOVE.

ANSWER: "THE IMPORTANCE AND UNIMPORTANCE OF THE SELF CANNOT BE EXAGGERATED."

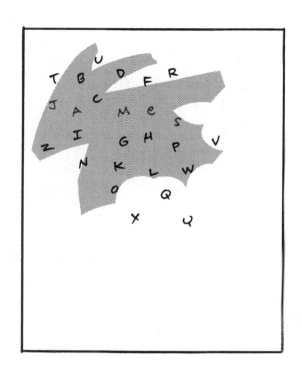

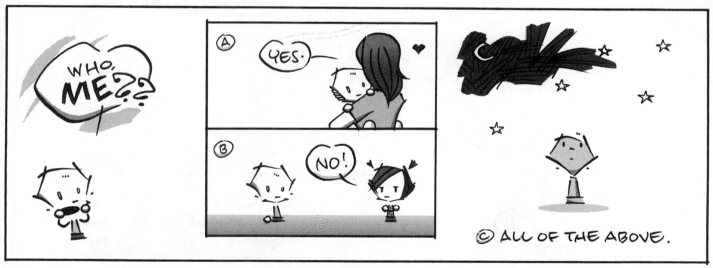

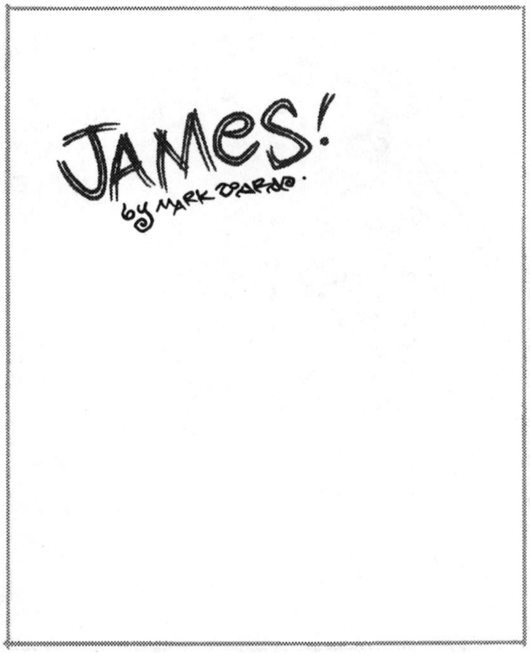
JAMES!
by MARK TATULLI

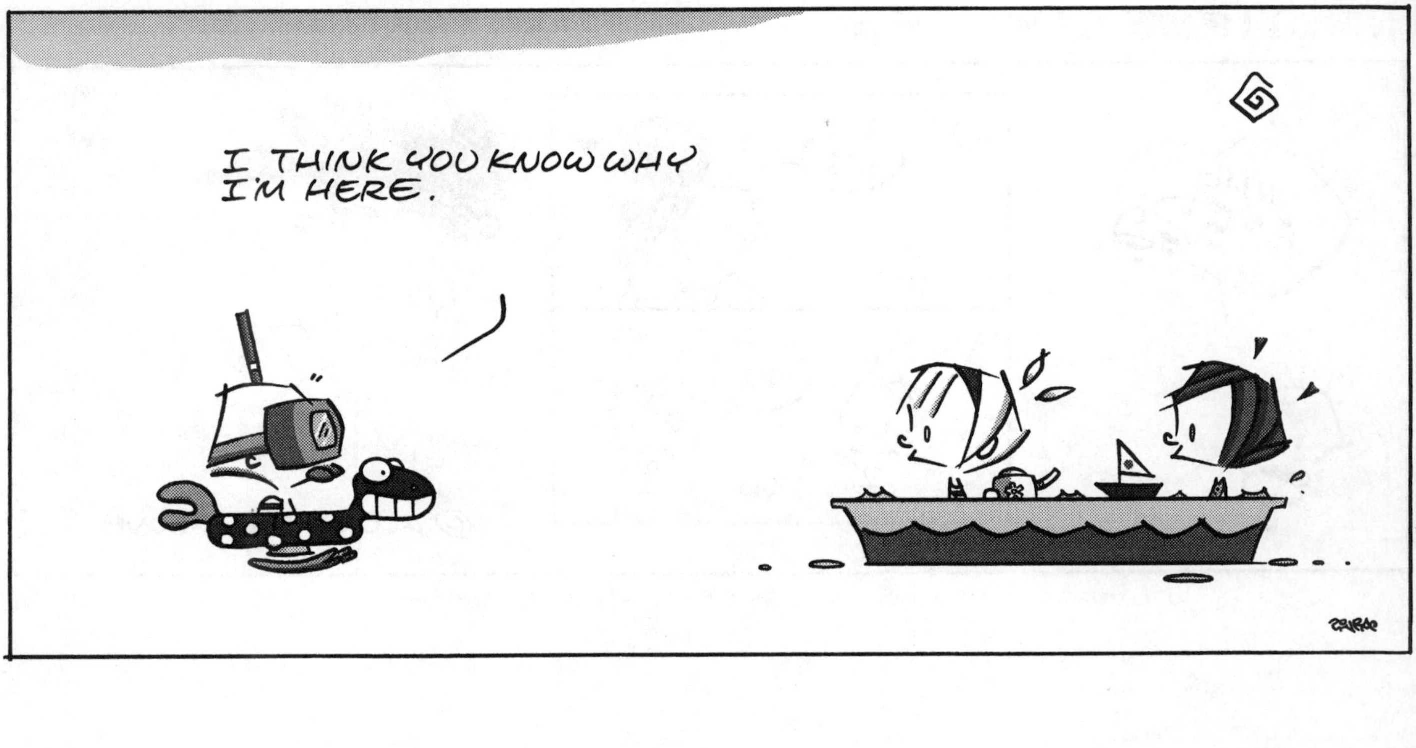
I THINK YOU KNOW WHY I'M HERE.

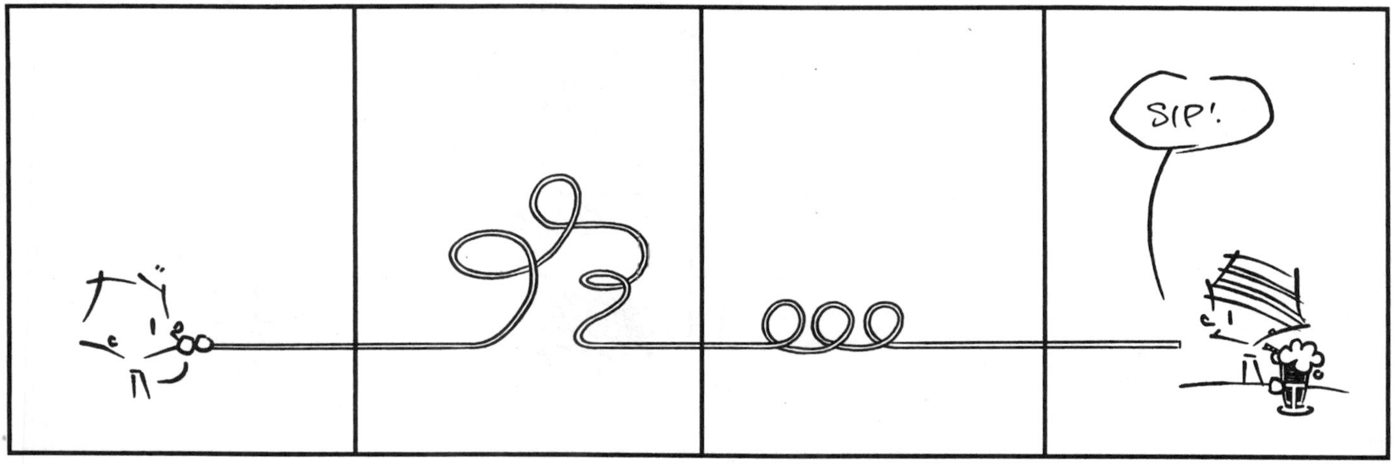
SIP!

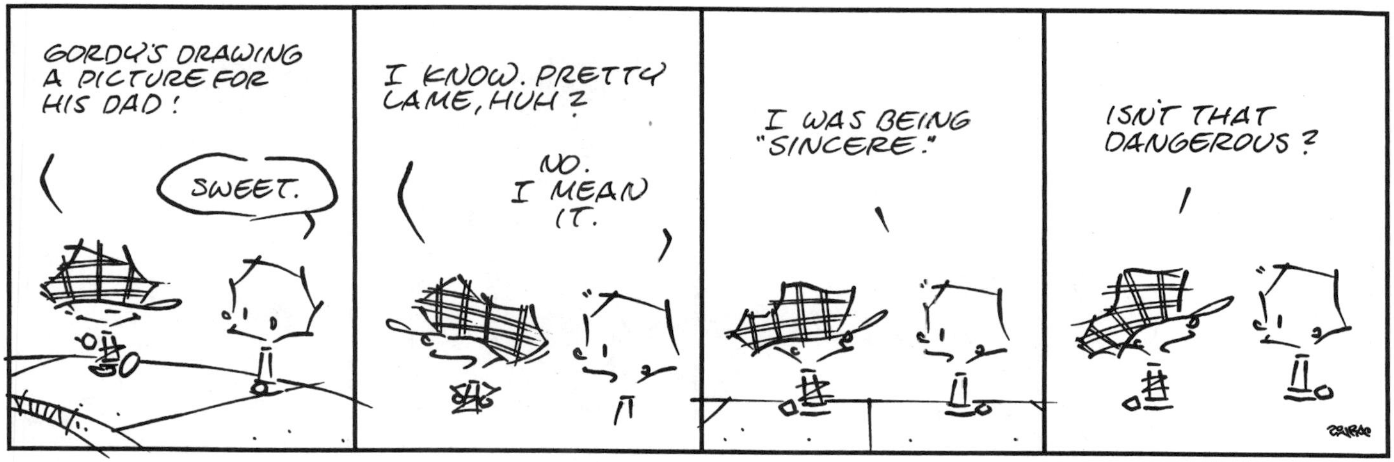
GORDY'S DRAWING A PICTURE FOR HIS DAD!
SWEET.
I KNOW. PRETTY LAME, HUH?
NO. I MEAN IT.
I WAS BEING "SINCERE."
ISN'T THAT DANGEROUS?

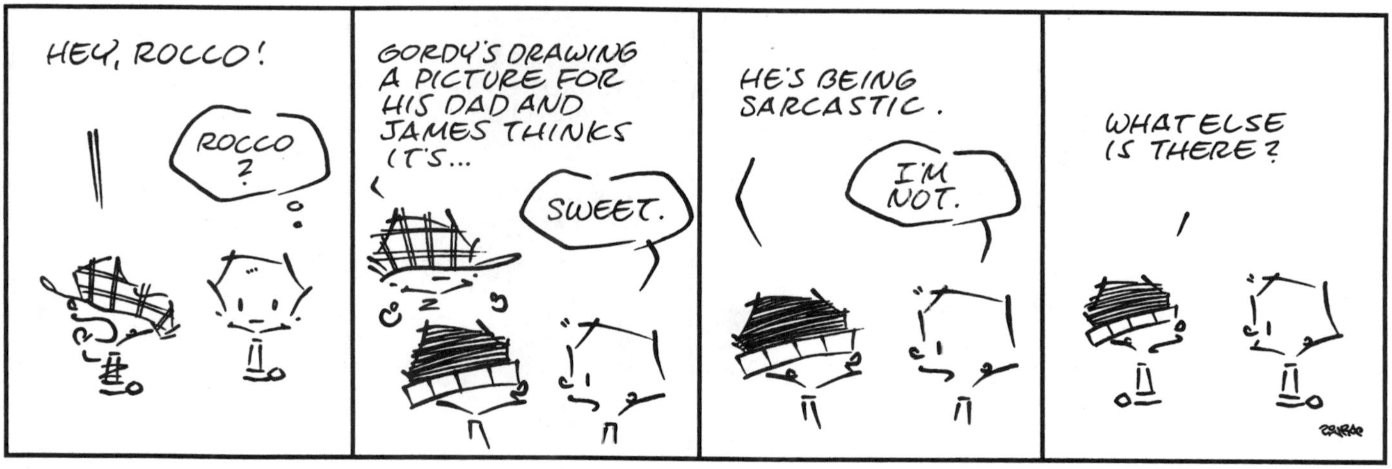
HEY, ROCCO!
ROCCO?
GORDY'S DRAWING A PICTURE FOR HIS DAD AND JAMES THINKS IT'S...
SWEET.
HE'S BEING SARCASTIC.
I'M NOT.
WHAT ELSE IS THERE?

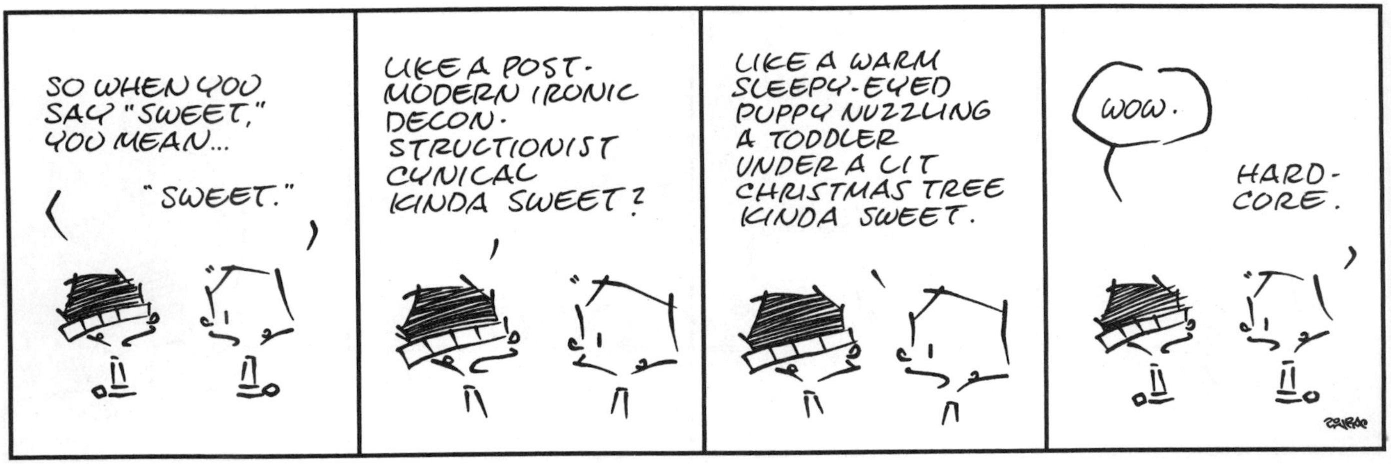
SO WHEN YOU SAY "SWEET," YOU MEAN...
"SWEET."
LIKE A POST-MODERN IRONIC DECON-STRUCTIONIST CYNICAL KINDA SWEET?
LIKE A WARM SLEEPY-EYED PUPPY NUZZLING A TODDLER UNDER A LIT CHRISTMAS TREE KINDA SWEET.
WOW.
HARD-CORE.

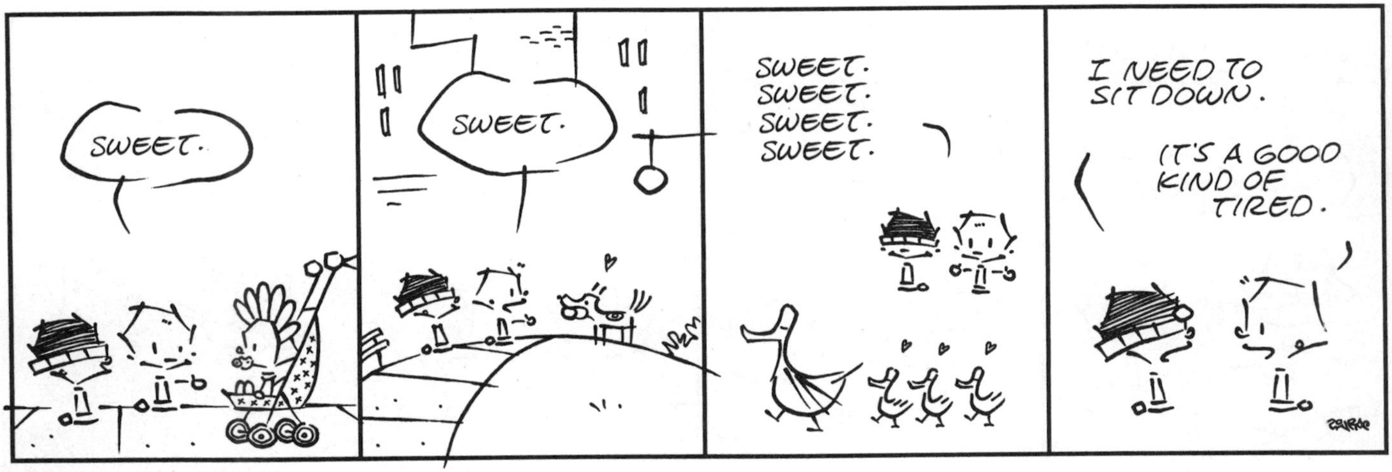
SWEET.
SWEET.
SWEET. SWEET. SWEET. SWEET.
I NEED TO SIT DOWN.
IT'S A GOOD KIND OF TIRED.

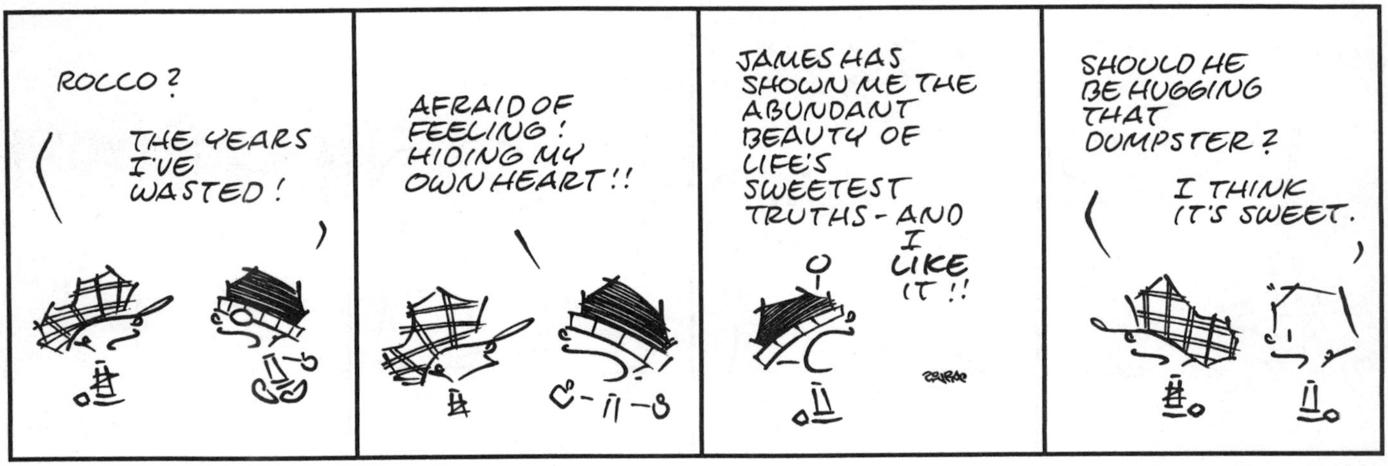
ROCCO?
THE YEARS I'VE WASTED!
AFRAID OF FEELING! HIDING MY OWN HEART!!
JAMES HAS SHOWN ME THE ABUNDANT BEAUTY OF LIFE'S SWEETEST TRUTHS - AND I LIKE IT!!
SHOULD HE BE HUGGING THAT DUMPSTER?
I THINK IT'S SWEET.

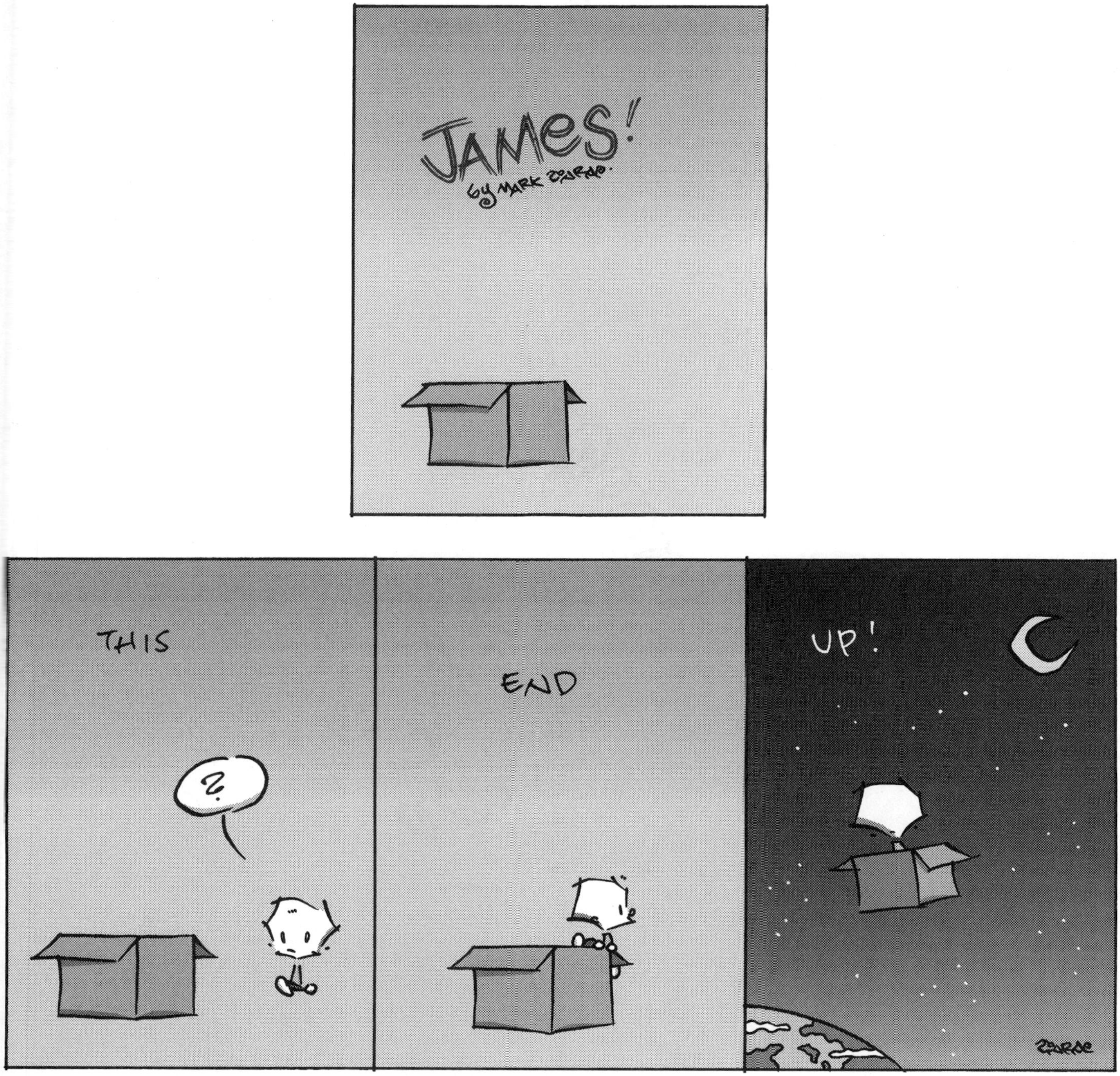
JAMES!
by MARK
THIS
?
END
UP!

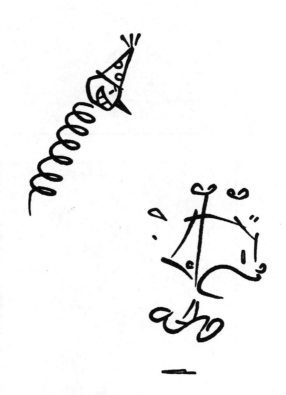